Formal Linguistics and Law

Trends in Linguistics
Studies and Monographs 212

Editors

Walter Bisang
(main editor for this volume)
Hans Henrich Hock
Werner Winter

Mouton de Gruyter
Berlin · New York

Formal Linguistics and Law

Edited by

Günther Grewendorf
Monika Rathert

Mouton de Gruyter
Berlin · New York

Mouton de Gruyter (formerly Mouton, The Hague)
is a Division of Walter de Gruyter GmbH & Co. KG, Berlin.

♾ Printed on acid-free paper which falls within the guidelines
of the ANSI to ensure permanence and durability.

Library of Congress Cataloging-in-Publication Data

Formal linguistics and law / edited by Günther Grewendorf, Monika Rathert.
p. cm. – (Trends in linguistics : studies and monographs ; v. 212)
Includes bibliographical references and index.
ISBN 978-3-11-021838-1 (hardcover : alk. paper)
1. Law – Language. 2. Law – Interpretation and construction.
I. Grewendorf, Günther. II. Rathert, Monika, 1972–
K213.F668 2009
340'.14–dc22
2009028432

ISBN 978-3-11-021838-1

ISSN 1861-4302

Bibliographic information published by the Deutsche Nationalbibliothek

The Deutsche Nationalbibliothek lists this publication in the Deutsche Nationalbibliografie; detailed bibliographic data are available in the Internet at http://dnb.d-nb.de.

Cover design: Christopher Schneider, Laufen.
Printed in Germany.

Table of contents

Part 3. Organizing legal systems: The contribution of computational linguistics and artificial intelligence

Part 4. Multilingualism and the law: The contribution of translation studies

Acknowledgements

The chapters in this volume are updated versions of talks presented at the workshop "Language and Law" that we organized at Bielefeld University, Germany, in February 2006. The connections between language and (formal) linguistics on the one hand, and law and jurisprudence, on the other, were long observed in the literature, and our aim at the Bielefeld workshop was to bring leading experts and practitioners together. We invited discussions among the central approaches in psycholinguistics, semantics, phonetics, text/corpus linguistics, computational linguistics, artificial intelligence and translation studies in so far as they were relevant to legal issues such as understanding the law, identifying the criminal, organizing legal systems and multilingualism and the law.

The result was a lively and engaging workshop, with papers addressing the core issues that we wanted to tackle. Most contributions in this volume are papers presented at this workshop, but we also asked other experts who were not present in Bielefeld to contribute to the volume. Our aim in compiling the volume was to give a good overview about the current work in formal linguistics and law in Europe.

Given the breadth of empirical coverage and expertise, we expect this volume to be useful to linguists and jurists working in the area of language and law, and, given the broad domain of discussion, it should be equally valuable to psycholinguists, semanticists, phoneticians, text linguists, computational linguists and translators. The volume can also be used for graduate and undergraduate level teaching.

It was an enormous pleasure for both of us to prepare this volume. We would like to thank our authors for their contributions, we have benefited enormously from reading their chapters. Many thanks also to our reviewers who did a great job. We would like to thank Walter Bisang, Hans Henrich Hock and Werner Winter for including this volume in the series "Trends in Linguistics. Studies and Monographs [TiLSM]".

Finally, we would like to thank Anke Beck, Birgit Sievert and Ursula Kleinhenz at Mouton de Gruyter for their valuable editorial assistance and guidance. Thanks also to Jan Köpping for proofreading and taking care of the formatting of the manuscripts.

Günther Grewendorf and Monika Rathert
Frankfurt a.M./ Wuppertal, August 2009

List of contributors

Angelika Braun is Full Professor of Phonetics at the University of Trier and interested in the forensic applications of phonetics and in socio-phonetics with a focus on the communication of emotions and irony and on dysfluencies as indicators of cognitive (mal)function. – She is chair of the *International Association for Forensic Phonetics.*

Agnieszka Doczekalska holds a doctorate in law from the European University Institute, Florence, Italy and diplomas in translation from the University of Lodz, Poland and Université des Sciences Humaines de Strasbourg, France. Her research focuses on legal multilingualism and legal translation, especially on legislative drafting in the European Union and Canada.

Tom van Engers is the Director of the Leibniz Center for Law and holds a chair in Legal Knowledge Management at the Law Faculty of the University of Amsterdam. He also is employed by the Dutch Tax and Customs Administration, beginning in 1983, where he among other positions was the program manager of the POWER program.

Stefan Friebis studied phonetics, computerlinguistics and German linguistics at the University of Trier. After his M.A. he worked as an employee in the field of public relations and as a Sales Manager in the digital signal processing and speech recognition industry. Presently he is a lecturer in adult education.

Günther Grewendorf is Professor of Linguistics at the University of Frankfurt/Main. His research interests lie in generative syntax and universal grammar, pragmatics, philosophy of language and forensic linguistics. He is editor of the journal *Linguistische Berichte* (together with Arnim von Stechow). His books include *Noam Chomsky* (Beck, 2006), *Minimalistische Syntax* (Francke, 2002), *Ergativity in German* (Foris, 1989), *Aspekte der deutschen Syntax* (Narr, 1988) and *Sprachliches Wissen* (Suhrkamp, 1987, together with Fritz Hamm and Wolfgang Sternefeld); he has edited *Speech acts, mind, and social reality* (Kluwer, 2002) together with Georg Meggle, *Rechtskultur als Sprachkultur* (Suhrkamp, 1992), and *Scrambling and barriers* (Benjamins, 1990) together with Wolfgang Sternefeld.

Michael Jessen is a Research Associate at the Speaker Identification and Audio Analysis Department of the National Forensic Science Institute (Kriminaltechnisches Institut) of Bundeskriminalamt, Germany. He is involved in casework and research in the domain of forensic speaker identification. His research focuses on speaker characteristics and the multitude of sources in which they can be observed in natural speech – including vocal tract factors, global prosodic features, as well as linguistic-phonetic and phonological aspects.

Doris Liebwald (PhD 2002, University of Vienna), Legal Expert for Computers and Law. Presently employed at the Federal Chancellery of Austria, Dep. I/13, E-Government. Furthermore Director of the Vienna Centre for Computers and Law VCCL, Vice-spokesman of the Professional Group "Juristische Informatiksysteme" within the (German) Gesellschaft für Informatik GI e.V., and Private Lecturer at the University of Applied Science "Technikum Kärnten". Her research focuses on legal information retrieval, AI & law, legal expert systems, legal ontologies, and on Austrian, European and international ICT-law.

Andreas Lötscher was associate professor at the University of Basel for German Linguistics and collaborator at the central linguistic services of the Swiss Federal Chancery at Berne and has been retired since 2009. His main fields of interest in linguistics include the linguistics of legal texts, text linguistics in general, historical syntax and dialectology.

Karin Luttermann studied German, Romance languages and law in Germany as well as abroad (Münster, Besancon, Berkeley, CA). She habilitated at the University Eichstätt-Ingolstadt, where currently she gives lectures in German Linguistics and European Studies. Her research focuses on linguistic discourse analysis, text linguistics, intelligibility, languages for special purposes, legal language and legislation on language in the European Union.

Emile de Maat is PhD student at the Leibniz Center for Law. His research focuses on the structure and semantics of legal texts, as well as the use of natural language processing to detect such structures and semantics.

Stella Neumann is Associate Professor of Modern English Linguistics at Saarland University, Saarbrücken. Her main research interests are linguistic variation, language for specialised purposes and empirical translation studies in English and German. Her recent research projects include work on optimising the comprehensibility of legal language, contrastive register variation, corpus-based analyses of linguistic properties of translations and experimental studies of the translation process.

Monika Rathert (PhD 2003, University of Tübingen) is Professor of Linguistics at Bergische Universität Wuppertal. Her research interests lie in morphosyntax, semantics, and language and the law. Her books include *Textures of Time* (Akademie, 2004), and *Sprache und Recht* (Winter, 2006); she has edited *Perfect Explorations* (Mouton, 2003) together with Artemis Alexiadou and Arnim von Stechow, and *Quantification, Definiteness, and Nominalization* (Oxford, 2009) together with Anastasia Giannakidou. Her Habilitation thesis is on deverbal nominalizations in German and English.

Erich Schweighofer is Associate Professor of Legal Informatics, International and European Law at University of Vienna. His research interests lie in international and European governance, European competition law, common agricultural policy, internet law, legal information retrieval, legal ontologies, text analysis and text categorization. His books include *Legal Knowledge Representation* (Kluwer Law International 1999, Springer 1999) and the joint publication of the conference proceedings of IRIS Internationales Rechtsinformatik Symposion, the main yearly related conference in Central Europe (2000 -). He is also speaker of the legal informatics groups in the German and Austrian computing societies and the main organizer of related conferences (in particular IRIS and KnowRight).

Jan Seifert is Assistant Professor at Bonn University, Germany, Department for German Linguistics. His current fields of research are forensic authorship analysis, archaisms, and gerontolinguistics.

Jacqueline Visconti is associate Professor of Italian linguistics at the University of Genova. Her interests include historical linguistics, with focus on grammaticalization and semantic change theory, and text-linguistics, with focus on the analysis of legal texts in a comparative perspective.

Carl Vogel is Senior Lecturer in Computational Linguistics at Trinity College, Dublin. His work in syntax and semantics investigates the ramifications of metaphor and genericity in language and quirky distributions of syntactic constructions that make authorship attribution, computational styolometry, and other forms of automatic text categorization feasible. These ramifications include the legal consequences of creative, idiosyncratic, dialectal, ungrammatical or otherwise anomalous use of language.

Stephan Walter worked as a researcher in Computational Linguistics at Saarland University until 2008. His research focused on the semantics of legal language and on legal information extraction. He is now doing research and development as a Linguistic Solutions Architect at euroscript Luxembourg S.à r.l..

Radboud Winkels is associate professor in Computer Science & Law at the Leibniz Center for Law, president of the JURIX foundation of Legal Knowledge and Information Systems and vice-president of the International Association of AI and Law.

Language and Law – new applications of formal linguistics

Günther Grewendorf and Monika Rathert

1. Introduction

Law always has a linguistic form; there would be no law without language. There would be no way to establish legal validity without language, as justice needs communication. In this respect, the laws of society and the laws of nature differ. The laws of nature are valid although their correct formulations are not known entirely; they would also be valid if nobody had ever tried to put them in formulas. The laws of society are different, they only come about via human communication; they depend on communication and do not exist as such. The laws of nature are truly universal and eternal whereas the laws of society are state-bound and prone to be changed. Imagine a society without any law or rules; sooner or later someone will feel disturbed by what someone else does and he will communicate this. Rules of living together will be negotiated and law comes into a previously lawless society.

Law is mediated through language, partially through spoken language (e.g. at court), partially through written language (e.g. written statutory regulations, ordinances). Litigation is a process that is oriented towards the text of the written law and that results in new texts, judgments. Language and law are intimately linked, and so are linguistics and jurisprudence.

The aim of this book is to show how different formal linguistic disciplines can fruitfully contribute to legal issues. The book wants to show the many interfaces between linguistics and jurisprudence.

Before having a look at the interfaces, let us present the daily work of a forensic linguist. What can linguists do for jurists? A company from the Ruhr area is blackmailed, the following letter arrives (Dern 2003: 55ff.):

G. Grewendorf and M. Rathert (eds.): Formal Linguistics and Law, 1–22

AN DIE
GESCHÄFTSLEITUNG IHRES UNTERNEHMENS
[redacted]

FAX 000 49 [redacted]

DAMEN UND HERRN.

WENN SIE DIESE ZEILEN IHREN FAXGERÄT ENTNOMMEN HABEN.EMPFEHLEN
WIR IHNEN DIESE AUFMERKSAM ZU LESEN UND VORALLEM SEHR.SEHR ERNST
ZU NEHMEN.DENN WIR SIND KEINE "DAGOBERTS" ODER SONSTIGE ANFÄNGER
UND WIR MACHEN KEINE WITZE.
WIR SIND EINE ORGANISATION DIE WELTWEIT TÄTIG IST,ABER IM PRINZIP
GEWALT IN JEGLICHER FORM ABLEHNT.SOLLTE MAN UNS JEDOCH ZUR GEWALT
ZWINGEN.HABEN WIR KEINE ANDERE WAHL WIE GEWALT ZUR VERWIRKLICHUNG
UNSERER ZIELE ANZUWENDEN.
WIR WOLLEN VON IHNEN NUR GELIEHEN FÜR EINEN ZEITRAUM VON 2 JAHREN
DEN BETRAG VON DM 1 MILLION. NACH UNSEREN UMFANGREICHEN INFORMATIONEN
FÄLLT EINEN UNTERNEHMEN WIE DAS IHRIGE DIES NICHT ALZU SCHWER.
WIR WOLLEN DIESES GELD WIE BEREITS ERWÄHNT NICHT GESCHENCKT HABEN,
SONNDERN ES WIRKLICH ZURÜCK ZAHLEN AN SIE.
WEITERHIN WOLLEN [illegible] WIR DAS GELD NICHT IN EINEN VOLLEN CASH
BETRAG,SONDERN IN FORM VON ZWEI GUTEN,INTERNATIONAL AKTZEPTIERTEN
KREDITKARTEN ZUR VERWENDUNG AN WELTWEITEN GELDAUTOMATEN.
ALS KREDITKARTEN STELLEN WIR UNS VOR Z.B. MASTERCARD,VISACARD.
DIE KARTEN SIND OHNE NAMEN DES KONTOINHABERS GEDRUCKT.SONDERN NUR
KREBITKARTENNUMMER UND KONTONUMMER.
WICHTIG IST   DAS BEIDE KARTEN DIE HÖCHSTMÖGLICHE AUSZAHLUNG AM
GELDAUTOMATEN PRO TAG HABEN,BIS BEIDE KARTEN BIS ZUM GESAMTBETRAG
VON DM 1 MIO. VERBRAUCHT WORDEN,DANACH VERLIEREN BEIDE KARTEN
IHRE GÜLDIGKEIT FÜR UNS UND KÖNNEN VERNICHTET WERDEN.
DAMEN UND HERRN UND BITTE ALLES OHNE TRICKS Z.B. SPERRUNG DER KARTEN
VORFRISTIG U.S.W. ODER ÄHNLICHE DINGE. DIE KREDITKARTEN SOLLEN
NUR MIT ENTSPRECHENDER GEHEIMZAHL AN UNS GELIEFERT WERDEN.
DA SIE DAMEN UND HERRN.DAS ALLES NICHT UNBEDINGT FREIWILLIG TUN
WERDEN FÜR UNS.HIER UNSER ACTIONSPLAN.FALLS SIE UNS NICHT HELFEN
WOLLEN.
WIR WOLLEN DIE KREBITKARTEN INCL. DER ENTSPRECHENDEN GEHEIMZAHL
BIS SPÄTESTENS MITTWOCH 25.10[redacted] AUS SICHERHEITSGRÜNDEN AN
EINE ANONYME ADRESSE ;DIE WIR IHNEN NOCH NENNEN WERDEN GESCHICKT
HABEN.B.Z.W. GELIEFERT HABEN, PER DHL-WORLDWIDEEXPRESS.
IM STANDARTUMSCHLAG VON DHL - EXPRESS SOLLTE FOLGENDES ENTHALTEN
SEIN , EIN NORMALER VERSIEGELTER BRIEFUMSCHLAG MIT DEN KREDITKARTEN
UND DER GEHEIMZAHL.EINE ORIGINALRECHNUNG ÜBER DEN VOLLEN BETRAG
INCL. ZINSEN FÜR ZWEI JAHRE.ANGABE DER BANKVERBINDUNG WOHIN DAS
GELD SOLL NACH ZWEI JAHREN,SOWIE ENTSPRECHENDES PROSPEKTMATERIAL
IHRER FIRMA. SIE DEKLARIEREN ALLES BEI DHL-WELTWEIT EXPRESS
VERSANT IN DEUTSCHLAND ALS GESCHÄFTSPOST/DOCUMENTE.
SOLLTE DIE GESAMTE POST PER DHL NICHT BIS ALLERSPÄTESTENS
AM DONNERSTAG MORGEN 26.10.[redacted] AM ZIELORT SEIN,GIBT ES DIE ERSTE
ACTION/ANSCHLAG AUF EINE IHRER FILIALEN,WAS WIR WIRKLICH NICHT
WOLLEN,ABER SIE WERDEN DANN SEHEN.DAS WIR KEINE WITZE MACHEN
WENN MAN UNS DAZU ZWINGT. WEITERE ACTIONEN WERDEN DANN SCHLAG AUF
SCHLAG FOLGEN OHNE VORWARNUNGEN.DIES GESCHIEHT ALLES NUR,WENN
SIE NICHT FREIWILLIG BEREIT SIND FRIEDLICHE WEGE ZU GEHEN,OHNE
GEWALT.

Figure 1. Part of a blackmailing letter (Dern 2003: 74)

The local police only have this letter, with no fingerprints or secretions on it. The only trace to the offender is the language of the letter.

The local police ask the Bundeskriminalamt (BKA) for a linguistic analysis. The BKA observes the following:

(1) a. a major insecurity with regard to orthography, particularly with consonant doubling and with the separate/ compound spelling of words
b. frequent omission of spaces after commas
c. *k* is wrongly substituted for *c* in foreign words
d. errors with the dative
e. errors with *t* and *d*; in most cases, the written form is identical with the spoken one

With this analysis at hand, a profile of the offender is sketched. Most probably, the offender is from Hesse, Thuringia or Saxony; he does not write much in his job and he did not have a higher education. In part 2 of this book, the reader will see how such a concrete profiling like this is developed from the analysis in (1). The next step is to consult the database at BKA for blackmailing letters with similar features like those in (1). Luckily, there is a similar letter:

Geehrter Herr [redacted],
zunächst möchten wir uns recht herzlich bedanken für Ihre
gelungene Verarschung! Sie müssen doch alle Leute für total
bescheuert halten,aber glauben Sie uns,auch Sie werden Ihren
Meister finden oder sogar kennen lernen.Über Ihr schreiben im
brannt neuen Koffer,(Sie haben keine Kosten gescheut)sogar die
Verpackung war erstklassig,kann man doch nur lächeln.Unsere Kosten
waren höher,denn viele Leute arbeiteten für uns die wir noch nicht
mal kennen.Aber im Gegensatz zu Ihnen haben wir dafür bezahlt
1:0 wie im Fußball für Sie.Wir glauben Ihnen sogar obwohl uns das
sehr schwer fällt,daß Sie mit großer Mühe die bekannte Summe
beschaft haben,aber das Risiko dabei die Summe nicht zu bekommen
lag auf unserer Seite,denn für Sie war bekannt,daß Sie sich von
dieser Summe trennen müssen.Alles andere war unser Problem und
unser Risiko. Aber das nur nebenbei!
Wie stellen Sie sich so eine Abwicklung vor? Das wir uns mit
Ihnen in Ihren Büro zum Kaffe treffen,und Sie uns freundlichst die
Summe überreichen! Oder das wir Sie Stundenlang mit Ihnen am
Telefon plaudern und so entsprechende Fangschaltungen der Polizei
gemacht werden könne u.s.w.
Da Sie so wie Sie schreiben Angst haben,daß wir das Geld nicht
bekommen könnten,und es möglicherweise in falsche Hände kommen
könnte sowohl an einer zügigen Abwicklung unbedingt interesiert
sind machen wir Ihnen folgenden und letzten Vorschlag!
Bringen Sie Ihr mühevoll beschafftes Geld zurück zur Bank da ist
es sicher. Sie eröffnen ein neues Konto,Oder haben vieleicht ein
Konto was Sie dafür was wir Ihnen vorschlagen werden verwenden
können.Für einen einflußreichen Geschäftsmann wie Sie es sind
dürfte folgendes kein Problem darstellen.Das ist für Sie unser
wirklich letztes Angebot! Wir wollen zwei sehr gute Kreditkarten.
Z.B. VISA-GOLD,und AMERICAN EXPRESS.Diese Karten müssen höchste
Auszahlungsmöglichkeit an internationalen Geldautomaten besitzen.
Die Kreditkarten tragen keinen aufgedruckten Namen,sondern nur
Kartennummer und Kontonummer. Die Karten können genutzt werden
bis der bekannte Betrag erschöpft ist,danach sind die Karten
unguldig und warden vernichtet.Wir werden Ihnen rechtzeitig mitteilen

Figure 2: Part of a blackmailing letter (Dern 2003: 77)

Besides the features in (1), there are even more correspondences between the two blackmailing letters in content, particularly with regards to transferring the money via credit cards. The BKA thus believes that the letters have the same author. As the author of the letter in figure 2 is already known, the blackmailing case in the Ruhr area is solved. Indeed, the offender was a German man, born in 1956 in Saxony, he had worked as a mechanic and as a salesman after the German reunification.

The linguists at the BKA perform important tasks, but they are not representative of the majority of forensic linguists; the majority writes reports for a case at court. Insults, libel, defamation, slander – these are the most frequent issues where linguists are asked for reports; here is an example (Kniffka 1981: 584):

(2) A housemate Y repeatedly writes letters to the caretaker; he complains about housemate X. The letters include passages like the following:
 1. Mr X and his concubine have used the laundry at times when they had no permission.
 2. Mr X and his concubine have repeatedly allowed their dog to urinate on the lawn of the house.

The woman Z who is dubbed 'concubine' in the letters sues a declaration of discontinuance against Y, she feels insulted by the term 'concubine'. Now linguistics comes into play. Y asks a linguist for a report, and this report states that 'concubine' is no insulting term anymore, instead, it is neutral now. With this at hand, Y starts an appeal against the declaration of discontinuance. Now Z also asks a linguist for a report, and this report argues for 'concubine' still being a derogatory, insulting term. The court follows the second report and Y loses the case.

This may suffice as an illustration of the daily work of a forensic linguist. Useful introductions to the topic include Rathert (2006), Gibbons (2005), Coulthard and Cotterill (2004), Olsson (2004). Very useful for getting a research oriented overview are the following edited volumes: Grewendorf (1992), Kniffka (1990), Haß-Zumkehr (2002); annotated bibliographies are Nussbaumer (1997), Levi (1994), Reitemeier (1985). For lay persons with no background in law, Haft (1986), Wesel (2002) and Wesel (2006) are helpful.

2. Overview of the volume

In this section, we present a brief overview of the main ideas expressed in the parts of this volume.

Part 1: Understanding the law: the contribution of semantics and psycholinguistics

The interpretation of law is as old as law itself. Jurists and laypersons always ask for the precise meaning of a certain piece of the law, they are engaged in a steady process of *understanding the law*. In linguistics, the discipline investigating 'meaning' (of words or sentences or texts) is *semantics*; thus, it is to be expected that semantics can contribute to a correct understanding of the law. Part 1 also investigates the alleged incomprehensibility of legal language. Many features are claimed to be responsible for this: embeddings, complex noun phrases, nominalizations etc. It is the task of *psycholinguistics* to investigate these features.

CARL VOGEL's paper *Law matters, syntax matters and semantics matters* argues that the formal semanticist can usefully interact with legal experts during the process of formulating legal texts, and that the semanticist can provide relevant advice for interpretive purposes. Vogel addresses a huge set of examples from Irish constitutional and statutory issues. Judges often explicitly appeal to linguistic principles of interpretation in justifying legal opinions and decisions, yet they do so inconsistently. The linguistic topics Vogel highlights as relevant for the interpretation of legal texts include the meaning relation between conjunction (*and*) and disjunction (*or*), readings of the plural (collective versus distributive readings), the interpretation of relative clauses, underspecification and vagueness, aspectual ambiguity, and lexical semantics. To pick out an example, in some jurisdictions (e.g. in New York), an interpretation statute specifies that *and* and *or* are equivalent, referring to De Morgan's laws in linguistics. As the following holds $\neg(\phi \vee \psi) \leftrightarrow \neg\phi \wedge \neg\psi$, exemplified with *You must not smoke* or *eat in the library* $\leftrightarrow$ *You must not smoke* and *you must not eat in the library*, the misunderstanding is motivated. Obviously, the lawyers responsible for the interpretation statute did not see the role of negation in De Morgan, they only saw that conjunction and disjunction enter an equivalence relation. Vogel also elucidates the merits and limitations of recent attempts in Ireland's legislation to provide semantic interpretation principles, among them the guidelines of the *Law Reform Committee* (2000) and the rules supplied by the *Interpretation Act* (2005).

In her paper *Improving the comprehensibility of German court decisions*, STELLA NEUMANN investigates how legal texts can be optimized in comprehensibility for laymen. Neumann starts out with example sentences from a corpus of German court decisions and then rewrites them in two variants, one with a mild syntactic simplification (version B) and another with a radical simplification (version C). The simplifications concern sentence complexity, NP complexity, and nominalizations in *–ung*. A set of 45 test persons is then exposed to the three variants. Tests measure three parameters of comprehension: the reading time, the time needed to answer questions on the text, and the correctness of these answers. Version A (the original text) proves least favourable in all respects. It results in the longest reading times, the longest response latencies and the lowest degree of correct answers. Interestingly, version B participants take as long as their version A counterparts to read the sentences. However, they need significantly less time to think about their response and then are most likely to give the correct response. Finally, when only looking at reading times and response latencies, version C seems to offer the most efficient sentences for lay persons. However, as for correctness of the responses, C is not any better than A. This means that version C participants obviously run through the simple sentences without thoroughly processing what they are reading. The performance for correctness of responses in version B offers the decisive factor suggesting that version B works best with lay persons.

MONIKA RATHERT's paper *Understanding a Riester-pension: A reply to Becker & Klein (2008)* is a critical response to a study carried out by an interdisciplinary research group at the Academy of Science at Berlin-Brandenburg. The aim of the study was to investigate the comprehension of insurance conditions by different individuals. The test persons were asked to "think aloud" about their understanding of the insurance conditions; the correctness of their understanding was checked with questionnaires. These showed very good results (80-90% of correct answers), whereas the "think aloud" protocols displayed severe misunderstandings. The authors of the study are sceptical about the questionnaires, but Rathert raises scepticism about the "think aloud" protocols. The "think aloud" situation is unnatural for most readers, commenting on comprehension usually influences comprehension as reported by many psycholinguistic studies. Often, test persons are nearly unable to report on their problem solving strategies, i.e. they do not have introspective access to their own comprehension which is nevertheless attested. In addition, the studies show that "thinking aloud" pushes test persons to a rigid and less creative way of solving tasks. Thus, as Rathert argues, it comes as no surprise that the test persons in (Becker and Klein 2008) did not show many revisions of their false beliefs. A basic criticism raised by Rathert concerns the point that there is no principled way to predict comprehension with the methods of the study; instead, comprehension is just measured empirically. Rathert proposes to use semantic models from *FrameNet* that allow these predictions and that open up the margin for an automatized comprehension analysis.

Part 2: Identifying the criminal: the contribution of phonetics and text/ corpus linguistics

The example of the blackmailing letter from above already highlighted the topic of part 2: *identifying the criminal.* The analysis of the blackmailer's letter is an example of author identification, and *text/ corpus linguistics* was instrumental in solving the case. If the blackmailer would have used the telephone instead of the letter, speaker identification would have been necessary with the help of *phonetics.*

MICHAEL JESSEN's paper *Forensic phonetics and the influence of speaking style on global measures of fundamental frequency* presents results of a study in which 100 German-speaking men produced read and spontaneous speech under normal and increased vocal loudness. The focus lies on the difference in speaking style between read and spontaneous speech and how it influences fundamental frequency (f0) behavior. On the average across all 100 speakers, mean f0 was higher in spontaneous than read speech, but this difference was significant only within the loud speech condition. Secondly, f0 variability was higher in spontaneous than read speech; this effect was significant only within normal-loudness speech. These results are compared to those in the literature. Most frequently in the literature, mean f0 is higher in read than in spontaneous speech; the opposite was found in the study. However, several studies concur with the present results. As a possible explanation for the discrepancies it is argued that psychological stress, which usually raises f0, acts as an intervening variable. For some speakers or in some experimental settings, the reading task is more stressful whereas for other speakers or settings, the spontaneous speech task is the more stressful one. A similar discussion is provided for f0 variability, which was investigated less frequently in the literature. Forensically it is concluded that if no strong influence from stress or other intervening factors occurs, average and variability of fundamental frequency are very similar in read and spontaneous speech.

The paper *Phonetic cues to speaker age: A longitudinal study*, ANGELIKA BRAUN and SEFAN FRIEBIS is on speaker age, the estimation of which forms an essential element in forensic speaker profiling and voice comparison. The processes going on within the human vocal apparatus with increasing age are of prime interest to any forensic phonetician. Specifically, if any reference material for a given speaker is non-contemporary, the issue of its usability for forensic speaker identification purposes arises frequently. While there is an abundance of cross-sectional studies on the subject of vocal manifestation of speaker age (different subject groups at different ages), there is a striking paucity of longitudinal studies. Only the latter will of course truly represent developments within the individual speaker. The study presented by Braun and Friebis focuses on the development of famous voices over time, the recordings of whom are readily available over a considerable time span. The voices of eight male German politicians were selected for the study. Recordings extending over a period of 20–30 years were obtained from the archives of various German radio stations. The variables studied were speech rate, mean fundamental frequency, its standard deviation, voice onset time (VOT), and jitter and shimmer. The main results indicate that the speech rate clearly decreases with advancing age. The VOT measurements demonstrate a decrease with increasing age. Shimmer shows a statistically significant increase with age. With respect to the forensic setting, the results of the present study demonstrate that certain changes within the vocal apparatus as well as changes in speech timing can reliably be linked to the age of a given speaker.

The topic of the next paper is also age, but the age of writers, not of speakers. JAN SEIFERT's paper *Does speech reveal one's age? On the use of gerontolinguistic topics for forensic authorship analysis* discusses to what extent the findings of gerontolinguistics can be utilized for forensic linguistic purposes. There are only few and only very general considerations on potential age markers in the forensic linguistic literature. Researchers often confine themselves to the categories 'young person', 'mature-aged adult' and 'old person'. As criteria they propose fashion words, the use of phraseologisms and patterns of word formation. The synonymous adjectives *geil*, *toll* and *knorke* may serve as examples of diachronically marked lexemes, representing contemporary (*geil*), established (*toll*) and antiquated (*knorke*) usage. Inferring the age of writers from diachronically labelled linguistic elements seems to be plausible; nonetheless, it is lacking a theoretical foundation. Whereas research on German youth language has become common since the late 19th century, gerontolinguistics started only in the nineties of the 20th century. Seifert discusses the forensic relevance of recent findings from gerontolinguistics as well as from areal linguistics, which also carries out longitudinal studies. In many cases, lexemes belong to different registers and cannot be used as diagnostics; this can be shown for *geil* and *knorke*. *Geil* is common among young people (where it is nearly synonymous with *kraß* or *fett*), it is not 'contemporary' in the sense of standard German. *Knorke* is marked diachronically, diatopically and diastratically as Berlin colloquiual German of the 1920ies.

Part 3: Organizing legal systems: the contribution of computational linguistics and artificial intelligence

The database with blackmailing letters at the BKA has already been mentioned. Databases are only one possibility of *organizing legal systems*; another possibility is the application of tools from *computational linguistics* and *artificial intelligence*. These tools can be useful to handle terminology, to retrieve information, or to model legal theorizing in a formal system. Part 3 demonstrates a variety of examples in these fields.

STEPHAN WALTER's paper *Definition Extraction from Court Decisions Using Computational Linguistic Technology* scrutinizes definitions in court decisions. Discussions in court are in large parts devoted to pinning down whether certain concepts apply. Central arguments are definitions or definition-like statements. Controversies arise because not all relevant concepts are defined within statutes, and because the terms used in legal definitions are often in need of clarification themselves. This is true for principled reasons for evaluative concepts such as *significant value*. However, even relatively concrete descriptive concepts, such as *water* or *electricity* often need to be supported with further definitions in courts' decisions. Definitions are open to revision, still they remain binding beyond the case at hand. Easy access to definitions in decisions is thus of great importance to the legal practitioner. Judges need to know such definitions in order to achieve a uniform application of the law over time, and lawyers may be provided with valuable arguments to make their clients' case. Finally, definition extraction is a prerequisite to building up an information system that allows for concept-centered access to the interpretational knowledge spread over court documents. First, Walter presents a corpus-based survey of the various realizations of definitions in court decisions. He then provides a structural segmentation scheme for definitions and discusses a method of applying computational linguistic analysis techniques for their text-based extraction and automatic segmentation. Finally, Walter shows that a large number of definitions can in fact be extracted at high precision using this method, and that the quality of extraction results can be improved with an induced ranking. Walter also discusses methods for acquiring further extractor patterns automatically.

As in the previous paper, information extraction is also at issue in *Making sense of legal texts.* However, EMILE DE MAAT, RADBOUD WINKELS and TOM VAN ENGERS do not have a focus on definitions. Instead, they treat the overall translation of legal texts into a formal machine executable language; this translation process is called 'making sense'. The authors develop an inter-coder independent and repeatable procedure for translating the legal sources into formal representations, leading to more uniformity and consequently better maintainability of the systems that are based upon those representations. The process of 'making sense' of legal texts is divided into three steps: first, structuring the text; second, identifying the source and its references; third, interpreting. In the past, legal texts were hardly structured in a systematic way. Nowadays this is less of a problem; even XML formats are often available. The authors use a parser based on a context-free grammar for this purpose. Once the source is structured, the next step is identifying which legal source it actually is, of which type (legislation, case law or legal doctrine for instance) and resolve all references, both internally and to external other legal sources. The authors use parsing techniques to perform this task. When we have a structured source with known identity and resolved references, we can start interpreting the text meaning. The authors tackle this problem in two steps: (a) Use parsing techniques to suggest translations from single provisions to formal model fragments, and (b) integrate these model fragments into a single model representing the entire legal source.

DORIS LIEBWALD's paper *Interfacing between different legal systems using the examples of N-Lex and EUR-Lex* is about information retrieval in the legal domain. Since the classic "Handbook of Legal Information Retrieval" was published in 1984, improvement in legal information retrieval has not seen any major advancement. Quite to the contrary, information overload and increased demand for cross-national and cross-lingual legal information have amplified the basic problems. The handbook already points out many of the shortcomings a lawyer typically has to struggle with when searching for relevant legal documents. Legal information retrieval systems still do not represent legal structural and conceptual knowledge, user friendliness regarding search strategies and input formats is lacking, and information about system functions and information content is often not sufficient. Liebwald demonstrates and explains the typical shortcomings of legal information retrieval systems. Since the emphasis is on multilingual and cross-national information retrieval, the experimental prototype N-Lex, the new common access portal for national law, EUR-Lex, the gateway to EU law, and the N-Lex and EUR-Lex implemented EUROVOC thesaurus serve as case study examples. These applications are maintained by the *Office for Official Publications* of the EC and are freely available on the internet. Whereas EUR-Lex supplies legal texts produced by the EU institutions, N-Lex is a new attempt to provide a common gateway to the national law of the EU member states. In its current state, N-Lex is an experimental prototype which is publicly available on the internet for free test use.

LOIS Project and Beyond is the topic of ERICH SCHWEIGHOFER's paper; as the previous paper, multilingual information retrieval is at issue. The main task of the EU-funded e-Content LOIS project (*L*exical *O*ntologies for legal *I*nformation *S*haring) was the building of a multilingual legal WordNet for the purpose of facilitating legal information retrieval. Thesaurus and lexical ontologies research were used to develop a crosslingual ontology with 5000 thesaurus entries in seven languages in order to improve crosslingual legal information retrieval. This approach could face the problem of lack of knowledge of a certain language that prevents users from formulating queries, and thus from finding relevant results but also provide some support to lawyers having to cope with EU's multilingualism. Manual construction of concepts and automatic extraction of legal definitions from European directives were used for creating this lexical ontology. The LOIS WordNet consists of both lexical and legal definitions. With this approach, crosslingual information could be attained both on a more general, lexical level, and on a more specific, legal level. Lexical definitions were translated manually on the basis of JurWordNet and its English translation. Legal definitions were based on the authoritative language versions of all European regulations and directives. This offered the possibility of introducing an equivalence relation between legal concepts in different languages. An equivalence relation and a near-equivalence relation (for related concepts) established links between concepts in different languages. If no equivalence or near-equivalence relation was present, analogous hierarchical structures could help in finding relations between terms in different languages; for instance in comparative law research.

Part 4: Multilingualism and the law: the contribution of translation studies

The last two papers from the previous part already alluded to the topic of part 4, *multilingualism and the law*. The European legislation is a product of legal and linguistic diversity, as the member states do not only differ in languages but also in their legal systems; two papers in this part treat EU's multilingualism. Another paper shows how Switzerland handles its multilingualism in legal drafting. The input of *translation studies* is of course vital in this field of research.

KARIN LUTTERMANN's paper *Multilingualism in the European Union. Status quo and perspectives: The reference language model* features the "Language Babel of Brussels" and the linguistic integration of Europe. "Unity in diversity" is the motto of the European Union, thus EU language law is in a tension: To preserve the national identity of each member state and meet the requirements of everyday communication. In practice, the limits of the translation services and also their costs are remarkable. The Community authorities and independent European institutions such as the Trademark Office and the Court of Auditors already reduce the general use of official and working languages to a great degree, in order to be able to work efficiently. In the long run, the EU is unthinkable without a working language regulation. In statistics: The EU comprises more than 450 million inhabitants, 23 official languages and 506 language combinations. The central part of Luttermann's paper deals with the reference language model, which takes maximal account of cultural identities. The reference language model is a system consisting of reference languages and mother tongues. The European legal acts are translated at all levels (treaty, official, working languages and languages of a case) authentically into two reference languages. This necessitates translation right from the start, which is methodologically the means for intercultural communication. The model is developed from a legal-linguistic perspective and is founded on the mother tongue basis, the jurisdiction of the European Court of Justice, the necessary legal certainty and in contradistinction to conventional language models.

In her paper *Drafting and interpretation of EU law – paradoxes of legal multilingualism,* AGNIESZKA DOCZEKALSKA explains why and how multilingual law is paradoxical. On the one hand, no two languages are identical; syntax and morphology vary from language to language. The semantics of a word in one language rarely matches exactly with the semantics of its closest equivalent in another language, not to mention words that are untranslatable. Hence, if there can be no absolute correspondence between languages, two and especially more than two language versions of the same text cannot be identical and some, at least, slight divergences are inevitable. On the other hand, the semantic equivalence of all the authentic language versions of a legal act is the main presumption of legal multilingualism and the prerequisite of the existence and functioning of multilingual law. In other words, all language versions of a legal act should have the same meaning. The law of the European Union expressed in twenty-three and soon possibly in more languages is an interesting example of such a paradox. Doczekalska demonstrates that the paradoxes of legal multilingualism appear when the practice of production and application of multilingual law is confronted with legal requirements and presumptions stemming from the principle of equal authenticity. Doczekalska demonstrates that legal requirements and the practice of legal multilingualism are more congruent than may appear at first glance. The insight into the drafting process and application of multilingual law and the thorough comprehension of the principle of equal authenticity reveals that contradictions creating paradoxes are to large extent just ostensible.

Like the previous two papers in this part, ANDREAS LÖTSCHER's paper *Multilingual law drafting in Switzerland* deals with multilingualism, but not on the European level. Instead, the conditions and problems of multilingual law drafting in Switzerland are discussed. The paper is full of examples of law drafting and has its merits in showing authentic empirical material. Apart from Switzerland, there are only a few other multilingual states and institutions that have established forms of multilingual legislation, above all Canada, Belgium and the European Union. The closest case to Switzerland is Canada, which has, however, other traditions of laws and legislation, with a mixture between civil law and common law. The European Union with its unique political and linguistic structure has developed its own special informal and formal procedures in negotiating and elaborating enactments. One may doubt whether the European Union has procedures of multilingual law drafting in a strict sense, as acts are often drafted in one or two languages only and translated later into the other languages. In this sense, Switzerland is a unique case, too, both in its policies of multilingualism and its traditions of legislation and legal language. Nevertheless, it seems worth to have a closer look at it, as in Switzerland, due to its tradition of direct democracy and having a multitude of language minorities, a high degree of consciousness of the problems of multilingualism has been developed, and the necessity of a good quality of the language of laws has resulted in specific methods of quality assurance. Thus, Switzerland may represent a prototypical case for demonstrating general problems. The paper presents reflections on the daily work and the practical problems of law drafting in Switzerland.

A modular approach to legal drafting and translation is the topic of JACQUELINE VISCONTI's paper. Most literature discussing multilingualism and translation in the legal domain focuses on terminological issues. The problems at stake revolve around questions such as: is the translation of terms mirroring different legal conceptions legitimate? How is a term used in a European Union context related to the corresponding terminology in a national context? Lawyers, in particular, comparatists, have been reflecting on the translation of terms such as trust, contract, property, etc. across legal systems. Visconti, however, widens and deepens the scope of reflection to other linguistic structures of legal texts. The problematic character of legal translation is shown to concern not only terminology, but also the semantic relationships expressed by connectives linking the propositions of a text. A fine-grained analysis of all linguistic levels of legal texts is argued to be a prerequisite for both translation and a good drafting practice in multilingual contexts. The analysis is grounded in a modular approach, where lexical, morphosyntactic and textual levels are seen as autonomous yet interacting modules. The textual dimension in its various facets (logical, argumentative, and informational) is shown to be of primary importance in shaping form and function of legal documents. Visconti's attempt to formalize the modular descriptions as lexical entries or information unit labels makes the proposal suitable to computational implementation.

3. Research projects on 'Language and Law'

After having sketched the content of the parts, we want to broaden the view on the topic of the book by presenting an overview about the most important past and current research projects in Germany and abroad, cf. also Rathert (2006: 87ff.).

The oldest project on 'Language and Law' is the *Deutsches Rechtswörterbuch* (www.rzuser.uni-heidelberg.de/~cd2/drw/). It was founded 1896 at the former *Königlich Preußische Akademie der Wissenschaften* and is still going on, now located at the *Heidelberger Akademie der Wissenschaften*. The *Rechtswörterbuch* treats legal terms from the beginning of the written tradition in Latin official documents in the Migration Period, also called Barbarian Invasions or Völkerwanderung until 1800.

In Germany, an intensive cooperation between jurists and linguists started in the 1970ies, when the language of law and administration was investigated in terms of comprehensibility and citizen-friendliness.

The project *Schlichtung – Gesprächs- und Interaktionsanalyse eines Verfahrens zur Lösung sozialer Konflikte* (1983–1990, conducted by Werner Kallmeyer and Werner Nothdurft) was located at the *Institut für Deutsche Sprache* (IDS). This project investigated mediation as a complex action pattern and described characteristic styles and variations of this pattern. Relevant project publications include Nothdurft (1995), Nothdurft (1997), Röhl (1987) and Schröder (1997).

Klaus F. Röhl, a jurist who was researcher in this project, later on was principal investigator of a project funded by Volkswagenstiftung on *Visuelle Rechtskommunikation* (Bochum University, 2001–2003). Röhl tracked the historical development of image and text in jurisprudence. The Roman law was without any visual elements, but many legal texts from the Middle Ages included images; e.g. the manuscript of the *Herforder Rechtsbuch* or the *Soester Nequam-Buch* (14th century both). The legal texts with the richest illustrations are the manuscripts of the *Sachsenspiegel*.

The *Sachsenspiegel* is the most important legal text in the Middle Ages. It is also the first bigger legal text in German. The title *Sachsenspiegel* ('Saxons-mirror') is an analogy; as one sees oneself in the mirror, so should one see justice and injustice just by looking into the book. The original *Sachsenspiegel* manuscript was written by Eike von Repgow between 1220 and 1235. Other legal texts were modelled on the *Sachsenspiegel*, e.g. the *Augsburger Sachsenspiegel*, the *Deutschenspiegel* or the *Schwabenspiegel*. In Prussia, the *Sachsenspiegel* was valid until common law was enacted in 1794; in Saxony, the *Sachsenspiegel* was in force even until 1865. Saxony-Anhalt applied it until 1900 and it was cited in court decisions in Leipzig until 1932.

The *Sachsenspiegel* contained two domains of law, the *Landrecht* (roughly equivalent to today's civil and crimial law) and the *Lehnrecht* (comparable to today's constitutional law). The *Sachsenspiegel* exists in the form of 460 manuscripts, the prettiest being the ones from Heidelberg, Oldenburg, Dresden and Wolfenbüttel. These four manuscripts were produced between 1295 and 1371; although they differ in many points, they all display a unique combination of image and text. Each page is divided in two columns for text and illustration; image and text illuminate each other (cf. the arrows, pointing from the initials of the text to the illustrations):

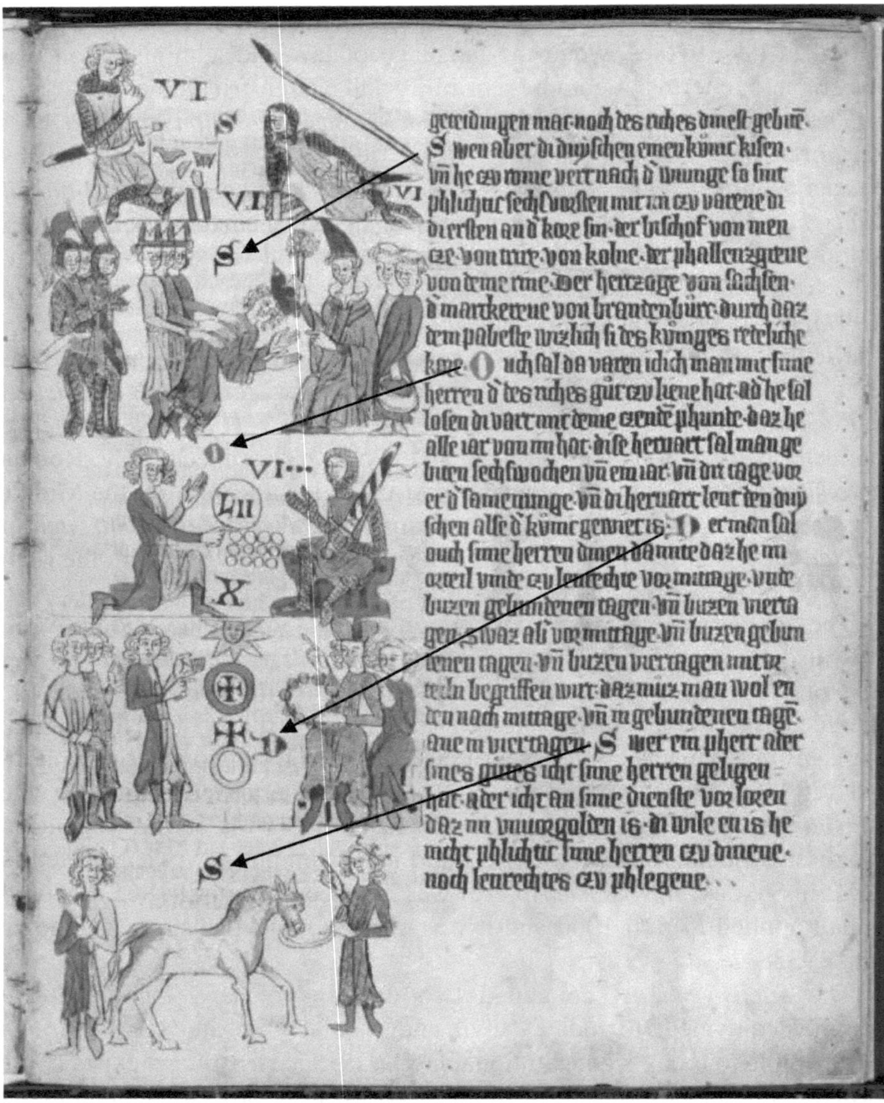

Figure 3. Heidelberg Sachsenspiegel, part of the Lehnrecht, digi.ub.uni-heidelberg.de/cpg164/0003, Cod. Pal. germ. 164, fol. 2r. With friendly permission of Universitätsbibliothek Heidelberg

Today's law is teached without images and illustrations of this kind; nevertheless, we live in a time where images play a major role in everyday life. Images are eye-catching, they can also provide distraction; often they activate schematic knowledge. Eyewitnesses are prone to report details they never saw, but which they added from their schematic world knowledge. Despite the well-known fact that a picture may lie, people tend to trust images more than text. The distinctive property of text is abstraction, and if this abstraction is reduced by adding concrete images, the outcome is unclear. Images have a scandalizing potential in the context of human rights abuse or global environmental devastation. The U.S. is known for images in court as a trigger for 'court room dramas', attracting both public and media attention.

The Academy of Science at Berlin-Brandenburg established an interdisciplinary research group with the permanent members Manfred Bierwisch, Rainer Dietrich, Wolfgang Klein (principal investigator), Hans-Peter Schwintowski, Dieter Simon and Christine Windbichler (www.bbaw.de/sdr/). The aim of the group was to investigate the comprehension of legal texts by different individuals. As an example of a legal text, the insurance conditions of a Riester-pension were chosen; Rathert's paper in this volume reports on this study. The research group existed from 1999 to 2004, the findings are published as Dietrich and Klein (2000), Klein (2002), Lerch (2004/2005), and Becker and Klein (2008).

Another project that is focused on the comprehensibility of legal texts is the IDEMA project (Internet-Dienst für eine moderne Amtssprache) in Bochum (www.ruhr-uni-bochum.de/idema/). IDEMA started in 2006 and is still going on. The theoretical part is carried out by Hans-Rüdiger Fluck from the German department of Bochum University. Fluck cooperates with Federal and Länder Authorities, with city administrations and with companies in optimizing the comprehensibility of legal texts.

There have been many interdisciplinary workshops on 'Language and Law' in Germany, e.g. at the annual meetings of the *Deutsche Gesellschaft für Sprachwissenschaft* (DGfS), 1985 in Hamburg (cf. Hoffmann 1989) and 2006 in Bielefeld (this volume). The BKA organized conferences on forensic linguistics and on authorship attribution in 1988 and 2000. The annual meeting at the *Institut für Deutsche Sprache* (IDS) in Mannheim in 2001 featured the topic 'Language and Law', cf. Haß-Zumkehr (2002). The *Gesellschaft für Angewandte Linguistik* (GAL) has a section on languages for special purposes at every annual meeting; in most cases, 'Language and Law' is represented there.

There are many linguists and jurists in Germany who work on 'Language and Law', but there is no umbrella organization and local initiatives hardly cooperate. At the beginning of the 1970ies, an interdisciplinary group 'Analyse der juristischen Sprache' existed; the 'Heidelberger

Gruppe' (www.recht-und-sprache.de/) has been founded in the 1980ies; there is a 'Regensburger Arbeitskreis' founded in 2006 and a law-oriented project in the *Heidelberger Forschungsnetzwerk* 'Sprache und Wissen – Probleme öffentlicher und professioneller Kommunikation'. Besides these research oriented initiatives, there are some incorporated societies. The *Deutsche Gesellschaft für Gesetzgebung e.V.* (www.dggev.de/, founded in 1987), is engaged on a better jurisdiction and advertizes a prize for a good and effective law. The aim of the society *Recht-Verständlich e.V.* (www.verein-rechtverstaendlich.de/, founded in 2005) is to explain those parts of the law that are of everyday relevance; the society is oriented towards new entrepreneurs and lay persons. The *Deutsche Gesellschaft für Kriminalistik e.V.* (www.kriminalistik.info/) was founded in 2002 by lecturers of criminal sciences and lecturers from the police academy; it is more or less fostering criminalistics in practice and research.

In 2009, Dieter Stein founded the e-journal *Language and Law*, hostet at DIPP (Cologne), http://www.languageandlaw.de/. It is an open-access, double-blind peer-reviewed e-journal which offers a forum for research on the interdependence of language and law in all of its facets, from theoretical approaches to the resolution of practical issues.

In the Anglo-American area, 'Language and Law' is defined and organized in a different manner. In most cases, the topic is identified with criminalistics, as an ancillary science of police investigation. In the U.S., the biggest research ressources are federal, there are big forensic departments at the FBI and other institutions; linguists work together with other crime scene investigators. In Great Britain, the *Forensic Science Service* is even part of the Home Office; its task is also supporting the police. Research on 'Language and Law' in the Anglo-American area is thus mostly forensic in nature, with a focus on speaker or author identification.

The Anglo-American focus on the courtroom situation and everything that is relevant there has a long tradition. Like in Germany, more intensive collaboration of linguists and jurists started in the 1970ies. The project *Law and Language* at Duke University was groundbreaking; it investigated communication at court. The result was that those men and women who were rated as untrustworthy by the jury used a special kind of language that was hitherto classified as women-specific. It contained many hesitations, hedges and politeness markers.

The well-known forensic work by Jan Svartvik and Malcolm Coulthard also contributed to highlighting the usefulness of linguistics for jurists. The rationale was the following: like a DNA test may prove the innocence of a defendant, a linguistic-forensic report can do the same. Malcolm Coulthard founded the *International Summer School in Forensic Linguistic Analysis* in 2000 (www.forensiclinguistics.net/); its focus is forensic linguistics, it takes place almost exclusively in Great Britain.

Many international research umbrella organizations in the field of 'Language and Law' have their origin in the Anglo-American area. The *International Association of Forensic Linguists* (IAFL, www.iafl.org/) was founded in 1992 in Birmingham. It is an organization whose members have some linguistic training (or, at least, are interested in language) and who also have an interest in language and law. Members tend to do research in areas like forensic linguistics (linguistic evidence and expertise), linguistic interaction in the courtroom, analysis and interpretation of legal texts, court interpreting, multilingualism, language policy, ethics of testifying on linguistic matters, and corpus-based approaches to legal issues. The IAFL holds a meeting once every two years; past conferences have been in Malta, Australia, Great Britain, and Seattle. The *International Association for Forensic Phonetics and Acoustics* (IAFPA, www.iafpa.net/) was founded in York in 1991. The journal that is edited jointly by the IAFL and the IAFPA is the *International Journal of Speech, Language and Law* (formerly *Journal of Forensic Linguistics*).

The *Law and Society Association* (LSA, www.lawandsociety.org/) was founded in 1964 in the U.S. The LSA is a relatively large organization that includes legal academics, sociologists, political scientists, and linguists. The annual meetings of the LSA are also outside the U.S.; their focus is on the interaction between law and politics, society, economy and culture.

The International Round Table for the Semiotics of Law (IRSL) is a consolidation of the European, Greimas-oriented International Association of the Semiotics of Law with the U.S. American Peirce-oriented Roundtable for the Semiotics of Law. The focus of the organization is on different forms of textual analysis to the discourses of the law, including the semiotics of Greimas, Peirce and Lacan, rhetorics, visual semiotics, philosophy of language, pragmatics, sociolinguistics and deconstructionism, as well as more traditional legal philosophical approaches to the language of the law. The journal edited by the IRSL is the *International Journal for the Semiotics of Law*. The annual conferences of the IRSL alternate between Europe and the Americas.

The *Plain-English-* or *Plain-Language-Movement* is devoted to improving the language of the legal profession. Many of its members are lawyers and judges. These movements are located in the U.S., in Australia, Canada and Great Britain. The goals of the movements include avoiding archaic, obscure, and over-elaborate language in legal work; drafting legal documents in a language that is both certain in meaning and easily understandable; exerting a firm, responsible influence on the style of legal language, with the hope of achieving a change in fashion.

There is a growing interest in law from computer science, language technology and artificial intelligence. In Germany, this new research field is still at the beginning; there are only very few chairs for legal informatics. The *German Association for Computing in the Judiciary* (*Deutscher EDV-Gerichtstag e. V.*, edvgt.jura.uni-sb.de/) was founded in 1989 in Saarbrücken and has become famous and important also outside of Germany. It cooperates regularly with the Bund-Länder Commission; the association develops standards for the XML-structuring of judgment transcripts in databases and fosters electronic data processing in the administration of justice, including advocacy.

In the Netherlands, the *Leibniz Center for Law* (www.leibnizcenter.org/, cf. the paper by de Maat, Winkels and van Engers in this volume) develops technology to support legal practice both in the private and in the public sector. The Leibniz Center applies artificial intelligence techniques to problems in legal theory, legal knowledge management and the field of law in general. The Leibniz Center has experience in the development of legal ontologies, automatic legal reasoning and legal knowledge-based systems, (standard) languages for representing legal knowledge and information, user-friendly disclosure of legal data, and the application of information technology in education and legal practice.

The *Foundation for Legal Knowledge Based Systems* (JURIX, www.jurix.nl/) is a forum for researchers in the field of law and computer science in the Netherlands and Flanders. Its members are research groups from most Dutch universities and a Flemish university, KU Leuven. JURIX organizes quarterly meetings that comprise of a number of lectures on artificial intelligence and law topics from both academics and practitioners. Since 1988, JURIX has held annual international conferences on legal knowledge and information systems.

In Austria, the *International Legal Informatics Symposium* (IRIS) takes place annually. IRIS is one of the largest academic conferences on computers and law in Austria and central Europe; topics include e-government, telecommunications law, e-tax and legal informatics.

Let us conclude with a huge European research project: *Lexical Ontologies for legal Information Sharing* (LOIS, www.loisproject.org/, cf. also the paper by Schweighofer in this volume). The aim of the LOIS project is to develop a multilingual access facility for European legal databases. This will enable citizens and professional users to search for European legislation and other legal documents (such as court cases) across six European languages (Italian, English, German, Czech, Portuguese and Dutch). To achieve this goal, the project uses formal representations of the WordNet technique. Similar concepts in different languages (synsets) are cross-linked in such a way that users can enter queries to a legal documentation base in his/her language and retrieve also documents written in different languages. The research results are taken on by the industry partners in the LOIS consortium to develop actual information products for European citizens.

4. References

Becker, Angelika and Wolfgang Klein. 2008. *Recht verstehen. Wie Laien, Juristen und Versicherungsagenten die "Riester-Rente" interpretieren.* Berlin: Akademie.

Coulthard, Malcolm and Janet Cotterill. 2004. *Introducing forensic linguistics.* London: Routledge.

Dern, Christa. 2003. "Sprachwissenschaft und Kriminalistik: zur Praxis der Autorenerkennung". *Zeitschrift für Germanistische Linguistik* 31. 44–77.

Dietrich, Rainer and Wolfgang Klein. 2000. "Sprache des Rechts". *Themenheft der 'Zeitschrift für Literaturwissenschaft und Linguistik'* 118 (30). Stuttgart: Metzler.

Gibbons, John. 2005. *Forensic linguistics: an introduction to language in the justice system.* Oxford: Blackwell.

Grewendorf, Günther (ed.) 1992. *Rechtskultur als Sprachkultur. Zur forensischen Funktion der Sprachanalyse.* Frankfurt am Main: Suhrkamp.

Haft, Fritjof. 1986. *Aus der Waagschale der Justitia. Ein Lesebuch aus 2000 Jahren Rechtsgeschichte.* München: C.H.Beck.

Haß-Zumkehr, Ulrike (ed.) 2002. *Sprache und Recht.* Berlin: Walter de Gruyter.

Hoffmann, Ludger (ed.) 1989. *Rechtsdiskurse. Untersuchungen zur Kommunikation in Gerichtsverfahren.* Tübingen: Narr.

Klein, Wolfgang (ed.) 2002. "Sprache des Rechts II". *Themenheft der 'Zeitschrift für Literaturwissenschaft und Linguistik'*, 128 (32). Stuttgart: Metzler.

Kniffka, Hannes. 1981. "Der Linguist als Gutachter bei Gericht. Überlegungen und Materialien zu einer 'Angewandten Soziolinguistik'". *Angewandte Sprachwissenschaft. Grundfragen – Bereiche – Methoden*, ed. by Günter Peuser and Stefan Winter, Bonn: Bouvier. 584–634.

Kniffka, Hannes (ed.) 1990. *Texte zu Theorie und Praxis forensischer Linguistik.* Tübingen: Niemeyer.

Lerch, Kent (ed.) 2004/ 2005. *Sprache des Rechts.* 3 Bände. Berlin: Walter de Gruyter.

Levi, Judith N. 1994. *Language and law. A bibliographic guide to social science research in the USA*. Chicago: American Bar Association.

Nothdurft, Werner (ed.) 1995. *Streit schlichten. Gesprächsanalytische Untersuchungen zu institutionellen Formen konsensueller Konfliktregelung*. Berlin: Walter de Gruyter.

Nothdurft, Werner. 1997. *Konfliktstoff – Gesprächsanalyse der Konfliktbearbeitung in Schlichtungsgesprächen*. Berlin: Walter de Gruyter.

Nussbaumer, Markus. 1997. *Sprache und Recht*. Heidelberg: Groos.

Olsson, John. 2004. *Forensic Linguistics. An Introduction to Language, Crime, and the Law*. London: Continuum.

Rathert, Monika. 2006. *Sprache und Recht*. Heidelberg: Universitätsverlag Winter.

Reitemeier, Ulrich. 1985. *Studien zur juristischen Kommunikation. Eine kommentierte Bibliographie*. Tübingen: Narr.

Röhl, Klaus Friedrich (ed.) 1987. *Das Güteverfahren vor dem Schiedsmann. Soziologische und kommunikationswissenschaftliche Untersuchungen*. Köln: Carl Heymanns.

Schröder, Peter (ed.) 1997. *Schlichtungsgespräche. Ein Textband mit einer exemplarischen Analyse*. Berlin: Walter de Gruyter.

Wesel, Uwe. 2002. *Fast alles, was Recht ist. Jura für Nichtjuristen*. Frankfurt am Main: Eichborn.

Wesel, Uwe. 2006. *Geschichte des Rechts*. München: C.H.Beck.

Part 1

Understanding the law: The contribution of semantics and psycholinguistics

Law matters, syntax matters and semantics matters

Carl Vogel

1. Background

For decades, people have taken automatic spelling checking for granted, and become increasingly accepting of the diagnostics provided by automated grammar checkers and style monitors. The next tool in the progression will be automatic meaning checkers to spot ambiguity, vagueness, (in)consistency, absurdity.[1] An assumption of this paper is that one role of the semanticist during the intervening period is to do the work that automated meaning checkers would do: dispassionately digest the composite meaning of texts (drawing on appropriately explicit contexts) to mark the locations within the texts that may have undesired implication. Where the text is of a legal nature, a difference between a semanticist and a lawyer is that the semanticist is not on retainer to find a desired interpretation, but to enumerate the possibilities. From among those possibilities, a judge must make a selection. A recent report on statutory drafting in Ireland articulates a clear aesthetic (The Law Reform Committee 2000: 8):

(1) Clearly, the ideal to be pursued in law should be that a particular legal question will always be resolved in the same way, irrespective of which judge hears the case. Of course, this ideal is not always achievable in practice. However, the law should be designed in such a way as to make it more, rather than less, likely to happen.

1. That this claim is not ridiculous finds evidence in the fact that sentiment analysis is an enormous activity using the tools of corpus linguistics. The "Recognising Textual Entailment Challenge", organized by the PASCAL Pattern Analysis, Statistical Modelling and Computational Learning network (http://www.pascal-network.org/Challenges/RTE3/ – last verified, February 2009) provides stronger evidence that this is a concrete possibility.

G. Grewendorf and M. Rathert (eds.): Formal Linguistics and Law, 25–54

Thus, the semanticist's most natural partner is on the legal drafting team. It has been noted that the language of law is constructed using devices akin to those in logic programming (e.g. Kowalski 1992), and the drafting team independently operates with formal guidelines, logical connectives and operators. However, sometimes the drafted text would benefit from a formalist's perusal and comment. Notwithstanding issues of interpretation that involve issues external to the text of laws (see §2), the text remains paramount. The Law Reform Committee (2000: 10) points out, "It is important to state, at the outset, that the literal rule [of interpretation] is, and must remain, the general governing principle in this area: anything else would lead to chaos."

Consider the extant relationships between linguists and the legal system. Chaski (1997) noted that the reluctance of courts to accept expert linguistic opinion, at least in the case of authorship attribution, derived from the methods often failing the *Daubert* test of admissibility of expert evidence. Expert evidence must be drawn from methods that are scientific in the sense of having been subject to empirical evaluation, with established criteria for applicability, conduct, and quantification of certainty; reliable in the sense that anyone performing the analysis would reach the same conclusions; and acknowledged as valid in the scientific community through peer reviewed publication.[2] However, despite an acknowledged reluctance of courts to accept expert linguistic opinion (*particularly on the meaning of ordinary English expressions* in statutes or contracts, for example), Tiersma and Solan (2002) point out several areas of linguistics in which judges have been known to accept expert witness: second language interpretation, dialectology, proficiency assessment, phonetics. In other areas, such as readability evaluation and semantics of natural language for statutory interpretation, expert testimony from linguists has been less welcome.

Solan (1993) notes that judges often explicitly appeal to linguistic principles of interpretation in justifying legal opinions and decisions, yet inconsistently. A number of interpretive rules that he discusses involve ambiguities of syntax and semantics, including anaphora. Consider the large issue that Solan raises is about the "and/or" rule, which is that in some jurisdictions (e.g. New York), an interpretation statute specifies that the two words

2. In her own work, she has investigated the reliability of methods (Chaski 2001) for authorship attribution, and has suggested letter unigram distributions as a level of linguistic description that will at least achieve reliability.

may be used interchangeably. The examples (2–5) demonstrate the common usage which makes this rational.

(2) At the conference dinner tonight, you can have stuffed artichoke with asparagus and also lamb chops with mashed potatoes.

(3) Would you like olives, or pretzels, or crisps, or beer or anything?

(4) You must not smoke or eat in the library.

(5) You must not smoke and you must not eat in the library.

In (2) the interaction of *and* with the modal *can* is such that there is a conjoint possibility of two different dinners, but the natural interpretation is that there is an "either/or but not both" for any actual dinner choice. Stacy (2005) discusses the issue with respect to the phrase prohibiting "cruel and unusual punishment", where many prefer to interpret the phrase as if *and* had been *or*. Similarly, in (3) there is no presumed exclusivity of the options, thus they may naturally in many settings all be conjointly accepted. The De Morgan's equivalences entail that (4) implies (5). It is not that *or* and *and* are synonyms, but examples like those motivate the interpretive rule. That anaphor resolution rules may be inconsistently applied is no surprise. It is even less a surprise that the "and/or" rule could lead to litigation. Adams and Kaye (2006) describe at length and depth the ambiguities that emerge in the interpretation of "and" and "or", as a function of the grammatical category of constituents that those connectives join.

Adams and Kaye (2006) also discuss the ambiguity of plurals. One issue is whether provisions associated with plurals are meant to apply collectively or distributively over each individual. Coles-Bjerre (2006) demonstrates the consequences of this ambiguity with respect to transfer of money to creditors in the context of bankruptcy. This discussion independently draws out in the legal context of disbursal of funds to creditors in the context of bankruptcy the fact that there is not a clear dichotomy between collective and fully distributive readings of plurals (Verkuyl 1994). In coarse terms, "three creditors received one hundred dollars" is a true sentence if two received forty-five each, and one received ten; it is also true if three creditors received one hundred dollars each; and so on. It is slightly taxing to imagine all of the permutations of distribution that make such a statement true, but it easy to see that there are many. The Irish Interpretation Act (2005) makes statement about plurals and singulars, but one that cannot be read as providing a rule on how distributivity is meant to be resolved (see (6)).

(6) Section 18 (a)
Singular and plural. A word importing singular shall be read as also importing the plural, and a word importing the plural shall be read as also importing the singular.

To see this, consider the Constitution of Ireland again. Article 45 §2 states, "The State shall, in particular, direct its policy towards securing: –"

(7) Art 45 §2 (ii)
That the ownership and control of the material resources of the community may be so distributed amongst private individuals and the various classes as best to subserve the common good.

In order to effect full distributivity, some quantification invoking "each" private individual and class would be necessary. Here, what is "best to subserve the common good" is left open and vague, with a rather large number of configurations of distribution to choose from.

Another principle of interpretation is called "the last antecedent rule" and meant to address scope ambiguity if conditions applying to complex clauses arising from structural attachment ambiguity. Solan (1993: 29)[3] provides the formal statement of the rule: "A limiting clause is to be confined to the last antecedent, unless the context or evident meaning requires a different construction." Rather than discussing the particulars of the case around which he makes the point, one can see the import from (8), a schematic of the case, *a* and *b* are potential distinct individuals with some shared quality *p*; Π is a proviso associated with the predicate *p*; and Ω is an outcome that follows if the non-atomic antecedent of (8) is satisfied.

(8) $p(a) \wedge (p(b) \wedge a \neq b) \wedge \Pi \rightarrow \Omega$

(9) $(p(a) \wedge (p(b) \wedge a \neq b) \wedge \Pi)$

(10) $((p(a) \wedge (p(b) \wedge a \neq b)) \wedge \Pi)$

This issue is that the natural language counterpart also lacks bracketing. The rule dictates the disambiguation in (9) while (10) also provides a natu-

3. He has quoted directly from Anderson vs. State Farm Mutual Automobile Insurance Co. 75 California Reporter 739, 741 (2nd District 1969).

ral interpretation, in which the proviso is a condition on the entire prior conjoint phrase.

(11) The possibility of admission is available to girls and boys under six years of age.

It is more natural to read (11) as requiring all of the children to be under six years of age, and not just the boys, although, of course, both readings are available. Solan demonstrates that judges are not consistent in their application of these interpretive rules, even though they are accepted interpretive principles. The key issue that is at stake is that the when the rules are applied, the judge tends to argue that the decision is based upon a linguistic rule of interpretation, and when the rule is not applied, it is drawn on legislative intent or other extra-textual considerations, when actually in both cases, the reasons for the decision are likely to be exterior to the texts, and happen to be consistent with a linguistic rule in the former.

This article is largely an exercise in meaning checking over legal texts. Schane (2002) provides a comparable look at case law demonstrating lexical ambiguity, reference resolution dispute, and vagueness, in developing an argument for subjective, purposive, interpretation of legal texts. The different issues considered here in §3 also highlight forms of ambiguity, but with the intent of arguing for the role of natural language semanticists working with legal experts in the drafting process particularly, and also interpretation. Of course, the scope of formal semantic approaches to texts has advanced a great deal since Tarskian foundations – contexts are relevant, and not just for anaphora resolution, but also, and particularly, for the interpretation of plain language.

The article mainly (but not exclusively) addresses Irish constitutional and statutory issues, not because the Irish situation is markedly different from any other jurisdiction, but because it is ready to hand for the author. The discussion involves close readings of texts for reasonable, literal everyday meanings, and Section 2 is provided to acknowledge the thorough awareness within the legal domain of theoretical and practical ramifications of exercises like this.

2. Principles of drafting and interpreting text

The principles that guide legal drafting and interpretation have been outlined and evaluated in countless monographs and articles. The purpose of this section is to highlight issues that are germane to the textual focus of §3. In particular, a natural response to some of the readings that are perhaps unintended by the drafters is to argue that some other purposive form of interpretation would rule the reading out, or some other interpretive rule would override in face of absurdity. Thus, the main role of this section is to highlight what some of those remedies might be. However, as noted in §1, where alternatives have equal support, it is likely that inconsistent resolutions would emerge, depending on the adjudicator.

2.1 Basic principles

A number of basic principles guide the understanding of texts, where a decision might be made from them, at odds with their literal contents. The Law Reform Committee (2000) distinguishes between literal and purposive rules. One example is the "mischief rule", which is called into play when a blatant error has emerged, for example via printing error. Another is the "golden rule" which is used when literal interpretation leads to an absurd meaning or inconsistency. Other rules address literal issues associated with polysemy. "A word is known by its associates" (*noscitur a sociis*) provides a dictum to take context into account, thus partly resolving lexical ambiguity. "Of the same kind" (*ejusdem generis*) addresses the absence of words, such that if constraints are placed on a series of explicitly named items, then they apply to other instances of the same kind.[4] However, a contrasting rule applied to cases rather than kinds works differently (*expressio unius est exclusio alterius*) in that a statute constraining one situation without mentioning a related situation is not allowed to automatically be generalized to cover the related case. Another basic principle (*generalia specialibus non derogant*) is that a general provision can be explicitly canceled through a statute applying to a more specific set of situations. These are basic principles that come to mind when addressing textual oddities in stat-

---

4. This limited open world assumption works against the construal of law as logic programs, which generally operate on a closed world assumption (see mention of Kowalski (1992) above).

utes. One considers that one or more of them will resolve the oddity. However, because there is not a unique solution, one is left with a situation in which different adjudicators will achieve different conclusions when interpreting the relevant text.

2.2 Drafting clarity

As noted in the introduction, it is desirable for interpretation to be reliable in the sense of not depending significantly on which person does the interpreting, and (1) "the law should be designed in such a way as to make it more, rather than less, likely to happen" that way.

Style guides exist for legal drafting, of course, with guidelines to be clear, unambiguous, avoid complex constructions, and so on. The Law Reform Committee (2000: Ch. 6.) proposed guidelines for statutory drafting in Ireland, suggesting that it should follow the principles encapsulated in (12)

(12)
1. Familiar vocabulary should be used in legislative drafting
2. Shorter sentences should be used in legislative drafting
3. Complex and obscure sentence structures should be avoided
4. Excessive cross reference among sections should be avoided
5. Unnecessary concepts should be avoided[5]
6. Examples should be provided
7. Maps, diagrams and mathematical formulae should be employed[6]

A specific thread of legal drafting thought involves the ideal of plain language that laypeople can understand. Notwithstanding the fact that plain language is the normal discourse that semanticists address, lawyers have also made significant critiques of this aesthetic. Tanner (2004), for exam-

---

5. This refers to constructions like "the relevant period" which tend to require cross reference outside the explicit provision, and thus, it is claimed, "obscure the significance" (p. 75). While acknowledging that over-precision is counter-productive, it does seem like exactly qualifications of "the relevant period" are the stuff of litigation and should be made precise to the greatest extent possible. Witness the dispute between Larry Silverstein and the insurers of the World Trade Center, and the billions of dollars that depended on whether there was one event or two.

6. For example, it is much clearer to stipulate the manner by which compensation among multiple parties is to be calculated using mathematical formulae than to describe the algorithm in natural language sentences.

ple, considers the style guide of Butts and Castle (2001), and complains that the notion of favoring "small meaning bites" is ill-defined, although the intuition behind it is sensible enough.[7] Hunt (2002) draws attention to an analogy between medical doctors and lawyers. Medical jargon is not put into plain language either, because it would not abet efficient communication among experts. So, too, with lawyers, the argument goes. However, it is not so clear that one should reasonably expect settling an insurance claim oneself to be as prohibitively involved as reading the instructions to perform surgery on oneself.

An uncontested dimension of clarity is that terms should be defined within statutes where neologisms, and more particularly, ordinary words, are provided with senses peculiar to the statutory domain. The first section of statutory acts is devoted to this. For the discussion which follows in §3, it is relevant to provide some of the articles of the Irish constitutions as examples (13–15). These articles define the nation, the state, the national language and the official languages of Ireland.

(13) Article 1
The Irish nation hereby affirms its inalienable, indefeasible, and sovereign right to choose its own form of Government, to determine its relations with other nations, and to develop its life, political, economic and cultural, in accordance with its own genius and traditions.

(14) Article 4
The name of the State is *Éire*, or, in the English language, *Ireland.*

(15) Article 8
1. The Irish language as the national language is the first official language.
2. The English language is recognised as a second official language.
3. Provision may, however, be made by law for the exclusive use of either of the said languages for any one or more official purposes, either throughout the State or in any part thereof.

---

7. Nonetheless, Tanner (2006) applies this to the EC Directive 2002/2/EC of the European Parliament, and finds it lacking in exactly this respect. The directive is of 28 January 2002, and amends Council Directive 79/373/EEC, which set rules on "circulation of compound feeding stuffs within the Community."

It is common for statutory drafters to provide accompanying margin notes that in a few words summarize what the relevant passage of the annotated statute is about, as in (16) which indicates the way §6 of the Interpretation Act (2005) of Ireland appears on the page. Importantly, these words in the right are supplied by the drafter and are not subject to debate by legislators.

(16)	6. – In construing a provision of any Act or statutory instrument, a court may make allowances for any changes in the law, social conditions, technology, the meaning of words used in that Act or statutory instrument and other relevant matters, which have occurred since the date of the passing of that Act or the making of that statutory instrument, but only in so far as its text, purpose and context permit.	Construing provisions in changing circumstances

Nonetheless, the margin notes provide limited insight into the intent of a phrasing, if not the intent of the legislative body deciding the measure.

2.3 Intended ambiguity

While drafting guidelines sensibly suggest eliminating ambiguity[8] and maximizing clarity, Solan (1993: 118–138) discusses the contrast of too much precision in legal texts, and the propensity of the search for precision to lead to unnatural syntax that can confound interpretation in a different way. Moreover, there is also a healthy role for allowing ambiguity, particularly in diplomatic contexts. However, these examples make clear why legislative intent and the history of discussions leading to legal enactment are a contentious source of guidance in legal interpretation, since, in fact, virtually every law that is passed involves debate and negotiation.

Byers (2004) discusses intended ambiguity in United Nations Security Council Resolution 1441 (adopted on November 8, 2002) "deploring" Iraq's substantial breaches of prior UN Resolutions, and whether Resolution

8. The title of this article, with one reading as a conjoined series of declarative sentences with finite intransitive verbs, and another as a heavy conjoined noun phrase, is an example of intended ambiguity more welcome in newspaper headlines than in drafting of legal texts.

1441 provided authorization for the 2003 invasion. In view of text such as in paragraph 13, "the Council has repeatedly warned Iraq that it will face serious consequences as a result of its continued violations of its obligations" which does not specify what those consequences might be, the US and UK saw the text as supporting invasion, while France and Russia did not. The text was the product of eight weeks of negotiation (Byers 2004: 165), evidently a construct whose ambiguity all parties could be satisfied with even with knowledge of differing intent (explicitly discernible in the differences in the texts of the resolution in French and English).

(17) ... all of the Council's members likely believed that their particular understanding of the resolution was legally correct. The differing interpretations were not necessarily the result of bad legal advice. They derived at least in part from the subtle, preexisting differences in interpretive approach – differences that only become significant in situations of textual ambiguity and that become all the more significant when, as in the case of Resolution 1441, there is no international court or tribunal with jurisdiction to resolve the resulting dispute.

The international lawyers who work for governments are aware of these differing interpretive approaches and their potential effects. The members of the Security Council agreed to the ambiguities of Resolution 1441 with their eyes open, knowing that they were neither resolving nor papering over their differences. Instead, they were simply agreeing to disagree.

Thus, in a way, the ambiguous text in its construction at the time allows all parties to feel that their own interests are protected, perhaps in the hope that the ambiguity ultimately would not be tested. Pehar (2005) considers the nature of diplomatic ambiguity in considerable depth, and with the optimistic perspective that the correct interpretive response to ambiguity is continued negotiation rather than a "power-centric" resolution of the ambiguity; that is, apart from face saving consequences of agreeing to an ambiguous text, it is rational to adopt a principle of charity during negotiations, accepting ambiguity as a way of avoiding irreparable breaks.

2.4 Multilinguality

A side issue in the last section was the fact that many legal texts are presented in more than one language. This is certainly not the only dimension in which multilinguality is a concern in the legal process. It certainly figures into matters of interrogation and evidence, down to the level of dialect and intercultural differences of interpretation of the pragmatic function of discourse particles like "Mm" and "Yeh" (Berk-Seligson 1990; Eades 2002). Here, the focus is on the enrolment of law in a bilingual jurisdiction, and potential priority of one language over another.

The Irish Constitution makes a number of provisions about the official bilingual status of Ireland, in addition to that of Article 8 (see (15) above). Articles 25 §4(3) and §4(4) ensure that laws are enacted in both of the official languages, with the provision that the bill might be debated and agreed in both languages (18) or in only one language (19).

(18) Article 25 §4(3)
Every Bill shall be signed by the President in the text in which it was passed or deemed to have been passed by both Houses of the Oireachtas, and if a Bill is so passed or deemed to have been passed in both the official languages, the President shall sign the text of the Bill in each of those languages.

(19) Article 25 §4(4)
Where the President signs the text of a Bill in one only of the official languages, an official translation shall be issued in the other official language.

Article 25, §4(5) of the Constitution of Ireland makes the texts in both languages binding and provides a constitutionalized guideline on interpretation:[9]

(20) Article 25 §4(5)
As soon as may be after the signature and promulgation of a Bill as a law, the text of such law which was signed by the President, or where the President has signed the text of such law in each of the official languages, both the signed texts shall be enrolled for record in the office of the Registrar of the Supreme Court, and *the text, or*

9. Emphasis added.

both the texts so enrolled shall be conclusive evidence of the provisions of such law

This principle is generalized to the status of the Constitution itself in Article 25, §5(3), thus establishing a coherent state of affairs in which it is legal texts, rather than hearsay, opinion, margin notes, debate records, etc., that determine the law. In making a commitment to the status of individual texts, the Constitution has a concomitant reliance on the language comprising the texts. It is interesting that the constitution allows that the translated text need not be debated and explicitly agreed, for it is certain that in the process of translation the meaning of the text could be modulated or ambiguities introduced. However, neither is it clear that the translated text is to be signed by the President. If the President does sign the undebated translation, the second disjunct of Article 24 §4(5) unambiguously has force. Without a signature on the translation, it depends on whether "both the texts" finds its antecedent within the scope of just this clause or also §4(4), the signed text and its official translation. A "last antecedent" interpretation suggests the former, such that if the text is debated in English, translated to Irish and not signed, only the English text determines interpretation since the expression, "both the texts so enrolled", fails to denote if enrolment requires debate and signature. Here, "the text, or both the texts so enrolled" is another example where "or" is probably not intended to offer choice.

The Constitution makes explicit the potential for alternative forms of expression to arise between phrasings stipulated in the national language and the second language, and provides for conflicting interpretations by settling with the interpretation expressed in the national language, Irish.

(21) Article 25 §5(4)
In case of conflict between the texts of any copy of this Constitution enrolled under this section, the text in the national language shall prevail.

Note that this provision holds even in case the phrase in question was composed first in the second language and subsequently translated into the national language. Section 25 §4(6) provides the same provision for laws enrolled under the Constitution: if there is a difference between the texts the Irish version takes priority. Given the point mentioned above, that the Irish text may not actually have been debated, and that appeal may be made only to the text for interpretation, this gives drafters engaged in translation into Irish considerable responsibility. Note that it is not necessary in bilingual jurisdictions for one language to be given priority. For example, the Canadian Charter of Rights and Freedoms, from the Canadian Constitution Act, 1982, provides in Article 18 §1 that "The Statutes, records and journals of Parliament shall be printed and published in English and French and both language versions are equally authoritative". The multilinguality issues are raised here are relevant to the issues named in §3.3.1 and §3.3.2.

2.5 Theoretical stances on interpretation

Thus far, this section has pointed out a number of basic principles of interpreting legal texts in light of some of the textual issues that have been enumerated. The last section points out that the Irish Constitution offers a strong constraint on what may be construed as the content of the law: it amounts to the Irish text of the law as it is enacted. In general, where law is codified, the judiciary may be disposed at some point in a cline between literal textual readings and contextualized purposive analyses of texts.

Although it is natural to conflate "intent" and "purpose", a distinction is often made between legislative intent and legislative purpose (see Dickerson 1975), in that the former is taken to refer to the immediate context of the act and the provisions within that context, while the latter encompasses the principled motive behind the act: some specific enactment (intent) may be provided to achieve a larger goal of policy (purpose).[10] Thus, in appealing to legislative purpose, one is typically applying a policy to a novel context. However, laws do not typically convey their purpose in their text. To some extent, this is documented in the marginalia that accompany laws, but it is noted above (see (16)) that those margin texts are not debated and agreed, and are not a reliable indication of purpose as a result. Further, records of parliamentary debate on matters are not reliable indications of purpose either. Recall from §2.3 that there are times in which text is left ambiguous in order to resolve dispute, and thus the text that is achieved may be the artifact of an equivocal purpose. Thus, full legislative history of an act is also not a perfect communicator of the final product either.

In its review, The Law Reform Committee (2000) proposed for Ireland a "moderately purposive approach to statutory interpretation." As mentioned

10. The application to novel contexts is often anticipated by the statutes – recall (16).

before, they concluded that full abandonment of literal approaches would lead to "chaos". The suggestion was that some finite list of sources external to statutes could be provided for access to judges, as appropriate.

The Interpretation Act (2005) allows for interpretation to for diverge from the text of the act. Section 5 provides:

1. In construing a provision of any Act (other than a provision that relates to the imposition of a penal or other sanction) –
   (a) that is obscure or ambiguous, or
   (b) that on a literal interpretation would be absurd or would fail to reflect the plain intention of –
      i. in the case of an Act to which paragraph (a) of the definition of "Act" in section 2(1) relates, the Oireachtas, or
      ii. in the case of an Act to which paragraph (b) of that definition relates, the parliament concerned, the provision shall be given a construction that reflects the plain intention of the Oireachtas or parliament concerned, as the case may be, where that intention can be ascertained from the Act as a whole.
2. In construing a provision of a statutory instrument (other than a provision that relates to the imposition of a penal or other sanction) –
   (a) that is obscure or ambiguous, or
   (b) that on a literal interpretation would be absurd or would fail to reflect the plain intention of the instrument as a whole in the context of the enactment (including the Act) under which it was made, the provision shall be given a construction that reflects the plain intention of the maker of the instrument where that intention can be ascertained from the instrument as a whole in the context of that enactment.

Notice that statutory instruments are treated differently from Acts in that intent must be discerned solely from the Act, while interpretation of other statutory supports may appeal to the context of enactment.

More specific rules of interpretation are supplied by the Interpretation Act (2005) in §18(a). These address issues of general definitions (e.g. "person"), and conventions for equating singulars and plurals,[11] assuming that provisions associated with words bearing solely masculine or feminine

11. Recall (6) in §1.

equally apply to the other gender, distance measuring conventions, application of constraints applied to a consecutive series or to temporal durations to the endpoints of the series and durations, time standards, etc. Here, perhaps one can see best how the interacting principles are meant to work rationally together. For example, on gender,

(22) Section 18 (b) stipulates
   (i) A word importing the masculine gender shall be read as also importing the feminine gender;
   (ii) In an Act passed on or after 22 December 1993, and in a statutory instrument made after that date, a word importing the feminine gender shall be read as also importing the masculine gender;

Certainly, "mother" is a word that imports feminine gender, but Statutory Instrument No. 654/2004 – *Maternity Protection (Protection of Mothers Who Are Breastfeeding) Regulations* 2004, cannot be read from its title as also importing masculine gender without patent absurdity. However, the actual text of the statutory instrument is curiously not absurd. This is because the text consistently makes provisions for an "employee who is breastfeeding", and the restrictive relative clause modifier has the effect of making the rules vacuous in the case where masculine gender is imported since there are no men who breastfeed. Section 10 of the Maternity Protection (Amendment) act extends the number of weeks relevant to the Maternity Protection Act 1994 (14 to 24 weeks with respect to confinement, and 10 to 16 weeks for leave):

(23) Section 10(a):
If a woman who has been delivered of a living child (in this section referred to as 'the mother') dies at any time before the expiry of the twenty-fourth week following the week of her confinement, the father of the child (if he is employed under a contract of employment) shall be entitled in accordance with this section to leave from his employment for a period....

This construction has the effect of simplifying the amount of legislation requiring amendment should Ireland provide legal definition and protection for same-sex unions, and the possibility of a child being born within one. In the tragic circumstances in which the birth mother dies during the relevant period, her partner would (unless legislated otherwise in any enactment of same-sex union) have access to the protection of this act, since "father" imports the feminine gender as well as the masculine.

The point here is that even with this statutory instrument it is possible on the basis of the interpretation rules and the text of the act alone to diagnose absurdity and feel confident about the purpose of the regulations and how to use them. It is when the text does not convey intent clearly, and when there is independent rationality for each of the alternatives that may be unintended, that the moderately purposive interpretations strategy may equally not yield anticipated results.

2.6 Synthesis

It is arguably the case that the constitutional provision for a Supreme Court is an implicit acknowledgement that a multiplicity of meanings for a phrase can exist within a single language and without statutory "mischief". Certainly, by committing to a given text, and thus the phrasing that forms the text, the state of the law on particular issues depends precisely on the interpretation of the phrasing given. There are common sense remedies, but they do not always yield expected results.

3. Formal linguistic approaches to specific texts

3.1 Syntactic ambiguity and Article 4

A visitor to Ireland who had received postage from Ireland whose stamp has *Éire* incorporated into the design will likely be puzzled at causing offense by saying to someone, "I'm enjoying my visit to *Éire*". Furlong (2006) describes the history behind this evaluation, the history containing better explanation of the offense caused than interpretive principles, and notes some of the same interpretive issues described here. The content of the *faux pas* is to use *Éire* as the name of Ireland in an English sentence. Recall Article 4 of the constitution (14):

(14) Article 4
The name of the State is *Éire*, or, in the English language, *Ireland.*

The emphasis is in the original: italicization cannot be used to diagnose that the word *Éire* is not an English word, since both names are emphasized. Indeed, Irish names are used throughout the English text of the constitution (see (26) and (27) below). It is common usage in public discourse to refer in an English sentence to the sole legislative body in Ireland responsible for the introduction of money bills as the "*Dáil*". Article 4 constitutes another case where "or" is involved in a confusing use, here in conjunction with ambiguity about punctuation, and the overall resulting syntactic ambiguity. In English, non-restrictive phrasal modifiers (non-restrictive relative clauses, appositives, etc.) are marked by commas; restrictive phrasal modifiers are not marked by commas. The semantic issue of a non-restrictive modifier is that it does not contribute information that narrows possible reference, and thus could be omitted without loss of information about reference.

(14') Article 4'
The name of the State is *Éire*, or, *Ireland*.

This interpretation is such that it favors a reading in which there is optionality on how to refer to the name of the State, in English. A natural understanding of the text is that there are two ways to refer to the State, and that this is special with reference to other issues that pertain to Ireland's internal operations. Precedent within the constitution for such use exists.

(24) Article 12 §1
There shall be a President of Ireland (Uachtarán na hÉireann), hereinafter called the President,....

In the excerpt of Article 12 given in (24) a parenthetical is used to provide another non-restrictive modification, an alternative proper description in English for the individual fulfilling the role. Evidently, the preferred reading of Article 4 is:

(14'') Article 4''
The name of the State in the National language is "*Éire*", and, the name State in the other official language is "*Ireland*".

However, applying the principles of interpretation in place, there is no method of formal syntax or semantics to justify this within the text. There is certainly ample sociolinguistic reason, but that appeals to information specifically extrinsic to the text.

Presumably, issues like this underlie The Law Reform Committee's (2000: 73) advice which suggests eliminating non-restrictive modification constructions from statutory drafting:

(25) Very often, too, draftsmen include words that appear superfluous. This is probably a symptom of an excess of the traditional care taken to ensure that there is no omission in a section. The common practice of using two or three words, with a similar meaning, in succession, when one noun would suffice, seems to us to be equally unnecessary.

3.2 Underspecification, aspectual ambiguity and Article 18 §2

Consider (26), an example of underspecification. This is from Article 18 §2 of the Constitution.

(26) A person to be eligible for membership of Seanad Éireann must be eligible to become a member of Dáil Éireann.

It seems that the text is underconstrained with respect to probable intent associated with the temporal aspect of "BE". For reference, Article 16 §1(1) provides for eligibility to be a member of Dáil Éireann as in (27):

(27) Every citizen without distinction of sex who has reached the age of twenty-one years, and who is not placed under disability or incapacity by this Constitution or by law, shall be eligible for membership of Dáil Éireann.

The issue at stake here is that, regardless of intended interpretations, the text (26) of Article 18 §2 is ambiguous. One reading of the text is that eligibility for membership in Seanad is identical with prerequisites to eligibility for membership in Dáil Éireann. The more readily available reading is that membership in Seanad is determined solely by potential to become eligible for membership in the other house. This reading is provided for by use of the infinitive *to become* in the predication *must be eligible to be-*

come. In order to have been unambiguous, the text would have to have been[12] stated as in (28):

(28) A person to be eligible for membership of Seanad Éireann must be eligible to be a member of Dáil Éireann.

The problem with (26) is that unless no citizen under the age of 21 can ever hope to be a member of Dáil Éireann and if no one over 21 can ever become a naturalized citizen and eligible, (in which case there could be no future members of Seanad) then anyone who can become a member of the Dáil Éireann in the future (but not now) is now eligible to be member of Seanad. An Irish national who today is a child is eligible to *become* a member of Dáil Éireann, by virtue of potential to become 21 years of age, even if that same child is not eligible to be a member of Dáil Éireann.

All this might seem like something that the "golden rule" of interpretation would rule out on the basis of its being absurd for a child to be allowed to hold public office, or inconsistent for a child to be allowed as a member of the Seanad but not the Dáil. However, contexts change, and norms about expectations of legal voting ages, eligibility for armed services, consent and responsibility can be modified over time. Presumably, if it does become an expectation that individuals under the age of 21 are allowed in the Seanad, they will also be allowed in the Dáil, by virtue of the "golden rule" eliminating inconsistency.

To take this further, contrast the statements of qualifications for the Dáil and Seanad with those stipulating qualifications to be President.

(29) Article 12 §4(1)
Every citizen who has reached his thirty-fifth year of age is eligible for election to the office of President.

This Article is unambiguous. Like Article 16 §1(1), only citizens of the Irish state are eligible. However, Article 18 §2 (see (26)) makes no refer-

12. Of course, there are an uncountable infinity of alternative phrasings that would have yielded the intended meaning unambiguously, however the suggestion given is minimally different from the original.

ence to citizenship[13]. Thus, in addition to there being no age constraint on Seanad Éireann, neither is there a citizenship requirement for anyone who is not Irish. The text of Article 2, wholly within the constitution, could be cited as actually emphasizing openness in this regard, at least with respect to some non-Nationals with Irish ancestry.

(30) Article 2
It is the entitlement and birthright of every person born in the island of Ireland, which includes its islands and seas, to be part of the Irish Nation. That is also the entitlement of all persons otherwise qualified in accordance with law to be citizens of Ireland. Furthermore, the Irish nation cherishes its special affinity with people of Irish ancestry living abroad who share its cultural identity and heritage.

As a result, it seems that anyone who is not ineligible to become an Irish citizen, regardless of age, is eligible to be a member of Seanad Éireann. The strength of this reading comes in no small part from Article 25, particularly the emphasized clause in (20) which places focus on the text of the constitution as the source of guidance on its interpretation.

The text of the Constitution in Article 18 §2 is not vague: it prescribes two possible forms of eligibility to the Seanad, one actual and the other potential[14].

---

13. Article 16 §1(1), on eligibility to be a member of the Dáil, does not mention citizenship (see (27)); however, the point here, too, is the difference between be and become.
14. Handily, by virtue of Article 25 §5 (4), the constitution is in the end unambiguous on exactly this point by virtue of the fact that the Irish version expresses the sense of (28) rather than the sense given by the actual English text (26) (Rósmáire Nic Aodha, personal communication): the English and Irish drafts of the constitution differ on precisely this point, as discussed above.

3.3 Lexical semantics, ambiguity and the Family Law Act (1996)

In this section, another article of the Constitution[15] is demonstrated to be ambiguous in a way that interacts interestingly with intentions surrounding the Family Law Act (1996), and other aspects of the Constitution[16]. The main argument of this section is that the legal instruments at stake provide for more divorces than has been hitherto observed, is within certain interesting parameters more permissive of no-fault divorce than is provided for by corresponding British legislation[17], and that this permissiveness is in general concert with the Constitutional provision for primacy of the Family[18] as well as the Constitution's declaration of social policy that includes maximization of the number of families in the State.[19]

Following the 1995 referendum, Article 41 §3(2) of the Constitution provides:

(31) A Court designated by law may grant of a dissolution of marriage where, but only where, it is satisfied that –
  (i) at the date of the institution of the proceedings, the spouses have lived apart from one another for a period of, or periods amounting to, at least four years during the previous five years,
  (ii) there is no reasonable prospect of a reconciliation between the spouses,
  (iii) such provision as the Court considers proper having regard to the circumstances exists or will be made for the spouses, any children of either or both of them and any other person prescribed by law, and
  (iv) any further conditions prescribed by law are complied with.

Moreover, the Family Law (Divorce) Act (1996) provides in §5(1):

15. Article 41 makes special provisions for the "family" as a societal unit, and Article 41 §3(2.i) spells out conditions for divorce, as discussed in the rest of this section.
16. Article 42 §1 and Article 45 §2(v)
17. Family Law Act (1996)
18. Article 41 §1
19. Article 45 §2(v)

(32) Subject to the provisions of this Act, where, on application to it in that behalf either of the spouses concerned, the court is satisfied that –
(a) at the date of the institution of the proceedings the spouses have lived apart from one another for a period of, or periods amounting to, at least four years during the previous five years,
(b) there is no reasonable prospect of a reconciliation between the spouses, and
(c) such provision as the court considers proper having regard to the circumstances exists or will be made for the spouses and any dependent members of the family,
the court may, in exercise of the jurisdiction conferred by Article 41.3.2 of the Constitution, grant a decree of divorce in respect of the marriage concerned.

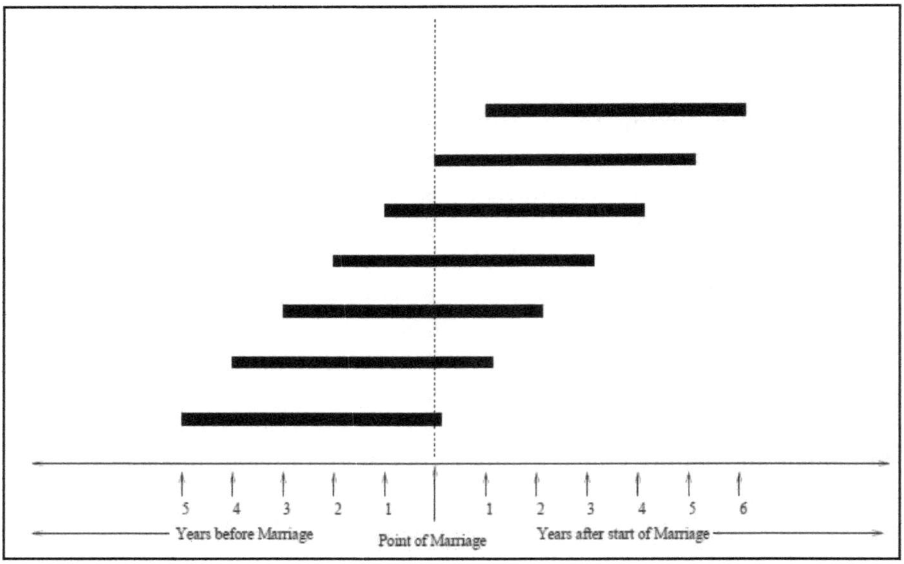

Figure 1. Discrete five year intervals of interest to the Family Law Act 1996

Popular[20] and scholarly[21] perception has it that the minimum time "living apart" required by Article 41 §3(2.i) is four of the five years preceding the date of application. This is indeed patently the case. Walls and Bergin (1997: 11) allude to the interesting fact that provided the other conditions are met, nothing here requires that even the year antecedent to application be included in the four years of separation[22]. What has not been pointed out before is that there is no stipulation in the Constitution or in the Act of the Oireachtas of the starting point in measuring the five years preceding the application. A popular predilection seems to assume that this reckoning commences with the start of the marriage; however, there is no such provision in the text of the Constitution or the relevant Act. On the other hand, the text is not especially vague either: there is a prescribed period of "living apart" that must be demonstrated to have existed among four of the five years prior to the application. While the corresponding act in Britain[23] entails a minimum of 93 weeks of marriage prior to divorce because of a stated prohibition against application within the first year of marriage (along with prescribed periods for various procedures), the text of the Irish laws entail no such minimum.

Figure 1 depicts five-year intervals that are salient to the issue at hand. For clarity of presentation only intervals beginning at discrete numbers of years relative to the point of marriage are depicted – the discussion applies equally to intervals which commence at interim points as well. The dark horizontal bars indicate five year spans prior to filing during which four years of "living apart" must be demonstrated. The illustration indicates that "living apart" does not entail "separation" until after the point of marriage; that is, provided that the spouses did not live together prior to the marriage, a divorce can be applied for immediately after marriage, and, in fact, at any point during the first year of marriage. If the spouses need only demonstrate that they have lived apart for four years (and not that they lived together as spouses and then separated), which is what the text of the Constitution and related Act stipulated, then all that is necessary (in addition to

20. "Divorce Bill Passes Second Stage in Dáil," The Irish Times. Home News. Friday, June 28, 1996; Carol Coulter, "'No Fault' Divorce Basis Not Debated," The Irish Times. Opinion. Friday, June 21, 1996.
21. See Conneely (1997) and Walls and Bergin (1997).
22. The Judicial Separation Act 1989 §2(d) does require a minimum of one year of living apart immediately prior to application.
23. Family Law Act (1996).

the other provisions, none of which stipulate periods of wait) is to demonstrate that they did not live together prior to the marriage. Obviously, the longer a couple has been married, the greater the length of separation is required and the less the time prior to marriage has an effect. After five years of marriage, none of the time prior to marriage is relevant to the law, and the full four years of "living apart" in the five years prior to application must be separation[24].

Two issues of lexical semantics are worthy of discussion at this point. The first is a reiteration: the legal texts stipulate "living apart" is essential, not "separation". Only the latter has any implication of a state of prior "togetherness", and even "separation" does not entail that the prior unity be conjugal. The second and more interesting point is the use of the definite description, "the spouses". One potential argument against the point made in this paper is that "spouse" conveys the requisite sense of conjugal relation that entails that the period of living apart must actually be separation after the commencement of marriage. The putative argument runs thusly: if the pair of individuals is not married, then they are not spouses, so the time prior to marriage is irrelevant.

However, this argument fails for two reasons, both of which pertain to the potential for the expression "the spouses" to designate a definite pair of individuals who are not conjugally related to each other. The most technical reason is that "the spouses" can in fact be used as a term to designate a definite pair of individuals who are not married to each other nor related in any conjugal sense. Consider the Pension Schemes (Family Law) Regulations 1997 (S.I. No. 107 of 1997; pt 1, §3 (definitions) 1)

(33) "Spouse" includes a person who is party to a marriage that has been dissolved under the Act of 1996 or under the law of a country or jurisdiction other than the State.

However, an even more obvious fact is that definite descriptions in general are characterized by designating a particular individual or set of individuals with particular members. "The spouses" in the Act is not, of course, designating a particular set of individuals, but instead specifies a function which in any case at hand does properly denote the two individuals who are ap-

24. This discussion is wholly orthogonal to the issue of what counts as "living apart" (cf. Walls and Bergin 1997). For example, living in separate rooms in the same house, given limiting financial circumstances, may be sufficient.

plying for a divorce. Thus, in a particular case, those individuals will have to demonstrate the requisite period of living apart: "the spouses" designates those two individuals uniquely, and having specified them in this fashion they remain uniquely identified in the period prior to the marriage and subsequent to the divorce. Consider another example of a definite description: "the current President of Ireland". The current President of Ireland is not a man – the individual designated by the expression "the current President of Ireland" (at the time of writing) is a woman, and (to the best of everyone's knowledge) has always been female, even prior to being the current President of Ireland: the description uniquely picks out an individual, yet the diagnostic property of the individual contained in the expression need not always have been a property of that unique individual. Thus, "the spouses" designates two individuals at the time of application for divorce, subsequent to marriage, and so also picks out the same the time of application for divorce, subsequent to marriage, and so also picks out the same individuals at times prior to the marriage. As one final example of this phenomenon, consider another passage from the Constitution[25]:

(34) If a member of either House of the Oireachtas be elected President, he shall be deemed to have vacated his seat in that House.

Article 12, §6 (1) stipulates that "the President shall not be a member of either House of the Oireachtas". This sentence makes §6 (2) interesting in that two pronouns are used, "he" and "his". Either those anaphors lack antecedents, or they refer to the "member" or to the "President". It's an interesting case because the preceding clause §6 (1) stipulates that a single individual can't hold a seat in one of the Houses at the same time as being President, yet intuitively the pronouns both pick out the individual at stake who might have been in such a position. If the pronouns do not pick out the individual in question, then they do not refer at all, as if an individual has vacated his seat he cannot be a member in the corresponding house. That is, the pronoun refers to a potential individual that fits the description, "elected President, former member of a House of the Oireachtas", as that person cannot without contradiction be a member of a House of the Oireachtas and President-elect. The essential point demonstrated here is that a definite description allows the designation of a particular individual, and having denoted that individual the same individual is uniquely identified for the peri-

25. Article 12, §6 (2)

ods prior to and subsequent to the period during which the definite description is accurate. Similarly, there is nothing in the text of the Constitution nor the corresponding Act[26] which stipulates that the spouses who must "have lived apart from each other for a period of, or periods amounting to, at least four of the five years during the previous five years" to have at the time of application been married for any length of time subsequent to commencement of the marriage, provided that it can be demonstrated that "there is no reasonable prospect of a reconciliation between the spouses".

The Constitution and Act are both ambiguous with respect to the minimum duration of "living apart" required relative to the commencement of the marriage[27]. This entails that the requisite period of separation after the marriage is also ambiguous (but not vague). Vagueness enters into the proceedings by virtue of Article 41 §3 (2.ii) quoted at the end of the preceding paragraph. It is not specified what can constitute a reasonable prospect for reconciliation, and presumably the judiciary is at some liberty to use this clause to prohibit what might be deemed a frivolously short period following commencement of the marriage before application. On the other hand, while "frivolously short" is also vague, it is outwith the texts at issue to require that the full five years be reckoned as the minimum bound. The next paragraphs argue why this is the case.

The Constitution has declared for itself an interesting pair of principles. On one hand, the Family is proclaimed as "the natural primary and fundamental unit group of Society"[28], and on the other hand it is indicated as a principle of social policy that there should be "as many families as the circumstances shall be practicable"[29]. Vagueness enters at this point, on exactly what constitutes the "Family". It would cause riot to declare that a single-parent household does not constitute a family. Thus, provided that Article 41 §3 (2.iii) is met in each case, access to divorce and subsequent remarriage does further the State's policy toward the proliferation of families as stated in Article 45, §2(v). This entails that given that no-fault divorce is constitutionally available, coupled with the finite span of human

26. Neither explicitly as in the corresponding British Family Act (1996), nor implicitly via lexical semantics.
27. Unlike the issue of eligibility for Seanad as discussed above for which the Irish text resolves the issue, the same ambiguity persists in both the English and the Irish texts on this point (Rósmáire Nic Aodha, personal communication).
28. Article 41, §1
29. Article 45, §2 (v)

life, there is a constitutional imperative to minimize any period of time at issue in the demonstration that Article 41 §3 (2.ii) is satisfied; that is, the phrase "no reasonable prospect of a reconciliation" cannot within the spirit of the Constitution be deemed to specify a duration of time for assessment "reasonable prospect" independent of the duration specified by Article 41 §3 (2.i). Incorporating a period of time into the interpretation of Article 41 §3 (2.ii) independent of that specified by Article 41 §3 (2.i) would violate both Article 45 §2 (v) and Article 25 §5 (3).

What is more deeply interesting is that while the letter of the law maximizes the number of potential marriages, and via correlation the number of families, extant in the State, there is a less sophisticated sense in which the structure of the text with its ambiguity[30] about the required length of time of living apart subsequent to commencement of marriage. The more interesting point is that the current phrasing of the Constitution and corresponding Act on the relevant points is such that there is an increasing commitment to a particular marriage continuing as a marriage in approximate proportion to the length of time of the marriage, with relatively less commitment at the start, and relatively more after the first five years. This is a rather liberal and strikingly sound design given general sociological and psychological principles about break-ups of commitments like marriage as a function of the time during which the married state is in force. That is, a divorce is likely to be more devastating to the individuals involved (dependents included) after more time of marriage than less (Catron et al. 1980; Palosaari and Aro 1994). It is sound that the Constitution respects both the maximization of quantity of families in the state as well as the increasing seriousness of a potential divorce as the union matures.

4. Generalizations

This article has suggested that the formal semanticist can usefully interact with legal experts during the process of formulating legal texts, and that the semanticist can provide relevant advice for interpretive purposes. A reason to subject legal texts to such scrutiny is in the potential for a document to stand, for example as a constitution, across generations, beyond periods of

30. Again, it is ambiguous how many of the four years need be subsequent to the commencement of marriage. It is not vague, the text allows a number of possibilities.

time in which extra-textual arguments for interpretation are severely challenged. This is perhaps at the heart of current agonization in the US over the "right to bear arms" under second amendment to the US constitution. There is reason to be clear and in conformance with communicative conventions in other contexts as well, of course (Cushing 1994). However, the difference is in the immediacy of interpretation. In general, there are cognitive propensities that are parameterized to contexts that determine the likelihood of any particular reading. An air traffic controller does not need a semanticist as an advisor, but possibly could benefit from advice from a sociolinguist.

This is not to say that linguist should write statutes, or that semanticists are always useful. Linguists working with lawyers often note that they discover that ordinary words have rather special meanings according to interpretation rules in particular jurisdictions, for example. Nonetheless, interactions would be mutually beneficial.

In contexts that permit time for reflection (and those that do not), semantic analysis is relevant, as it depends on syntax, semantics, local and global contexts (including law and legal convention), and matters.

5. Acknowledgements

I thank Cécile Bouchet for introducing me to family law and contributing to the unpublished article (Vogel and Bouchet 1998) that this paper draws on. Monika Rathert has my eternal gratitude for her kind encouragement, understanding and patience with contributing delinquents.

6. References

Adams, Kenneth A. and Kaye, Alan S. 2006. "Revisiting the Ambiguity of "And" and "Or" in Legal Drafting". *St. John's Law Review*, 80(4), 1167–1195.

Berk-Seligson, Susan. 1990. "Bilingual Court Proceedings: The Role of the Court Interpreter". *Language in the Judicial Process*, Vol. 5 of *Law, Society and Policy*, ed. by J. N. Levi and A. G. Walker, New York: Plenum. 155–201.

Butts, Peter and Castle, Richard. 2001. *Modern Legal Drafting*. Cambridge: Cambridge University Press.

Byers, Michael. 2004. "Agreeing to Disagree: Security Resolution 1441 and Intentional Ambiguity". *Global Governance* 10, 165–186.

Catron, Linda S., Chiriboga, David. A., and Krystal, Sheila. 1980. "Divorce at Midlife: Psychic Dangers of the Liminal Period. Part I. Empirical Considerations". *Maturitas* 2(2), 131–139.

Chaski, Carole E. 1997. "Who wrote it? Steps toward a science of authorship identification". *National Institute of Justice Journal* 233, 15–22.

Chaski, Carole E. 2001. "Empirical Evaluations of Language-based Author Identification Techniques". *Forensic Linguistics* 8(1), 1–65.

Coles-Bjerre, Andrea. 2006. "Bankruptcy Theory and the Acceptance of Ambiguity". *The American Bankruptcy Law Journal* 80(4), 327–376.

Conneely, Sinead. 1997. "The Family Law (Divorce) Act 1996: Some Observations". *Irish Law Times* 15(4), 78–81.

Cushing, Steven. 1994. *Fatal Words: Communication Clashes and Aircraft Crashes*. University of Chicago Press.

Dickerson, F. Reed. 1975. *The Interpretation and Application of Statutes*. Boston: Little, Brown and Company.

Eades, Diana. 2002. "'Evidence Given in Unequivocal Terms': Gaining Consent of Aboriginal Young People in Court". *Language in the Legal Process*, ed. by J. Cotterill, Hampshire: Palgrave Macmillan. 162–179.

Furlong, John. 2006. "Ireland – the Name of the State". *Legal Information Management* 6, 297–301.

Hunt, Brian. 2002. "Plain Language in Legislative Drafting: An Achievable Objective or A Laudable Ideal". *Fourth Biennial Conference Proceedings. Plain Language Association International*. Toronto, Canada. September 2002. 26–29.

Kowalski, Robert A. 1992. "Legislation as logic programs". *Logic Programming in Action, Lecture Notes in Computer Science*, ed. by G. Comyn, N. E. Fuchs and M. J. Ratcliff, Springer: Berlin-Heidelberg. 203–230.

Palosaari, Ulla and Aro, Hillevi. 1994. "Effect of Timing of Parental Divorce on the Vulnerability of Children to Depression in Young Adulthood". *Adolescence* 29(115), 681–90.

Pehar, Drazen. 2005. *Language, Power, Law: Groundwork for the Theory of Diplomatic Ambiguity*. Ph.D. thesis, Keele University.

Schane, Sanford. 2002. "Ambiguity and Misunderstanding in the Law". *Thomas Jefferson Law Revew* 25, 167–193.

Solan, Lawrence M. 1993. *The Language of Judges*. University of Chicago Press.

Stacy, Thomas G. 2005. "Cleaning up the Eighth Amendment Mess". *William and Mary Bill of Rights Journal* 14, 475–573.

Tanner, Edwin. 2004. "Clear, Simple and Precise Legislative Drafting: Australian Guidelines Explicated Using an EU Directive". *Statute Law Review* 25(3), 223–250.

Tanner, Edwin. 2006." Clear, Simple, and Precise Legislative Drafting: How Does a European Community Directive Fare?". *Statute Law Review* 27(3), 150–175.

The Law Reform Committee. 2000. *Statutory Drafting and Interpretation: Plain Language and the Law*. Ireland.

Tiersma, Peter and Solan, Lawrence. M. 2002. "The Linguist on the Witness Stand: Forensic Linguistics in American Courts". *Language* 78(2), 221–239.

Verkuyl, Henk. 1994. "Distributivity and Collectivity: A Couple at Odds". *Dynamics, Polarity and Quantification*, ed. by M. Kanazawa and C. Piñon, Stanford: CSLI Publications. 49–80.

Vogel, Carl and Bouchet, Cécile. 1998. "Semantic Ambiguity, Vagueness and Constitutional Ramifications of the Family Law Act of 1996". Tech. rep. TCD-CS-1998-04, Department of Computer Science, Trinity College, University of Dublin.

Walls, Muriel and Bergin, David. 1997. *The Law of Divorce in Ireland*. Bristol: Jordans.

Improving the comprehensibility of German court decisions

Stella Neumann

1. Introduction

Throughout the years many legal scholars have discussed the difficulties of understanding the structure of the law, the way it is negotiated and conveyed (see Viehweg and Rotter 1977, also Haß-Zumkehr 2002). Most recently this discussion had a forum in the working group "Sprache des Rechts" at the Berlin-Brandenburgische Akademie der Wissenschaften (see Lerch 2005a, b). While some of the scholars argue that legal texts are not meant to be understood by the lay public and that it should rely on professional "translation" (see Ogorek 2004), i.e. by lawyers, many jurists seem to feel a strong need to improve the comprehensibility of legal texts for lay readers.[1] One of the reasons could be that even legal professionals have difficulties explaining complex legal questions to their clients. Part of this problem is inherent in the way the law has evolved into such a complex structure that is hard to handle even for experts. However, there is also a part having more to do with the way the law is expressed linguistically. Some of the methods linguists can contribute to investigating the comprehensibility of legal texts are

1. identifying and explaining the linguistic phenomena that distinguish legal texts from other registers,
2. manipulating these phenomena in legal texts and
3. testing their processing with both jurists and lay persons.

1. One indicator is the interest the present work received from the German Federal Constitutional Court as well as the reactions of the legal experts participating in the experiment described here.

G. Grewendorf and M. Rathert (eds.): Formal Linguistics and Law, 55–80

Strategy 1 may use the instruments corpus linguistics offers in order to make general statements on the basis of empirical analyses. Strategy 2 involves experimenting with the linguistic phenomena under the supervision of jurists. Finally, strategy 3 draws upon methods of psycholinguistic research. The work presented here combines these three steps on a very small scale picking out the example of German court decisions.

Some caveats are in place. First of all, it has to be ensured that the legal contents of the texts remain unchanged during the process of varying legal texts for the purpose of improving their comprehensibility. This aspect is taken into account in the present work by the participation of a jurist in the rephrasing process (see section 4). Furthermore, it should be stressed that the scope of the present work does not allow covering all linguistic phenomena that would deserve attention. We narrowed down the range of linguistic phenomena arguably affecting the comprehensibility of legal texts to some prominent syntactic features. As will be seen in section 3, these features have overall consequences for the texts beyond just syntactic structures. The study thus exemplifies a methodology dealing with linguistic obstacles to understanding legal texts particularly by lay readers.

It should be pointed out that the discussion on legal comprehensibility is an important topic in many languages and legal systems.[2] In the Anglophone world this has led to the emergence of the Plain Language Movement that promotes the use of simple language not only in a legal context but beyond that in all areas of public life. Rather than getting its impetus from academic research, this movement has more in common with an action group. In German speaking countries, the topic is discussed almost exclusively in a scholarly context (e.g. Grewendorf 1992, Dietrich and Klein 2000, Klein 2001, Haß-Zumkehr 2002, Lerch 2004a). In what follows, we will focus on this latter context not least because the research described here is concerned with the German language. Nevertheless, the overall methodology presented here should be transferable to other languages, particularly to the English language since the syntactic features we investigate roughly correspond to features discussed for the English legal language as well (see Hülper 2004).

The paper is organised as follows. First we will give a brief account of existing work particularly on measuring the comprehensibility of legal texts

2. The International Association of Forensic Linguists offers an online bibliography on this strand of research at http://www.iafl.bham.uk/bib/biblio.html#CAT030000 (last visited: 10 November 2006).

(section 2). Looking closer at German court decisions we will then consider some frequent syntactic features of this register in section 3, complementing it by some thoughts on the contribution of these features to the way German court decisions function. Section 4 presents our experiment of varying the features discussed previously and testing the rephrasings in a psycholinguistic experiment including a brief assessment of the merits and limitations of our methodology. We will then come to some conclusions combined with an outlook on a profile of a text optimised for the lay reader in section 5.

2. State of the art

So far our account may suggest that the language of law is a coherent complex. This is not very plausible because different texts in the legal domain serve quite different purposes which ought to be reflected in different linguistic realisations (see Eriksen 2002). Legislative texts, for instance, define in general terms what is lawful and what is not. The focus of these texts is to cover as many different cases as possible in as general a wording as possible. It even transcends existing cases having to encompass all future events that could arise in those situations addressed by the legislation.

Contracts, on the other hand, regulate the internal relationship between the parties involved. While also covering events in the future these are – or at least should be – defined as clearly as possible. Contracts may refer to legislation, but they (or rather the contract parties) are ultimately also subject to it.

The present work is concerned with yet another register, court decisions. These texts differ from the two previously mentioned registers in that a concrete event in the past is addressed by an independent institution (Eriksen 2002). The institution's task is to consider and decide the case in view of the existing legislation and precedence cases[3]. Instead of instructing the recipient how to act in accordance with the law (or a contract), the behaviour of the litigants in a concrete case is appraised. The recipients are both jurists working with the decision as well as lay persons in terms of the litigants involved.[4] This characterisation entails specific features of court decisions that have been described for German by Altehenger (1983) in an ex-

3. This latter aspect only plays a minor role in the German legal system.
4. Eriksen (2002:17) calls this the janus-faced character of the language of courts.

ample based way, Engberg (1997) with a focus on activity patterns expressed by classes of verbs in German and Danish court decisions, and Hansen-Schirra and Neumann (2004) using corpus-linguistic methods to quantify typical features of German court decisions. Additionally, we may find recommendations for writing court decisions in textbooks for law students (for instance Anders and Gehle 2005).

One strand of research into legal language aims at measuring the comprehensibility of legal texts. This can be approached from different angles targeting different units of analysis and using different kinds of experimental methods.

Firstly, we can measure the length of words and the numbers of syllables per word and compute these figures with the help of readability formulas (e.g. the Flesch test; Flesch 1948), assuming that the longer the words are and the more syllables they contain the more processing effort the recipient will have to invest. Basedow (1999) applies the Flesch test to texts from the field of insurance law – an area that is of major importance to the lay reader and therefore receives much attention in studies on legal comprehensibility. The advantage of methods like the Flesch test is that they are easy to compute and that they result in ratios that allow easy comparison across texts. However, one of the many problems with the readability approach is that short words favoured by this approach are not necessarily easy to understand. Therefore readability is not considered a state of the art methodology anymore (see Rickheit 1995; Davison and Green 1988 from within the paradigm; Lerch 2004b for an exhaustive discussion of applying readability tests to legal language).

Looking at units within syntactic structures, Neumann and Hansen-Schirra (2004) focus on the German conjunctive, the verb mood expressing reported speech, wishes, unreality and other kinds of modal meaning in German legal language and discuss a rating experiment of sentences featuring verbs in conjunctive mood. This study can be seen as a pilot study of the methodology used in the present study. It starts with a quantitative examination of a corpus of court decisions before testing different versions of the structure under investigation in view of their comprehensibility both for legal experts and for lay readers. However, while acceptability rating is suited to get a first idea of a phenomenon, it does not give comprehensive insight into the way language is processed.

The above mentioned working group "Sprache des Rechts" employed more elaborate experimental methods in their research (see Berliner Arbeitsgruppe 2000). The group looked at complex comprehension processes of whole texts rather than at smaller units within the texts. Focussing on the comprehensibility of terms and conditions of insurances, the members of the group used a range of methods: free recall task, semantic differential, questionnaire (Dietrich and Kühn 2000), free linearisation (Dietrich and Schmidt 2002), think-aloud protocol (Becker 2002) and most recently eye tracking (Hillebrand et al. 2006).

While all of these studies offer valuable insights, they do not attempt to investigate how the recipients would process rephrased versions of the texts improved for their comprehensibility.

3. Frequent syntactic features of German court decisions

Syntactic features typically mentioned in descriptions of legal and administrative texts are overly long and complex sentences as well as nominal style (see Wagner 1981, Oksaar 1988). Nominal style can be viewed in terms of noun phrases used to pack information otherwise contained in whole clauses as well as in terms of nominalisations. These features are investigated in linguistic studies of legal language. An alternative – and promising – approach would be deriving features from psycholinguistic studies of language processing. This would require selecting those features impairing language processing that can be assumed to be of particular interest in the language of the law.

3.1 Corpus analysis of syntactic features

The present study picks out three of the features discussed in Hansen-Schirra and Neumann (2004) for court decisions, i.e. complex sentences, complex noun phrases including prepositional phrases and nominalisations, and puts them to more scrutiny by not only analysing corpora but rather by annotating the texts in order to yield richer linguistic information.

In order to identify the typical usage of the three features, we have to compare the court decisions to a more general language usage. The corpus used for this purpose therefore does not only consist of court decisions but also of newspaper reports on the same decisions. The corpus of decisions by the German Federal Constitutional Court[5] contains 35,636 words in total. This corpus was chosen because it is particularly these decisions that

5. Taken from the Court's website (http://www.bundesverfassungsgericht.de)

have an impact not only on the litigants in the concrete case but potentially affect a wider public (see Jaspersen 1998). The corpus of newspaper reports totals 5,304 words taken from a range of nationwide broadsheet newspapers.[6] The smaller size of the newspaper sub-corpus is due to two factors. Firstly, not all of the decisions in the corpus are covered by newspaper reports and, secondly, the reports are much shorter than the decisions. They focus on the judgement and cover only the most important reasons detailed in the decision.

The annotation involves a range of tools adapted to the needs of the three features under investigation. Firstly, the corpus was annotated with the help of Christian Braun's topological parser (Braun 1999) based on the field theory ordering the German sentence into fields organised around the verbal bracket (see Höhle 1983). This topological analysis is particularly suited to examine embedding and nesting in complex sentential structures. The automatic annotation is checked and corrected manually.

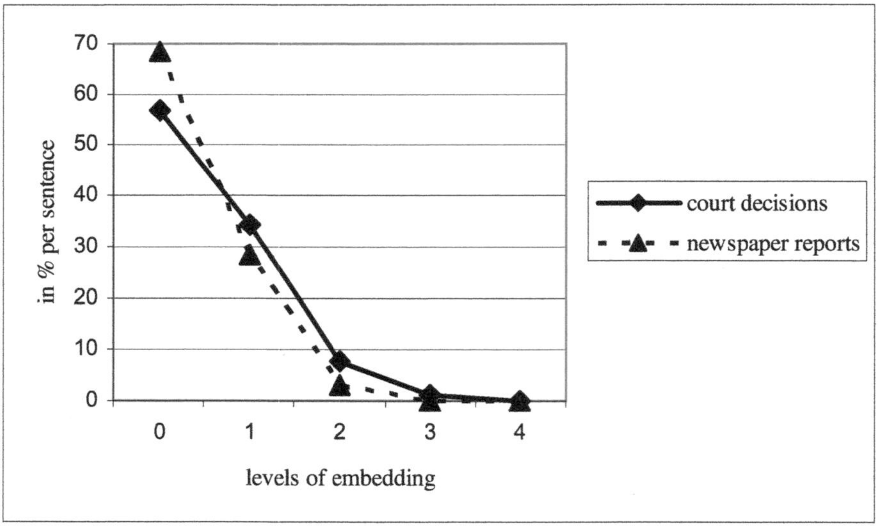

Figure 1. Sentence embedding

6. Hansen et al. (2006) also include press releases by the Court reporting on the decisions. They come to the conclusion that these press releases represent summaries for expert recipients rather than simplified reports for a lay audience. This register therefore does not appear suited as a yardstick for varying the features in view of their comprehensibility for a lay audience (see section 3).

The results as displayed in figure 1 show that in total more sentences are embedded in the court decisions than in the newspaper reports. 56.8% of the sentences in the court decisions contain no embedding compared to 68.3% in the newspaper reports. While the amount of embedding in the newspaper reports declines massively already on level 1 and does not go beyond level 2, the sentences in the court decisions contain more embedding going as deep as level 4. (1) exemplifies the highly complex sentences in the corpus of court decisions. This example does not only contain three levels of embedding (represented by subscript numbers) but is also heavily nested going back and forth between different levels embedding.

(1) [Der Gesetzgeber durfte davon ausgehen,]$_0$[dass eine Mutter,]$_1$[gerade wenn sie mit dem Vater und dem Kind zusammenlebt,]$_2$[sich nur ausnahmsweise und nur dann dem Wunsch des Vaters nach einer gemeinsamen Sorge verweigert,]$_1$[wenn sie dafür schwerwiegende Gründe hat,]$_2$[die von der Wahrung des Kindeswohls getragen werden,]$_3$[dass sie also die Möglichkeit der Verweigerung einer Sorgeerklärung nicht etwa als Machtposition gegenüber dem Vater missbraucht.]$_1$

Noun phrases are analysed manually using an XML editor to store the annotation in a machine-readable form. To this purpose we first extract noun phrases of at least 10 tokens for the decisions and 7 tokens for the newspaper reports[7] from the parsed corpus. These are then annotated formally focussing on pre- and postmodification. Like the sentence annotation this manual annotation is also checked and corrected manually.

7. We reduced the threshold in newspaper reports, because they did not contain longer phrases.

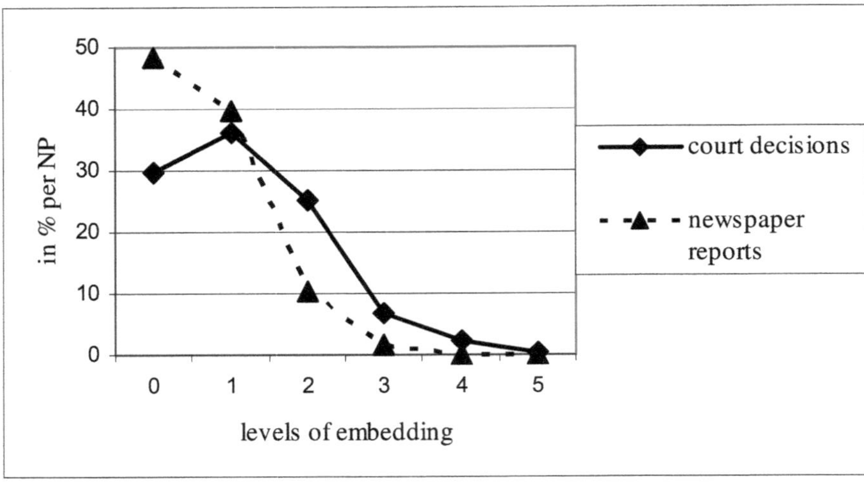

Figure 2. NP embedding

The results show that there are more noun phrases in the court decisions containing one embedded modification (36.11%) than there are without any modification (29.70%). This contrasts with the newspaper reports in which almost half of the NPs (48.51%) are not embedded at all and, if so, mostly on level 1 (39.55%). The amount of embedding beyond this level drops sharply. The difference between the two corpora becomes obvious in figure 2. Deep NP embedding is a clear indicator of the way authors of court decisions convey information within nominal elements rather than in clauses. (2) shows a heavily postmodified prepositional phrase (italicised) from the corpus of court decisions.

(2) *Bei der Umsetzung der Vorgaben der Gerichte für eine verfassungskonforme Regelung der Überführung von Ansprüchen und Anwartschaften aus den Zusatz- und Sonderversorgungssystemen der ehemaligen DDR* lässt sich der Gesetzgeber von der befriedenden Wirkung dieser Entscheidungen leiten.

Finally, for retrieving nominalisations the corpus is tagged with part-of-speech information using the TnT tagger (Brants 2000). We query derivations on "-ung", "-ion", "-ismus", "-heit", "-keit", "-ität", "-schaft" as well as the respective plural forms in the concordance tool WordSmith (Scott 1996). Queries of the following type are done: *[derivational suffix][plural marker] [part of speech tag for nouns].* (3) displays some concordance lines from the corpus of court decisions.

(3) a. Es entspreche der *Bedeutung* der Feststellung durch das ...
b. ... Tatbestandsseite an die *Befolgung* oder Nichtbefolgung ...
c. ... Gesetzgeber für die *Beurteilung* der Eignung und ...
d. ... Finanzvolumen der *Budgetplanung* und –entscheidung ...
e. ... einer staatlichen *Einrichtung* oder Leistung erhoben ...
f. ... über die *Entkriminalisierung* bzw. Entpönalisierung von ...
g. ... die alternative *Entsorgung* durch Verbrennung seien ...
h. ... Person an der *Erlangung* der Rechtsstellung als ...
i. ... oder Aufhebung der *Gebührenermäßigung* durch ...
j. ... typisierende *Gesamtbetrachtung* und Gesamtwürdigung ...

For the purpose of the present study we concentrate on deverbal derivations in "-ung", because they constitute by far the largest group of nominalisations, particularly in the court decisions, as can be seen from table 1. There are more "-ung" nominalisations in the court decisions than there are nominalisations of all kinds in the newspaper reports. This can be interpreted as a way of condensing information.

Table 1. Nominalisations

corpus	all	"-ung"
court decisions	7.15 %	5.31 %
newspaper reports	4.54 %	3.30 %

The analysis presented here concentrated on a broad characterisation of the three features. It would be interesting to investigate the respective feature more closely. For example, positional aspects of the embedding structures would deserve attention.

3.2 Interpretation

If we look at the syntactic features in a broader perspective we can see that they have an impact beyond the scope of grammar. First of all, the prime linguistic function of court decisions is to communicate the legal information in an efficient, i.e. concise way. A convenient way to achieve this is to pack information into nominal elements rather than into complete clauses which have to contain all arguments required by the verb.[8] In this sense, legal language is not different from any other language for specific purposes (LSP; see Roelcke 2005).

At a closer look, the functions can be examined from three perspectives on the text, focussing on the referential meaning, the interpersonal relationship between author and recipient and, finally, the textual structure.

With respect to referential meaning we can ask what the features under investigation contribute to the conveyed meaning. Can we find any reasons why highly complex sentences could be useful in the court decisions? Let us go back to example 1 in its immediate context italicised in (4) to find an explanation.

(4) Ziel des Kindschaftsrechtsreformgesetzes, mit dem § 1626 a BGB eingeführt worden ist, war es, im Interesse der Kinder die gemeinsame elterliche Sorge auch für nicht miteinander verheiratete Eltern zu ermöglichen, diese Sorgeform zu fördern und dabei die Elternautonomie zu stärken. Durch diese Regelung ist dem Elternrecht des Vaters aus Art. 6 Abs. 2 GG hinreichend Rechnung getragen worden. *Der Gesetzgeber durfte davon ausgehen, dass eine Mutter, gerade wenn sie mit dem Vater und dem Kind zusammenlebt, sich nur ausnahmsweise und nur dann dem Wunsch des Vaters nach einer gemeinsamen Sorge verweigert, wenn sie dafür schwerwiegende Gründe hat, die von der Wahrung des Kindeswohls getragen werden, dass sie also die Möglichkeit der Verweigerung einer Sorgeerklärung nicht etwa als Machtposition gegenüber dem Vater missbraucht.* Zwar hat die Studie von Proksch inzwischen bestätigt, dass auch nach einer Trennung von Eltern deren gemeinsame Sorge dem Kindeswohl in vielen Fällen dienlich ist.

One factor prompting the authors to pack all the information in one sentence could be portioning of information within the legal reasoning. From the point of view of the referential meaning it is obvious that the authors try to describe the object as clearly as possible and delineate it from any other constellation. Each of the sentences elaborates one point in the argumentation (in our target sentence “eine Mutter”) with parataxis and hypotaxis used to specify it as exactly as possible. The authors employ the complex

8. Moreover, grammatical information contained in the verbal group like tense, mood and voice is underspecified.

sentence as an efficient tool to compress this specification. The relevant aspects are thus linked to each other as closely as possible. If we break this sentence into several units, cohesion is more difficult to achieve (see section 4). The frequency of nominalisations in the court decisions can be attributed at least in part to the need to assign specific denotations in the specific legal context (see Roelcke 2005:79).

Looking at the relationship between author and reader, the interesting question is: Can we infer a recipient assumed by the authors from the syntax of the text? Of course this is only one aspect of the interpretation. The mere high frequency of complex sentences in the court decisions as compared to the newspaper reports can be interpreted as targeting the expert recipient. Experts accustomed to this kind of wording will have fewer difficulties in processing a sequence like (4). Novices are only occasionally exposed to this kind of logical relations between portions of information. They can be expected to lose track within the complex constructions and will therefore need more processing effort (this was tested in the experiment described in section 4).

Nominalisations can also be viewed as a means of addressing the expert reader. They are an efficient device for packing the information as concisely as possible thus making it difficult for the lay reader to unpack the information, particularly because the nominalisations offer the possibility to leave information like semantic relations, tense, voice etc. implicit (see Halliday 1993). In legal language this has the additional effect of intentionally allowing different readings of the information given. This information may be evident to the expert, but poses a major obstacle to the novice.

Finally, the third aspect to be taken into account is the impact the respective feature has on the texture of the wording. Deverbal derivations like "-ung" nominalisations do not only help condensing the information. They also help extending reference chains throughout the text which would be more difficult to maintain with verbs representing ideas of states or events. These ideas are rather transient and are constantly replaced by other ideas of states and events again expressed by verbs (Chafe 1994). Nominalisations can even be part of compounds, thus still remaining active in the working memory of the reader (sometimes even if they do not build the semantic head of the compound). In (5), an example taken from a decision on children's names, the lemma "bestimmen" first occurs as a verb and is subsequently taken up in various compounds.

(5) Die Vorlage betrifft die Frage, ob es mit dem Grundgesetz vereinbar ist, dass gemeinsam sorgeberechtigte Eltern, die keinen Ehe-

> namen führen, zum Geburtsnamen ihres Kindes (...) einen aus ihren beiden Namen zusammengesetzten Doppelnamen *bestimmen* können. Darüber hinaus wirft die Vorlage die Frage auf, ob die gesetzliche Ermächtigung des zuständigen Gerichts, bei Nicht*bestimmung* des Geburtsnamens durch die Eltern einem Elternteil das *Bestimmungs*recht zu übertragen mit der Folge, dass bei weiterer Nicht*bestimmung* des Namens das Kind den Namen dieses Elternteils erhält, verfassungsgemäß ist.

However, it is questionable whether these reference chains are of help to the lay reader due to the above mentioned ambiguity of the semantic relations of nominalisations. Moreover, nominalisations contribute to making the court decisions so dense that the inexperienced reader probably cannot keep track of all the different chains.

Example (5) also highlights another function of nominalisations. They have been described as an efficient means of summing up the information in the preceding sentence (see Halliday 1993), i.e. in some kind of transcategorisation. In (5) the sequence begins with a sentence introducing the question of the case. In this sentence the authors go to some lengths explaining the process of naming ("zum Geburtsnamen ... bestimmen"). In the following sentence this process initially expressed by a verb is summarised in the form of nominalisations allowing referring to the process of naming in a condensed form. Lambrecht (1994) describes this as the prolonged persistence of an event by conversion into a referent.

Of course, most of the functions only briefly touched upon here have been discussed in more detail elsewhere (concerned with LSPs Roelcke 2005). What we hope to have shown here is that syntactic peculiarities should not be seen in isolation but rather as a building block of the overall make up of the texts and as such contributing to the relative incomprehensibility of the court decisions as LSP texts.

All three features examined here display characteristic differences in their realisation between court decisions and newspaper reports and – as Hansen et al. (2006) show – also to press releases on court decisions. It thus seems plausible to modify them in order to make the texts more in line with the lay reader's reading habits as described in the following section.

4. Testing the comprehensibility of rephrased decisions

Our knowledge of the described features as distinguished from their realisation in texts aimed at a general (lay) public allows us to manipulate the features assumed to impair the lay reader's understanding of the legal text because their frequencies contrast in the two corpora.

4.1 Rephrasing

The rephrasing process is limited to creating two rephrasings on the basis of the complex versions (hereafter referred to as version A). The two rephrasings are geared to two approaches to comprehensibility. The approach proposed by Langer et al. (1974) favours radically resolving complex structures in view of the four dimensions 'linguistic simplicity', 'structure-organisation', 'brevity-shortness' and 'interest-liveliness'. The authors report on a study in which experts scored texts in view of these dimensions, arguing that the higher scores a text receives the better the text will be memorised. Ultimately, this may result in radically simple syntactic structures. In the present study we concentrated on Langer et al.'s dimension of simplicity for the maximally resolved version C.

Groeben and Christmann (1989) oppose to this strategy. They argue that texts conforming to the recipient's expectations do not offer enough cognitive stimuli. Groeben and Christmann claim that extremely simplified texts may destruct the recipient's motivation to continue reading.

This reasoning is used as the basis for creating the medium version B. It is particularly this version B that draws on the quantitative findings for the newspaper reports in the corpus study (section 3), building on the assumption that newspapers reflect – or even influence – their readers' reading habits. Structures typically used in newspapers should be familiar to recipients of court decisions while still instigating enough motivation to 'struggle' with the unfolding text.

For the reformulation the following strategies are used. With respect to sentence complexity we divide the sentences. The strategy for the nominal parameters is to convert nominal into verbal structures either by introducing a verb or by transforming nominalisations back into verbs.

Examples (6) to (8) display the rephrasing process for sentence complexity. (6) shows the original sentence retrieved from the corpus of court decisions, (7) displays the version based on the newspaper reports. The original sentence is divided into three sentences each containing one subordinate clause.

(6) Paragraph 1626 BGB ist mit Artikel 6 Grundgesetz insoweit nicht vereinbar, als eine Übergangsregelung fehlt, die eine gerichtliche Einzelfallprüfung, ob das Wohl des Kindes einer gemeinsamen elterlichen Sorge der nicht miteinander verheirateten Eltern entgegensteht, für die Fälle vorsieht, in denen die Eltern mit dem Kind zusammengelebt, sich aber noch vor In-Kraft-Treten des Kindschaftsrechtsreformgesetzes am 1. Juli 1998 getrennt haben.

(7) Paragraph 1626 BGB ist mit Artikel 6 Grundgesetz insoweit nicht vereinbar, als eine Übergangsregelung fehlt. Diese müsste eine gerichtliche Einzelfallprüfung für die Fälle vorsehen, in denen die Eltern mit dem Kind zusammengelebt haben, sich aber vor dem Inkrafttreten des Kindschaftsrechtsreformgesetzes am 1. Juli 1998 getrennt haben. In diesem Fall wäre zu prüfen, ob das Wohl des Kindes einer gemeinsamen elterlichen Sorge der nicht miteinander verheirateten Eltern entgegensteht.

In the final rephrasing (8) the subordinate clauses have also been resolved into individual sentences.

(8) Paragraph 1626 BGB ist mit Artikel 6 Grundgesetz in einem Punkt nicht vereinbar: Eine Übergangsregelung fehlt. Diese müsste eine gerichtliche Einzelfallprüfung unter zwei Bedingungen vorsehen. Erstens müssten die Eltern mit dem Kind zusammengelebt haben. Zweitens müssten diese sich vor dem Inkrafttreten des Kindschaftsrechtsreformgesetzes am 1. Juli 1998 getrennt haben. In diesem Fall könnte das Wohl des Kindes einer gemeinsamen elterlichen Sorge der nicht miteinander verheirateten Eltern entgegenstehen.

This example shows one of the problems in the rephrasing process. The logical relations within the sentence are difficult to maintain in rephrased versions, because the intersentential reference may be ambiguous and less cohesive. This results in major restructuring of the clauses. In (7), for instance, the postmodification of "Einzelfallprüfung" ("ob das Wohl ... entgegensteht") is shifted to a new sentence at the end of the sequence adding an introductory anaphoric prepositional phrase "in diesem Fall". This phrase refers back to the lemma "Fall" within the compound "Einzelfallprüfung".

The reformulation of complex phrases is exemplified in (9) to (11). First, the premodifying participial constructions are transformed into finite relative clauses. In the second step a nominalisation within this (former) premodification is rephrased as a finite verb in an additional subordinate clause.

(9) *Die vom Bundesverfassungsgericht zur Zulässigkeit von Sonderabgaben geforderten und nach dem 31. Dezember 2003 zu erfüllenden haushaltsrechtlichen Informationspflichten* gelten auch für die Beiträge zum Klärschlamm-Entschädigungsfonds.

(10) Die haushaltsrechtlichen Informationspflichten, die vom Bundesverfassungsgericht zur Zulässigkeit von Sonderabgaben gefordert wurden, und die nach dem 31. Dezember 2003 erfüllt werden müssen, gelten auch für die Beiträge zum Klärschlamm-Entschädigungsfonds.

(11) Die haushaltsrechtlichen Informationspflichten, die vom Bundesverfassungsgericht gefordert wurden, damit Sonderabgaben zulässig sind, und die nach dem 31. Dezember 2003 erfüllt werden müssen, gelten auch für die Beiträge zum Klärschlamm-Entschädigungsfonds.

Deverbal derivations with the suffix "-ung" are so frequent in the court decisions that not all of the occurrences can be rephrased. We thus focused on those occurrences where at least two nominalisations are part of one phrase (see also the concordance lines in (3)). (12) to (14) show that the first step of rephrasing is to build a clause with the verbal form of the nominalisation in question. In the second step non-finite subordinate clauses created in the first step are rephrased into finite clauses where applicable.

(12) Bei der Abwägung zwischen den Belangen der Beschwerdeführerin einerseits und dem Persönlichkeitsrecht der Kläger andererseits gebühre dem Interesse der Kläger an einer *Veröffentlichung der Richtigstellung* auf der Titelseite der Vorrang.

(13) Bei der Abwägung zwischen den Belangen der Beschwerdeführerin einerseits und dem Persönlichkeitsrecht der Kläger andererseits gebühre dem Interesse der Kläger daran, eine Richtigstellung auf der Titelseite zu veröffentlichen, der Vorrang.

(14) Bei der Abwägung zwischen den Belangen der Beschwerdeführerin einerseits und dem Persönlichkeitsrecht der Kläger andererseits gebühre dem Interesse der Kläger daran, dass eine Richtigstellung auf der Titelseite veröffentlicht wird, der Vorrang.

As can be seen from these examples, rephrasing one feature often leads to new problems: Re-verbalising the nominal structures creates complex sentences which then have to be treated again by splitting sentences. And, as previously mentioned, creating new sentences makes the sequence less cohesive. The scope of the present work did not allow solving these issues. They will have to be addressed in future work.

4.2 Method of psycholinguistic testing

The rephrasing process resulted in three versions A (complex), B (medium) and C (simplified) for the three syntactic parameters sentence complexity (hereafter abbreviated S), noun phrase complexity (P) and nominalisation (N). The three versions were subjected to a psycholinguistic experiment in order to assess the respective impact on processing by lay recipients. Self-paced reading was chosen as the experimental method (see Mitchell 1987), the underlying assumption being that longer reading times are caused by either deeper processing or more complex texts. The recorded reading times for the different versions are interpreted as indicating the processing efforts for the respective version. Comprehension questions are posed following each item to check whether the participants actually understand what they just read. These yes/no questions remained unchanged in all three versions. Finally, the time the participants took to answer the comprehension question was also recorded.

The test consists of 10 sentences taken from the corpus of court decisions for each parameter, i.e. 30 sentences in total. In preparation of the experiment some of the original A version sentences are revised to delete a few structures assumed to distort the focus on the respective syntactic parameter. (15) shows an example of additional noun phrases crossed out in the target sentence testing parameter P. In the example the target phrase is italicised.

(15) Allerdings stehe der familienrechtlichen Lösung ~~in § 1626 a BGB~~ *im Falle einer Trennung der Eltern eines nichtehelichen Kindes nach längerem Zusammenleben mit diesem* ~~die verfassungsrechtli-~~

~~che Wertung~~ entgegen, dass weder dem Elternrecht der Mutter noch dem des Vaters ein Vorrang eingeräumt werden könne.

Furthermore, we inserted filler sentences in between the randomly ordered target sentences. These fillers serve to give some context for the target sentence in order to avoid prolonged processing times resulting from adjusting to the topic of the target sentence. The filler sentences (see(16)) are mildly complex in structure and remain unchanged in all three versions.

(16) *Filler*
Ein Automatismus, dass der Vater eines nichtehelichen Kindes immer das Mitsorgerecht erhält, sei grundrechtlich nicht gefordert.

Target sentence, parameter P, version A
Allerdings stehe der familienrechtlichen Lösung im Falle einer Trennung der Eltern eines nichtehelichen Kindes nach längerem Zusammenleben mit diesem entgegen, dass weder der Mutter noch dem Vaters ein Vorrang eingeräumt werden könne.

We thus obtain a 3x2 factorial design with three complexity conditions, i.e. our versions A, B and C, and two expertise conditions (novices and experts). The experiment is run on two portable computers using the software DMDX[9]. The participant reads the test sentences on the screen with each subsequent word appearing on request by mouse click. The programme logs all mouse clicks and records the time span from one click to the next. Typically in self-paced reading experiments the previous word disappears when the next is requested. However, we did not adhere to this moving windows paradigm, because we expected the sentences – particularly in the complex version A – to be too complex to be memorised. Instead, the words of one sentence remain on the screen until the sentence is complete. This means that we were not able to interpret the reading times for individual words because the participant might first request all the words of one sentence and only afterwards start processing the sentence.

45 persons participated in the study, 36 of which were novices, i.e. neither legal experts nor linguists, the remaining 9 were legal experts and advanced law students. Each subject was paid 5 Euro for participating. Each

9. http://www.u.arizona.edu/~kforster/dmdx/dmdx.htm (last visited: 10 November 2006)

participant was randomly assigned to one of the versions resulting in 15 participants (12 novices and 3 experts) per version.

In general we expected that the novices would perform better reading the rephrased versions (B and C) than the original versions (A). The subjects were expected to read faster with every step of the rephrasing because the structures become simpler and ultimately shortest in version C. Assuming that this version C does not stimulate the reader's motivation to engage with the text (corresponding to Groeben and Christmann's (1989) line of argument), we expected the subjects not to be the group thinking briefest about their response to the comprehension question. Since version A is judged to be too complex subjects reading this version ought to think longest about the questions in version A. The shortest latencies were thus expected for version B. In the same vein, we expected to find the most questions answered correctly in version B. The cognitive stimulus in this mildly complex version whose structure is familiar to newspaper readers should help subjects exposed to this version to process the target sentences in such a way as to be able to answer the questions well. Subjects reading version C therefore should be in a worse position to answer the questions correctly, while readers of version A should face the most difficult task resulting in the fewest correct answers.

Expressed formally, we stated the following hypotheses for the lay persons[10]:

(H1)	Reading times:	A > B > C
(H2)	Response latency:	A > C > B
(H3)	Correctness of responses:	A < C < B

The research design used here is not suited to make reliable statements on the individual contribution of the three parameters (see below). Thus, no specific hypotheses are established to this end. We will, however, give a brief account of the tendencies found in the experiment in the following section.

10. We focussed on the lay participants because the group of jurists was too small to make any general statements.

4.3 Findings

All of our hypotheses were confirmed only in part. As to H1 on reading times, our assumption that version A should require the longest reading times is confirmed, however version B is not read significantly faster than version A. Version C proves to pose the least processing efforts, since it is read significantly faster than the two more complex versions. Breaking down the overall comparison into the three syntactic parameters, this result is reflected both in S and in N. P results in even longer reading times in version B, a finding that must be attributed to the fact that in version B the complex phrases are resolved into clauses increasing the complexity of the respective sentences.

The response latencies (H2) are significantly longer in version A, but do not differ significantly in versions B and C. Participants reading these two versions thus do not think very long before attempting to answer the comprehension question, while version A subjects need considerably more time to think about how to relate the question to what they have just read. Parameter S confirms this overall finding. As to P, this parameter results in the longest latency for version C followed by A. B affords the shortest response latency. Parameter N, by contrast, results in the shortest latency in version C followed by B. As in all other conditions, version A produces the longest latency.

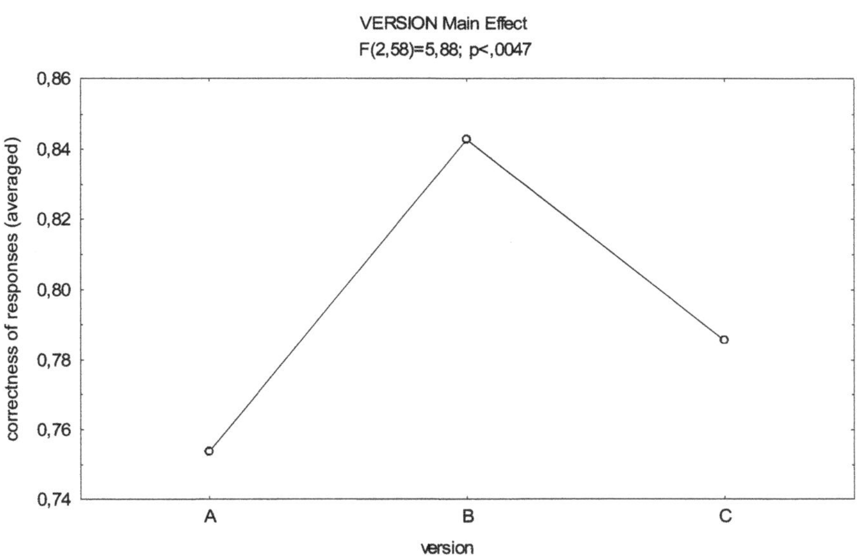

Figure 3. Correctness of responses

Finally, correctness of responses (H3) does not differ as expected between version A and C, however, responses in version B are significantly more often correct than in the other two versions, as can be seen in figure 3. Both A and C participants do not succeed well in answering the question, whereas the mildly complex version B seems to pave the way for more correct responses. This overall finding also applies to the individual parameters S and N. For parameter P, version C results in the most mistake, whereas versions A and B produce higher scores yielding equally many correct answers.

4.4 Discussion

Our interpretation takes into account that the three dependent variables can only be viewed in combination. Reading times may reflect how long a person needs to process the given sentence, it does not allow statements on how well the sentences are understood. Again, response latencies indicate how long the subjects considered their answers which can be seen as continued processing of the sentence read previously. It is the correctness of the responses which tells us whether the subjects actually understood what the have read. Keeping this in mind the findings of the experiment offer an interesting perspective on the comprehensibility of the three syntactic features under investigation.

As expected, version A proves least favourable in all respects. It results in the longest reading times. Participants obviously still have not finished processing when the comprehension question appears and therefore have to think longest about the right answer and in the end still frequently choose the wrong answer. Interestingly, version B participants take as long as their version A counterparts to read the sentences, so in this respect version B does not outperform version A. However, they need significantly less time to think about their response and then are most likely to give the correct response.

Finally, when only looking at reading times and response latencies, version C seems to offer the most efficient sentences for novices. They read fastest and also answer quickly. However, when taking into account the correctness of the responses as well, the picture changes dramatically. The correctness of the responses is not any better than in version A. This means that version C participants obviously run through the simple sentences without thoroughly processing what they are reading. The brief response latencies suggest that readers of version C feel apt to answer correctly.[11]

The performance for correctness of responses in version B offers the decisive factor suggesting that version B works best with legal novices. This result supports Groeben and Christmann's (1989) claim of the use of some cognitive challenge on comprehensibility. Version C built with the dimension of simplicity by Langer et al. (1974) in mind is outperformed by the B version. However, this statement is of limited merit. First of all, the results might have been different when attempting to cover all four dimensions described by Langer and colleagues. Furthermore, version C is rather improbable from the linguistic point of view. This issue was already mentioned in the description of the rephrasing process with respect to C's lacking cohesion. Shifting the cohesive ties from within the sentence to larger units makes it difficult to make up – and read – a text.

As mentioned before, the limitations of the research described here did not allow us to look at a more fine-grained analysis of sentence and phrase complexity. However, this would be necessary in order to improve the rephrasing process. Rephrasing the characteristic structures into more mainstream features as guided by the corpus frequencies proved difficult and needs some linguistic fine tuning in future work. This fine tuning should focus on variations of our B version. Finally, a necessary practical decision arising from financial limitations was to focus on novices. This means that we are not able to make generalisable statements on how the legal experts processed the test sentences. It would be highly interesting to compare the results of lay persons with those for jurists. It can be expected that the experts would not process the manipulated versions as well as the novices. This would be in line with the argument that it is not possible to adequately address both recipient groups within one text and that two separate texts are needed. The advantages of condensed writing that have been mentioned in section 3 make the original versions still preferable to the legal experts. The variation brought in by rephrasing the court decisions results in a new and different text adapted specifically to the needs of novices.

11. An accompanying questionnaire covering this aspect could help with this interpretation.

5. Conclusions and outlook

The psycholinguistic experiment has shown that it is not necessary to create overly simple versions of the court decisions[12] in order to increase their comprehensibility. A realistic version would still require a considerable amount of processing effort. We can assume that a mildly complex variant like our version B represents the optimal text for lay readers of court decisions, allowing us to model this optimal text with respect to the three perspectives on the functions of our syntactic parameters discussed in section 3. This consideration will also clarify where other linguistic features that were not part of the present study would come into play giving us a first view on the comprehensive research set-up needed to manipulate all features of legal texts that constitute the main obstacles to comprehensibility.

With respect to referential meaning, the results of the psycholinguistic experiment suggest that the information should be spread over sentences with one level of embedding. The challenge here is to maintain clear logical relationships between the increasing numbers of sentences. In the same vein, the phrases should not contain more than one level of embedding.

An important feature we did not take into account is legal terminology or, more generally, lexis. It is a major factor for the way referential meaning is made up. Legal terminology is an interesting mixture of standard language expressions with a specific legal meaning and fully-fledged terms (see Eckardt 2000:26ff. who also mentions "half" terms which are not as abstract as terms proper). In the legal context the problem of indeterminacy of terms is further aggravated by the fact that not everything is or even can be clearly defined and therefore needs to be interpreted (Eckardt 2000:27). The expert reader recognises both specific meanings of expressions used in standard language as well as terms requiring interpretation. The lay reader, in contrast, will probably have difficulties in understanding the legal meaning of the familiar sounding lexical items and will not be able to understand, let alone interpret, the abstract terms. The optimised text will therefore have to address the issue of flagging and explaining terminology.

The last factor to be considered is the impact of the parameters on the texture of the optimised text. Reducing the complexity of sentences will require adding more cohesive devices to clarify the logical relationship

12. This of course presupposes a rather well educated lay readership as reflected in our experiment. It remains to be seen whether this statement still holds when testing the same items with a representative sample of the population.

between the different sentences. This becomes even more pressing when also reducing the complexity of phrases because this may lead to increased complexity of the sentences. In section 3, we questioned the benefit of reference chains made up of nominalisations for the lay reader. It might be better to reduce the lexical density of the court decisions by using less nominalisations and rather employ other cohesive devices to maintain reference, for instance pronominalisation.

Among the aspects not covered by the present study is the macrostructure of the court decisions. It is quite obvious that headings supplementing the numbering would make the organisation of the text more explicit and thus arguably more comprehensible. In fact, the Federal Constitutional Judges reading the decision add headings during the oral pronunciation marking them as additions to the written text by their intonation.

All of the possible changes mentioned here can be seen as a contribution to improving the relationship between expert author and lay reader.

The corpus we built up and enriched linguistically is a valuable resource for different research questions concerned with comparing a legal register with non-specialist registers. The work presented here offers a first step into a methodology not only concerned with the difficult legal texts but attempting to work out improvements of these texts for lay citizens.

In future work, the interdisciplinary aspect of the research on legal comprehensibility needs strengthening. Our research was conducted jointly by linguists and jurists, particularly in the rephrasing process. Nevertheless, the cooperation should extend to more fundamental aspects looking at points of contact between the two disciplines spending more effort on how the respective methods could be combined.

Finally, it would be highly interesting to examine which of the linguistic features contributes most to improving a text's comprehensibility. The findings presented here only give a first idea of each parameter's contribution. A more elaborate examination of this question requires a research design concentrating on the processing of the respective feature irrespective of the language of the law.

6. Acknowledgements

The author would like to thank the anonymous reviewers for their valuable suggestions. The work presented here was funded by the Saarland University in the framework of the project "Verständlichkeitsoptimierung von Rechtstexten: grammatisch-stilistische Parameter". This paper would not exist without the hard work of the project team: Ralph Dirksen, Sandra Hansen, Martin Küchler and Kerstin Kunz. Silvia Hansen-Schirra and Erich Steiner helped frame the layout of the study with their continual contributions. Finally, Stefan Baumann gave helpful comments on the final version.

7. References

Altehenger, Bernhard. 1983. "Die richterliche Entscheidung als Texttyp". *Texte und Sachverhalte*, ed. by János Petöfi, Hamburg: Buske. 185–227.

Anders, Monika and Burkhard Gehle. 2005. *Das Assessorexamen im Zivilrecht*. 8th edition. München: Werner.

Basedow, Jürgen. 1999. "Transparenz als Prinzip des (Versicherungs-) Vertragsrechts". *Zeitschrift für Versicherungsrecht, Haftungs- und Schadensrecht* (VersR) 50 (1999), 25. 1045–1054.

Becker, Angelika. 2002. "Interdisziplinäre Arbeitsgruppe 'Sprache des Rechts' an der Berlin-Brandenburgischen Akademie der Wissenschaften: Projektdarstellung". *Sprache und Recht. Jahrbuch 2001 Institut für Deutsche Sprache*, ed. by Ulrike Haß-Zumkehr, Berlin-New York: de Gruyter. 361–365.

Berliner Arbeitsgruppe. 2000. "Sprache des Rechts. Vermitteln, Verstehen, Verwechseln". *Zeitschrift für Literaturwissenschaft und Linguistik* 118, 7–33.

Brants, Thorsten. 2000. "TNT – A statistical part-of-speech tagger". *Proceedings of the 6th Conference on Applied Natural Language Processing (ANLP 2000)*. Seattle: WA. 224–231.

Braun, Christian. 1999. "Flaches und robustes Parsen deutscher Satzgefüge". *Diplom thesis. Saarbrücken: Universität des Saarlandes.*

Chafe, Wallace. 1994. *Discourse, Consciousness, and Time*. Chicago; London: University of Chicago Press.

Davison, Alice and Georgia M. Green (eds.). 1988. *Linguistic Complexity and Text Comprehension: Readability Issues Reconsidered*. London: Erlbaum.

Dietrich, Rainer and Wolfgang Klein (eds.). 2000. *Sprache des Rechts. Special issue of Zeitschrift für Literaturwissenschaft und Linguistik* 118.

Dietrich, Rainer. and Katja Kühn. 2000. "Transparent oder verständlich oder wie was verstanden wird – Eine empirische Untersuchung zum Verstehen eines juristischen Textes". *Zeitschrift für Literaturwissenschaft und Linguistik* 118, 67–95.

Dietrich, Rainer. and Carolin Schmidt. 2002. "Zur Lesbarkeit von Verbrauchertexten. Ein Beitrag aus der Sicht der Textproduktion". *Zeitschrift für Literaturwissenschaft und Linguistik* 128, 34–62.

Eckardt, Birgit. 2000. *Fachsprache als Kommunikationsbarriere? Verständigungsprobleme zwischen Juristen und Laien*. Wiesbaden: DUV.

Engberg, Jan. 1997. *Konventionen von Fachtextsorten. Kontrastive Analysen zu deutschen und dänischen Gerichtsurteilen*. Tübingen: Narr.

Eriksen, Lars. 2002. "Einführung in die Systematik der juristischen Fachsprache". *Juristische Fachsprache. Kongressberichte des 12th European Symposium on Language for Special Purposes, Brixen/Bressanone 1999*, ed. by Lars Eriksen and Karin Luttermann, Münster-Hamburg-London: LIT Verlag. 1–19.

Flesch, Rudolph F. 1948. "A new readability yardstick". *Journal of Applied Psychology* 32. 221–233.

Grewendorf, Günther (ed.). 1992. *Rechtskultur als Sprachkultur – zur forensischen Funktion der Sprachanalyse*. Frankfurt a.M.: Suhrkamp.

Groeben, Norbert and Ursula Christmann. 1989. "Textoptimierung unter Verständlichkeitsperspektive". *Textproduktion. Ein interdisziplinärer Forschungsüberblick*, ed. by Gerd Antos and Hans Peter Krings, Tübingen: Niemeyer. 165–196.

Halliday, Michael A. K. 1993. "On the language of Physical Science". *Writing Science: Literacy and Discursive Power*, ed. by Michael A. K. Halliday and John R. Martin, London-Washington D.C.: The Falmer Press. 54–68.

Hansen, Sandra, Ralph Dirksen, Martin Küchler, Kerstin Kunz and Stella Neumann. 2006. "Comprehensible legal texts – utopia or a question of wording? On processing rephrased German court decisions". *Hermes – Journal of Language and Communication Studies*, 36. 15–40.

Hansen-Schirra, Silvia and Stella Neumann. 2004. "Linguistische Verständlichmachung in der juristischen Realität". *Recht verstehen. Verständlichkeit, Missverständlichkeit und Unverständlichkeit von Recht*, ed. by Kent D. Lerch, Berlin-New York: de Gruyter. 167–184.

Haß-Zumkehr, Ulrike (ed.). 2002. *Sprache und Recht. Jahrbuch 2001 des Instituts für Deutsche Sprache*. Berlin/New York: de Gruyter.

Hillebrand, Julia, Rainer Dietrich and Yvonne Stakic. (2006) "Syntaktische Komplexität in Rechtstexten: Tragen Reformulierungen zur Verständlichkeit von Gerichtsentscheidungen bei?". Paper presented to the DGfS-AG 'Sprache und Recht', Bielefeld 2006.

Höhle, Tilman N. 1983. "Topologische Felder". Manuskript. Köln. (Downloadable at http://www.linguistik.uni-tuebingen.de/hoehle/manuskripte/Topologische_Felder.pdf)

Hülper, Markus. 2004. *Die englische Rechtssprache – Verständlichkeit für Laien und Sprachkundige*. Münster: LIT Verlag.

Jaspersen, Andrea. 1998. *Über die mangelnde Verständlichkeit des Rechts für den Laien*. PhD dissertation. Bonn: Rheinische Friedrich-Wilhelms-Universität.

Klein, Wolfgang (ed.). 2001. *Sprache des Rechts II. Special issue of Zeitschrift für Literaturwissenschaft und Linguistik* 128.

Lambrecht, Knud. 1994. *Information Structure and Sentence Form*. Cambridge: Cambridge University Press.

Langer, Inghard, Schulz von Thun, Friedemann and Reinhard Tausch. 1974. *Verständlichkeit in Schule, Verwaltung, Politik und Wissenschaft*. München: Reinhardt.

Lerch, Kent D. (ed.). 2004a. *Recht verstehen. Verständlichkeit, Missverständlichkeit und Unverständlichkeit von Recht*. Berlin-New York: de Gruyter.

Lerch, Kent D. 2004b. "Verständlichkeit als Pflicht? Zur Intransparenz des Transparenzgebots". *Recht verstehen. Verständlichkeit, Missverständlichkeit und Unverständlichkeit von Recht*, ed. by Kent D. Lerch, Berlin-New York: de Gruyter. 239–283.

Lerch, Kent D. (ed.). 2005a. *Recht verhandeln: Argumentieren, Begründen und Entscheiden im Diskurs des Rechts*. Berlin-New York: de Gruyter.

Lerch, Kent D. (ed.). 2005b. *Recht vermitteln: Strukturen, Formen und Medien der Kommunikation im Recht*. Berlin-New York: de Gruyter.

Mitchell, D. C. 1987. "Reading and syntactic analysis". *Cognitive Approaches to Reading*, ed. by John R. Beech and Ann M. Colley, Chichester, UK: Wiley. 87–112.

Neumann, Stella and Silvia Hansen-Schirra. 2004. "Der Konjunktiv als Verständnisproblem in Rechtstexten". *Zeitschrift für Angewandte Linguistik* 41. 67–87.

Ogorek, Regina. 2004. "'Ich kenne das Reglement nicht, habe es aber immer befolgt!' Metatheoretische Anmerkungen zur Verständnisdebatte". *Recht verstehen. Verständlichkeit, Missverständlichkeit und Unverständlichkeit von Recht*, ed. by Kent D. Lerch, Berlin-New York: de Gruyter. 297–305.

Oksaar, Els. 1988. *Fachsprachliche Dimensionen*. Tübingen: Narr.

Rickheit, Gert. 1995. "Verstehen und Verständlichkeit von Sprache". *Verstehen und Verständlichkeit*, ed. by Bernd Spillner, Frankfurt am Main-Berlin-Bern: Lang. 15–30.

Roelcke, Thorsten. 2005. *Fachsprachen*. 2nd ed. Berlin: Erich Schmidt Verlag.

Scott, Mike. 1996. *WordSmith Tools Manual*. Oxford: Oxford University Press.

Viehweg, Theodor and Frank Rotter (eds.). 1977. *Recht und Sprache. Vorträge auf der Tagung der deutschen Sektion der Internationalen Vereinigung für Rechts- und Sozialphilosophie (IVR) in der Bundesrepublik Deutschland, Mainz, 3.-5.10.1974*. Wiesbaden: Franz Steiner Verlag.

Wagner, Hildegard. 1981. *Die deutsche Verwaltungssprache der Gegenwart*. 3rd ed. Düsseldorf: Schwann.

Understanding a Riester-pension: A reply to Becker and Klein (2008)

Monika Rathert

1. Introduction

Consumer contracts have to be drafted in plain and intelligible language. This is stated in the European Council Directive 93/13/EEC of 5 April 1993 on unfair terms in consumer contracts. Article 5 of this Directive says:

> "In the case of contracts where all or certain terms offered to the consumer are in writing, these terms must always be drafted in plain, intelligible language. Where there is doubt about the meaning of a term, the interpretation most favourable to the consumer shall prevail [...]."

Is the following sentence from the insurance conditions of a Riester-pension plain and intelligible?

> "Der Abzug beträgt 0,2 Prozent der Differenz zwischen dem zum vereinbarten Rentenbeginn vorhandenen Deckungskapital und dem zum Zeitpunkt der Beitragsfreistellung vorhandenen Deckungskapital."
>
> (The discount is 0.2 percent of the difference between the coverage capital at the agreed starting point of the pension and the coverage capital at the time of exemption of payment.)

For many people, this sentence is not easy to comprehend. This is one of the findings of a study on 'Language of the Law' carried out by an interdisciplinary research group at the Academy of Science at Berlin-Brandenburg, published as Becker and Klein (2008). The Academy of Science established the interdisciplinary group in 1999 with the permanent members Manfred Bierwisch, Rainer Dietrich, Wolfgang Klein (principal investigator), Hans-Peter Schwintowski, Dieter Simon and Christine Windbichler. The aim of

G. Grewendorf and M. Rathert (eds.): Formal Linguistics and Law, 81–111

the group was to investigate the comprehension of legal texts by different individuals. As an example of a legal text, the insurance conditions of a Riester-pension were chosen, and the test persons were jurists, insurance agents and laymen.

This paper is structured as follows. Section 1 is on the context, aims and design of Becker and Klein (2008). The study elucidated three parameters of comprehension each of which was tested separately. All test persons received the same task, they were asked to give advice in the following situation: A client is no longer able or willing to pay the monthly insurance contributions, what should she do about her insurance? First, the test persons had to find relevant pieces of information in the insurance conditions in order to find the necessary information to be able to give the advice. Second, the test persons had to report on their understanding of the information found, they had to comment on how they solve the problem. Third, the correctness of the test persons' comprehension of the insurance conditions was tested with two questionnaires. – Section 2 of this paper summarizes the findings concerning the questionnaires and the information searching task. – Section 3 of this paper is on the main point of the study, namely the process of understanding the insurance conditions and solving the task. Section 4 is the main point of this paper, namely a critical assessment of the study, including suggestions for future research on the topic.

2. Context, aims and design of the study

There is a long tradition of complaints about the incomprehensibility of legal texts. Frederick the Great already said about the Prussian law "Es ist aber sehr Dikke und gesetze müssen kurz und nicht Weitläufig seindt (*It is very bulky, but laws should be short and not extensive*)."[1] He demanded that the "möglichste Deutlichkeit und Simplicite eines natürlichen und ungezwungenen Erzählerstyls" (*utmost clarity and simplicity of a natural and effortless narrative style*) should be attained and that the following must be avoided: "affectirte Wendungen, neu gemachte Worte ... imgleichen Termini technici, wenn sie nicht allgemein bekannter Verständlichkeit seien" (*affected style, neologisms... technical terms if they are not generally known*).[2]

1. Cited according to Grewendorf (1992: 37).
2. Cited according to Lorenz (1991: 295f.).

The most frequent complaints raised in the German context are the following[3]:

(1)
a. nominal style (nominalizations, nominal compounds)
b. impersonal style (passive)
c. abbreviations
d. long sentences with many embeddings
e. official style ("Kanzleistil", *stylum curiae*)
f. outdated terms (e.g. "Kraftdroschke" meaning *car*)
g. terms with a meaning differing from the usual one (e.g. "Sache" has a terminological meaning in the legal context which it does not have in everyday's speech)
h. vage terms (e.g. "geringe Menge", "niedrige Beweggründe")

All issues in (1) refer to style, and most of them could be amended. But comprehensibility problems in the legal context go beyond style; they have a very serious background. Incomprehensible laws threaten the separation of powers:

> "Within a state that established the separation of powers, the legislature has de jure a leading function against the other powers. This leading power is executed with the instrument of the law. In adjudication this is called "being bound by the law". The association with this is that the judge may only execute the law; he is not allowed to add his own thoughts to it. In case the legislature is unable to produce precise laws, the judiciary and the executive must take the power of the legislature. The separation of powers no longer exists in this situation. Nobody knows where the responsibilities of the different powers start and end because the boundaries between them fade. These boundaries are to a large degree linguistic in nature."
> Hassemer (1992: 73), translation mine, MR[4]

Thus, the aim of comprehensibility seems to be intimately linked to the enlightened type of state in which powers are separated. However, Herberger (1983: 20) has shown that there is no correlation between a certain type

3. Cf. Hoffmann (1992), Lerch (2004/2005), Pfeiffer et al. (1987) and Jaspersen (1998).
4. Cf. also Grewendorf (1992: 35).

of state and the aim of comprehensibility: rather, he found that comprehensibility has been regarded as valuable as such, independent of the form of government.

The struggle for comprehensibility has been made explicit in a number of ways. In Germany, the *Gemeinsame Geschäftsordnung der Bundesministerien zur Gesetzgebung* states that "Gesetze müssen sprachlich einwandfrei und sollen so weit wie möglich für jedermann verständlich gefasst sein" (*laws must be linguistically correct and should be intelligible to everyone*).[5] The famous principle of civil freedom *nullum crimen, nulla poena sine lege* (Art. 103 II GG, §1 StGB) breaks down into several principles, among them the *lex certa* principle ("Bestimmtheitsgebot"): the legislative powers must formulate norms as precise as possible.

However, comprehensibility or incomprehensibility does not exist as such. It depends on the addressee and his/ her knowledge and interests. Objective features of texts (like sentence length, frequency of nominalizations, depth of embeddings etc) are no predictors of comprehensibility.[6]

Empirical studies on the comprehension of legal texts are rare, cf. Schendera (2000). As far as law written in German is concerned, the only larger studies are Pfeiffer et al. (1987) and Becker and Klein (2008).

There are two possible directions for comprehension studies. Either, a given text is changed and both the resulting variant and the original text are tested empirically for comprehensibility. Researchers following this strategy are Charrow and Charrow (1979), Pfeiffer et al. (1987), Hansen-Schirra and Neumann (2004), Neumann and Hansen-Schirra (2004) and Gunnarsson (1984). The other approach to comprehension is to vary the knowledge of the recipients (i.e. to use test persons with different background knowledge) and check whether this has an impact on text comprehension. Examples of this kind of studies are Dietrich and Kühn (2000) or Lundeberg (1987).

To illustrate the differences between the two kinds of comprehension studies, a comparison between Pfeiffer et al. (1987) and Dietrich and Kühn (2000) is useful. Pfeiffer et al. (1987) investigated a legislative text (the Northern Austrian Building Regulations of 1976) and possibilities of its addressee-oriented text optimization. In a first step, the Building Regulations were rewritten by a non-jurist person. Based on a comparison of the two versions, the researchers developed a catalogue of criteria that could be relevant to comprehension, including syntax, terminology, information

5. GGO II § 35 Abs. 1, cited from Hoffmann (1992).
6. See Chall (1958), Weber and Noschka-Roos (1988), Hoffmann (1992).

structure and ordering of text passages. With these criteria at hand, jurists were asked to rewrite the original Building Regulations. The variants that were finally compared empirically with regard to comprehension were A) the original Building Regulations of 1976 and B) the version of this text that was created by the jurists. The 127 test persons were asked questions relating to terminology. In addition, the test persons had to solve cloze tests, their reading speed was measured, they were asked to solve little problem solving tasks. The clear result of the study was that the B-variant of the text was easier to comprehend.

Dietrich and Kühn (2000) focused not on text variations but on reader oriented factors of comprehension. They varied the background knowledge and worked with a constant text, a portion of liability insurance conditions. The first experiment was carried out with students with no background in law. Their comprehension of the text was measured by free recall, question answering and small problem solving tasks. The result was that although the test persons were good in recalling the content, they were bad in understanding it. They applied schemata relating to insurances that were not relevant to the case at hand. The second experiment was carried out with the same text, but with two different kinds of test persons, law students and students of subjects other than law. The law students had no special background in insurances. The result was that there was no difference in comprehension. Both kinds of students had no background knowledge about insurances, which could be an explanation of their equal performance in the comprehension tests.

Becker and Klein (2008) follow the approach in Dietrich and Kühn (2000) in that they understand text comprehension as an interaction between the text and its features (like terminology, syntax etc.) on the one hand and the cognitive preconditions of the reader on the other hand (like e.g. background knowledge). The aim of Becker and Klein (2008) is to elucidate the process of understanding a legal text by exposing three different kinds of test persons to it

The legal text that was investigated in Becker and Klein (2008) was part of the insurance conditions of a Riester-pension. It is of practical relevance that these conditions are plain and intelligible, as insurances are consumer contracts subject to the European Council Directive 93/13/EEC cited at the beginning of this paper. The situation the test persons were confronted with was the following (cf. Becker and Klein 2008: 215):

> A friend asks you for an advice. She has signed a contract for a Riester-pension in January. She pays € 150 per month for this

> insurance. She is 32 now and she will have to pay the monthly contributions until she reaches the age of 65. She fears that the monthly contributions could be too strenuous for her. What should she do?

The situation is realistic as almost half of all life insurances are cancelled ahead of schedule. The test persons received the insurance conditions and the certificate of insurance. There were three groups of test persons: ten jurists, ten insurance agents and ten laymen. As for the laymen, it was required that they had finished a non-academic professional training and that they did not have more than an average knowledge of legal or insurance matters. The jurists were required to be no experts on insurance matters. The insurance agents were only required to be informed about the Riester-pension, it was not required that they had sold this product to clients before. The latter would have been unrealistic, as the Riester-pension was new on the market at the time of the study.

3. Paragraph search and questionnaires

The first task the test persons had to solve was to find the relevant paragraphs in the insurance conditions. It was checked whether the search for the relevant paragraphs was successful and how much time the test persons needed for it. The insurance conditions were presented as a booklet with one paragraph on each page, the conditions consisted of 19 paragraphs in total. The test persons were asked to search for the relevant paragraphs and to tell the instructor when they had finished. They were video recorded while reading, thus the reading time per paragraph and the overall reading time could be measured. Finally, the test persons were asked to name the relevant paragraphs and to give a short explanation for their choice.

The two relevant paragraphs were §6 Suspending the insurance and §7 Cancellation of the insurance:

§ 6 Suspending the insurance

1. You can suspend your insurance before the agreed start of the pension anytime at the end of the ongoing year of insurance, in case of paying by installments also during the ongoing year of insurance (at the end of each installment, cf. §3, 2). In this case, we lower the insured pension down to a non-contributory pension. The non-contributory pension is calculated in accordance

with the usual rules of insurance mathematics for the time of the suspension. The amount of money that is used for the noncontributory pension out of this insurance is decreased by the following rate. The discount is 0.2 percent of the difference between the coverage capital at the agreed starting point of the pension and the coverage capital at the time of exemption of payment.

There is an overview of the guaranteed non-contributory pension in your certificate of insurance.

2. After having suspended your insurance, you can restart it again any time by paying the contributions. In this case, the rate that was valid at the time of signing the contract applies.

§ 7 Cancellation of the insurance

1. You can cancel your insurance in written form before the agreed start of the pension anytime at the end of the ongoing year of insurance, in case of paying by installments also during the ongoing year of insurance (at the end of each installment, cf. §3, 2). After the cancellation you receive the redemption value.

2. In case you cancel your insurance, the redemption value is calculated on the base of § 176 of the insurance law in accordance with the usual rules of insurance mathematics. The redemption value is decreased by the same rate that applies in §6 1. Premium arrears are considered. There is no decrease with noncontributory pensions.

   The minimum of the redemption value is the amount guaranteed at the time of signing the contract. This guaranteed amount depends on the time of the cancellation of the insurance and on the time of ceasing the contributions. There is an overview of the guaranteed redemption values plus the benefits derived from profit distribution in your certificate of insurance.

3. After the start of the pension, a cancellation of the insurance to pay the redemption value is no longer possible.

4. You have no right to demand the return of the contributions.

Becker and Klein (2008: 231f.), translation mine, MR

Nearly everybody found these paragraphs; 97% of the test persons found §6, 90% found §7. However, the test persons differed with respect to reading times. As expected, the laymen needed a lot of time to read the text as a whole, between 4 and 14 minutes. Compared to this, the variance in overall reading time among jurists and insurance agents was low, as 90% of the jurists and the insurance agents needed less than 4 minutes. The insurance agents were just a little quicker in overall reading time than the jurists. 60% of the insurance agents needed less than 2 minutes while 60% of the jurists needed more than 2 minutes.

The three groups varied with respect to rereading single paragraphs. Altogether, the jurists reread 44 paragraphs, the insurance agents reread 22 paragraphs and the laymen only 15. The small number of rereadings among the laymen can be explained with the long overall reading time in this group. The laymen read the text so slowly and thoroughly that repetitions were not necessary. The fact that jurists reread so much material finds a natural explanation in the jurists' reading habits: they did not read the text as a whole, but first only leafed through the booklet, not paying attention to the content of the paragraphs but only to their headlines. When finished, the jurists jumped back to the relevant headlines, thus the high number of repetitions. The insurance agents showed a similar behavior, but in contrast to the jurists, they left out more material without rereading it later. Most agents started reading only with §6, they leafed through the paragraphs before and did not come back to them later.

In general, all test persons spent more reading time on paragraphs that they thought to be relevant in contrast to those paragraphs that had no relevance with respect to the task at hand. However, the groups differed in reading times. On average, the laymen spent 46 seconds on relevant paragraphs and 19 seconds on irrelevant ones. Jurists spent only 27 seconds on relevant and 5 seconds on irrelevant paragraphs. The insurance agents had a similar reading time for the relevant paragraphs (26 seconds), but they were a little slower with irrelevant passages (11 seconds).

The central part of the study was to elucidate in which ways the test persons understood the relevant paragraphs §6 and §7; this is reported in the next section of this paper. Finally, the correctness of the test persons' comprehension was tested. To check this, two questionnaires were used, one questionnaire with 13 multiple choice questions, and another questionnaire with 18 yes/no questions. In addition to this, the test persons were requested to give confidence judgments expressing how sure they were about the correctness of each of their answers. For this purpose, a scale with five degrees of certainty was used (1: absolutely certain, 5: very uncertain).

There were three kinds of questions: a) text-based questions (i.e. questions that can be answered directly by consulting the text), b) inference questions (i.e. questions which require inferences from the text), and c) nontext questions (i.e. questions that have something to do with the topic of the text, but answers to them cannot be inferred or directly taken from the text).

As for the questionnaire with the multiple choice questions, this was fairly simple, because altogether 83% of the questions were answered correctly. The arithmetic mean of all confidence values is also high (4.4 out of 5), the test persons were quite certain about their answers. Only three questions of this multiple choice questionnaire caused problems.

The questionnaire with the yes/no questions was also relatively easy to deal with, as altogether 79% of the answers were answered correctly. The three groups of test persons varied a little in performance. With laymen, 71% of the answers were correct, 79% of the jurists' answers were correct and 88% of the insurance agents' answers. The arithmetic mean of all confidence values is even a little higher than it was in the multiple choice questionnaire (4.6 out of 5), the test persons were very certain about their answers.

The relationship between (subjective) confidence and (objective) correctness of the answers is called calibration (Jonsson and Allwood 2003: 564f.). If confidence is higher than correctness, this is called overconfidence; the opposite is underconfidence. The ideal is that confidence and correctness match, of course – people should be sure only about what is right, and unsure about what is actually wrong. Only the insurance agents showed this good kind of calibration in both questionnaires, i.e. they were realistic, neither over- nor underconfident. The jurists and the laymen were either over- or underconfident.

4. The process of comprehension

The central part of the study was to elucidate in which ways the test persons understood the two relevant paragraphs §6 *Suspending the insurance* and §7 *Cancellation of the insurance*. It was an aim of the study to get hold of the test persons' comprehension under real-time conditions, i.e. during the comprehension process itself. To achieve this goal, the method of "think aloud" was used, cf. e.g. Graesser et al. (1997: 166):

> "In a "think aloud" task, the reader expresses ideas that come to mind as each clause in the text is comprehended. The content extracted from think aloud protocols is a very rich source of data for discovering possible comprehension strategies".

"Think aloud" tasks reflect deeper level comprehension, as Olson et al. (1984: 255) say:

> "(the) TOL [= Think Out Loud, M.R./A.B.] task is best used to study the higher level processes in reading: the inferences, predictions, schema elaborations, and other complex cognitions that occur as part of skilled reading. We assume that these processes are most available to consciousness as the reader reads."

The "think aloud" data of the test persons were tape-recorded and transcribed by one person and this transcript was checked by another person.[7] Some part of the transcribed data is cited in Becker and Klein (2008) in chapter 5, pp. 59 onwards.

The test persons' "think aloud" utterances referred to different aspects of understanding (Becker and Klein 2008: 44):

(2) a. *Utterances with an interpretive function that refer to the* content *of the text*
Some of these utterances are mere paraphrases of text passages; some explain terminology occurring in the text. Elaborations of the text also belong to this category, i.e. utterances that elaborate on the content of the text. Elaborations are based on previous knowledge or on inferences drawn from the text.

b. *Utterances with an interpretive function that refer to the* structure *of the text*
This kind of utterances expresses relations between the sentences or text passages.

7. It is not clear if some standard like GAT (Selting et al. 1998) was used for the transcription.

c. *Utterances with a* metacognitive *function*
Some of these utterances express a self-assessment of the test persons' comprehension of the text; others are judgments on the text's comprehensibility as such.

d. *Utterances with an* evaluative *function*
These utterances include verbalized emotions, opinions and statements that were (obviously) triggered by reading the text. These utterances were not considered in the analysis of the test persons' comprehension.

To compare the test persons' understanding of the text with the actual meaning of the text, a *tertium comparationis* was needed. The text was 'translated' into a set of propositions in the style of Kintsch (1998). The propositional approach of Kintsch and his collaborators tries to apply a simplified version of formal semantics to ordinary texts. In the style of Fillmore (1968), propositions are defined as n-tuples of *concepts*, with a concept consisting of a *predicate* P and *arguments* $A_1, \ldots, A_n$. Here is an example:

(3) *John loves Mary* → (LOVE, John, Mary) – proposition (p)/ concept
| | |
predicate arguments

Propositions may be *predicative*, *modifying* or *connective*. With a predicative proposition, the verb has the role of the predicate, (3) serving as an example. Modifying propositions are those where arguments are modified, connective propositions express relations between propositions:

(4) modifying propositions
All PhD students sleep badly □
p1 (SLEEP, PhD students)
p2 (quantification: PhD students, all)
p3 (attribute of, p1, badly)

(5) connective propositions
Schools are important for children not to stupefy □
p1 (IMPORTANT, schools)
p2 (STUPEFY, children)
p3 (negation, p2)
p4 (in order to, p3, p1)

The propositional approach is not only interested in the semantics of individual sentences like those in (3)–(5), but is heading for semantic representations of texts. This is the reason why the approach was chosen in Becker and Klein (2008).

To illustrate what the propositional approach means in the context of this study, a sentence from §6 *Suspending the insurance* is rewritten in propositions here (cf. Becker and Klein 2008: 45):

(6) a. *original text* (cf. section 3 of this paper for the whole paragraph)
The discount is 0.2 percent of the difference between the coverage capital at the agreed starting point of the pension and the coverage capital at the time of exemption of payment.

b. *set of propositions*[8]
p1 IS (discount, p2)
p2 QUANT (DIFFERENCE-BETWEEN (p3, p4))
p3 AT (AGREED (starting point of the pension), EXIST (coverage capital))
p4 AT (TIME-OF (exemption of payment), EXIST (coverage capital))

The transcribed "think aloud" data were annotated with different aspects of understanding. To this end, a coding scheme was developed with the aim to encompass as many utterances of the test persons as possible and also to highlight the differences between the three types of test persons.

The coding made explicit reference to the aspects listed in (2a–c) above. As far as (2a) (utterances with an interpretive function that refer to the *content* of the text) is concerned, the coding referred to the following subtypes of aspects:

(7) a. completeness of the interpretation
– utterance was interpreted completely[9]
– utterance was interpreted incompletely
– utterance was not interpreted
– it is unclear whether there is an interpretation[10]

8. Note that "0.2 percent" is in fact missing in (6b), cf. Becker and Klein (2008: 45).

9. This coding is used when all propositions of the text occurred in the test persons' transcript.

b. correctness of the interpretation and of the elaborations
   – the interpretation and the elaborations (if any) are correct
   – the interpretation and/or the elaborations are partially incorrect
   – the interpretation is totally wrong
   – it is unclear whether the interpretation is correct[11]

c. elaborations
   – no elaborations occur
   – concretising elaborations occur, referring…[12]
     i. … to a personal experience
     ii. … to a hypothetical example
     iii. … to other paragraphs in the insurance conditions
   – extending elaborations occur, adding…
     i. … a reason for a text statement
     ii. … a condition for a text statement
     iii. … a consequence that follows from the text
     iv. … a regulation that is not mentioned in the text
     v. … general background in insurances

With (2b) (utterances with an interpretive function that refer to the *structure* of the text), the coding distinguished the following subtypes:

(8) a. theme
   – the theme of the paragraph is recognized
   – the theme of the paragraph is not recognized

b. establishing cross references
   – … backwards in §§ 6 and 7
   – … forwards in §§ 6 and 7
   – … to other paragraphs in the conditions

c. recognizing existing cross references
   – existing cross references are not noticed
   – existing cross references are mentioned
   – existing cross references are read out

---

10. This coding was used for passages where the test persons merely repeated phrases from the insurance conditions.

11. This coding was reserved for unclear and inconsistent passages.

12. Elaborations of this kind illustrate an abstract statement from the text with concrete examples or with other means.

Utterances with a *metacognitive* function (cf. (2c) above) directly indicate the subjective comprehension of the test persons; partly, reasons for bad comprehension are also given. The coding referred to the following aspects:

(9) a. subjective comprehension rating
   – no rating
   – positive rating
   – negative rating
   – the test person is unsure

b. named comprehension problems
   – with reference to a concrete term or a special phrase in the text
   – without this reference (generalized comprehension problem)

c. rating of the text's comprehensibility
   – no rating
   – positive rating
   – negative rating
   – the test person is unsure

d. indirect evidence for comprehension problems[13]
   – pauses
   – rereading
   – scanning the text

The coding of the transcript was done very thoroughly as can be taken from this overview. It highlights a huge set of comprehension issues in three domains: content, structure and metacognition. It may a problem, though, that the coding was only done by one person; only 20% of the coded data were checked by another person. Actually, it does not even suffice to have someone check someone else's codings, there should be two independent codings that are unified into one in the end. Also, it would have been interesting to see at least a passage of coded text; the book presents only the results but not the coded transcript itself. A passage of coded text would have been interesting also for other reasons. There are several obvious in-

13. Becker and Klein (2008: 50) mention another piece of indirect evidence for comprehension problems, namely the test persons' uttering something like "now this question requires the consultation of an expert, an insurance agent or someone else". This sounds more like a direct evidence for a comprehension problem and can easily be subsumed under (9c).

consistencies and vague points in the coding schema. For example, what does it mean that an interpretation is 'incomplete' or 'partially incorrect' (cf. (7a) and (7b), second bullet points)? Are 5%, 10%, 20% of the propositions missing or incorrect if this coding is applied?

To see how the analysis of "think aloud" data works, we pick out the sentence about the 0.2 percent discount which is part of §6 *Suspending the insurance* (cf. (6) above, repeated here for convenience):

(10) *Original text*
The discount is 0.2 percent of the difference between the coverage capital at the agreed starting point of the pension and the coverage capital at the time of exemption of payment.

The analysis of the "think aloud" data on this sentence in Becker and Klein (2008: 83–93) is summarized here. As far as the dimension *content* is concerned (cf.(7) above), 57% of the interpretations were complete. This is a high percentage compared to the average reached in the study which is 45% (Becker and Klein 2008: 160). There was no difference between the three kinds of test persons as far as completeness is concerned. However, only 20% of the interpretations were correct. This is not much compared to the average of 32% (Becker and Klein 2008: 161). Jurists and insurance agents each contributed 10% of the correct interpretations, the laymen were wrong in all cases. It is striking that this sentence evoked only few elaborations, 18 altogether, on average there were 36 per sentence (cf. Becker and Klein 2008). As elaborations presuppose some understanding of the text (at least if they are extending or concretising), this comes as no surprise.

As far as the dimension *metacognition* (cf. (9) above) is concerned, the subjective comprehension rating was quite negative, 53% of the test persons said they did not understand the sentence. Corresponding to this, the rating of the sentence's comprehensibility was also bad, 43% of the test persons gave a negative rating. No other sentence got such negative ratings in these two aspects. Also, this sentence displayed by far the greatest number of indirect pieces of evidence for comprehension problems (pauses, rereadings etc.).

The obvious tension between the high percentage of complete interpretations and the low percentage of correct interpretations (combined with the negative estimations concerning metacognition and the low number of elaborations) is not resolved in Becker and Klein (2008). It is stated that the sentence shows that "complex linguistic structure need not result in incomprehensibility" (Becker and Klein 2008: 86). First, how do we know that the sentence has a "complex linguistic structure", which criteria do we have for complexity? Second, what is the heuristic meaning of "comprehensibility" or "incomprehensibility" in this context? Facing the low percentage of correct interpretations and the low number of elaborations, we have to assume incomprehensibility. Maybe checking whether the test persons verbalize all propositions is just not very instrumental for measuring comprehension. Keeping in mind that Kintsch's theory is a model for comprehension, not reality, this could resolve the tension. The *tertium comparationis* that is needed to compare the test persons' understanding of the text with the actual meaning of the text does not seem to be apt.

There are some terms in the sentence in (10) that seem to have caused more trouble than others, among them "discount" and "coverage capital". The discount is a sum that is taken by the insurance company as a fee for the benefit that is lost because the client stops the monthly insurance contributions. The test persons came up with different ideas on the meaning of "discount" here and partially admitted that they did not understand it at all:

(11) a. an insurance agent (Becker and Klein 2008: 93)
"ich weiß nicht, was das soll; ich kenn das üblicherweise nicht von privaten rentenversicherungen oder kapitallebensversicherungen; da gibt's, wenn der vertrag beitragsfrei gestellt wird, gibt's keinen abzug, keinen zusätzlichen (...) *wofür*? erklärt ja nicht mal, *wofür*"

(I don't understand what is going on [...] there is no discount, no additional discount? Why should there be one?)

b. a layman (Becker and Klein 2008: 93)
"davon werden null komma zwei prozent abzug berechnet, die ich zahlen muss + als +++ ja + strafe, oder was weiß ich"

(there is a discount of 0.2 percent, and I have to pay this as a penalty or whatever)

The concept of "coverage capital" was likewise ill understood, although there is a footnote in the conditions that explains it. Nobody seems to understand this footnote:

(12) a. a layman (Becker and Klein 2008: 89))
"also das kann ich nun überhaupt nicht mehr so nachvollziehen (…); da müsst ich erst mal wissen, wie definiert sich das vorhandene deckungskapital"

(I do not understand this anymore. I would need to know how the existing coverage capital is defined)

b. a layman (Becker and Klein 2008: 89))
"ich weiß hier nicht von welchem deckungskapital geredet wird; zum vereinbarten rentenbeginn muss n deckungskapital vorhanden sein und zum zeitpunkt der freistellung muss auch n deckungskapital vorhanden sein; ich weiß nicht, wie gross eins von beiden ist und ich weiß auch nicht, wo diese deckungskapitale herkommen; deshalb erklärt sich mir der Satz nicht"

(I do not know which coverage capital they are talking about; at the agreed starting time of the pension there must be a coverage capital and there is also one at the time of stopping the contributions. I do not know the amount of either of them, and I do not know where they come from, and this is why I cannot understand the sentence)

Each sentence in the two relevant paragraphs §6 *Suspending the insurance* and §7 *Cancellation of the insurance* is treated in this detail in the book, this takes 100 pages, cf. Becker and Klein (2008: 59–158).

5. A critical assessment

5.1 Introduction

It was the declared aim of Becker and Klein (2008) to show with a concrete example how legal texts are really understood and which difficulties occur among different readers of these texts. Becker and Klein (2008: 217) come to the conclusion that the insurance conditions of the investigated Riester-pension are not plain and intelligible and thus do not conform to the European Council Directive 93/13/EEC on consumer contracts. This conclusion is irritating given the high percentages of correct answers in the questionnaires. So either the authors of the study have to claim that their questionnaires do not constitute an apt method to test plainness and intelligibility or the conclusion is wrong.

But even if the conclusion were true, it is unclear what would follow from it. If an insurance company sets up a new Riester-pension product, should the company engage a team of linguists that sets up "think aloud" experiments and questionnaires of the kind described here? This would at least be quite expensive and it would take an enormous amount of time, given the methods of this study. Also, these methods not seem to be applicable to other legal texts. A lawyer who wants to check a letter to his client in terms of comprehensibility does not have time to write up all the propositions, then let someone "think aloud" about the text, record this, compare the (transcribed) result to his set of propositions and then do one or two questionnaires. In short, the methods of this study are not applicable in everyday life. Professionals in the domain of drafting legal will not be able to apply these methods.

Surely, not every study that deserves consideration and that reports research on an interesting and highly relevant issue (which the study does) must necessarily be applicable in everyday life. What are the scientific merits of Becker and Klein (2008)? There is no principled way to predict comprehension with the methods of the study. Instead, comprehension is just measured empirically, by comparing "think aloud" protocols with sets of propositions, doing questionnaires etc. We demand more from a linguistic theory. Where can we get more? To answer this question, a deeper investigation of the present study is necessary. I focus on five aspects: the Riester-pension, the questionnaires, the "think aloud" method, and the propositional approach.

5.2 The Riester-pension

Maybe it was not very wise to choose the Riester-pension for the study. As this pension was new on the market, the insurance agents had no selling experience with it, and many puzzling results of this study can be explained by taking the agents' lacking routine into account. The missing routine is mirrored in the first task about finding the relevant paragraph, where jurists and insurance agents had nearly the same overall reading time. With a familiar product, the insurance agents would have been quicker.

The ratio of reading relevant to irrelevant paragraphs among insurance agents was 26:11[14], or 2.4 to 1. This is identical to the ratio found with

---

14. This means that on average, the insurance agents spent 26 seconds reading a relevant paragraph and 11 seconds reading an irrelevant one.

laymen, which was 46:19, or 2.4 to 1. In other words, it is very difficult for the agents to distinguish between relevant and irrelevant passages, as difficult as it is for laymen. The difficulties of the agents are quite probably due to their lacking selling experience with this pension. Jurists have better ratios, 27:5, or 5.4 to 1. They are skilled readers and can easily decide between relevant and irrelevant passages.

5.3 The questionnaires

The questionnaires used in the study are not very helpful in detecting the correctness of the test persons' understanding. The multiple choice questionnaire was too easy, with 10 out of 13 questions answered correctly in 93% (taken all test persons together). The three remaining questions in the multiple choice questionnaire were insurance specific questions that were however not specific to a Riester-pension. They were of course only answered correctly by the insurance agents, with the laymen and the jurists performing badly. This comes as no surprise, but the results are not indicative of a correct or incorrect understanding of the concrete Riester-pension insurance conditions at hand. Thus, the multiple choice questionnaire does not seem to have a real function in the study.

One of these difficult questions (question A4, cf. Becker and Klein 2008: 198) was about the definition of "coverage capital". This is a term not specific to a Riester-pension, it is a general term used in insurances of many types (e.g. in life and health insurances). Laymen and jurists with no background in insurances performed badly with it, being right in only 45%[15]. As the insurance agents have a good knowledge about insurances, they were right in 70%[16]. The next difficult question (question A9, cf. Becker and Klein 2008: 199) was about the "redemption value". As with A4, this term not specific to a Riester-pension, it is a general term used in life insurances. Again, the insurance agents were right in 90% whereas the jurists and the laymen made mistakes here. The third difficult question

15. I.e., 5 laymen and 4 jurists gave the correct answer, and 9 out of 20 persons is 45%.
16. I.e., 7 agents gave the correct answer, and 7 out of 10 persons is 70%.

(question A13, cf. Becker and Klein (2008: 199) was about the term "insured pension". As this term is common in all private pensions and also in disability insurances, the insurance agents have a good performance (70% right answers) whereas the jurists and laymen have a bad one (50% right answers).

The questionnaire with the yes/no questions was also too easy, with 79% of the questions answered correctly. The authors themselves are skeptical about the validity of the results (cf. Becker and Klein 2008: 210), as the "think aloud" data reveal misunderstandings of the insurance conditions whereas the corresponding yes/no questions in the questionnaire were answered correctly. Thus, the questionnaire seems to be rather superficial, not apt to test deeper understanding.

As far as confidence and calibration in the questionnaires is concerned, we also just find what we expect anyway. The more difficult a question is, the more likely it is that overconfidence occurs. If a question is easy, underconfidence is likely to happen. This is knows as the *hard-easy effect* in the literature (Lichtenstein et al. 1982). The multiple choice questionnaire was so easy that the test persons showed a high degree of confidence (4.4 out of 5). This was even surpassed by the yes/no questionnaire, with 4.6 out of 5. Thus, it is probable that the the yes/no questionnaire was more difficult, and this is confirmed by the correctness of the answers: 'only' 79% compared to 93% in the other questionnaire.[17]

5.4 The "think aloud" method

The "think aloud" method does not seem to be suited to meet the aims of the investigation. It would have been very interesting to have a look at comprehension while it happens, i.e., under real-time conditions. But as Olson et al. (1984: 285) admit, not all test persons are able to deliver reliable data and "think aloud" may influence the comprehension process itself. As for the first point, this is more than obvious. But even the reliable data have to be taken with care, keeping in mind that thinking is faster than

17. The introduction to the presentation of the questionnaires is misleading about this point (Becker and Klein 2008: 193). The authors claim that multiple choice questionnaires are generally more difficult and thus get higher confidence values than 'simple' yes/no questionnaires. This is not warranted by the confidence values discussed a few pages thereafter. Also, I could not come up with positive evidence for this claim in the literature. The point is not taken up again in Becker and Klein (2008).

articulating one's thoughts and that many thoughts cannot be properly articulated. Thus, it is quite possible that test persons understand more than they report. The "think aloud" situation is unnatural for most readers, who rarely think so awarely or aloud about their understanding of a text.

The second point of Olson et al. (1984) is even more important. When you have to comment on your comprehension, comprehension is influenced either negatively or positively. Visual tasks profit from "think aloud", as Merz (1969), Hussy (1987) and Franzen and Merz (1979) have shown. The authors of the mentioned studies argue that "think aloud" structures the solving of the task; instead of approaching the problem in a holistic or perceptual way, test persons tend to apply their analytic abilities. "Think aloud" also enhances the results in experiments where memory plays an important role (cf. Riley 1963), as verbalizing something itself is a way to memorize the content.

But it need not be the case that comprehension is facilitated by "think aloud". This is shown in Haak et al. (2003), a study on "think aloud" protocols in usability testing. Haak et al. (2003) describe an experiment that compares concurrent and retrospective "think aloud" protocols for a usability test of an online library catalogue. Results show that concurrent and retrospective "think aloud" protocols reveal comparable sets of usability problems, but that these problems come to light in different ways. In retrospective "think aloud" protocols, more problems were detected by means of verbalization, while in concurrent "think aloud" protocols; more problems were detected by means of observation. Moreover, in the concurrent "think aloud" protocols, the requirement to think aloud while working had a negative effect on the task performance.

There is a long tradition of skepticism about "think aloud" data, and it is astonishing that this is not even mentioned in Becker and Klein (2008). In their seminal paper, Nisbett and Wilson (1977) reviewed ample evidence that there is little or no direct introspective access to higher order cognitive processes. Nisbett and Wilson argue that "think aloud" data are not based on true introspection but rather on a priori, implicit causal theories, or judgments. Similar results are reported in Lüer et al. (1990) (cf. also Lüer et al. 1989) in a task about anagrams. The test persons solved the task partially in silence (their eye movements being recorded) and partially with "think aloud"; they were also interviewed about their strategies after the task. The eye movement recordings showed that the test persons developed good strategies to deal with the anagrams. However, the test persons were nearly unable to report on their strategies in the interviews, i.e., their strategies were unconscious. Also, the strategies did not come out in the "think aloud" data, i.e. they did not have introspective access to their own comprehension.

This offers another perspective on the findings in Becker and Klein (2008). We saw above that the test persons were good in the questionnaires but seemed to have severe problems in the "think aloud" task. Either the questionnaires were too easy as I suggested above or the "think aloud" data do not tell much about comprehension because the test persons do not have access to their comprehension in this mode. If the latter were true (and only additional empirical data, like recorded eye movements or something else could tell whether it is true), the questionnaires would show what they show: that the test persons had a good understanding of the insurance conditions. This result would contradict the aims of Becker and Klein (2008), though.

The study by Lüer et al. (1990) shows something else that offers a new interpretation for the findings in Becker and Klein (2008). When test persons were required to "think aloud", they became inflexible with new anagrams. "Think aloud" pushed them to a rigid and less creative way of solving the task. This aspect was also highlighted in Deffner (1987) and Deffner (1989). Thus, it comes as no surprise that the test persons in Becker and Klein (2008) did not show many revisions of their false beliefs (a fact that is highlighted again and again in the study), although the text of the insurance conditions suggests that they should revise them. The method of "think aloud" leads to unflexibility. Lüer et al. (1989) come to the conclusion that although "think aloud" is a useful method for some tasks, it is not applicable for analyzing higher order cognitive processes. Definitely, the understanding of a Riester-pension is such a processes.

Kaakinen and Hyönä (2005) argue for a combination of complementary measuring techniques such as eye tracking, the "think aloud" and free recall. In this study, 36 participants read an expository text describing rare illnesses. As far as eyetracking is concerned, readers invested more attentional resources to relevant text information and slowed down the pace of reading immediately when they encountered relevant information in the text. The test persons also reread the relevant sentences more than irrelevant sentences. "Think alouds" showed a different result: relevant and irrelevant text information probed overall very similar responses. However, there was a correlation between the different fixation time measures and the "think aloud" response types. Responses that are thought to reflect deeper level comprehension activities (self-explaining and elaborative questioning) were coupled with longer eye fixation times than responses indexing shallower processing (associations and paraphrasing).

Other researchers also move into this direction of combining "think aloud" with other methods, e.g. Whitney and Budd (1996) or Long and Bourg (1996). Long and Bourg argue that much of the information contained in verbal protocols reflect processes specific to the "think aloud" task instead of reflecting details of comprehension itself. In their study, the "think aloud" report of their test persons was definitely not a veridical report on their mental processes. Rather, the test persons constructed a text representation and used it to "tell a story" about their understanding, conforming to the pragmatics of the experimental situation where such a "story" was required. – I think it would be very interesting to try the Riester-pension study again, combining "think aloud" with eye movements, for instance.

5.5 The propositional approach

The propositional approach to comprehensibility developed by Kintsch and his collaborators (cf. Kintsch 1998; Kiontsch and Dijk 1978; Kintsch and Vipond 1979) surely is an innovation in comprehensibility research. However, the assumed semantics is very abstract; there is no connection to syntax. This can be seen in the partial rewriting of §6 *Suspending the insurance* in (6). The semantics as such is relatively primitive, compared to the standard of formal semantics e.g. in Heim and Kratzer (1998). The mode of description in this propositional approach is semi-formal. As arguments of predicates we have mere words or whole propositions. Quantification, modalization, tense, polarity and similar notions cannot be formalized here. Grabowski (1991) already explains why sentences like *Geißler called the Greens slobs* cannot be treated with this semantics – the correct propositional representation demands too much, namely that the pragmatics of the sentence is understood, it must be clear that the representation differs from *Geißler called Mrs Wright Jenny.* Well-known example sentences like *The morning star is the evening star* (where *morning star* and *evening star* have the same meaning but a different sense) or John Perry's example *Heimson believes that he is Hume* (where *he* cannot be just anaphoric, Heimson is not as crazy to believe that Heimson is Hume; on the other hand, Heimson does not only believe that Hume is Hume) cannot be treated.

It is stated in Becker and Klein (2008) that all sentences in §6 *Suspending the insurance* and §7 *Cancellation of the insurance* were rewritten in propositions. As the test persons' comprehension is measured against this representation of the text, it would have been interesting to look at the rewritten paragraphs. Unfortunately, they are not given in Becker and Klein (2008).

I agree with Becker and Klein (2008) that we need to have a model for the maximally understandable content of a text. The propositional approach by Kintsch and his collaborators is one way to go. However, there are alternatives to it, discussed also in Rathert (2006). Within computational linguistics, "shallow" modelling of meaning in terms of predicate-argument structures has lately regained interest. For example, the Berkeley *FrameNet* project (Fillmore et al. 2003) is developing a semantic lexicon for a core set of English, based on Fillmore's *Frame Semantics* (Fillmore 1976). Frame semantics models the semantics of predicates in terms of *frames*. A frame describes a conceptual structure or a prototypical situation together with a set of involved semantic roles or *frame elements*. Frame elements thus identify the participants of the situation. Taking the example of VERDICT, the frame VERDICT has the roles CASE, CHARGES, DEFENDANT, JUDGE, FINDING:

(13) [The jury]$_{\text{JUDGE}}$ convicted [him]$_{\text{DEFENDANT}}$ [on the counts of theft]$_{\text{CHARGES}}$

Elements like verbs, nouns, or adjectives evoke certain frames with their lexical semantics. As *FrameNet* currently focuses on these three open categories, the meaning representation is necessarily partial. The partiality of the Kintsch-type of meaning representation was discussed above.

How a combination of *FrameNet's* frame semantics with a deep syntactic analysis can be used as a shallow meaning representation of texts has been discussed in Burchardt et al. (2005). Remember that the Kintsch-type of semantics has no relation whatsoever to syntax. In Burchardt et al. (2005), frames are not only evoked by the lexicon, but also in the course of inferential processes, or via meaning postulates. This is something a Kintsch-semantics cannot come up with in principle, as the propositions are only descriptions. To show how such an analysis is represented, the essentials from the case study in Burchardt et al. (2005) are reproduced here. This is the text:

(14) In the first trial in the world in connection with the terrorist attacks of 11 September 2001, the Higher Regional Court of Hamburg has passed down the maximum sentence. Mounir al Motassadeq will spend 15 years in prison. The 28-year-old Moroccan was found guilty as an accessory to murder in more than 3000 cases.

A partial representation with local roles will look like this:

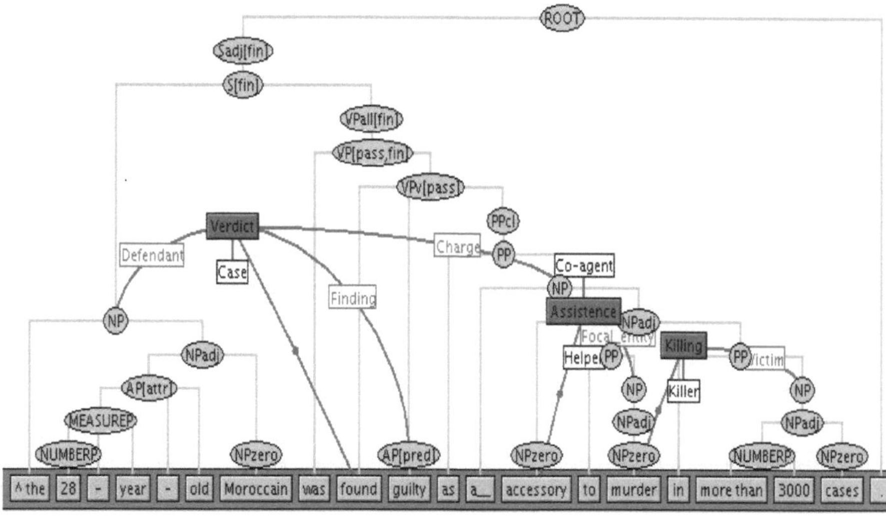

Figure 1: Semantic and syntactic annotation

The last sentence from (14) is printed at the bottom. An LFG parser produces the syntactic structure for the sentence, the frames and their roles associated with it are provided automatically, see Erk and Padó (2006). This is something that the Kintsch-type of meaning representation cannot achieve; the writing-up of the propositions has to be done manually. In the Kintsch-system, there are no generalizations about prototypical situations that would allow a semi-automatic way of dealing with the propositions.

In the diagram above, frames are in grey rectangles (like VERDICT at the left. ASSISTENCE and KILLING at the right), roles are in white rectangles with a grey margin (like DEFENDANT, CASE, FINDING, CHARGE as roles of the frame VERDICT). Erk and Pado's *Shalmaneser* is used in the RTE-system of Burchardt and Frank for robust, broad-coverage semantic annotation (Burchardt and Frank 2006).

The frame VERDICT (see left hand side) has the filler-NP *The 28-year-old Moroccan* for its role DEFENDANT, whereas its role CASE has no filler. What does this give us? I believe it is the first usable tool with which a new model of comprehensibility can be developed. In the spirit of Kintsch's propositional approach, we have a model for the maximally understandable content of a text. This model allows predictions.

The denser the frame net is (with super- and sub-frames), the better a text should be understood. It would be interesting to check whether relations between frames as defined in *FrameNet* can be attested empirically in comprehensibility tests. Defined prominent relations are *inheritance* and *subframe*. If a frame *a* inherits from frame *b*, then all frame elements of *b* are also available for *a*. The frame ARREST inherits PATIENT and AGENT from the frame INTENTIONALLY_AFFECT. The *subframe* relation is involved in larger frames, often called 'scenario frames', which represent complex events being composed of temporally ordered sub-events. As an example, CRIMINAL_PROCESS contains the subframes ARREST, TRIAL, SENTENCING (among others), having a fixed causal and temporal order with respect to each other. Frame elements are usually also inherited to the subframes. To stay with the example subframes ARREST and TRIAL, the same person who is arrested will also be the 'patient' in the trial.

Frames that cannot be integrated should cause comprehensibility problems. In the diagram above, the role CASE of the frame VERDICT cannot be filled. This should decrease comprehensibility. On the other hand, syntactic material that fills no frame should also decrease comprehensibility, because it adds material that does not contribute to conceptual structure. Of course, this does not apply to nodes whose daughters are fillers: in the diagram above, the node S[fin] is no filler, but its daughter NP bears the role DEFENDANT.

Inferences, i.e., inferred relations between frames, can also be shown. One would expect a difference in comprehensibility between overt and inferred relation, and also differences between sub- and super-frames.

The frame annotations leading to partial text meaning representations as described in Burchardt et al. (2005) aim at applications in practical NLP tasks, such as information extraction or question answering. No one from Frame Semantics has ever looked for an application like forensic linguistics, and forensic linguists have not started using the methods from computational linguistics. This is a concrete point where interdisciplinary collaboration should start.

The declared aim of FrameNet and Frame Semantics is to build up lexical databases, to do lexicography. A newer aim is to annotate continuous texts, as a demonstration of how this tool can contribute to text understanding.[18] However, as this research is empirically based on written corpora only, it is not clear what the psycholinguistic correlates of the frames (and

---

18. See the Berkeley site for current work carried out: http://framenet.icsi.berkeley.edu/.

their hierarchical and inferred relations) are. In other words: FrameNet and Frame Semantics should expose themselves to an empirical validation of their powerful and promising model.

5.6 Conclusion

To conclude, let me emphasize the merits of Becker and Klein (2008). It is one of the very few elaborate psycholinguistic studies carried out so far on German written law. For projects on 'Language of the Law', it is indispensable to have access to an interdisciplinary research group. The Berlin-Brandenburg group was lucky to be interdisciplinary from the beginning, and this is mirrored in the quality of the book discussed here. The content of the legal texts investigated in studies like this definitely needs to be checked by jurists, and the experiments can only be designed and carried out by psycholinguists. Both of this was done successfully in Becker and Klein (2008). Considering three different kinds of test persons was also a wise decision of the Berlin-Brandenburg group. Observing comprehension while it happens is absolutely exciting and reading the protocols in the book is very illuminating (and also funny). Finally, evaluating the test persons' comprehension with questionnaires is also a necessary and indispensable task.

To sum it up, future studies on 'Language of the Law' will have to expose themselves to the high standards that are met in this publication.

Hopefully, the ideas and the spirit of the interdisciplinary research group at the Academy of Science at Berlin-Brandenburg will be taken up by other groups working empirically or theoretically on the topic of 'Language of the Law'. The ideas that were developed in this group are inspiring and definitely worth pursuing. They are highly relevant to practitioners of legal drafting as well as to theoretical linguistics working on comprehension.

6. References

Becker, Angelika and Wolfgang Klein. 2008. *Recht verstehen. Wie Laien, Juristen und Versicherungsagenten die „Riester-Rente" interpretieren.* Berlin: Akademie.

Burchardt, Aljoscha and Anette Frank. 2006. "Approximating Textual Entailment with LFG and FrameNet Frames". *Proceedings of the second PASCAL Recognizing Textual Entailment Workshop, Venice, Italy*, 92–97.

Burchardt, Aljoscha, Anette Frank and Manfred Pinkal. 2005. "Building Text Meaning Representations from Contextually Related Frames". *Proceedings of IWCS 6, Tilburg.*

Chall, J.S. 1958. *Readability: an appraisal of research and application.* Columbus: Ohio State University.

Charrow, Robert P. and Veda R. Charrow. 1979. "Making Legal Language Understandable: A Psycholinguistic Study of Jury Instructions". *Columbia Law Review* 79. 1306–1374.

Deffner, Gerhard. 1987. Eye movement patterns as an indicator of solution strategy in solving n-term series task. Paper presented to the the Fourth European conference on eye moevements, 1987.

Deffner, Gerhard. 1989. "Interaktion zwischen Lautem Denken, Bearbeitungsstrategien und Aufgabenmerkmalen? Eine experimentelle Prüfung des Modells von Ericsson und Simon". *Sprache & Kognition* 8. 98–111.

Dietrich, Rainer and Katja Kühn. 2000. "Transparent oder verständlich oder wie was verstanden wird – Eine empirische Untersuchung zum Verstehen eines juristischen Textes.". *Zeitschrift für Literaturwissenschaft und Linguistik 118.* 67–95.

Erk, Katrin and Sebastian Padó. 2006. Shalmaneser – a toolchain for shallow semantic parsing. Paper presented to the Language resources and evaluation (LREC), Genua, 2006.

Fillmore, Charles J. 1968. "The case for case". *Universals of Linguistic Theory*, ed. by E. Bach and R.T. Harms, New York: Holt, Rinehart amd Winston. 1–88.

Fillmore, Charles J. 1976. "Frame semantics and the nature of language". *Annals of the New York Academy of Sciences: Conference on the origin and development of Language and Speech* 280. 20–32.

Fillmore, Charles J., Christopher R. Johnson and Miriam R.L. Petruck. 2003. "Background to FrameNet". *International Journal of Lexicography* 16. 235–250.

Franzen, U. and F. Merz. 1976. "Der Einfluß des Verbalisierens auf die Leistung bei Intelligenzprüfungen: neue Untersuchungen". *Zeitschrift für Entwicklungspsychologie und Pädagogische Psychologie* 8. 117–34.

Grabowski, Joachim. 1991. *Der propositionale Ansatz der Textverständlichkeit: Kohärenz, Interessantheit und Behalten.* Münster: Aschendorff.

Graesser, Arthur C., Keith K. Millis and Rolf A. Zwaan. 1997. "Discourse comprehension". *Annual Review of Psychology* 48. 163–189.

Grewendorf, Günther. 1992. "Rechtskultur als Sprachkultur. Der sprachanalytische Sachverstand im Recht". *Rechtskultur als Sprachkultur. Zur forensischen Funktion der Sprachanalyse*, ed. by G. Grewendorf, Frankfurt am Main: Suhrkamp. 11–41.

Gunnarsson, Britt-Louise. 1984. "Functional comprehensibility of legislative texts: experiments with a Swedish act of parliament". *Text* 4. 71–105.

Haak, Maaike J. van den, Menno D. T. de Jong and Peter Jan Schellens. 2003. "Retrospective vs. concurrent think-aloud protocols: testing the usability of an online library catalogue". *Behaviour & information technology* 22. 339–351.
Hansen-Schirra, Silvia and Stella Neumann. 2004. "Linguistische Verständlichmachung in der juristischen Realität". *Die Sprache des Rechts. Band 1: Recht verstehen. Verständlichkeit, Missverständlichkeit und Unverständlichkeit von Recht*, ed. by K. Lerch, Berlin: Walter de Gruyter. 167–184.
Hassemer, Winfried. 1992. "Richtiges Recht durch richtiges Sprechen? Zum Analogieverbot im Strafrecht". *Rechtskultur als Sprachkultur. Zur Forensischen Funktion der Sprachanalyse*, ed. by G. Grewendorf, Frankfurt am Main: Suhrkamp. 71–92.
Heim, Irene and Angelika Kratzer. 1998. *Semantics in Generative Grammar*. Oxford: Blackwell.
Herberger, Maximilian. 1983. "Unverständlichkeit des Rechts. Anmerkungen zur historischen Entwicklung des Problems und des Problembewußtseins.". *Recht und Sprache*, ed. by R. Wassermann and J. Petersen, Heidelberg: C. F. Müller. 19–40.
Hoffmann, Ludger. 1992. "Wie verständlich können Gesetze sein?". *Rechtskultur als Sprachkultur. Zur forensischen Funktion der Sprachanalyse*, ed. by G. Grewendorf, Frankfurt am Main: Suhrkamp. 122–154.
Hussy, Walter. 1987. "Zur Steuerfunktion der Sprache beim Problemlösen". *Sprache & Kognition* 1. 14–22.
Jaspersen, Andrea. 1998. Über die mangelnde Verständlichkeit des Rechts für den Laien: University of Bonn PhD Thesis.
Jonsson, Anna-Carin and Carl Martin Allwood. 2003. "Stability and variability in the realism of confidence judgments over time, content domain, and gender". *Personality and individual differences* 34. 559–574.
Kaakinen, Johanna K. and Jukka Hyönä. 2005. "Perspective Effects on Expository Text Comprehension: Evidence From Think-Aloud Protocols, Eyetracking, and Recall". *Discourse Processes* 40. 239–257.
Kintsch, Walter. 1988. "The role of knowledge in discourse comprehension: a construction-integration model". *Psychological review* 95. 163–82.
Kintsch, Walter. 1998. *Comprehension. A paradigm for cognition*. Cambridge: Cambridge University Press.
Kintsch, Walter and T. van Dijk. 1978. "Toward a model of text comprehension and production". *Psychological review* 85. 363–394.
Kintsch, Walter and D. Vipond. 1979. "Reading comprehension and readability in educational practice and psychological theory". *Perspectives on memory research*, ed. by L. Nilsson, Hillsdale: Erslbaum. 329–365.
Lerch, Kent (ed.) 2004/2005. *Sprache des Rechts. 3 Bände*. Berlin: Walter de Gruyter.
Lichtenstein, Sarah, Baruch Fischhoff and Lawrence D. Philipps. 1982. "Calibration of Probabilities: The State of the Art to 1980". *Judgement under Un-*

certainty: Heuristics and Biases, ed. by D. Kahneman, P. Slovic and A. Tversky, Cambridge: Cambridge University Press. 306–334.

Long, Debra L. and Tammy Bourg. 1996. "Thinking aloud: Telling a story about a story". *Discourse Processes* 21. 329–39.

Lorenz, Reinhard. 1991. "Recht – Sprache – Begriff". *Sprache – Recht – Geschichte. Rechtshistorisches Kolloquium* 5.-9.6.1990, ed. by J. Eckert and H. Hattenhauer, Heidelberg: C. F. Müller. 295–311.

Lüer, Gerd, Uta Lass and Peter Ruhlender. 1989. "Denken und lautes Denken". *Idola fori et idola theatri : Festschrift aus Anlass der Emeritierung von Prof. Dr. phil. et Dr. med. Hermann Wegener*, ed. by D. Dörner and W. Michaelis, Göttingen: Hogrefe. 71–86.

Lüer, Gerd, P. Ruhlender, W. Klettke and Uta Lass. 1990. "The construction of procedural knowledge independent of declarative factual knowledge: An experimental study". *From Eye to Mind. Information Acquisition in Perception, Search and Reading*, ed. by R. Groner, G. d'Ydewalle and R. Parham, Amsterdam: North-Holland. 141–152.

Lundeberg, Mary A. 1987. "Metacognitive Aspects of Reading Comprehension: Studying Understanding in Legal Case Analysis". *Reading Research Quarterly* 22. 407–432.

Merz, F. 1969. "Der Einfluß des Verbalisierens auf die Leistung bei Intelligenzaufgaben". *Zeitschrift für Experimentelle und Angewandte Psychologie* 16. 114–137.

Neumann, Stella and Silvia Hansen-Schirra. 2004. "Der Konjunktiv als Verständnisproblem in Rechtstexten". *Zeitschrift für Angewandte Linguistik* 41. 67–87.

Nisbett, Richard and Timothy deCamp Wilson. 1977. "Telling more than we can know: Verbal reports on mental processes". *Psychological review* 84. 231–259.

Olson, G.M., S.A. Duffy and R.L. Mack. 1984. "Thinking-out-loud as a method for studying real-time comprehension processes". *New Methods in reading comprehension research*, ed. by D. Kieras and M. Just, Hillsdale: Erlbaum. 253–286.

Pfeiffer, Oskar E., Ernst Strouhal and Ruth Wodak. 1987. *Recht auf Sprache. Verstehen und Verständlichkeit von Gesetzen*. Wien: Orac.

Rathert, Monika. 2006. "Comprehensibility in forensic linguistics – new perspectives for Frame Semantics". *Form, Structure, and Grammar. A Festschrift presented to Günther Grewendorf on occasion of his 60th birthday*, ed. by P. Brandt and E. Fuß, Berlin: Akademie. 337–352.

Riley, Donald A. 1963. "Memory for form". *Psychology in the making*, ed. by L. Postman, New York: Knopf. 402–465.

Schendera, Christian F.G. 2000. "Die Verständlichkeit normativer Texte: eine kritische Darstellung der Forschungslage". *Leges* 2. 99–134.

Selting, Margaret, Peter Auer, Birgit Barden, Jörg Bergmann, Elisabeth Couper-Kuhlen, Susanne Günthner, Christoph Meier, Uta Quasthoff, Peter Schlobinski and Susanne Uhmann. 1998. "Gesprächsanalytisches Transkriptionssystem (GAT)". *Linguistische Berichte* 173. 91– 122.

Weber, Traudel and Annette Noschka-Roos. 1988. *Texte im Technischen Museum. Textformulierung und Gestaltung, Verständlichkeit, Testmöglichkeiten* Berlin: Materialien aus dem Institut für Museumskunde, Staatliche Museen Preußischer Kulturbesitz Berlin

Whitney, Paul and Desiree Budd. 1996. "Think-aloud protocols and the study of comprehension". *Discourse Processes* 21. 341–51

Part 2

Identifying the criminal: The contribution of phonetics and text/corpus linguistics

Forensic phonetics and the influence of speaking style on global measures of fundamental frequency

Michael Jessen

1. Introduction

Forensic phonetics is a scientific and practical discipline in which phonetic and linguistic knowledge and methodology are applied in order to provide helpful information in police investigations and to prepare and present forensic expert witness reports in court. More broadly defined, this discipline includes aspects of acoustic analysis which are addressed in collaboration with speech engineers and acousticians and comprise tasks such as tape authentication, the analysis of non-speech signals like gunshot sounds, audio enhancement, and – with gaining interest over the past years – automatic speaker recognition. The international organization dealing with forensic phonetics has recently added "acoustics" to its name in order to express greater appreciation of these speech-technological aspects of forensic phonetics and is now called "International Association for Forensic Phonetics and Acoustics" (IAFPA). An alternative label for this discipline is "Forensic Speech and Audio Analysis" – a name used for example by the "European Network of Forensic Science Institutes" (ENFSI). Since the more speech-technological aspects of forensic analysis are not addressed in this paper, the name "forensic phonetics" will be kept.

Not the only but certainly the central task of forensic phonetics is speaker recognition (cf. Künzel 1987, 2004; Hollien 1990; Nolan 1997; Gfroerer 2006 for overviews of the entire scope of forensic phonetics). Speaker recognition, in turn, can be subdivided into voice comparison, voice profiling, and speaker recognition by victims and witnesses, the latter of which also includes the design and application of voice line ups (also called voice parades). Fundamental frequency analysis, which is the topic of this paper, is not equally relevant to all three of these speaker recognition tasks: It is very important for voice comparisons, it is of more limited importance for the preparation of voice lines ups, and it is currently of no practical relevance in voice profiling, unless fundamental frequency meas-

G. Grewendorf and M. Rathert (eds.): Formal Linguistics and Law, 115–139
© Berlin, New York: Mouton deGruyter

urements could provide some information on speaker classification features such as age, gender, dialect, and speech pathology, that cannot be achieved by auditory analysis alone.

Focussing on voice comparison in forensic phonetics, recorded speech material from an unknown speaker (i.e. the criminal) and a suspect are compared with respect to a variety of phonetic and linguistic features. Based on this feature analysis, a probabilistic statement is made as to whether or not the unknown speaker and the suspect are identical. Künzel (1987) has provided convincing arguments and illustrations for the requirement that forensic-phonetic analysis should include both auditory-phonetic and acoustic-phonetic features (see also Nolan 1983). This combined auditory-acoustic approach has been adopted on an international level by a wide variety of institutes and experts involved in forensic phonetics (see Nolan 1997; Gfroerer 2003). According to this approach the initial analysis of the speech material is performed auditorily. Acoustic measurements are made in areas where acoustic data can provide more detailed and more objective information than is possible with auditory methods alone. It is undisputed among practitioners of this approach that the acoustic side of this combined approach should include the measurement and analysis of fundamental frequency (f0).

In forensic phonetics, fundamental frequency is most commonly measured and evaluated under its "global" aspects, and the two most common global f0 parameters are average f0 and the variability of f0, which can be quantified in terms of the standard deviation of f0 values in a recording. From individual differences in the length of the vocal folds (Titze 1994: 172–173) it is expected that average f0 is subject to a high degree of interspeaker variation. That this is indeed the case has been shown by Künzel (1987), who – based on German speech – has provided Gaussian-shaped histograms of average f0 values from 100 men and 50 women. Less information is available on the interspeaker variation of variability measures of f0, such as f0 standard deviation. Furthermore, f0 variability does not have the same kind of anatomical motivation as average f0. Instead of being an anatomically predisposed feature, it is plausible to assume that f0 variability is primarily a habitual feature that captures speaker-specific preferences on the axis between a melodic and a monotonous manner of speaking (Künzel 1987). The common practice of selecting global f0 parameters instead of using more localised parameters that are motivated by intonational phonology and phonetics is not merely a matter of convenience and efficiency but is also motivated by empirical research which has shown that "intonationally intelligent" parameters do not necessarily lead to better speaker recognition than global f0 measures (Kraayeveld 1997), and that these intonationally motivated parameters are very sensitive to the kind of speech material that is used and work best in controlled experiments (Nolan 2002).

What makes the use of fundamental frequency in forensic phonetics difficult is the fact that f0 not only differs between speakers but that it is also subject to various sources of within-speaker variation (see Braun 1995 for overview). One of the most significant and forensically relevant sources of intraspeaker variation is the influence of vocal effort on average f0: When a speaker turns from normal to loud speech, the f0 level is increased. This effect was investigated in 100 male adult speakers of German, none of whom posed an exception to this effect. This study as well as a review of literature on that topic is presented by Jessen et al. (2005). The f0 data on which the study of Jessen et al. (2005) is based are identical to the ones analysed here. The difference between the two studies lies in the focus of the study: Whereas the focus of Jessen et al. (2005) was on the effect of loud speech production on f0, the focus of this study is on the difference between read and spontaneous speech.

The difference between read and spontaneous speech is forensically relevant when in a voice comparison the unknown speaker spoke in one of these speech styles whereas the suspect spoke in the other. The most common situation in which these stylistic mismatches occur is when the samples of spontaneous speech from an unknown speaker are transcribed by a police officer and then read aloud by the suspect. Although it is recommended by the German *Bundeskriminalamt* as well as other forensic institutes that not only read but also spontaneous speech samples should be obtained from a suspect, there are situations in which this recommendation is either not known or disregarded for various reasons. In such a situation it is very important to know how much and in which direction the global f0 measures taken in forensic phonetics are expected to differ from one style to the other.

The following section presents an overview of studies on the influence of read vs. spontaneous speech on the average and variability of fundamental frequency. In this survey, special attention will be given to the speech of male subjects, since all the subjects in the present study are male as well (which is a forensically motivated choice). Furthermore, results on German and results presented by researchers with a particular interest in forensic applications will be presented most explicitly. Results on average f0 and on f0 variability are addressed in separate subsections. In the following, average or mean fundamental frequency will be referred to as "f0mean", and the standard deviation of f0 values in a recording as "f0sd".

2. Literature on f0 in read vs. spontaneous speech

2.1 Average f0

Interest in the influence of speaking style on fundamental frequency dates back at least to Snidecor (1943). Snidecor investigated read and spontaneous speech in six male students with "superior voice usage", as selected by a panel of listeners who based their judgments on the "general effectiveness of the performances" in a preliminary reading task (p. 51). Fundamental frequency was determined manually by measuring the duration of the fundamental period in representative sections of the speech material. In both the reading and the spontaneous speech task subjects were asked to talk as if to an audience of 25 people. Across speakers Snidecor measured a mean f0 value of 120 Hz for spontaneous speech and 132 Hz for read speech.[1] In his conclusions Snidecor mentions that a higher mean f0 in read as opposed to spontaneous speech was found for five of his speakers, whereas for the sixth speaker there was no difference. This pattern according to which reading leads to higher mean f0 values than spontaneous speech was replicated in several subsequent studies on English. However, in some of these studies the difference was so small that it did not reach statistical significance (Sorensen and Horii 1982; Fitch 1990; Murry et al. 1995).

With special attention to forensic applications, Hirson et al. (1995) elicited spontaneous and read speech from 20 male speakers of English, aged between 21 and 37 years. The two speech styles were produced both in a face-to-face situation and on the telephone. Pooled across subjects f0mean was 121.2 Hz for read telephone speech, 121.5 Hz for read face-to-face speech, 108.9 Hz for spontaneous speech on the telephone and 106.9 Hz for spontaneous face-to-face speech. Statistical testing showed that f0mean was significantly higher in read speech than in spontaneous speech. This was the case both for the telephone setting and the face-to-face setting. In their discussion Hirson et al. say that they might have predicted f0mean in read speech to be lower, not higher, than in spontaneous speech. However, the

1. Compared to other studies, the values for both reading and spontaneous speech are slightly above average. This might be due to increased vocal effort induced by the 25-people-audience instruction.

opposite was the case and this was attributed in part to the fact that some passages of the text had been read in a rather dramatic way (probably leading to more or stronger pitch accents than in spontaneous speech). By eliminating the more dramatically read passages and re-running the f0 analysis, Hirson et al. found f0mean values in read speech that were very close to those in spontaneous speech.

Hollien et al. (1997) report results on f0mean from a total of 324 English-speaking male subjects, aged between approximately 18 and 30 years. These data were drawn from previously published or unpublished studies guided by Harry Hollien. In the pooled data of the first study they report, f0mean was at 129 Hz for read and 123 Hz for spontaneous speech, in the second study reading resulted in 122 Hz and spontaneous speech in 116 Hz, and in the third study the figures were 114 Hz for read speech and 110 Hz for spontaneous speech. From these results f0mean is higher in read speech than in spontaneous speech, which is consistent with the results obtained by Snidecor (1943) and Hirson et al. (1995). However, in a discussion of previous literature on f0mean in read versus spontaneous speech in English, Hollien et al. point out that the results from these older sources were "somewhat mixed", that "no clear patterns have emerged" and that "the differences were quite small" (pp. 2989–2990).They also mention that the trend of higher f0mean in read speech as opposed to spontaneous speech among their 324 males was not uniform across subjects, and that in about one out of five subjects the effect was reversed or no difference between the two speech styles occurred at all. Looking back at the data from Hirson et al. (1995: Table 16.1), the trend was not uniform across speakers in that study either, and the percentage of speakers with reversals and equalisations was comparable, though slightly lower than in Hollien et al. (1997). Laan (1997), in a study on Dutch speech, presents another case of speaker-specific differences. Both of her two speakers (male) showed higher f0mean in reading than in spontaneous speech, but for only one of her speakers this difference was statistically significant.

The remainder of this survey addresses research on German. Schultz-Coulon (1975) presents a study where f0mean was measured for read speech, spontaneous speech, and number counting. Female and male adult speakers, subdivided into singers, dysphonic patients, and normal speakers, were used as subjects. The number of normal male speakers was 11. Results pooled across the three subgroups showed that f0mean for the male speakers was 117 Hz in read speech, 110 Hz during number counting, and 107 Hz in spontaneous speech. When focussing specifically on the values for normal male speakers (which were expressed in semitones above the lower end of the f0 range, not in terms of Hz) the same order, i.e. reading > counting > spontaneous speech was noted. The higher values of f0mean in reading compared to spontaneous speech and the size of the difference found by Schultz-Coulon is comparable to the mentioned studies on English.

Batliner et al. (1995) recorded three females and one male speaker (probably students) who were speaking spontaneously in a dialogue where they had to solve problems in a "blocks world" (p. 321). Nine months later they were asked to read the dialogue, which had been transcribed in the meantime. It turned out that for all four speakers f0mean was higher in spontaneous than in read speech.

Künzel (1997) elicited spontaneous speech (presenting personal views on a controversial issue), semispontaneous speech (retelling the essentials of a previous discussion), and read speech by five male and five female subjects (students), both in a face-to-face context and during telephone conversation. Künzel found that for both the male and female speakers f0mean was significantly higher in read speech than in either spontaneous or semispontaneous speech. There was, however, a certain amount of speaker variation with respect to the direction of the effects. For two out of the five male speakers, f0mean was not the highest in read speech, and in most of these cases (considering both the telephone and the face-to-face condition) it was the spontaneous speech condition that lead to the highest values (see his Table 2). For the females, speaker variation was even higher. Hence, although the group effects point towards f0mean being highest in read speech the amount of speaker variation was substantial.

In the German Lombard study carried out by Köster (2002), three speech styles were used, among them "dialogue" (spontaneous speech) and "sentence".[2] It is not mentioned in that paper whether the "sentence" condition actually refers to the reading of sentences or perhaps to their repetition. But, assuming it was read speech, one can observe from her figure 2 that for non-Lombard speech f0mean was slightly higher in spontaneous than in read speech, whereas for Lombard speech f0mean was slightly higher in read than in spontaneous speech. The difference between read and sponta-

---

2. The "Lombard effect" is named after Etienne Lombard, who first described the phenomenon in 1911. It refers to the fact that a speaker raises the loudness level of her/his voice when speaking in a noisy environment. Several studies with the goal of investigating the phonetic/acoustic consequences of loud speech production make use of this effect, for example by presenting loud white noise over headphones (see Jessen et al. (2005) for overview and further literature).

neous speech was so small that it is unlikely it reached the level of statistical significance – neither within Lombard nor non-Lombard speech.

Mixdorff and Pfitzinger (2005) investigated speech samples from three female speakers and one male speaker of German (students) as they produced spontaneous speech in a German Map Task version and as they read scripts derived from their spontaneous speech productions. For two of the female speakers, f0mean was higher in spontaneous than in read speech. As to the male speaker, the opposite pattern occurred. For the remaining female subject f0mean was practically the same in both speech styles.

To summarise the foregoing, the studies that were reviewed here have revealed a tendency for mean f0 to be higher in read than in spontaneous speech. However, many of these studies show that some subjects deviate from this pattern. Furthermore, some studies show no significant difference (if significance was tested) or even show higher values in spontaneous than in read speech. The latter occurred more frequently in studies based on German than on English.

2.2 f0 variability

Compared to the literature on the parameter f0mean, less data are available on f0 variability, such as f0 standard deviation or f0 range (obtained separately for each speaker). In the study carried out by Snidecor (1943) f0sd, expressed in tones, was higher for the reading task than for spontaneous speech.[3] In the Dutch study by Laan (1997), 90% f0 range was significantly higher in read than in spontaneous speech for one of the two subjects (the same that also had a significant f0mean difference, as mentioned above), whereas the other speaker showed no significant f0 range difference. In two of the three studies reported by Hollien et al. (1997), f0sd (in tones) in spontaneous and in read speech are exactly the same. In the third study (on male military personnel), f0sd is slightly higher in spontaneous speech than in read speech.

Tjaden (2000) measured f0 range in a study about Parkinson speech. The nine healthy control speakers (of English) were males and aged between 59 and 80 years. Spontaneous speech was elicited in a session were the subjects spoke about their family, home or work. Excerpts from the

3. When using the adjectives "high" vs. "low" in connection with measures of f0 variability in this paper, it is meant that the variability is "large" or "wide" vs. "small" or "narrow", respectively.

Farm Passage (a text with 313 monosyllabic words; see Crystal and House 1982) were used to investigate read speech. Across all subjects, the average f0 range was 64 Hz for read speech (at habitual speech rate) and 55 Hz for spontaneous speech, i.e. somewhat higher in read than in spontaneous speech.

As to German, in the study by Batliner et al. (1995) f0sd was higher in read than in spontaneous speech for the two female and the male speaker, whereas is was higher in spontaneous than in read speech for one female speaker. In the data presented by Köster (2002), f0 interquartiles were very similar for read and spontaneous speech, although slightly lower for read than for spontaneous speech, both for Lombard and especially for non-Lombard speech. Mixdorff and Pfitzinger (2005) show that for the three female subjects in their study f0sd was higher in spontaneous than in read speech, whereas for the male subject f0sd was the same in both conditions.[4]

These results of f0 variability are even more heterogeneous than the results for average f0. Whereas there is a trend among the studies on English (and Dutch) indicating that f0 variability tends to be higher in read than in spontaneous speech, the data reported in Hollien et al. (1997) do not correspond to this trend. For the German data, there is not much of a trend at all. From the studies reported in section 2 one can notice a certain correspondence between the average and the variability data: If average f0 is higher in read than in spontaneous speech, f0 variability also tends to be higher, and if average f0 is lower in read than in spontaneous speech, the same applies to variability (with exceptions, especially in Batliner et al. 1995). It is possible that this observable correspondence is due to a positive correlation between average and variability of f0, if variability is not normalised against average. This point will be addressed in more detail in section 5.

2.3 Conclusion

The literature review has shown certain tendencies but no uniform patterns with respect to the question of whether and in what ways average funda-

4. For the studies by Snidecor, Tjaden, Batliner et al. as well as Mixdorff and Pfitzinger it is clear that f0 variability was measured separately for each speaker, which is the desired procedure in order to use f0 variability as an index of more mononotous vs. more melodic speaking. For the studies by Hollien et al. and Köster the same procedure was probably used as well, but due to lack of more explicit documentation it cannot be ruled out entirely that they calculated f0 variability as the variability (e.g. standard deviation) of f0mean or f0 raw values across all speakers.

mental frequency differs between read and spontaneous speech. It is possible that some of the discrepancies are due to the fact that different speakers behave differently in terms of the relative influence of speaking style on fundamental frequency behaviour. Furthermore, relatively little research turned out to be available on the relation between speech style and f0 variability. In order to capture possible speaker differences and in order to obtain more data not only on average f0 but also on f0 variability in relation to read vs. spontaneous speech, a new experiment based on a large number of speakers was carried out.

3. Method

Speech from 100 male native speakers of German aged between 21 and 63 (average age: 39 years) was recorded and analysed for average and variability of fundamental frequency. Most of the speakers had grown up in the area in and around Wiesbaden and often had weak dialectal features of Hessian German ("Hessisch"), whereas others had been brought up in other locations in Germany and often had weak dialectal features of the corresponding regions. The speakers' education level was average to above average and none of them had any noticeable voice or speech deficiencies.

Each speaker was recorded while performing two different speech tasks in three settings, which added up to six experimental conditions. The two speech tasks were spontaneous speech and read speech. Reading was based on the German version of "The Northwind and the Sun". Spontaneous speech was elicited with some form of quiz game in which the subjects had to describe a series of pictures to a conversation partner but avoid certain terms that were written under the picture (e.g. description of a picture showing a lion without using the words "king", "Africa", and "cat"). The description had to be accurate enough for the conversation partner to be able to name the content of the picture that the subject was describing. What the subjects did not know was that the conversation partner was part of the research team and knew the pictures. With this knowledge the conversation partner was able to pretend ignorance in a number of cases in order to make the picture description task slightly more difficult. It was expected that with this method fairly realistic spontaneous speech could be stimulated. Since investigation of speech under stress was not the aim of this experiment the conversation partner's feigned ignorance was still moderate and not pushed to an extreme. Furthermore, no time pressure was applied and the subjects were not given the feeling that the "success rate" of their picture descriptions was of any importance. It cannot be totally ruled out, however, that some speakers still felt some stress in carrying out the task – an issue that will be further addressed in the discussion.

The three settings are "neutral speech", "loud speech", and "telephone speech". Loud speech was elicited in the form of a Lombard experiment (cf. Lane and Tranel 1971; Van Summers et al. 1988; Junqua 1996). In the Lombard setting the speakers were exposed to 80 dB_{SPL} white noise over headphones in order to stimulate an increase in vocal effort, i.e. in order to make the subjects speak louder than normal. "Normal" loudness was recorded in the neutral speech setting, which was the same as the loud speech setting except that the subjects were not wearing headphones and no noise was played. In the telephone setting the speaker received a call from the conversation partner and performed the reading and spontaneous speech tasks over the phone. The results from the telephone setting are not further addressed in this paper.[5]

The order of the three settings of the experiment (neutral, loud, telephone) was varied randomly from subject to subject in order to prevent potential serial order effects. The order of the two tasks, however, was always kept the same (first spontaneous speech, then reading), due to a decision at an early stage of the experiment, when the investigation of loudness effects was given highest priority. Therefore a serial order effect regarding

---

5. Briefly, the results for spontaneous speech on the telephone were similar to those for direct spontaneous speech, in that the centre of distribution of f0mean values was very much the same (between 110 and 120 Hz; cf. fig. 2a). The only major difference was that in telephone speech a few more speakers had their mean f0 in the interval between 140 and 150 Hz and that two speakers even had values as high as 170 to 200 Hz. This result suggests that for a few speakers the telephone setting induced a certain Lombard effect but that for most speakers it did not. Perhaps in many forensically relevant telephone communications, where the telephone channel characteristics are worse than here and where background noise might be present as well, a stronger and more uniform Lombard effect is present than here. In the literature the effect of telephone speech on f0 has been investigated in the study by Hirson et al. (1995), mentioned above. Hirson et al. report that f0mean was significantly higher in telephone speech than in face-to-face speech. This, however, was the case only when spontaneous speech was used. In read speech it did not matter to f0mean whether the setting was face-to-face or telephone. In the German study by Künzel (1997) a similar result to that in Hirson et al. (1995) occurred for the male subjects (see his Table 2). However, for the female subjects spontaneous speech lead to mixed results, and for read speech there was a tendency for f0mean to be higher in direct than in telephone speech.

read versus spontaneous speech cannot be ruled out completely, but it is unlikely that such an effect had a significant impact on the results (see footnote 8).

DAT (digital audio tape) recordings were made and analysed with ESPS/waves+. A separate speech file was created for each of the 100 speakers and each of the six experimental conditions. The duration of the files from the reading task ranged from about 30 seconds to one minute; speaker-specific differences in speaking tempo were mainly responsible for this range of differences. The files containing spontaneous speech were between about 2 and 6 minutes long. Speaker differences in tempo could only partially account for this range; in addition, speakers differed in how verbose they were and where the conversation partner found it appropriate to end the conversation.

For each speech file the f0 signal was calculated, using the standard settings of the "get_ f0" command within ESPS/waves+. On the basis of this f0 signal and its labelling, mean f0 ("f0mean") and standard deviation of f0 ("f0sd") were determined for each file. Labelling was performed manually on the basis of the audio output and the graphic f0 representation. The aim of labelling was to exclude certain portions of the f0 signal from analysis. Excluded from analysis were f0 values from non-verbal vocalisations such as laughter and cough, from invalid measurements (e.g. f0 values appearing during voiceless portions of the signal), from abrupt f0 changes due to creaky voice, voiceless obstruents, etc., and, of course, from utterances produced by the conversation partner. This labelling procedure is illustrated in figure 1.

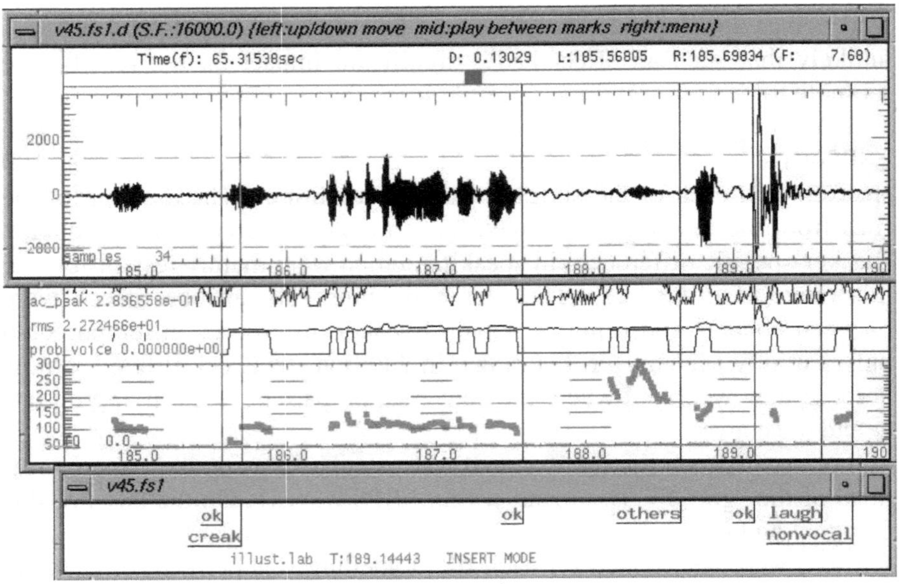

Figure 1. Printout of a representative portion of speech as displayed by the speech analysis package ESPS/waves+. The uppermost window shows the waveform of the speech signal, the window in the middle shows the fundamental frequency curve, and the bottom window shows the contents of the label file. The temporal scope of a labelled interval ends at the label that carries the label name and begins at the previous label or the beginning of the file. For this study, only intervals labelled "ok" were included in the analysis.

Based on the f0mean and f0sd value obtained for each speaker and condition, histograms were created which show how rare and how frequent different values are among the set of 100 speakers in the different conditions. Furthermore, statistical tests of the difference between read and spontaneous speech were carried out and individual variations in terms of this difference were examined. Some more methodological details – especially on the Lombard setting, which are not central to this paper – are given in Jessen et al. (2005).

4. Results for mean fundamental frequency (f0mean)

The results for f0mean in *spontaneous* speech produced at normal loudness (i.e. from the neutral speech setting) are shown in figure 2a. The histogram in figure 2a indicates, for each interval of values shown on the x-axis, how many speakers out of one hundred (a number which automatically corresponds to the percentage) produced an average f0 that fell into that interval. For example, for 31 percent of all 100 speakers f0mean is between 110 Hz and 120 Hz.

Fig. 2b shows the results for *read* speech at normal loudness. These results correspond closely to the results of an experiment on read normal-loudness speech in 100 male adult speakers carried out by Künzel (1987; see also Künzel, 1989, 1995, 2000 for further information on that experiment and its results).

a. f0mean in *spontaneous* speech (neutral)

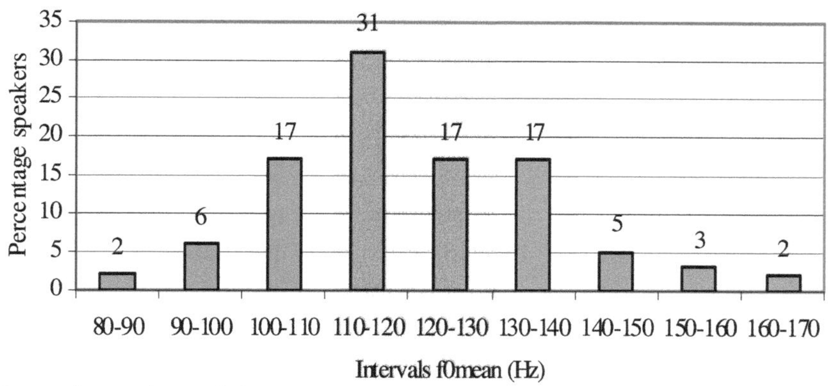

b. f0mean in *read* speech (neutral)

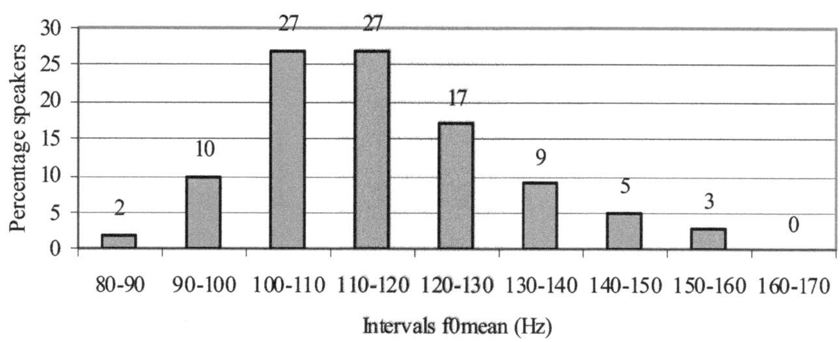

Figure 2. Histograms of mean fundamental frequency (f0mean) in Hz at *normal loudness* among 100 male speakers. Results for spontaneous speech are shown in the upper histogram (a.), results for read speech are shown in the lower histogram (b.). Intervals of f0mean values are plotted on the x-axis, number of speakers per interval on the y-axis and at the top side of the columns.

When comparing part a and b of fig. 2, it can be seen that at normal loudness the centre of the distribution of f0mean values is slightly higher in spontaneous speech than in read speech. Average f0mean across speakers is indeed higher in spontaneous neutral (120 Hz) than in read neutral speech (116 Hz). However, according to a one-factor ANOVA with task (spontaneous vs. reading) as the independent variable and f0mean as the dependent variable, the difference between spontaneous and read speech was slightly below significance on the 5% level [F(1, 198) = 3.4, p = 0.0647].

a. f0mean in *spontaneous* speech (loud)

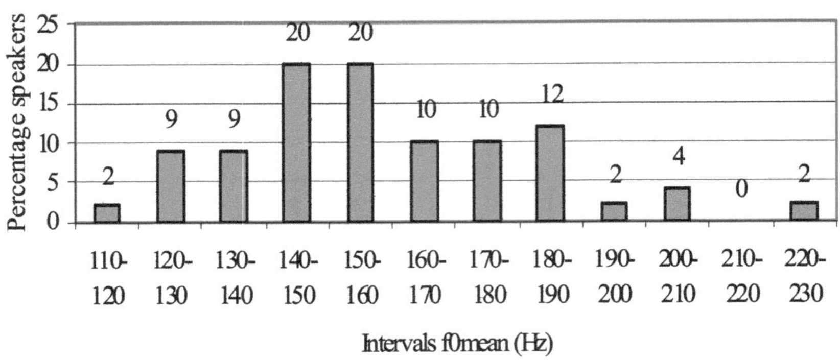

b. f0mean in *read* speech (loud)

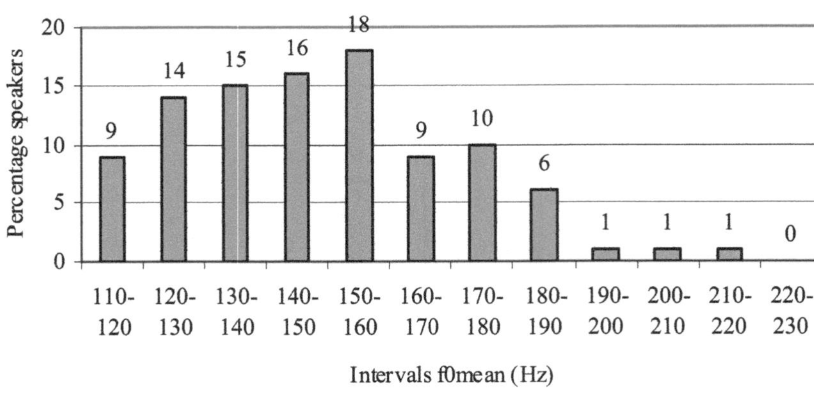

Figure 3. Histograms of mean fundamental frequency (f0mean) in Hz at *loud speech* among 100 male speakers (otherwise same conventions as in figure 2).

Figure 3 shows the results for spontaneous speech (a.) and read speech (b.), when, instead of speaking with normal loudness, the subjects spoke with increased loudness due to the Lombard setting. First of all, f0mean values are much higher at loud speech (fig. 3) than under normal loudness (fig. 2) – no matter whether the subjects were speaking spontaneously or carrying out the reading task. This substantial increase in average f0 due to loud speech production corresponds to the findings of many other studies and is addressed in Jessen et al. (2005). Secondly, and closer to the subject of the present paper, it can be observed that within loud speech there is a difference between read and spontaneous speech style. As in normal-loudness speech, the distribution of f0mean values in spontaneous loud speech is slightly higher than in read loud speech. A one-factor ANOVA with the factor task was carried out on the material from the Lombard setting and it turned out that f0mean is significantly higher in spontaneous than read speech [$F(1, 198) = 8.8$, $p = 0.0034$]. In this comparison average f0mean across speakers was 149 Hz for read and 159 Hz for spontaneous speech. These statistical results show that while in both loud and normal speech production spontaneous speech leads to higher f0mean values than read speech, it is only in loud speech production that this difference between read on spontaneous speech style is significant.

5. Results: relative standard deviation of fundamental frequency (f0varco)

Turning from average f0 (f0mean), as an index of anatomically predisposed pitch level, to f0 standard deviation (f0sd) as an index of habitual preferences between monotonous to melodic speaking, the question arises whether f0sd can be expressed directly or whether it needs to undergo some form of normalisation against f0mean. The results presented in Jessen et al. (2005) show that f0mean and f0sd are positively correlated.[6] Forensically,

6. A reviewer correctly points out that the correlation between f0sd and f0mean is to be expected on purely mathematical grounds. If, for example, all the f0 values of a speaker in a recording are multiplied by ten, not only the average of all f0 values will be increased by a factor of ten but the standard deviation of the f0 values will be increased by the same factor. Despite this mathematical principle it remains an empirical matter whether in fact differences in f0mean (between different speakers or between different conditions spoken by the same speaker, such as soft vs. loud) lead to proportional differences in f0sd. That this is only partially the case is shown in Jessen et al. (2005), where a correlation, although it was high (Pearson correlation of 0.77), did not reach the perfect value of 1 which one would expect if solely the mathematical principle applied. More importantly, it is possible that with other

such a correlation between two different parameters that are used as independent speaker-specific features is undesirable (cf. Rose 2002: 52 on the required independence of forensic-phonetic parameters). In order to avoid this dependence of f0sd from f0mean, Künzel (1987: 76) and Kraayeveld (1997: 24–25) recommend that f0sd standard should be expressed not in absolute terms but in the form of the coefficient of variation. If expressed as a percentage, the coefficient of variation is derived by the formula 100 * (f0sd [Hz]/f0mean [Hz]).[7]

The results for f0sd – expressed as coefficient of variation and abbreviated as f0varco – are presented in Figs. 4 and 5. Fig. 4 shows the data for spontaneous and read speech under normal loudness and fig. 5 the data for spontaneous and read speech in loud speech.

a. f0varco in *spontaneous* speech (neutral)

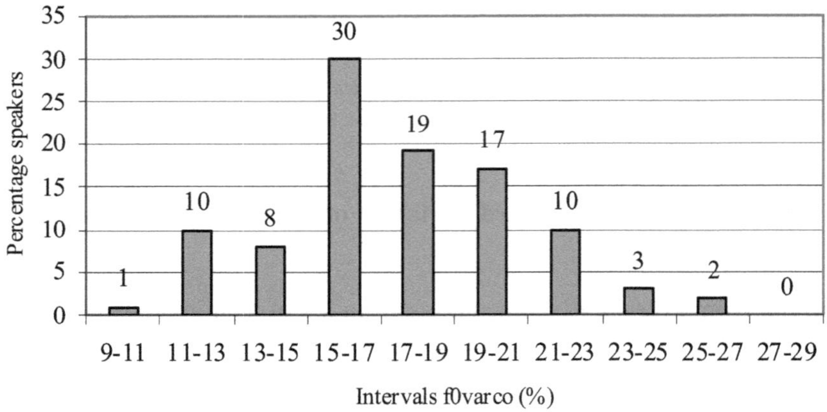

speech parameters the correlation between mean and standard deviation is smaller. That situation occurred with articulation rate (AR) in Jessen (2007), where the correlation between ARmean and ARsd was very small (0.15) and the correlation between ARmean and ARvarco was even negative (-0.29). In a situation like that it is better to leave the standard deviation unnormalised.

7. A reviewer acknowledges the importance of the coefficient of variation and asks about other methods, such as semitone-based normalisation. In fact, some authors, like Dromey and Ramig (1998), propose such a method. Their "semitone standard deviation" is calculated by the formula: $12*\log_2((f0mean+f0sd)/(f0mean-f0sd))$. This formula was applied to the data of this study and it was found that for the range of f0sd found here, semitone standard deviation and coefficient of variation are highly correlated. It is only at much higher f0sd values that the two functions begin to diverge.

b. f0varco in *read* speech (neutral)

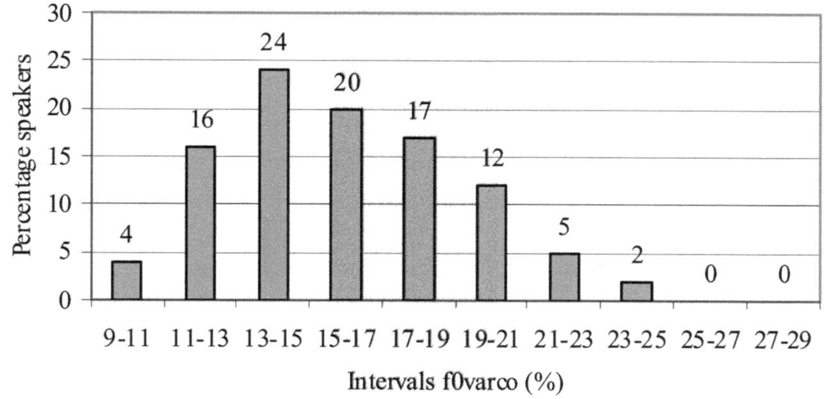

Figure 4. Histograms of f0 coefficient of variation (f0varco) in percent at *normal loudness* among 100 male speakers. Results for spontaneous speech are shown in the upper histogram (a.), results for read speech are shown in the lower histogram (b.). Intervals of f0varco values are plotted on the x-axis, the number of speakers per interval on the y-axis and above of the columns.

a. f0varco in *spontaneous* speech (loud)

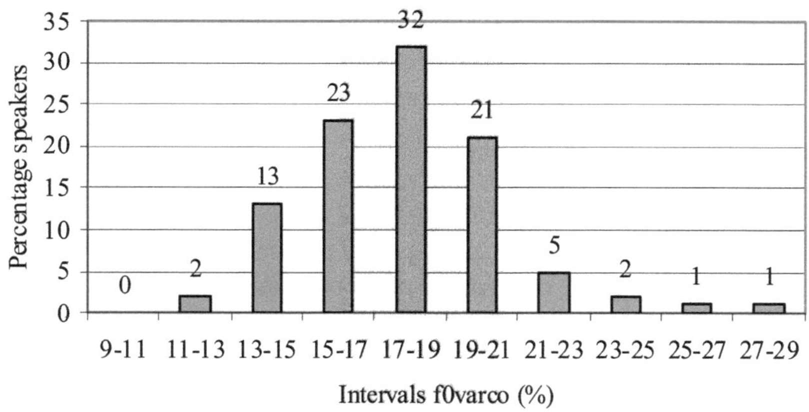

b. f0varco in *read* speech (loud)

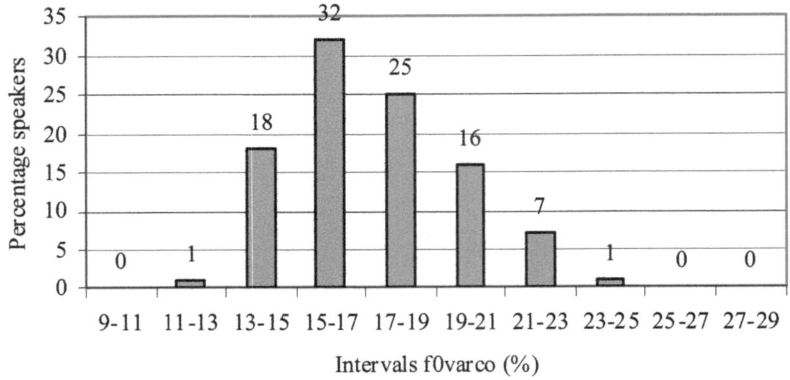

Figure 5. Histograms of coefficient of variation (f0varco) in percent at *loud* speech among 100 male speakers (otherwise same conventions as in figure 4).

According to a one-factor ANOVA with the factor task on the material from the neutral setting, f0varco was significantly higher in spontaneous speech (with an average of 17.5%) than in read speech (with an average of 15.9%) [$F(1, 198) = 11.7$, $p = 0.0007$]. When a one-factor ANOVA with the factor task was calculated on the material from the loud-speech setting, f0varco did not differ significantly between spontaneous speech (with an average of 17.8%) and read speech (with an average of 17.2%) [$F(1, 198) = 2.0$, $p = 0.1582$].

6. Results: individual patterns

So far, changes in f0mean and f0varco due to the difference between read and spontaneous speech have been reported as effects of the entire group of 100 speakers. However, individual speakers' results can deviate from the group effects. A summary of these individual patterns is provided in table 1.

Table 1. Types of individual patterns among 100 speakers

		f0mean			
		spont ≥ read	spont < read	spont ≥ read	spont < read
f0varco	spont ≥ read	54	20	46	12
	spont<read	16	10	36	6
		Neutral		Lombard	

Table 1 shows, for example, that in the neutral setting 54 speakers have equal or higher f0mean in spontaneous as opposed to read speech and at the same time equal or higher f0varco in spontaneous than in read speech, or it shows that in the Lombard setting 36 speakers have equal or higher f0mean in spontaneous as opposed to read speech and lower f0varco in spontaneous than in read speech.

These speaker-specific patterns correspond well to the results from the statistical tests. Beginning with the neutral setting, the most common combination is an increase in both f0mean and f0varco from read to spontaneous speech (54 speakers), which corresponds to the findings that on average both f0mean and f0varco were higher in spontaneous than in read speech. The effects that the number of speakers with higher f0varco but lower f0mean in spontaneous than in read speech (20) is higher than the one with lower f0varco but higher f0mean in spontaneous than in read speech (16) is consistent with the fact that the effect for the f0 parameters to be higher in spontaneous than in read speech was significant only for f0varco and (slightly) below significance for f0mean.

As to Lombard speech, again the largest number of speakers (46) have both higher f0mean and f0varco in spontaneous than in read speech, which corresponds to the result that both f0mean and f0varco were on average higher in spontaneous than in read speech. In contrast to normal-loudness speech, the number of speakers in Lombard speech with higher f0mean but lower f0varco in spontaneous than in read speech was higher (36) than the one with lower f0mean but higher f0varco in spontaneous than in read speech (12). This pattern is consistent with the findings that f0mean was significantly higher in spontaneous than in read Lombard speech, but that there was no significant difference regarding f0varco.

Despite these matches between the statistical results and the individual-speakers patterns shown in table 1 it should be emphasised that about 50% of the speakers show deviations from the most frequent of the four possible patterns. Therefore, the fact that both f0mean and f0varco are on average higher in spontaneous than in read speech is no more than a tendency that is not true for many speakers.

7. Discussion

The results of this study have shown that f0mean in read speech is lower than in spontaneous speech, although the difference is relatively small and significant only within Lombard speech. Substantial speaker differences were found, so that for many speakers f0mean was higher in read than in spontaneous speech. Probably most important for forensic purposes is the fact that on average, f0mean was actually quite similar in read and spontaneous speech, so that for most voice comparisons data obtained from spontaneous speech can be compared quite well to data obtained from a reading task.

When compared to the results on studies with speakers of English, reviewed in section 2, the present results are unusual since there is no tendency for f0mean to be higher in read as opposed to spontaneous speech; either the result is statistically the same (normal-loudness speech) or it is reversed (Lombard speech). However, when comparing the results with other studies on German speech, the present outcome is not so unusual. Among the German studies both phenomena were found, i.e. where f0mean is predominantly higher in read than in spontaneous speech (Schultz-Coulon, 1975; Künzel, 1997) and where f0mean is predominantly lower in read than in spontaneous speech (Batliner et al., 1995; Mixdorff and Pfitzinger, 2005). In the study carried out by Köster (2002), the influence of style depended on whether Lombard or non-Lombard speech was involved. One conclusion that could be drawn from the present results together with the existing literature is that the style dependence of f0mean is language-specific. It is true that f0mean in itself can differ between speakers of different languages. For example, f0mean is higher with speakers of Turkish than with speakers of German (Braun, 1994; Gfroerer and Wagner 1995). But whether or not the *style dependence* of f0mean differs between speakers of different languages is a separate question that would require more research. From what has been learned thus far, it would appear more reasonable to examine other explanations for why in the present study f0mean tends to be higher in spontaneous than in read speech whereas in most other studies the opposite pattern was found. One such explanation could be found in the influence of *stress* on fundamental frequency. As has been shown by a large body of literature, the presence of physical or psychological stress usually leads to an increase in f0mean (see Jessen 2006 for literature and the results of a study with German speakers).

Hollien et al. (1997), in the paper summarised in section 2, found that, in general, f0mean was higher in read than in spontaneous speech but that for some speakers the effect was reversed. In trying to explain these reversals they mention that some subjects, when speaking spontaneously, became somewhat exited about the topic they were talking about. Quoting the literature discussion in Hollien (1990), they point out that (psychological) stress and certain emotions can increase f0, which could explain the facts.

However, the argument that stress influences f0 could theoretically also be applied to the opposite, i.e. when explaining why f0 might be higher in read than in spontaneous speech. Imagine someone who has to read a text experiences stress perhaps because s/he is not used to reading aloud, while the same person is relaxed in spontaneous speech. In that case the stress factor could lead to the result that f0mean is higher in read than in spontaneous speech.

Indications that stress might be an intervening factor also emerge from the study of Schultz-Coulon (1975) mentioned above. In his discussion Schultz-Coulon recommends spontaneous speech as the most suitable way of eliciting average f0 because "apparently in this style speech is produced in the most relaxed manner" (p. 383, translated from German). Provided that this statement actually applies to his data and is not just meant as a general idea, the lower f0mean in spontaneous as opposed to read speech found in his study could at least partially be explained by the more relaxed, hence less stressful speaking situation during spontaneous in contrast to read speech. Another stress-related factor that could have played a role is the fact that the order in which the three tasks had to be carried out by the subjects was first the reading, second the number counting, and third the spontaneous speech task. This order corresponds to the descending order in which the f0mean values were found. It is possible that the speakers experienced stress at the beginning of the recording, where they had to perform the reading task, and that the stress level subsequently diminished – causing f0mean to become lower in the counting and lowest in the spontaneous speech task.[8]

---

8. In the present study the order was the opposite: Each speaker performed the spontaneous speech task before the reading task. Using the same argument as for Schulz-Coulon (1975), it is conceivable that f0mean was higher in spontaneous speech than in read speech here because from its serial position in the experiment it could have been more stressful. However, in the present experiment spontaneous and read speech were produced in the three settings neutral, telephone, and Lombard, which were ordered randomly across subjects. For example, if the order was Lombard-neutral-telephone, spontaneous speech in the neutral setting was already preceded by two conditions (spontaneous and read Lombard), at which point any possible stress at the beginning of the experiment was likely to have disappeared. In other words, even though the presentation order spontaneous > read speech might explain some proportion of the higher f0mean in the former than in the latter style, the overall design of the experiment would have dispersed most of this effect.

The argument that stress or emotional excitement might shift f0 towards higher values could be one reason why in the present study f0mean was in general higher in spontaneous than in read speech. As mentioned in section 3, spontaneous speech was elicited using a kind of quiz game. Since it was not intended to induce stress, the level of difficulty of the game was low and no time pressure was applied. Neither were the participants expected to score high. However, it is still possible that several speakers experienced stress at a degree that was higher than in the reading task and that this situation influenced the final results to the effect that f0mean was generally higher in spontaneous than in read speech. Stress might also explain why in the studies by Batliner et al. (1995) and Mixdorff and Pfitzinger (2005) f0mean was predominantly higher in spontaneous than in read speech. In the study by Batliner et al. the speakers had to solve a "blocks world" problem, and in the study by Mixdorff and Pfitzinger the Map Task might have been at least more exciting than the task of speaking casually about topics such as their hobbies, which is used in many other studies as the way of eliciting spontaneous speech.

Under forensic aspects these data and explanations concerning f0mean in read versus spontaneous speech imply that if spontaneous versus read is the only difference between the speech of the unknown speaker and the speech of the suspect, the f0 values derived from these speakers can be compared quite well. Similar f0 values then are evidence for the identity, whereas different values are evidence against the identity of the speakers. If, however, it seems that stress or emotional influence somehow co-varies with the distinction between read and spontaneous speech, a more cautious approach should be taken.

As to the parameter f0varco, the results have shown that f0varco is higher in spontaneous than in read speech. This was the case both within normal-loudness speech and within loud speech, but only for speech at normal vocal effort this difference was statistically significant. Towards the end of section 2 it was mentioned that in most studies the results for f0 average have the same direction as the results for f0 variability. If the average is higher in one speech style than the other so tends to be the variability of f0 and vice versa. The present study shows the same kind of pattern: Both average and variability of f0 were higher in spontaneous than in read speech (although sometimes the difference was not significant). This was so despite the fact that, in contrast to many other studies, f0 variability was normalised with respect to f0 average (coefficient of variation). This shows that the hypothesis, mentioned in section 2, i.e. that the correlation between f0 average and variability occurs because variability is not normalised, cannot explain the present results. Instead, the increase of f0 variability (f0varco) in spontaneous compared to read speech must have independent explanations. The result is intuitively plausible though: It is expected that spontaneous speech is rendered in a more lively, melodic manner and that read speech is produced in a less lively and more monotonous way. This cannot be more than a general rule of thumb because it is easily conceivable that spontaneous speaking is rendered monotonously, while reading is acted out in a lively manner (cf. Hirson et al. 1995). Perhaps "The North-wind and the Sun" used here for the reading task was not the kind of text to encourage the speakers to act out a story with zest.

Whether or not stress could explain the higher f0 variability found in spontaneous speech here is less clear than it is for f0 average. According to the literature review of Jessen (2006), f0 variability was investigated much less frequently in stress experiments than was f0 average. However, most studies that investigated this parameter found that f0 variability is higher in stressful than in non-stress situations. Therefore, stress could be part of the reason why f0varco was generally higher in spontaneous speech, where the potentially stressful quiz game was used, than in reading.

8. References

Batliner, A., R. Kompe, A. Kießling, E. Nöth, and H. Niemann. 1995. "Can you tell apart spontaneous and read speech if you just look at prosody?" *Speech Recognition and Coding. New Advances and Trends*, ed. by. A.J. Rubio Ayuso and J.M. López Soler, Berlin: Springer. 321–324.

Braun, Angelika. 1994. "Sprechstimmlage und Muttersprache". *Zeitschrift für Dialektologie und Linguistik* 61. 170–178.

Braun, Angelika. 1995. "Fundamental frequency – How speaker-specific is it?" *Studies in Forensic Phonetics*, ed. by Angelika Braun and J.-P. Köster, Trier: Wissenschaftlicher Verlag Trier. 9–23.

Crystal, Thomas H. and Arthur S. House. 1982. "Segmental durations in connected speech signals: Preliminary results". *Journal of the Acoustical Society of America* 72. 705–716.

Dromey, Christopher and Lorraine O. Ramig. 1998. "Intentional changes in sound pressure level and rate: Their impact on measures of respiration, phonation, and articulation". *Journal of Speech, Language, and Hearing Research* 41. 1003–1018.

Fitch, James L. 1990. "Consistency of fundamental frequency and perturbation in repeated phonations of sustained vowels, reading, and connected speech". *Journal of Speech and Hearing Disorders* 55. 360–363.

Gfroerer, Stefan. 2003. "Auditory-instrumental forensic speaker recognition". *Proceedings of EUROSPEECH 2003, Geneva*, 705–708. (on CD).

Gfroerer, Stefan. 2006. "Sprechererkennung und Tonträgerauswertung". *Münchener Anwaltshandbuch Strafverteidigung*, ed. By G. Widmaier, München: Beck. 2505–2526.

Gfroerer, Stefan and Isolde Wagner. 1995. "Fundamental frequency in forensic speech samples". *Studies in Forensic Phonetics*, ed. by Angelika Braun and J.-P. Köster, Trier: Wissenschaftlicher Verlag Trier. 41–48.

Hirson, Alan, Peter French, and David Howard. 1995. "Speech fundamental frequency over the telephone and face-to-face: some implications for forensic phonetics". *Studies in General and English Phonetics. Essays in Honour of Professor J.D. O'Connor*, ed. by Jack Windsor Lewis, London: Routledge. 230–240.

Hollien, Harry. 1990. *The Acoustics of Crime - The New Science of Forensic Phonetics*. New York: Plenum Press.

Hollien, Harry, Patricia A. Hollien, and Gea de Jong. 1997. "Effects of three parameters on speaking fundamental frequency". *Journal of the Acoustical Society of America* 102. 2984–2991.

Jessen, Marianne. 2006. *Einfluss von Stress auf Sprache und Stimme. Unter besonderer Berücksichtigung polizeidienstlicher Anforderungen*. Idstein: Schulz-Kirchner.

Jessen, Michael. 2007. "Forensic reference data on articulation rate in German". *Science and Justice* (in press).

Jessen, Michael, Olaf Köster, and Stefan Gfroerer. 2005. "Influence of vocal effort on average and variability of fundamental frequency". *International Journal of Speech, Language and the Law* 12. 174–213.

Junqua, Jean-Claude. 1996. "The influence of acoustics on speech production: A noise-induced stress phenomenon known as the Lombard reflex". *Speech Communication* 20. 13–22.

Köster, Stefanie. 2002. "Acoustic-phonetic aspects of Lombard Speech for different text styles". *The Phonetician* 85. 9–16.

Kraayeveld, Johannes. 1997. *Idiosyncrasy in prosody: speaker and speaker group identification in Dutch using melodic and temporal information*, PhD thesis, Catholic University Nijmegen [published under ISBN 90-9010846-7].

Künzel, Hermann J. 1987. *Sprechererkennung: Grundzüge forensischer Sprachverarbeitung*. Heidelberg: Kriminalistik Verlag.

Künzel, Hermann J. 1989. "How well does average fundamental frequency correlate with speaker height and weight?" *Phonetica* 46. 117–125.

Künzel, Hermann J. 1995. "Field procedures in forensic speaker recognition". *Studies in General and English Phonetics, Essays in Honour of Professor J.D. O'Connor*, ed. by Jack Windsor Lewis, London: Routledge. 68–84

Künzel, Hermann J. 1997. "Some general phonetic and forensic aspects of speaking tempo". *Forensic Linguistics* 4. 48–83.

Künzel, Hermann J. 2000. "Effects of voice disguise on speaking fundamental frequency". *Forensic Linguistics* 7. 149–179.
Künzel, Hermann J. 2004. "Tasks in forensic speech and audio analysis: A tutorial". *The Phonetician* 90. 9–22.
Laan, Gitta P.M. 1997. "The contribution of intonation, segmental durations, and spectral features to the perception of a spontaneous and a read speaking style". *Speech Communication* 22. 43–65.
Lane, Harlan and Bernard Tranel. 1971. "The Lombard sign and the role of hearing in speech". *Journal of Speech and Hearing Research* 14. 677–709.
Mixdorff, Hansjörg and Hartmut R. Pfitzinger. 2005. "Analysing fundamental frequency contours and local speech rate in map task dialogs". *Speech Communication* 46. 310–325.
Murry, Thomas, William S. Brown, Jr., and Richard J. Morris. 1995. "Patterns of fundamental frequency for three types of voice samples". *Journal of Voice* 9: 282–289.
Nolan, Francis. 1983. *The Phonetic Bases of Speaker Recognition*. Cambridge: Cambridge University Press.
Nolan, Francis. 1997. "Speaker recognition and forensic phonetics". *The Handbook of the Phonetic Sciences*, ed. by William J. Hardcastle and John Laver, Oxford: Blackwell. 744–767.
Nolan, Francis. 2002. "Intonation in speaker identification: an experiment on pitch alignment features". *Forensic Linguistics* 9. 1–21.
Rose, Philip. 2002. *Forensic Speaker Identification*. London: Taylor & Francis.
Schultz-Coulon, H.-J. 1975. "Bestimmung und Beurteilung der individuellen mittleren Sprechstimmlage". *Folia Phoniatrica* 27. 375–386.
Snidecor, John C. 1943. "A comparative study of the pitch and duration characteristics of impromptu speaking and oral reading". *Speech Monographs* 10. 50–56.
Sorensen, David and Yoshiyuki Horii. 1982. "Cigarette smoking and voice fundamental frequency". *Journal of Communication Disorders* 15. 135–144.
Titze, Ingo. 1994. *Principles of Voice Production*. Englewood Cliffs, NJ: Prentice Hall.
Tjaden, Kris. 2000. "A preliminary study of factors influencing perception of articulatory rate in Parkinson disease". *Journal of Speech, Language, and Hearing Research* 43. 997–1010.
Van Summers, W., David B. Pisoni, Robert H. Bernacki, Robert I. Pedlow, and Michael A. Stokes. 1988. "Effects of noise on speech production: Acoustic and perceptual analyses". *Journal of the Acoustical Society of America* 84. 917–928.

Phonetic cues to speaker age: A longitudinal study

Angelika Braun and Stefan Friebis

1. Introduction

Forensic speaker identification entails a wide variety of tasks like voice comparison, disputed utterances, speech enhancement, and speaker profiling (Braun 1995a). The latter is called for whenever the only or prime lead in an investigation consists in the recording of an unknown speaker, from which a maximum of information needs to be derived by the expert. One essential element in speaker profiling is the estimation of speaker age. In many cases, this parameter alone has directed the investigation away from certain suspect groups and towards others and has thus helped to focus investigational activities. Extreme examples would be phone calls in a case of food-poisoning being carried out by pre-puberty children or calls for ransom in a kidnapping case by a male whose age was estimated to be well beyond 60. At any rate, the estimation of speaker age has an essential bearing on forensic phonetic casework in that it serves to enable the expert to assist in directing the investigation process and forms an important element in voice comparison.

At first glance, it would seem fairly simple to make an assessment with respect to a given speaker's age, assuming that ageing processes which generally apply to the human body will also extend to the organs of speech. This view is supported by a number of studies which demonstrate that there is a reasonably acceptable correlation between the actual age of a given speaker and his age as estimated by human listeners (cf. e.g. Shipp and Hollien 1969; Ryan and Burk 1974; Hartman and Danhauer 1976; Horii and Ryan 1981; Neiman and Applegate 1990).

While this seems reassuring from a forensic point of view, several questions remain:

- Will previous results which were established largely on the basis of cross-sectional studies hold true also in a longitudinal investigation?

G. Grewendorf and M. Rathert (eds.): Formal Linguistics and Law, 141–162

- What – if any – acoustic phonetic parameters correlate best with chronological age?

2. The ageing vocal apparatus

2.1 Production

Ageing can generally be looked at as an involutional process affecting various bodily structures. This process will affect all stages of speech production: the verbal planning process in the brain, respiratory activity, phonation, articulation, and the feedback mechanism which is largely carried out through the auditory pathway. However, the vast majority of studies on these topics has been cross-sectional, i.e. different populations were studied at one point in time (e.g. Böhme and Hecker 1970). The disadvantage of this procedure is evident – one does not really learn anything about the process going on in the individual organs of speech production over time. Therefore, the sparse findings of longitudinal studies will be discussed separately.

2.1.1 Central nervous system

Age-related changes in the human brain structure include the loss of nerve cells which may begin in middle age as well as the lack of the ability of neurons to recover from lesions, i.e. by forming new synapses. A number of morphological changes in the brains of aged subjects have been described (for a summary see Valenstein 1981), but it has proven to be difficult to distinguish between changes which can simply be attributed to old age and those which are due to disease. Some of the changes were observed in the superior temporal gyrus, an area which is closely linked to speech processing (Valenstein 1981: 91; 100).

2.1.2 Peripheral nervous system

Beside the osseous and muscular systems, it is the peripheral nervous system which guarantees a smooth functioning of the speech production process. An impaired functioning of peripheral nerve fibers has been observed with increasing age. This may be complemented by a central impairment in efferent and afferent nervous processing which is held responsible for the voice tremor which has been described as a consequence of old age (Segre 1971). Figure 1 shows the changes in dendrites during senescence.

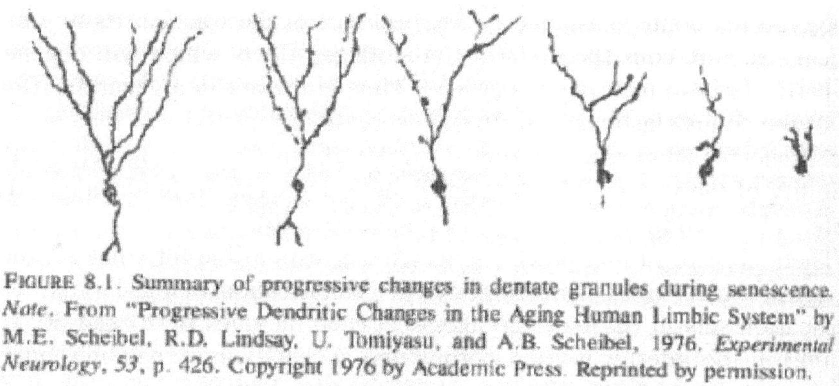

Figure 1. Changes in dendrites during senescense (Whitebourne 1985: 134)

2.1.3 Respiration

As far as the lungs are concerned, emphysema will result in an increase in residual capacity at the expense of vital capacity. This will result in a reduction of expiratory pressure. Furthermore, is has been demonstrated (Ptacek et al. 1966; Turner et al. 1968) that due to the deterioration of the elastin fibers the elasticity of the lungs and of the rib cage as a whole will substantially decrease with age. Thus the rib cage can no longer fully expand, which in turn will result in a reduced respiratory force and thus a reduced subglottal pressure. This may in the end affect voice production as well as speaking tempo: "In addition, degenerative changes in the laryngeal muscles, interacting with respiratory muscles, may have adversely affected both the vowel duration and vowel performances of older subjects" (Ptacek et al. 1966: 358). Hoit and Hixon (1987) found a significant difference in the number of syllables per breath group between their 25 and 75-year-old subjects, the younger subjects exhibiting more syllables per breath group, but not between the 25-year-old and the 50 year-old subjects. It thus seems that a rather large time span is necessary for this development to take effect.

2.1.4 Phonation

However, not only the lungs are affected by the ageing process. The same applies to the conus elasticus, i.e. the top part of the trachea. Its morphological structure consists in elastic and collagen fibers which will degenerate particularly in men beyond age 60. This will result in a general stiffening of the conus elasticus as well as a decrease in sensitivity of the connective tissue to subglottal pressure: “Increased stiffness would reduce the pliability of the vocal folds and contribute to increases in fundamental frequency observed in elderly men” (Linville 2001: 46).

There are two further processes which are responsible for what is called the senile voice: the ossification and the calcification of the larynx. The ossification sets in (in male larynges) between the ages of 20 and 30, beginning in the inferior thyroid cornua and successively expanding anteriorly within that cartilage (Kahane 1983; see also Figure 2). Similar ossifications have been observed in the posterior lamina and the arch of the cricoid cartilage and in the arytenoids. Here, the body muscular processes will ossify, whereas the vocal processes remain cartilaginous (Kahane 1983).

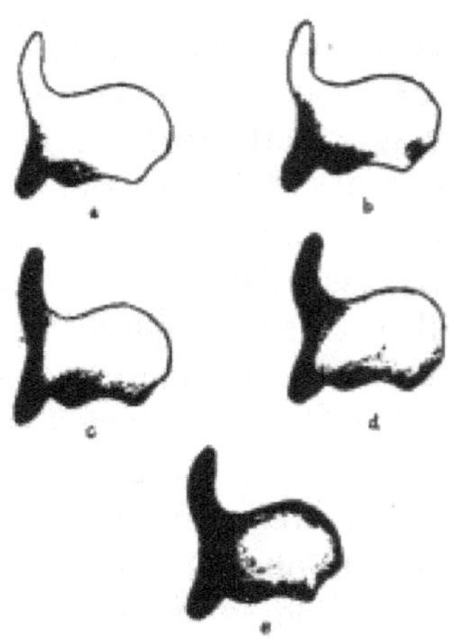

Figure 2. Progression of ossification in the thyroid cartilage (Hecker 1969: 56)

In addition to the processes described above the cricoarytenoid joint will degenerate with age, resulting in a wear of its articular surface. This may cause a reduced tension of the vocal folds and a reduced vocal closure, which is commonly perceived as hoarseness (Kahane 1981: 24). Furthermore, atrophy of the mucous glands will affect the ageing voice. The reduced amount of secretion in the false vocal folds and the Morgagni folds will cause the vocal folds to dry out, which may in turn result in irregular voicing patterns: "Changes in the cricoarytenoid joint include thinning of articular surfaces, breakdown and disorganisation of collagen fibers in cartilage matrix and surface irregularities; it has been suggested that these changes may influence the extent of approximation of vocal folds and smoothness of adjustments during voicing" (Ramig et al. 2001: 256).

Another element which ought to be considered in conjunction with vocal ageing is the intrinsic laryngeal musculature. Changes in the distribution and size of the muscle fibers as well as a reduction in muscle mass have been observed (Kahane 1981). This atrophy of the intrinsic laryngeal muscles is attributed to reduced blood flow (Linville 2001: 41). It was demonstrated that age-related changes in the deep layer of the lamina propria will cause disturbances in the collagen fibers which in turn will result in irregularities of vocal fold vibration (Linville 2001: 43) and a more clearly visible mucosal wave (Hertegård 1994). There are a number of severe consequences for voice production including an insufficient closure phase and aperiodicity of the voice signal.

A much less known but yet important tissue which is subject to degenerative processes is the macula flava. It consists of densely structured elastic fibers which are located at the front and back ends of the vocal folds and is regarded as a continuation of the lamina propria. It has been argued that it serves a "buffer function", protecting the ends of the vocal folds from mechanical damage during the phonation process (Linville 2001). In this tissue, an age-related reduction of the fibrous components as well as an abnormal metabolism thereof has been observed:

> "With these age-related changes in the macula flava, a decrease in synthesis of fibrous components in the vocal fold mucosa would be expected and an increase in stiffness of the vocal fold would result. The changes in stiffness of the vocal fold resulting from age-related changes in the macula flava are felt to be of sufficient magnitude to contribute to aging of the voice" (Linville 2001: 45).

2.1.5 Articulation

The most immediate age-related cause for articulatory adaptations is the loss of dentition (Kent and Burkard 1981). Gum retraction and/or dentures may lead to a marked change in the acoustic shape of alveolar sounds like /s/, /t/, /d/, and /ʃ/ in particular.[1]

The physiological change of the supralaryngeal tract as a whole with age is characterized by an increase in muscle relaxation which will result in an effective expansion of the oral cavity, a reduction of the elasticity of its walls and in turn in a substantial change in vocal tract resonances. Furthermore, there is a general decrease in motor and sensory innervation. This will primarily affect the tongue. Not only is there a decrease in salivation but also in tongue muscle mass which will cause a reduced velocity of tongue movement and thus result in a loss of precision in sound production. In addition, lacking teeth, the degeneration of the mandibular joint and a progressive reduction of facial and mandibular muscle power will result in a change in vocal tract diameter: "The tongue, facial muscles, temporomandibular joint, and associated musculature constitute a major group of articulatory structures. Their reduced efficiency of performance resulting from age-related changes may have measurable effects on speech adequacy" (Kahane 1981: 38). Even though the causes are not entirely clear, there is evidence for a lengthening of the vocal tract with increasing age (Kent and Burkard 1981: 54). This would result in a formant lowering, which has indeed been observed by Endres et al. (1971).

2.1.6 Hearing

The well-documented hearing loss – especially affecting high frequencies – with increasing age (cf. e.g. Nadol 1981; Meyerson 1976) is not something that will immediately come to mind as influencing speech production characteristics. However, one consequence of hearing loss beside the lack of discrimination between high-frequency speech sounds is an impaired auditory feedback loop. This may in turn cause articulatory imprecision.

2.1.7 Speaking tempo

A major effect of ageing on speech behavior which has to be attributed to a combination of several of the factors mentioned above is simply a slowed-down speech production. This is, in fact, the one most frequently observed

1. This effect was extremely notable in the late famous German actress Inge Meysel.

and probably one of the most reliable predictors of speaker age in cross-sectional studies and also has been proven to serve as an important cue for listeners estimating a speaker's age (e.g. Mysak 1959; Ptacek and Sander 1966; Ryan and Burk 1974; Hartman 1979; Shipp et al. 1992; Braun and Rietveld 1995). Several factors may contribute to this: a slowed-down conceptual planning and lexical retrieval, an increased time spent on speech breathing, and a reduction in neuronal motor activity.

It seems worthy of note at this point to utter a word of caution with respect to the anatomical and physiological findings cited in all the above sections. First of all, most of the anatomical studies which have been carried out so far are cadaver studies (e.g. Kahane 1983; Hirano et al. 1983) and thus cross-sectional by nature. Furthermore, several authors point to the fact that biological rather than chronological age (the former being influenced by physiological fitness, substance abuse etc.) may be the determining factor for vocal ageing (Horii and Ryan 1981; Ramig 1983; Ramig and Ringel 1983; Ramig 1986). Finally, researchers caution against expecting to find all the effects mentioned above in any one individual (e.g. Habermann 1972: 124). These considerations may serve to put longitudinal studies on vocal ageing into perspective.

2.2 Longitudinal studies of ageing

While there is a relatively large number of studies on the developmental voice changes during adolescence (e.g. Duffy 1970; Pedersen et al. 1982; Bennett 1983; Hollien et al. 1994), there are very few longitudinal studies on the adult voice, and those that there are provide limited information. Endres et al. (1971) analyzed four male and two female speakers several times (numbers vary across subjects) over a period of 13 to 15 years. They measured formants as well as fundamental frequencies (means and ranges). They report – without stating gender specificities – a general lowering of formants as well as a lowering of the mean fundamental frequency and a reduction in F0 range. A word of caution seems to be in order regarding their study, though. Three of their male subjects were relatively old to start with (60 and 73 years, respectively), which may mean that senescence instead of development during adulthood was captured by the study.

De Pinto and Hollien (1982) studied 11 female speakers at an interval of 35 years, admittedly with "little-to-no information about their use of cigarettes, drugs, alcohol and so on" (374). They found a substantial decrease in average F0 over age, thus confirming the results of cross-sectional studies

(Saxman and Burk 1967; Gilbert and Weismer 1974; Stoicheff 1981). No further measurements were taken in that study.

Künzel and Wagner (1993) studied 10 male speakers twice with a time lag of 11 years. (Their exact ages are not reported, but they were all at working age at both recording sessions.) Subjects were asked to read a mock kidnapper's message which lasted about 50 secs. The authors found a slight lowering of F0 in two speakers only, whereas eight speakers exhibited a higher F0 after 11 years, six of them even "surpassing the respective ranges of intra-individual variability" of the first recording (Künzel and Wagner 1993). Neither did they find a "conclusive pattern of change as a function of aging" in F0 standard deviation (Künzel and Wagner 1993, personal communication). These two were the only parameters analyzed by those authors.

It thus appears that (a) the only parameters studied in longitudinal studies so far are speaking fundamental frequency and its standard deviation as well as formant frequencies and (b) while the picture looks reasonably clear from a cross-sectional perspective for mean F0, results cannot simply be replicated in longitudinal studies.

3. The present experiment

3.1 Materials and methods

In order to study the long-term effects of vocal ageing, recordings of the same person from several decades had to be available. We decided to use "famous voices", i.e. the voices of German politicians, because (a) recordings from these personalities were available from various radio station archives from a time period of several decades and (b) owing to the wealth of recordings the situational settings used for analysis could be carefully selected and thus kept constant (e.g. it would have made no sense to compare fundamental frequency parameters of an emotional speech given in Parliament to those of a relaxed talk show performance – Braun 1995b).

The present study involves radio interviews of eight famous West German politicians over a time period of 20 to 30 years: two former Federal Presidents (Walter Scheel and Richard von Weizsäcker), three former Chancellors (Helmut Kohl, Helmut Schmidt, and Willy Brandt), and three former Cabinet Members (Hans-Jochen Vogel, Franz- Josef Strauß, and

Gerhard Schröder [CDU][2]). Three to four samples were analyzed for each politician, with a time interval of 10 years being aimed at. The samples basically consisted in radio interviews. Only monologous samples were analyzed, utterances which were interrupted by an interviewer were discarded. In order to avoid side effects caused by emotionally loaded speech only neutral, matter-of-fact parts of the conversation were analyzed. The following speech samples were considered for analysis:

Table 1. Speech samples[3]

politician (date of birth)	date of recording	age of the politician at the time of the interview	archives	period of time
Willy Brandt *1913 – 1992	19.12.1958	45	WDR	30 years
	Feb. 1970	57	WDR	
	28.07.1981	68	WDR	
	26.09.1989	76	NDR	
Helmut Kohl *1930	05.02.1973	43	DRA	20 years
	31.12.1982	52	WDR	
	Sep. 1992	62	DRA	
Walter Scheel *1919	26.01.1962	43	DRA	20 years
	21.01.1972	53	WDR	
	12.11.1981	62	WDR	
Helmut Schmidt *1918	04.12.1962	44	NDR	30 years
	26.02.1973	55	DRA	
	23.12.1982	64	NDR	
	09.09.1992	74	NDR	

2. Gerhard Schröder (CDU) is not confuse with Gerhard Schröder (SPD), the last Federal Chancellor of Germany.

3. WDR = Westdeutscher Rundfunk (Western German Broadcasting Service), NDR = Norddeutscher Rundfunk (Northern German Broadcasting Service), DRA = Deutsches Rundfunk-Archiv (German Archive of Broadcasting)

Gerhard Schröder *1910 – 1989	07.11.1951	41	WDR	20 years
	20.01.1963	53	WDR	
	July 1972	62	DRA	
Franz-Josef Strauß *1915 – 1988	26.08.1960	45	NDR	20 years
	17.10.1969	54	WDR	
	24.09.1980	65	WDR	
Hans-Jochen Vogel *1926	04.03.1964	38	NDR	30 years
	02.10.1972	46	NDR	
	26.01.1983	57	DRA	
	19.01.1993	67	DRA	
Richard von Weizsäcker *1920	14.05.1974	54	WDR	20 years
	19.02.1984	64	DRA	
	20.05.1992	72	DRA	

Most of the materials were originally stored on audio tape. They were digitized at 44.1 KHz and 16 bit. The rest were already available in digital format.

Based on the predictions derived from the physiological ageing process as well as the findings of previous studies, various acoustic analyses were carried out: F0 and related parameters, perturbation measures (jitter and shimmer), voice onset time (VOT), and speaking tempo were measured. The latter is expressed in terms of. syllable rate, the number of (linguistic) syllables per second including pauses and hesitations and articulation rate, the number of (linguistic) syllables per second without pauses and hesitations.

For calculating the mean fundamental frequency and related parameters the Kay Elemetrics Multispeech 2.2 software package was used. About one minute of net speech was analyzed from each recording. The perturbation measurements were carried out using the *voice protocol* option of Praat 4.2.2.1. For lack of sustained vowels, the perturbation measurements were based on hesitation markers. These are generally much longer than phonologically long vowels and can thus serve as a surrogate for sustained vowels. In case of jitter, the RAP (Relative Average Perturbation) algorithm was chosen; in view of the relatively short samples, APQ5 (Amplitude Perturbation Quotient averaging over five samples) was selected for shimmer analysis instead of APQ 9 or 11. Cool Edit Pro 2.0 as well as Multispeech were used to determine voice onset time (VOT) and speaking

tempo. The former was calculated from word-initial plosives before stressed vowels only. The bilabial, alveolar, and velar places of articulation were equally represented in number in order to avoid artifacts due to the fact that substantially longer VOTs have been observed in velar plosives as compared to the other two groups (Cho and Ladefoged 1999). The measurements of speaking tempo were based on about five minutes of speech (including pauses) for each recording.
Two kinds of statistical analysis were applied: ANOVAs and Pearson correlations were calculated. As a consequence of previously reported findings, 1-tailed hypotheses were applied. The significance level was set at 5% ($p = 0.05$).

3.2 Results and discussion

3.2.1 Fundamental frequency mean and standard deviation

Figure 3 shows the results for mean F0 and its standard deviation. The results for mean F0 are fairly inconclusive: Three subjects showed a linear increase, one exhibited a linear decrease, and the remaining four showed no clear pattern. Figure 3 shows examples of linear increase and decrease. While a trend towards higher mean F0 with advancing age is evident, no statistical testing was carried out under these circumstances.

This finding confirms earlier reports, which, based on large numbers of subjects in cross-sectional studies, argued that F0 remains essentially constant until senescence (Böhme and Hecker 1970). The small number of longitudinal studies did not find a clear tendency among their subjects either (Endres et al. 1971; de Pinto and Hollien 1982; Künzel and Wagner 1993).

As far as F0 variability is concerned, the picture is much the same: Once again, three out of eight subjects show a linear increase, three exhibited a fairly linear decrease, while two showed no clear tendency. No statistically significant results were obtained. This is in good agreement with previous findings (Linville 2001; Linville 2000; Orlikoff 1990).

From a physiological point of view, there are a number of good reasons to expect an increase in F0 and F0 variability with age. Due to changes in the lamina propria, muscular atrophy will occur in the vocal folds and lead to a stiffening. The fibers within the conus elasticus have shown to become thinner in males beyond age 60 (Linville 2001) due to a fragmentation of the elastic and collagenous fibers. Both these processes can be expected to lead to an increase in F0.

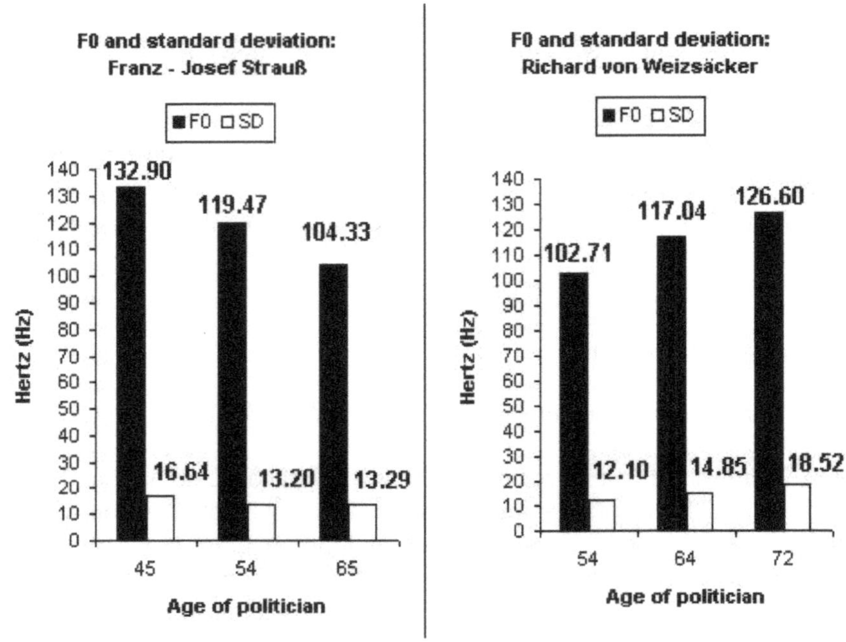

Figure 3. Mean fundamental frequency and standard deviation

However, these mechanisms may begin to be fully effective beyond the age of the subjects who were studied here. Incidentally, the one subject exhibiting a marked decrease (Strauß) was among the younger ones. It should be taken into account, though, that both the consumption of alcohol and cigarettes will influence F0, the former resulting in an increase, the latter in a lowering (Braun 1994; Künzel et al. 1992). The (ab) use of those substances could not be controlled for. Furthermore, F0 standard deviation is to some degree influenced by the conversational setting. We cannot be absolutely certain that some of the interviews were more "emotionally loaded" than others, and this may have affected the results.

3.2.2 Speaking tempo

As was mentioned above (cf. 3.1.), both syllable rate and articulation rate were measured. Since it incorporates pauses and hesitations, syllable rate is (in spontaneous speech) a good reflection of the mental planning stage, whereas articulation rate can be expected to form a better representation of the actual speed of articulator movements.

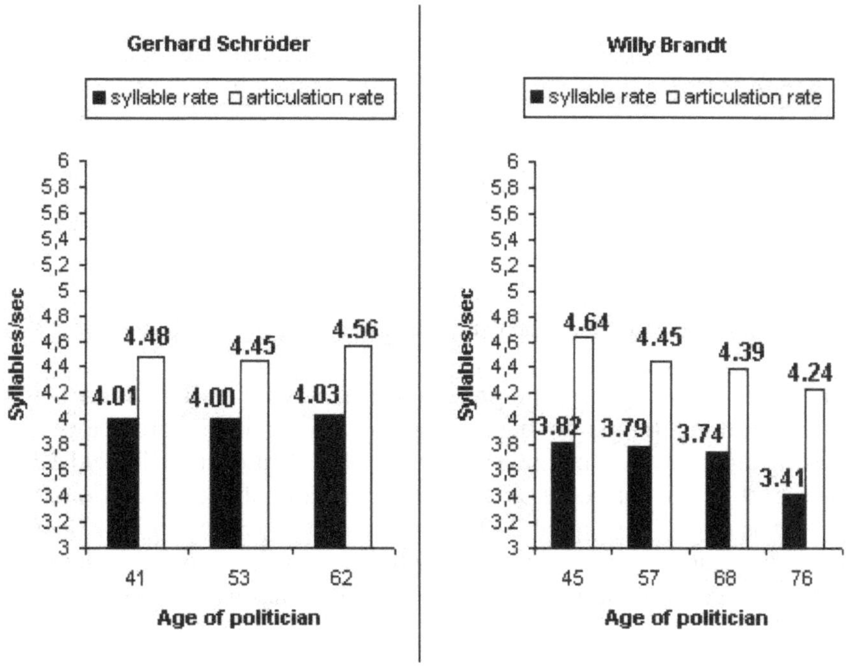

Figure 4. Syllable rates and articulation rates

Results demonstrate very clearly that both syllable rate and articulation rate show a sizeable decrease in six out of eight cases, the speaking tempo essentially remaining constant over time for the remaining two subjects. Figure 4 shows one example for a linear decrease (Brandt) and one in which there is practically no change in speaking tempo over a 20-year period (Schröder). Figure 5 demonstrates the development of AR and SR averaged over all speakers at a period of 20 years.

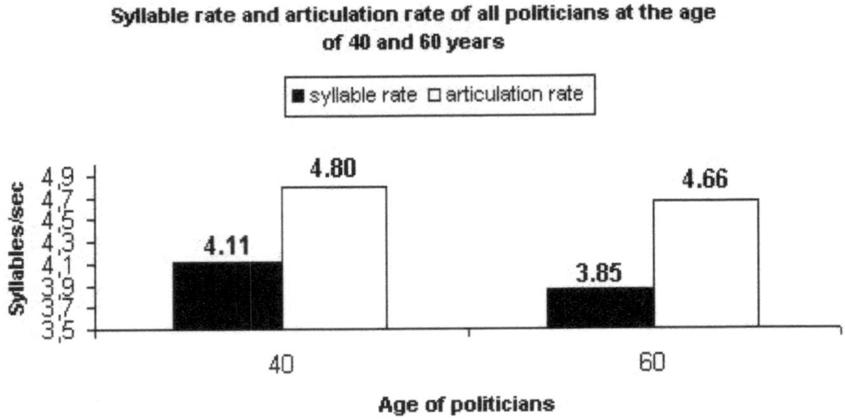

Figure 5. Syllable rates and articulation rates averaged over subjects

The present findings are in good agreement with earlier studies which found speaking tempo to be among the most reliable predictors of increasing age (cf. e.g. Dutchin and Mysak 1987; Braun and Rietveld 1995). These results do not come as a surprise in view of the involutional processes described in chapter 2. In particular, the reduction in nerve conductability and the loss of neurons will have affected mental planning as well as the coordination of articulators. The former as well as the decrease in respiratory activity may have lead to an increase in pause duration, as is reflected by the syllable rates. The importance of pausing for tempo reduction is emphasized by Benjamin (1997: 139): "In addition to increases in phonemic and syllable duration, increases in the number of pauses affect older persons' rate of speech. (…) When speaking at fast rates, older adults are not as effective as young adult speakers in reducing pause length to increase speaking rate."

The significance of our results was tested by analysis of variance and Pearson correlations. Both methods reveal a significant increase with age for syllable rate only (ANOVA $p = 0.01$; Pearson $r = -0.607$); the differences in articulation rate fall short of significance (ANOVA $p = 0.129$; Pearson $r = -0.312$). Even though the sample is not very large, it can with due caution be concluded that it is the mental planning stage more than the actual articulation which is slowed down by increasing age.

3.2.3 VOT

There is a three-way distinction in the presentation of VOT measurements (voiceless aspirated, voiceless unaspirated, and voiced) even though the phonological contrast between German plosives is only twofold (voiced vs. voiceless). However, the phonologically voiced phonemes can either be realized as voiced or as voiceless unaspirated, and it would have been inadequate to combine the two.

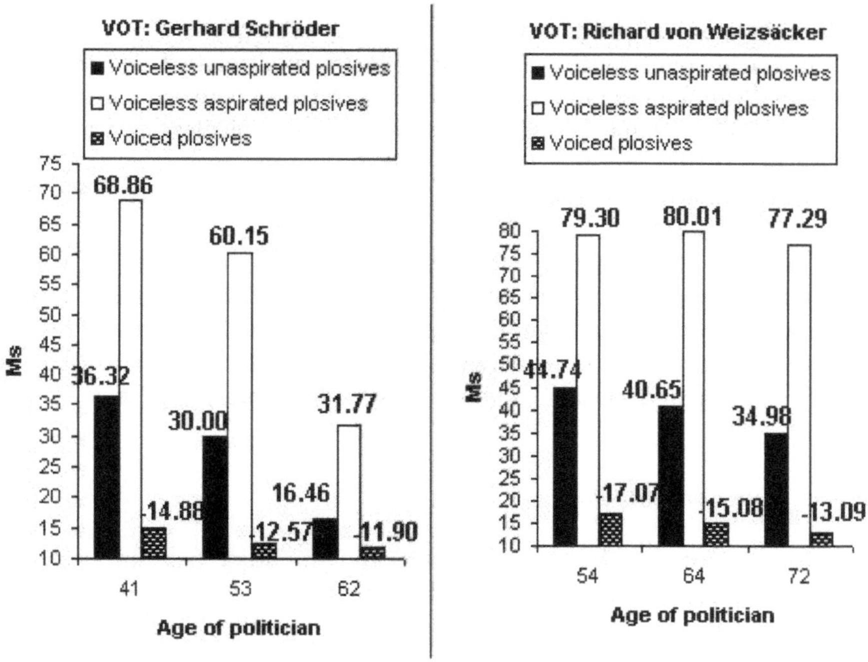

Figure 6. VOT measurements

The present results demonstrate that indeed the coordination between glottal and supraglottal activity is affected by age in a systematic way. VOT is shown to decrease with age. The same phenomenon has also been observed in cross-sectional studies (Benjamin 1982; Smith et al. 1987). Explanations for this behavior may once again be sought in the physiological domain. A major factor contributing to these results may be a reduction in subglottal pressure due to reduced respiratory power. This will lead to a faster drop in transglottal air pressure and thus an earlier onset of vocal fold vibrations. “Slow VOTs may result also from deficient respiratory functioning or an interaction between aberrant respiratory and laryngeal behaviours" (Tyler and Watterson 1991: 136).

A slackening of the pharyngeal musculature and – as a consequence – the widening of the larynx may have a similar result.

Additionally, the function of the intrinsic laryngeal muscles (m. cricoarytenoideus and antagonists) is reduced by decreasing elasticity, mass and the ability to move, which also causes decreasing VOTs. The permanent power-decrease of the neurons also contributes to the imprecise articulation. Immediate consequences are the contractions of muscles as well as the atony of phonatory and articulatory organs.

Statistical significance was tested by Pearson correlation and regression analyses. Although the trend is clear, the correlation between chronological age and VOT fell short of significance for both the voiceless aspirated ($r = -0.170$; $p = 0.198$) and the voiceless unaspirated plosives ($r = -0.229$; $p = 0.125$). It did, however, reach the 1% level for the phonetically voiced ones ($r = -0.592$; $p = 0.001$).

A number of explanations for this finding are conceivable. As was explained in chapter 3.1., even though the position of the plosive within the word was kept constant, running speech was examined, which will result in much less sharp distinctions between categories and also in increased variability as compared to isolated words (Lisker and Abramson 1967: 1).

3.2.4 Jitter and shimmer

Micro-perturbations of frequency (jitter) and amplitude (shimmer) are generally accepted features of vocal ageing. In the present study, the hesitation marker was used to study jitter and shimmer since they were the sustained vowels in the samples which had the longest durations. Both the jitter and shimmer measurements show a marked increase with age. Statistical analysis included ANOVAs and (Pearson) correlations. Whereas RAP values fell short of significance despite a weak positive correlation ($r = 0.187$; $p = 0.185$), the increase in APQ proved to be significant at the 5% level ($r = 0.401$; $p = 0.024$).

The following examples show two extremes: Hans-Jochen Vogel exhibits very little change in jitter and shimmer over a time span of 20 years while the change from the first to the last measurement is evident, whereas Helmut Schmidt shows a linear increase for both.

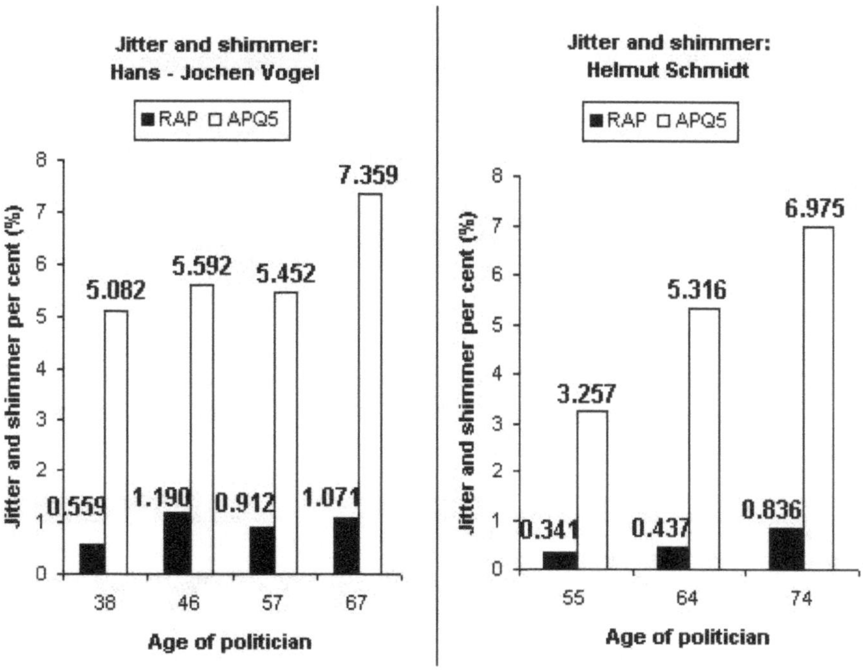

Figure 7. Jitter and shimmer measurements

The change of amplitude perturbation in particular is illustrated by samples taken from recordings of Germany's former chancellor Helmut Kohl at ages 43 (Figure 8) and 62 (Figure 9). In Figure 9 the oscillations from one peak in the signal to the next in the vertical dimension (amplitude) are considerable larger than in Figure 8).

Specifically, degenerative changes in the mucous glands within the Morgagni folds in particular are responsible for an insufficient lubrification of the vocal folds, resulting in their dehydration. The dehydrated surface of the vocal folds will cause vibrational irregularities. Another reason for the increase in jitter and shimmer may be a reduced elasticity of the vocal fold epithelium and a more closely visible mucosal wave. This is most commonly caused by age-related changes in the deep layer of the lamina propria and an atrophy of the m. vocalis. Evidently, the decrease in nerve fibres in the n. laryngeus superior must also be taken into account which is responsible for the sensitive innervation of that muscle which innervates the laryngeal mucosa and the cricothyroid muscle. Since the cricothyroid muscle regulates vocal fold tension, its malfunction will have an immediate effect on periodicity.

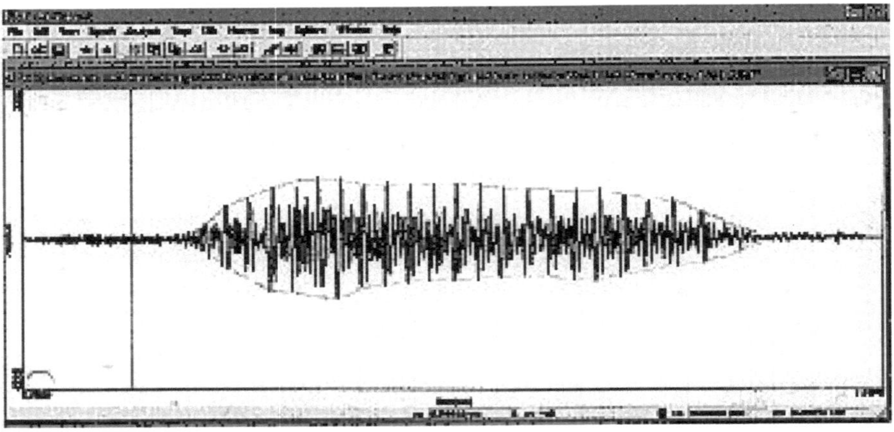

Figure 8. Regular vibrational pattern

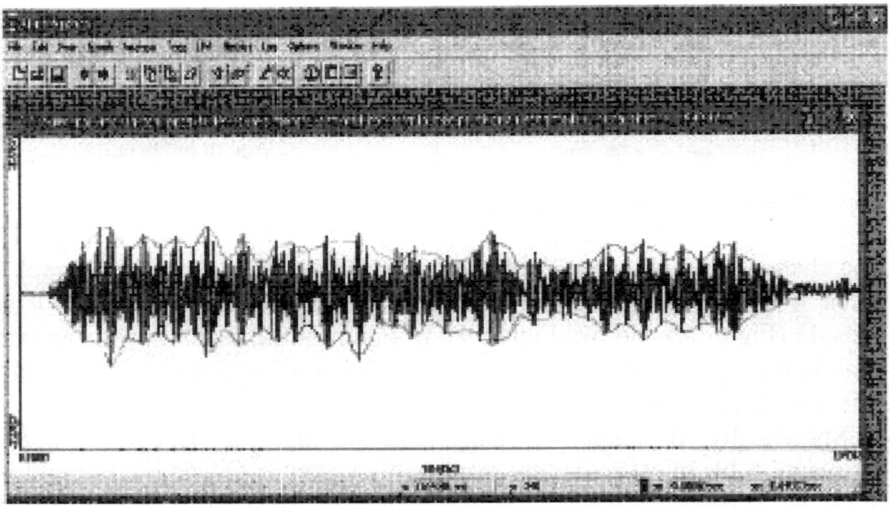

Figure 9. Highly irregular vibrational pattern

4. General discussion

This longitudinal study involves a relatively small sample of speakers (N=8) at three to four points in time. It is, however, by all means comparable to the longitudinal studies which have so far been published (cf. chapter 2) in that respect. The (ab)use of legal drugs may be assumed as an intrapersonal constant; no voice-related illnesses were reported for the period under investigation. Still, the relatively small number of speakers and of samples per speaker is not entirely satisfactory and may explain why some results showed a clear trend but did not reach statistical significance (VOT of voiceless plosives, articulation rate, jitter). This is one of many problems related to any longitudinal research on vocal behavior.

With respect to the research questions asked at the outset, it may be stated that a number of parameters were indeed found to be related to chronological age in a linear way. This includes the VOT in voiced plosives as a measure of supraglottal and glottal coordination, vocal shimmer as a measure of voicing irregularity and speaking tempo as an overall measure of verbal planning. The positive correlations found for these parameters as well as the absence of others (e.g. regarding F0 and F0sd) confirm the findings of cross-sectional studies but those results remained to be established as within-subject developments.

With regard to the forensic setting, we can safely conclude that non-contemporary speech samples do not present a serious problem as long as they are taken from pre-senescent adults and no illnesses and/or operations within the vocal tract are reported. Non-contemporary can in the present context be defined as exhibiting an age-difference of 10 years or less. Sensitive areas have been established by this study. They include the syllable rate, voice perturbation, and certain aspects of VOT. Forensic evidence in non-contemporary recordings running counter to these strong trends will have to be viewed with extra caution.

5. References

Benjamin, Barbaranne J. 1982. "Phonological performance in gerontological speech". *Journal of Psycholinguistic Research* 11. 159–167.

Benjamin, Barbaranne J. 1997. "Speech production of normally aging adults". *Seminars in Speech and Language* 18. 135–141.

Bennett, Suzanne. 1983. "A 3-year longitudinal study of school-aged children's fundamental frequencies". *Journal of Speech and Hearing Research* 26. 137–142.

Böhme, Gerhard and Gertrud Hecker. 1970. "Gerontologische Untersuchungen über Stimmumfang und Sprechstimmlage". *Folia Phoniatrica* 22. 176–184.

Braun, Angelika. 1994. "The Effect of Cigarette Smoking on Vocal Parameters". *Proceedings of the ESCA Conference on Speaker Identification Verification Recognition*, Martigny. 161–164.

Braun, Angelika. 1995a. "Procedures and Perspectives in Forensic Phonetics". *Proceedings of the XIIIth International Congress of Phonetic Sciences, Stockholm.* Vol. 3, 146–153.

Braun, Angelika. 1995b. "Fundamental frequency - how speaker-specific is it?" *Studies in Forensic Phonetics*, ed. by Angelika Braun and Jens-Peter Köster, Trier: Wissenschaftlicher Verlag. 9–23.

Braun, Angelika and Toni Rietveld. 1995. "The influence of smoking habits on perceived age". *Proceedings of the XIIIth International Congress of Phonetic Sciences, Stockholm.* Vol. 2, 294–297.

Cho, Taehong, and Peter Ladefoged. 1999. "Variation and universals in VOT: evidence from 18 languages". *Journal of Phonetics* 27. 207–229.

de Pinto, Olive and Harry Hollien. 1982. "Speaking fundamental frequency characteristics of Australian women: then and now". *Journal of Phonetics* 10. 367–375.

Duffy, R. J. 1970. "Fundamental frequency characteristics of adolescent females". *Language and Speech* 13. 14–24.

Dutchin, Sandra W. and Edward D. Mysak. 1987. "Disfluency and rate characteristics of young adult, middle-aged, and older males". *Journal of Communication Disorders* 20. 245–257.

Endres, W., W. Bambach, and G. Flösser. 1971. "Voice spectrograms as a function of age, voice disguise, and voice imitation". *Journal of the Acoustical Society of America* 49. 1842–1848.

Gilbert, H. R., and G. G. Weismer. 1974. "The effects of smoking on the speaking fundamental frequency of adult women". *Journal of Psycholinguistic Research* 3. 225–231.

Habermann, Günther. 1972. "Der alternde Larynx: Funktionelle Aspekte". *HNO* 20. 121–124.

Hartman, David E. 1979. "The perceptual identity and characteristics of aging in normal male adult speakers". *Journal of Communication Disorders* 12. 53–61.

Hartman, David E. and Jeffrey L. Danhauer. 1976. "Perceptual features of speech for males in four perceived age decades". *Journal of the Acoustical Society of America* 59. 713–715.

Hecker, Gudrun. 1969. *Gerontologische Untersuchungen über Stimmumfang, Sprechstimmlage und Kehlkopfossifikation.* Ph. D. diss., HNO-Klinik, Karl-Marx-Universität Leipzig.

Hertegård, S. 1994. "Normal and pathological glottal closure patterns at different ages". *Voice* 3. 17–26.

Hirano, Minoru, Shigejiro Kurita and Terujuki Nakashima. 1983. "Growth, Development, and Aging of Human Vocal Folds". *Vocal Fold Physiology: Contemporary Research and Clinical Issues*, ed. by Diane M. Bless, and James H. Abbs, San Diego: College-Hill Press. 22–43.

Hoit, Jeannette D. and Thomas J. Hixon. 1987. "Age and speech breathing". *Journal of Speech and Hearing Research* 30. 351–366.

Hollien, Harry, Rachel Green and Karen Massey. 1994. "Longitudinal research on adolescent voice change in males". *Journal of the Acoustical Society of America* 96. 2646–2654.

Horii, Yoshiyuki and J. Ryan William. 1981. "Fundamental frequency characteristics and perceived age of adult male speakers". *Folia Phoniatrica* 33. 227–233.

Kahane, Joel C. 1981. "Anatomic and physiologic changes in the aging peripheral speech mechanism". *Aging. Communication Processes and Disorders*, ed. by Daniel S. Beasley and G. Albyn Davis, New York et al.: Grune & Stratton. 21–45.

Kahane, Joel C. 1983. "A survey of age-related changes in the connective tissues of the human adult larynx". *Vocal Fold Physiology: Contemporary Research and Clinical Issues*, ed. by Diane M. Bless and James H. Abbs, San Diego: College-Hill Press. 44–49.

Kent, Raymond D. and Robert Burkard. 1981. "Changes in the acoustic correlates of speech production". *Aging. Communication Processes and Disorders*, ed. by Daniel S. Beasley and G. Albyn Davis, New York et al.: Grune & Stratton. 47–62.

Künzel, Hermann Angelika Braun and Ulrich Eysholdt. 1992. *Einfluß von Alkohol auf Stimme und Sprache*. Heidelberg: Kriminalistik Verlag.

Künzel, Hermann and Isolde Wagner. 1993. "Discrimination of speaker age from speech". Paper given at the *Annual Conference of the International Association for Forensic Phonetics*, Trier.

Linville, Sue Ellen. 2000. "The aging voice". *Voice Quality Measurement*, ed. by Raymond D. Kent, Martin J. Ball, San Diego: Singular Thomson Learning. 359–376.

Linville, Sue Ellen. 2001. *Vocal Aging*. San Diego: Singular Thomson Learning.

Lisker, Leigh and Arthur S. Abramson. 1967. "Some effects of context on voice onset time in English stops". *Language and Speech* 10. 1–28.

Meyerson, Marion D. 1976. "The effects of aging on communication". *Journal of Gerontology* 31. 29–38.

Mysak, Edward D. 1959. "Pitch and duration characteristics of older males". *Journal of Speech and Hearing Research* 2. 46–54.

Nadol, Joseph B. Jr. 1981. "The aging peripheral hearing mechanism". *Aging. Communication Processes and Disorders*, ed. by Daniel S. Beasley and G. Albyn Davis, New York et al.: Grune & Stratton. 63–85

Neiman, G.S. and J.A. Applegate. 1990. "Accuracy of listener judgements of perceived age relative to chronological age in adults". *Folia Phoniatrica* 42. 327–330.

Orlikoff, Robert F. 1990. "The relationship of age and cardiovascular health to certain acoustic characteristics of male voices". *Journal of Speech and Hearing Research* 33. 450–457.

Pedersen, M. F., P. Kitzing, S. Krabbe and S. Heramb. 1982. "The change of voice during puberty in 11 to 16 years old choir singers measured with elec-

troglottographic fundamental frequency analysis and compared to other phenomena of puberty". *Acta Otolaryngologica*, Suppl. 386. 189–192.
Ptacek, Paul H. and Eric K. Sander. 1966. "Age recognition from voice". *Journal of Speech and Hearing Research* 9. 273–277.
Ptacek, Paul H., Eric K. Sander, Walter H. Maloney and C. C. Roe Jackson. 1966. "Phonatory and related changes with advanced age". *Journal of Speech and Hearing Research* 9. 353–360.
Ramig, Lorraine A. 1983. "Effects of physiological aging on speaking and reading rates". *Journal of Communication Disorders* 16. 217–226.
Ramig, Lorraine A. 1986. "Aging speech: Physiological and sociological aspects". *Language & Communication* 6. 25–34.
Ramig, Lorraine A. and Robert L. Ringel. 1983. "Effects of physiological aging on selected acoustic characteristics of voice". *Journal of Speech and Hearing Research* 26. 22–30.
Ramig, Lorraine A., Steven Gray, Kristin Baker, Kim Corbin-Lewis, Eugene Buder, Erich Luschei, Hillary Coon and Marshall Smith. 2001. "The aging voice: A review, treatment data and familial and genetic perspectives". *Folia Phoniatrica et Logopaedica* 5. 252–263.
Ryan, William R. and Kenneth W. Burk. 1974. "Perceptual and acoustic correlates of aging in the speech of males". *Journal of Communication Disorders* 7 181–192.
Saxman, John H. and Kenneth W. Burk. 1967. "Speaking fundamental frequency characteristics of middle-aged females". *Folia Phoniatrica* 19. 167–172.
Segre, Renato. 1971. "Senescence of the voice". *The Eye, Ear, Nose and Throat Monthly* 50. 62–68.
Shipp, Thomas and Harry Hollien. 1969. "Perception of the aging male voice. *Journal of Speech and Hearing Research* 12. 703–710.
Shipp, Thomas, Qi Yingyong, Ruth Huntley and Harry Hollien. 1992. "Acoustic and temporal correlates of perceived age". *Journal of Voice* 6. 211–216.
Smith, Bruce L., Jan Wasowicz and Judy Preston. 1987. "Temporal characteristics of the speech of normal elderly adults". *Journal of Speech and Hearing Research* 30. 522–529.
Stoicheff, M. L. 1981. "Speaking fundamental frequency characteristics of non-smoking female adults". *Journal of Speech and Hearing Research* 24. 437–441.
Turner, James M., Jere Mead and Mary Ellen Wohl. 1968. "Elasticity of human lungs in relation to age". *Journal of Applied Physiology*, 25. 664–671.
Tyler, Ann A. and Thomas L. Watterson. 1991. "VOT as an indirect measure of laryngeal function". *Seminars in Speech and Language* 12. 131–141.
Whitebourne, Susan Krauss. 1985. *The Aging Body. Physiological Changes and Psychological Consequences*. New York: Springer.
Valenstein, Edward. 1981. "Age-related changes in the human central nervous system". *Aging. Communication Processes and Disorders*, ed. by Daniel S. Beasley and G. Albyn Davis, New York et al.: Grune & Stratton. 87–106.

Does speech reveal one's age? On the use of gerontolinguistic topics for forensic authorship analysis

Jan Seifert

1. Introduction

In the past years, the identification of authors (so-called *Autorenerkennung*, cf. Baldauf 2002; Dern 2003; Schall 2004) proved to be a helpful and broadly accepted procedure in the prosecution and enlightenment of offences. The purpose of *Autorenerkennung* is to examine an anonymous text (e.g. blackmail, threatening, or defamatory letter) for linguistic features and to draw conclusions concerning the author. Kniffka (1990: 438–447) mentions a case where the incriminated texts showed numerous faults in grammar and phraseology, which were explainable as English interferences. The case was solved, an English native speaker had written the incriminated letters. Faults can also be signs of missing native language competence and, furthermore, of the speaker's level of education (Schall 2004: 552).

Two fundamental restrictions have to be pointed out: 1. Any forensic linguistic authorship analysis is only able to yield indications for a description of a profile of an author; it cannot prove the identity of an author beyond doubt. The myth of a linguistic fingerprint against which Wolf (2002) polemicizes has been obsolete for a long time. The metaphor of a hint (Baldauf 2002: 327), however, seems to be quite apt. 2. There is still no comprehensive, genuine theory of forensic linguistic anonymous authorship analysis (Kniffka 2001: 76). The discipline can rather be considered as a methodically open subject (Kämper 1996: 563). However, it can be stated that any authorship analysis for advancing reliable and scientifically reasonable hypotheses on anonymous authors primarily depends on results of empirical linguistics, and that concerns all relevant linguistic subjects. So, Baldauf (1999: 100–101) lists a number of desiderata. She postulates, e.g., studies on the relationship between written language diction and the generation one belongs to (101).

G. Grewendorf and M. Rathert (eds.): Formal Linguistics and Law, 163–180

The considerations on potential age markers that are often discussed in articles on forensic linguistics are comparatively general. Schall (2004: 558) confines herself to a rough pattern containing the categories 'young person', 'mature-aged adult', and 'old person'. As criteria she proposes "Aspekte des Zeitstils", i.e. fashion words, the use of certain phraseologisms which are subject to vogue, and patterns of word formation. As an example for diachronically marked lexems, she quotes the synonymous adjectives *geil*, *toll*, and *knorke*, which she considers to represent contemporary (*geil*), established (*toll*) resp. antiquated (*knorke*) usage and therefore to point to speakers of three different generations. Baldauf (1999: 97) responds: On the one hand, she concedes linguistic features, "die auf generelle Tendenzen in der Entwicklung der deutschen Gegenwartssprache [...] zurückzuführen sind" – she proposes analytic forms of a verb's conjunctive mood, reduction of case markers, word order change – little significance. On the other hand, she takes the same features "als Norm zur groben Bestimmung von Generationszugehörigkeit von Textproduzenten". Intuitively, inferring the age of speakers resp. writers from diachronically labelled linguistic elements seems to be plausible. Nevertheless, for judging the validity of that kind of hypotheses, some reflections on theoretical foundations are required, as well as appropriate empirical research.

For several years, linguists have increasingly been dealing with language usage of elderly people. Whereas research in German youth language has become common since the late 19th century, studies on elderspeak concerning the German-speaking area started to appear only in the nineties of the 20th century (cf. e.g. Fiehler and Thimm 1998).[1] In the meantime, there are plenty of appropriate contributions, and gerontolinguistics seems to be firmly established as a branch of linguistics (Thimm 1996). The following article firstly discusses to what extent these studies and related studies can be utilized for forensic linguistic purposes; it also gives an outline of potential research perspectives.

1. Currently, there is a project "Lesen und Schreiben im Alter" (see http://www.ruhr-uni-bochum.de/alusia/), dealing with aspects of reading und writing by old-aged people. Among other things it is examined to what extent there are age specific linguistic features in conventionalized every-day text types like congratulatory cards. This is done by a text corpus analysis.

2. Theoretical presuppositions

For the purpose of examining the mode of manifestation of generation specific usage of language, one has to explicate some theoretical presuppositions about the linguistic status that is due to the specific features being described. It has been suggested to classify language behaviour of different age categories as varieties (Löffler 2005: 118: "transitorischer Sozioloekt"). However, implying the concept of a relative homogeneous system, this approach seems to be questionable. Another approach of description, which may be more appropriate, is using the concepts of style or register. Both are based on the axiom that speakers make a choice from a range of linguistic elements, according to the particular situation and communicative requirements. An adequate style analysis has to examine the chosen variants in comparison with potential competing elements (cf. Fiehler 1998: 45). It functions like the concept of register (Kohrt and Kucharczik 1998: 25–27) which is illustrated by an organ metaphor. It is supposed that both speaking and writing are intentional actions, i.e., text formation on principle is subject to the author's control. However, the autonomy of the author can be limited by superior norms, referring to situation or text type. The text type style, particularly in highly conventionalized text types, may require certain ritual patterns of style (e.g. nominalizations, passive constructions, etc. in technical language). In anonymous authorship analysis, texts or passages like that can be consulted - only with restriction -as comparison texts. Furthermore, one has to consider additional possibilities of variation, which are of particular interest to forensic linguists:

> "Sie sind in nur sehr geringem Maße der 'bewussten' Handhabung der Sprecher unterworfen und lediglich in Ausnahmefällen in begrenztem Maße überhaupt bewusst manipulierbar. Sie [...] werden von Sprechern/Schreibern nicht mit besonderer Aufmerksamkeit getätigt." (Kniffka 2001: 84)

That refers to different spellings in numeral compounds, use or no-use of linking morphemes in morphologically complex words, or use of (regional conditioned?) variants of phraseologisms. There is a difference between the stylistic relevant variants named above, being available to the speaker's awareness and chosen by intention, and those which are not to one's disposal. This essential distinction is part of a model of speech functions proposed by v. Polenz (1974), which is based on Bühler's organon model.

According to that, these markers or symptoms concern the "symptomatische Sprachfunktion [symptomatic function]" (v. Polenz 1974: 105):

> "Hörer nehmen in den Äußerungen des Sprechers Symptome für bestimmte Eigenschaften oder Verhaltensweisen des Sprechers wahr, auch ohne daß der Sprecher selbst dies beabsichtigt bzw. davon weiß, auch ohne daß der Sprecher auf Hervorbringung oder Vermeidung solcher Symptome Einfluß hat."

So "ist die kommunikative Realisierung eines Symptoms nicht eine intentionale Handlung des Senders, sondern der Sender ist hier nur unwillkürlicher Träger des Zeichens." In this sense, the symptoms enable a social estimation of the speaker – not only by auditors/readers, but also by forensic linguists, one can add. Thus, a category of group specific features (sociolect) is obtained, which may supply clues significant to authorship analysis. To give an example, there are deviations and faults mentioned above, but also those indications which suggest the level of education, regional origin – and possibly age, or the generation one belongs to.

However, it must be considered that anonymous authors may try to cover their tracks resp. to put readers on the wrong track (Dern 2003: 47–49). For example, an author may try to simulate a juvenile writer by using a supposed youth register. It does not yet seem to be shown whether those attempts to dissimulate one's own style resp. to imitate another person by pretence are provable at all.[2] Nevertheless, one may suppose that a consistent dissimulation of individual speech behaviour will require profound knowledge of linguistics, which is not to be expected from laymen.[3]

Considering these reflections, we have to specify the initial question. Those speech elements can be regarded as age-specific speech characteristics which are provably and significant more frequently used by members

2. Attempts at dissimulation are assumed to be provable on the basis of several indications, particularly non-consistent realization (Braun 1989: 162–163; Kniffka 1992: 187–188; Bungarten 1996: 191), with certain branches being dissimulated more easily (Grewendorf 2000: 83). An empirical pilot study is presented in Busch and Heitz (2006).

3. In many cases, linguistically naive speakers as well as experienced linguists do not consider which indications of identity speech behaviour may give. This can be seen in journalists' failed attempts on imitating "youth language" ("Disco-Deutsch", cf. Henne 1986: 61) and, on the other hand, in an experiment by Brandt (1988: 37–41) who showed that even members of academic staff in assigning anonymous texts were guided by lexical parallels, ignoring syntactic structures.

of a certain age group. It concerns less age-exclusive rather than age-preferential features. Specifics attributed to natural or biological changes during ageing are left out of consideration. It is rather supposed that individual speech competence is determinated by social factors (cf. Mattheier 1988). Hence, it seems to be sensible to consider the concept of generation, which supposes that people who are born in the same years have experienced similar historical, cultural, and political events and evolvements at certain times (Thimm 2000: 30). This implies that their registers are disposed in a different manner than those of members of younger generations. For a detailed description, several studies remain to be seen.

3. Generation specificness and language change

The considerations on significance of "Aspekten des Zeitstils" referred above, are based on the hypothesis that speakers preserve the stage of language once acquired in ontogenesis. This phenomenon can particularly be observed when speakers leave the primary language community and move to another speech resp. cultural area – still clinging to native tongue in cohesive circles. For example, interviews taken in the period 1989–1994 with German-Jewish people who had emigrated to Israel in the thirties, showed "daß sich in Israel die Sprache der Gebildeten des ersten Drittels unseres Jahrhunderts ziemlich unverändert erhalten hat" (Betten 1998: 131). Particularly noticeable are the complex syntactic structures, orientated towards norms of literary language with one informant recognizing his preference for sentence brackets and regarding them as archaic (cf. Betten 1998: 136). This unusual material is a matter of special case – not only as it results from a speech island situation but also because it reflects the usage of a certain, highly erudite class. To what extent age can be isolated as an influence factor from other social factors (such as level of education) needs to be examined (see below).

For answering the main question, whether linguistic features in a text can be rated as indicators for the author's age resp. generation s/he belongs to, more detailed research on the "normal case" is required, i.e. it has to be explored how the speech behaviour of members of a speech community who are in interchange and exposed several influences is changed by each influence factor. The idea that older persons represent an older stage of language implies two assumptions:

1. Language acquisition by individuals is concluded at a certain point of time, possibly at the end of schooldays.
2. Language change is primarly caused and beared by younger generations.

The first supposition is the base of the so-called plateau model in language acquisition theory (Fiehler 2002: 500–501). Certain indicators seem to confirm this hypothesis, for example the observation that speakers by the age of 20 tend to get linguistically conservative (Glück and Sauer 1997: 31) in the sense that they take a negative view of changes in language. However, this assumption disregards that speakers personally develop further, are in contact with others, and are confronted with recent developments in language by mass media etc. what means that language biographies can be written (cf. Tophinke 2002). Among social influence factors that determine one's speech, there are (beyond linguistic socialisation at home): education, employment, experiences in reading and writing, etc. Learning and modifying rules of situation-appropriate communication have to be assumed as a lifetime process.

Apart from studies on language acquisition in early age, it has not been examined exactly how language acquisition of individuals takes place. However, the individual is the principle quantity for all general propositions about language usage and language change and should be integrated within language change theory. Häcki Buhofer (2003a: 6) emphatically points out the desideratum of "Individuallinguistik" as a branch of linguistics:

> "Welchen Umgang ein Sprecher bzw. eine Sprecherin mit Gelerntem hat, welche Strategien des Neulernens unterschieden werden können, wer von wem welche sprachlichen Änderungen und Neuerungen übernimmt oder „aufsaugt" (wie ein Schwamm), wer konstant bleibt und zunehmend durch Veralten auffällt, wer konstant variiert und warum, das sind Fragen, die nicht einmal in Ansätzen beantwortet werden können."

The difficulties that stand in the way of such an approach are concerned with methodical questions – apart from the fact that many linguists strive to general propositions: Ideally, for describing changes in language usage of individuals diachronically, adequate longitudinal studies are required. As such investigations from obvious causes are out of question, there are other methods for doing research on recent developments in language, being evolved and applied in areal linguistics (Siebenhaar 2003: 313–315):

- In real-time-comparison, two data sets compiled at different times (and in most cases from different informants) are compared; language change is inferred from differences in data. It has to be assured that both clusters of informants reflect the same segment of speech community.
- In real-time-comparison, it is supposed that older informants represent an older stage of language (see above). Data is gathered from younger and older informants synchronously; differences in data are taken as an indication for language change. Hence, processes of individual language change in the elderly are disregarded inevitably.

Considering these methodical difficulties, particularly panel studies are worth paying attention to. This method's advantage is in enabling longitudinal observation of the individual through time by collecting data samples from the same informants at different times. For example, it was possible for Bausch (2000) to interview several informants of those who had already been recorded in the fifties. The comparison showed changes being explainable by biographical aspects. Something similar is seen in Siebenhaar's study (2003) examining recent changes in phonology and morphology of the Swiss German dialect spoken in Aarau. He had the rare chance to apply the three methods outlined above in combination. As a result, it is proved that the apparent time hypothesis should not be maintained just like that, since both informants of those existed long interval data sets made reversals and took diametrical positions within the elder generation (Siebenhaar 2003: 322): Whereas one of them linguistically behaves evidently conservatively, exactly the most aged informant shows a language usage being clearly orientated towards the younger generation.

> "Obwohl also Sprachwandel eine Veränderung der Sprache einer Sprachgemeinschaft über eine bestimmte Zeit darstellt und von den Individuen dieser Sprachgemeinschaft getragen wird, kann der Idiolekt der Sprachträger jeweils andere Entwicklungen durchmachen. Erst die Mittelwerte der Veränderungen über Generationen hinweg zeigen überindividuellen Sprachwandel." (Siebenhaar 2003: 322–323)

What is proved for the relatively steady grammatical subsystems of a variety applies probably even more to the open and flexible system of lexis of standard language: The assumption of apparent time differences levels the actual relations which are considerably more complicated.

In addition, it has to be warned about far too naive ideas regarding changes in language as linear processes, as Cherubim (1988: 544) points out in the connection with describing archaising processes. A questionnaire by Häcki Buhofer (2003b) on knowledge of several Swiss German phraseologisms shows clearly that in examinations of lexical aliveness not linear but u-shaped developments have to be taken into account: Three age groups were questioned; for the middle one, not simply the average arose but the data indicated that the middle-aged persons know resp. comprehend the given phraseologisms significantly better than both other groups. It follows that in research using the apparent time model at least three age groups are required for including and considering biographical learning processes and developments. In studying particular language biographies, it has to be examined which biographical influence factors in detail determine the development of speech behaviour. Regarding vocabulary, it has to be assumed that linguistic socialisation at home, education, employment, experiences in reading, etc. have considerable influence on the disposition of the registers.

4. Lexical age markers: On the significance of archaisms

Generally, so-called archaisms (Cherubim 1988) are assumed to be the main lexical age markers (cf. Thimm 2000: 164; 2002: 885). However, there must be considered a vicious circle as in describing antiquated lexems (e.g., in dictionaries which give diachronical information) the preference use by the elderly is almost taken as a criterion. As an example, see the ten volume Duden dictionary: The information "veraltend [becoming obsolete]" means "daß das damit bezeichnete Wort nicht mehr zum allgemein benutzten Wortschatz der Gegenwartssprache gehört, sondern, wie etwa *Backfisch*, meist oder fast ausschließlich von der älteren Generation verwendet wird" (GWDS 1999: 35; cf. Ludwig 2005). The lexicographical treatment of "archaisms" seems to be problematic, as the information is rather diffuse: It is vague what is to be understood by "elder generation", what distinguishes the lexemes classified as "becoming obsolete" from those which are regarded as "obsolete", and what relation these labels have with other pragmatical information (cf. Wiegand 1981), for example regional or situation related. In addition, that information not necessarily has an empirical basis – in most cases, the decision on diachronic labels seems to be based on intuition of lexicographers (cf. Ludwig 2005: 274).

Archaisms still are, regardless of the instructive contributions by Cherubim (1988; 1995) and Ludwig (recently 2005), a desideratum. The reason is that there are methodical difficulties on defining the topic and reconstructing processes of archaization. Another cause of the reserved interest in archaisms may be that for an adequate approach the dichotomy of synchronical versus diachronical linguistics has to be overcome. In addition, one has to consider that lexicology in the past has been orientated rather one-sided to theoretical problems (Geeraerts 1997). However that may be: A systematic, empirically based recording and description of archaisms in German is missing, as well as a detailed study on aspects of their use in present-day language.[4]

For exemplifying several methodical problems, the handbook article on generation specific vocabularies by Thimm (2002) is suitable, still representing the up-to-date state of research. According to Thimm, description of youth specific registers and therefore youth language vocabulary is assumed to be unproblematic (Thimm 2002: 884). In contrast, elderly specific lexis is thought to be "weniger leicht identifizierbar. Zugrunde gelegt wurde *daher* das Kriterium des Veraltens der betreffenden Lexeme" (Thimm 2002: 885, display J.S.). The wording shows how obviously a causal relation between old age and use of lexems becoming "antiquated" is presumed. The data presented in this connection is based on an empirical study by Thimm (2000). This work is worth paying attention to because it looks into lexical age markers using authentic material for the first time (cf. Thimm 2000: 163–165, 183–184, 196–197). The underlying corpus consists of 42 produced dialogues between 84 women of different age groups ("young": 24–35 years; "old": 60–85 years), bearing three constellations of discourse: old-young; old-old; young-young (Thimm 2000: 147). As a result, Thimm points out:

> "Das Ergebnis bestätigt die Hypothese, dass lexikalische Sprachmarker als wichtige Kategorie zur Erfassung altersdifferenzierenden Sprachgebrauchs heranzuziehen sind. So verwenden die jüngeren Sprecherinnen mehr als doppelt so viele der als *jugendsprachlich* bezeichneten Sprachmarker (m_{jung}=5.6/m_{alt}=2.7). Die älteren Sprecherinnen dagegen gebrauchen signifikant mehr der als *veraltet* oder *veraltend* bezeichneten Lexeme und Phraseme (m_{alt}=1.2/m_{jung}=0.4). Bemerkenswert an den genauen Werten ist die

4. A study dealing with these aspects is prepared currently by the author. It is designed to gather data by questionnaire as well as text corpus analysis.

> Tatsache, dass die veralteten Formen relativ selten auftreten, auch bei den Älteren sind die Mittelwerte gering." (Thimm 2000: 183; cf. 2002: 885f.)

The last sentence relativizes the entire findings. With detailed quantitative information missing, it is impossible to assess whether archaisms actually are a characteristic feature of the language usage of the elderly or how far idiosyncratic stylistic features of individual probationers are responsible for the statistical values. For examining validity of the survey, a qualitative study is required, which means an examination of the context the relevant lexems are used in, considering functional and stylistic aspects.

First of all, as a basic problem it has to be discussed which lexems may be considered as potential age markers and which criteria can be referred. In Thimm (2000: 164), classification is based on corresponding metalinguistic opinions of several persons (whose ages are not mentioned). As an example for age language resp. old-fashioned units the following words resp. expressions are given: *mir dünkt / Wochenbettpfleger / besinnen / Photokopieranstalt*[5] */ Jugendführer / Infanterieregiment* (Thimm 2000: 164; cf. 2002: 885).

How far the stock of examples reaches beyond these few ones remains open. As no further examples are quoted anywhere and archaisms are rated as comparatively rare anyway (see above) that suggests that the supply of archaisms found in the corpus is not much more extensive. However, the few given examples show the principle problematic nature of a procedure based on intuition:

- The word *Infanterieregiment* refers to a historical object that does not exist anymore. So far, the reason that this expression has moved to the periphery of usage is of extra linguistic kind; these cases are to be distinguished strictly from those concerning a linguistical archaization. For differentiation, in German terminology the term "Historismus" is often used (cf. Ludwig 2005: 262). In the handbook article mentioned above, Thimm (2002: 885) no longer quotes this word as an example for archaisms.
- The lexem *Jugendführer* is not obsolete, as Thimm (2000: 236) alleges ("heute nicht mehr gebräuchlich"), but domain specific – it is a term in

5. Obviously, the spelling <Ph> in transcription is meant to underscore the archaic character of the lexem.

pathfinder affairs.[6] The respective communication problems occuring in inter-generation dialogues (Thimm 2000: 236) are to be attributed to competence differences concerning technical language; it is not a matter of linguistic archaization.

– The verb *besinnen* is used in different ways, namely (among others) in the meanings a) 'reflect, consider'; b) 'call to mind'; c) 'meditate' etc. (cf. GWDS 1999: 554). Even if some ways of use seem to be stylistically marked, it is not sensible to classify the whole lexeme apodictically as "old-fashioned". Without information about the contexts of utterances, precise assessments are impossible.
– The verb *dünken* (cf. GWDS 1999: 881–882) is a lexeme marked in a high degree. Therefore, it should be examined whether an author/speaker uses the word in a neutral sense or whether he pursues a special purpose (e.g. elevated, pathetical or dissociating, caricaturing archaization: cf. Cherubim 1995: 33–35). Only in the first case, the word can justifiably be construed as a "symptom".
– The lexeme *Wochenbettpfleger* seems to be remarkable, especially because of its masculine form as nursing profession (while this job is mostly done by women). There is no entry in the recent Duden dictionary (GWDS 1999) but at least the feminine variant can be taken as a usual name of an occupational status resp. a business, which is gathered from a booklet by "Bundesagentur für Arbeit".[7] The example shows how questionable the method of introspection is in deciding on labels.

The discussion of the examples shows clearly that further differentiation in conditions of usage is required. Words beside their denotation have a pragmatical potential what means that their use is constrained by specific situation conditions. For avoiding the rather diffuse categories of stylistic layer ("Stilschicht") and stylistic shade ("Stilfärbung"), these constraints can be described with a model of communicative predispositions proposed by Ludwig (1991: 228): "Gemeint ist damit, daß ein Lexem prädisponiert ist, in bestimmten Bereichen der Kommunikation benutzt zu werden." These predispositions are indicated in dictionary articles by pragmatic la-

6. There is no corresponding lemma in the relevant dictionaries on contemporary German, but electronic corpora inquiries yield indications that the word is a common, well-accepted name of a pathfinder rank, cf. English *youth leader*.
7. "Hinweise zur Verschlüsselung der Angaben zur Tätigkeit": www.arbeitsagentur.de/RD-NSB/Bremen/A20-Intern/Publikation/pdf/Schluesselverz-f-priv-Haush-aktualisiert.pdf [25.10.06].

bels (cf. Wiegand 1981). Concerning archaisms, it has to be considered that the dimensions "diachrony" and "level" cannot be divided simply: Thus dictionaries operate with levels such as "gehoben", "dichterisch", or "bildungssprachlich" ("elevated", "poetic", and "educational"), partially combined with diachronic labels (cf. Ludwig 2005: 265–271). It is obvious that even such words belong to educationally labelled lexis that are not (no more) generally known but, for example, imparted especially by reading of literary works. If just archaisms are of "poetic" quality (examples in Ludwig 1991: 231–242), it needs to be asked how appreciated "old-fashioned" words are at all. Being willing to concede archaisms an exclusive status, one has to consider them not only as potential age markers but as indicators of a certain level of education.

Finally, a decision whether a word is labeled regionally or diachronically is frequently not simple, e.g. *Eisschrank* 'refrigerator'. Corresponding to the matter of archaisms, there is an empirical deficit in lexicographical practice concerning diatopical variation. For example, Piirainen (2002) showed in a study on diatopical distribution of phraseologisms that diatopic labels in dictionaries of contemporary German in part do not correspond with linguistic facts.

The aspect of variation is neglected also in the set of examples given by Schall (2004: 558; s. above): *knorke – toll – geil*. These value-adjectives are marked in more than diachronical respect. The word *geil* – at least in the meaning 'great' – is part of a youth specific register; it does not represent the "contemporary" usage within the meaning of unmarked standard language. (Considering that these registers change permanently, one will have to deliberate if *geil* even becomes obsolete in the presence of *krass* or *fett*, which adjectives are used synonymously...). The adjective *knorke*, being part of Berlin colloquial language in the twenties (Paul 2002: 546; Tucholsky 1924), is undoubtly labelled diachronically, diatopically, and diastratically. Finally, the word *toll*, which obviously is meant to function as a neutral, unmarked element, is to be classified as colloquial. Hence, from the beginning the lexemes are to be regarded as parts of different registers. They are not suited to be evidential diachronical variants of a variable "expression of 'great'" for purpose of forensic linguistics.

Similarly one should deal with considering "fashion words" (cf. Schall 2004: 558).. It is obvious that there are lexemes that shape public discourses at certain times. Listings of "Words of the year" etc. which are published regularly (cf. Förster 1991), reflect contemporary history; dictionaries of contemporary history even do so (cf. Stötzel and Eitz 2003). With a certain time distance, these words lose importance, which is reflected in lower frequency of use. This is explainable by changed communication requirements.

How far the use of such words at later times may be taken as an indication of age of a speaker/author, having experienced his/her linguistic socialization with them being ubiquitous and therefore adhering to them, must be left undecided at the moment. However, it seems to be questionable, as an example shows: The 'word of the year' 1971, the adjective *aufmüpfig* 'rebellious' (Paul 2002: 106) can be regarded as a fashion word of the early seventies, reflecting an established generation's attitude towards rebellious youth. 35 years later, the word is still frequently used (search engines and online text corpora supply numerous examples), but there are no indications that the authors of the current relevant texts are in their seventies, having belonged to 40-years-old established citizens in the early seventies. – As mentioned above, the apparent time hypothesis with individual conditions being considered, cannot be corroborated. What applies to phonology and morphology should all the more be heeded in lexis, which, being an open system, would follow biographical changes even more flexibly.

However, the critical comments given so far do not propose giving the impression that the assumption of generation-related differences is totally unfounded. Thus, specific studies on lexis change for purposes of areal linguistic research showed that there are evident differences in knowledge and usage of certain lexemes between speakers who belong to different age groups (e.g. Schmutz 1999 on Sensler German, Berroth 2001: 32–95 on Middle Swabian basis dialects). With this, one has to consider the special conditions of diatopical varieties which are permanently influenced by regional dialects resp. standard language and whose vocabulary changes, on the other hand, by real causes (e.g., abolition of agricultural objects).

With regard to the primary question, results from a more standard related topic are more productive. For example, a new inquiry on regional variation in standard lexis was able to yield indications that die Northern German form *Sonnabend* 'Saturday' is rather used by elder people, whereas younger ones prefer the form *Samstag* (cf. Elspaß 2005: 1, 11–12). To forensic text analysis, findings like that may be of importance.

Summing up, it may be said that dealing with supposed generation specific lexical features should be done very reservedly at the up-to-date state of research. Neither the status of archaisms in language system is clear, nor their importance in individuals' vocabulary. Hence, it is to be cautioned against supposition of language change in apparent time.

5. Desiderata and problems

Up to now, there are no definite indicators of linguistic features to be an age marker. At this point, future research has to start. Among several questions, the status of so-called archaisms is of special interest:

- Is there a relation at all between age and knowledge resp. use of "antiquated" language elements?
- Do old speakers use archaic forms to a higher degree than younger ones?
- In which cases and why do they do so?
- How big is the influence of linguistic socialisation?
- Which individual differences are to be found?

These questions go beyond the application related aspects, as on the one hand they concern problems of labelling in lexicography, on the other they touch on aspects of language change theory:

- How steady are individual language features for quite a long period?
- Which influence factors can be discovered?
- Are recent development trends concerning present-day language actually beard only by younger generations?

Given this, an important and promising field of research opens up. Without empirically examined theory, forensic authorship analysis using "age markers" as criteria is lost in mere speculation.

6. References

Baldauf, Christa. 1999. "Zur Signifikanz sprachlicher Merkmale im Rahmen des Autorschaftsnachweises: Ansätze und Desiderate der forensischen Linguistik". *Archiv für Kriminologie* 204. 93–105.

Baldauf, Christa. 2002. "Autorenerkennung im BKA – Linguistik unter Zugzwang?" *Sprache und Recht,* ed. by Ulrike Haß-Zumkehr, Berlin-New York: de Gruyter. 321–329.

Bausch, Karl-Heinz. 2000. *Wandel im gesprochenen Deutsch. Eine Pilotstudie zum diachronen Vergleich von Korpora gesprochener Sprache am Beispiel des Rhein-Neckar-Raums.* Mannheim: IDS.

Berroth, Daniela. 2001. *Altersbedingter Mundartgebrauch. Wandel und Kontinuität in einem mittelschwäbischen Dialekt.* Stuttgart: Steiner (Zeitschrift für Dialektologie und Linguistik. Beihefte, 116).

Betten, Anne. 1998. "Ist 'Altersstil' in der Sprechsprache wissenschaftlich nachweisbar? Überlegungen zu Interviews mit 70- bis 100jährigen Emigranten". *Sprache und Kommunikation im Alter*, ed. by Fiehler and Thimm, Opladen-Wiesbaden: Westdeutscher Verlag. 131–142.

Brandt, Wolfgang. 1989. "Grenzen und Möglichkeiten forensischer Linguistik. Ergebnisse und Folgerungen aus empirischen Reihenuntersuchungen". *Symposium: Forensischer linguistischer Textvergleich.* Wiesbaden: Bundeskriminalamt. 31–48.

Braun, Angelika. 1989. "Linguistische Analysen im forensischen Bereich – zu den Möglichkeiten einer Texturheberschaftsuntersuchung". *Symposium: Forensischer linguistischer Textvergleich.* Wiesbaden: Bundeskriminalamt, 143–166.

Bungarten, Theo. 1996. "Anonymität und Urheberschaft. Kommunikationswissenschaftliche, linguistische und informationstheoretische Modellierung möglicher Urheberschaften von anonymen Textdokumenten", *Recent Developments in Forensic Linguistics,* ed. by hannes Kniffka. Frankfurt (Main): Lang, 181–201.

Busch, Albert and Susanne Catharina Heitz. 2006. "Wissenstransfer und Verstellung in Erpresserschreiben: Zur Analyse von Verstellungsstrategien auf korpuslinguistischer Basis". *Wissenstransfer: Erfolgskontrolle und Rückmeldungen aus der Praxis*, ed. by Wichter, Sigurd and Albert Busch, Frankfurt u. a.: Lang. 83-100.

Cherubim, Dieter. 1988. "Sprach-Fossilien. Beobachtungen zum Gebrauch, zur Beschreibung und zur Bewertung der sogenannten Archaismen". *Deutscher Wortschatz. Lexikologische Studien. Ludwig Erich Schmitt zum 80. Geburtstag von seinen Marburger Schülern*, ed. by Horst Haider Munske, Peter v. Polenz, Oskar Reichmann, and Reiner Hildebrandt. Berlin-New York: de Gruyter. 525–552.

Cherubim, Dieter. 1995. "Archaisierung. Zur historischen Tiefe von Normierungen". *Sprachnormen und Sprachnormwandel in gegenwärtigen europäischen Sprachen. Beiträge zur gleichnamigen Fachkonferenz November 1994 am Fachbereich Sprach- und Literaturwissenschaften der Universität Rostock.* Rostock: Universität Rostock (Rostocker Beiträge zur Sprachwissenschaft 1), 29–45.

Dern, Christa. 2003. "Sprachwissenschaft und Kriminalistik: zur Praxis der Autorenerkennung". *Zeitschrift für germanistische Linguistik* 31. 44–77.

Elspaß, Stephan. 2005. "Zum Wandel im Gebrauch regionalsprachlicher Lexik. Ergebnisse einer Neuerhebung". *Zeitschrift für Dialektologie und Linguistik* 72. 1–51.

Fiehler, Reinhard. 1998. "Modelle zur Beschreibung und Erklärung altersspezifischer Sprache und Kommunikation". *Sprache und Kommunikation im Al-*

ter, ed. by Fiehler and Thimm, Opladen-Wiesbaden: Westdeutscher Verlag. 38–56.

Fiehler, Reinhard. 2002. "Der Stil des Alters". *Soziale Welten und kommunikative Stile. Festschrift für Werner Kallmeyer zum 60. Geburtstag*, ed. by Inken Keim and Wilfried Schütte, Tübingen: Narr. 499–511.

Fiehler, Reinhard and Caja Thimm. (eds.) 1998. *Sprache und Kommunikation im Alter*. Opladen/Wiesbaden: Westdeutscher Verlag.

Förster, Uwe. 1991/2000. "Wörter der achtziger Jahre". *Sprachpflege auf wissenschaftlicher Grundlage. Beiträge aus drei Jahrzehnten*, ed. by Gesellschaft für deutsche Sprache, Mannhein u.a.: Dudenverlag, 48–59.

Geeraerts, Dirk. 1997. "Entfernung, Fortschritt und Unvollständigkeit. Das historische Verhältnis von Lexikologie und Lexikographie". *Linguistische Theorie und lexikographische Praxis. Symposiumsvorträge, Heidelberg 1996*, ed. by Klaus-Peter Konerding and Andrea Lehr, Tübingen: Niemeyer (Lexicographica. Series Maior 82), 7–16.

Glück, Helmut and Wolfgang Werner Sauer 1997. *Gegenwartsdeutsch*. 2., überarb. u. erw. Auflage. Stuttgart/Weimar: Metzler.

Grewendorf, Günther. 2000. "Gibt es syntaktische Spuren?" *2. Symposion Autorenerkennung des Bundeskriminalamtes. Tagungsband*, ed. by Baldauf, Christa J., Wiesbaden: Bundeskriminalamt, 83–96.

GWDS 1999. *Duden. Das große Wörterbuch der deutschen Sprache*. 3., völlig neu bearb. und erw. Aufl. Mannheim u. a.: Dudenverlag.

Häcki Buhofer, Annelies. 2003a. "Einleitung: Spracherwerb und Lebensalter". *Spracherwerb und Lebensalter*, ed. by Annelies Häcki Buhofer, unter Mitarbeit von Lorenz Hofer et al., Tübingen-Basel: Francke (Basler Studien zur deutschen Sprache und Literatur 83). 1–17.

Häcki Buhofer, Annelies. 2003b. "Psycholinguistik der lexikalischen Lebendigkeit. Phraseologismenkenntnis in verschiedenen Lebensaltern am Beispiel einiger schweizerdeutscher Phraseologismen". *Spracherwerb und Lebensalter*, ed. by Annelies Häcki Buhofer, unter Mitarbeit von Lorenz Hofer et al., Tübingen-Basel: Francke (Basler Studien zur deutschen Sprache und Literatur 83), 279–292.

Henne, Helmut. 1986. *Jugend und ihre Sprache*. Berlin-New York: de Gruyter.

Kämper, Heidrun. 1996. "Nachweis der Autorschaft. Methodische Überlegungen zur linguistischen Textidentifizierung und Täterermittlung". *Kriminalistik* 50. 561–566.

Kniffka, Hannes. 1990. "Ein Autorschafts-Ausschluß: Ein 'Liquet' und ein 'Nonliquet'". *Texte zu Theorie und Praxis forensischer Linguistik*, ed. by Hannes Kniffka, Tübingen: Niemeyer. 437–456.

Kniffka, Hannes. 1992. "Sprachwissenschaftliche Hilfe bei der Täterermittlung". *Rechtskultur als Sprachkultur. Zur forensischen Funktion der Sprachanalyse*, ed. by Günther Grewendorf. Frankfurt (Main): Suhrkamp. 157–193.

Kniffka, Hannes. 2001. "Eine Zwischenbilanz aus der Werkstatt eines 'forensischen' Linguisten: Zur Analyse anonymer Autorschaft". *Linguistische Berichte* 185. 75–104.

Kohrt, Manfred and Kerstin Kucharczik. 1998. "'Sprache' – unter besonderer Berücksichtigung von 'Jugend' und 'Alter'". *Sprache und Kommunikation im Alter*, ed. by Fiehler and Thimm, Opladen-Wiesbaden: Westdeutscher Verlag. 17–37.

Löffler, Heinrich. 2005. *Germanistische Soziolinguistik*. 3., überarb. Aufl. Berlin: Schmidt (Grundlagen der Germanistik 28).

Ludwig, Klaus Dieter. 1991. *Markierungen im allgemeinen einsprachigen Wörterbuch des Deutschen. Ein Beitrag zur Metalexikographie*. Tübingen: Niemeyer (Lexicographica. Series Maior 38).

Ludwig, Klaus Dieter. 2005. "Archaismen im GWDS." *Untersuchungen zur kommerziellen Lexikographie der deutschen Gegenwartssprache II. Duden. Das große Wörterbuch der deutschen Sprache in zehn Bänden [GWDS]. Print- und CD-ROM-Version*, ed. by Herbert Ernst Wiegand, Vol. 2. Tübingen: Niemeyer (Lexicographica. Series Maior 121), 261–275.

Mattheier, Klaus J. 1988. "Das Verhältnis von sozialem und sprachlichem Wandel". *Sociolinguistics. An International Handbook of the Science of Language and Society*, ed. by Ulrich Ammon, Norbert Dittmar, Klaus J. Mattheier, Vol. 2. Berlin / New York: de Gruyter (HSK 3.2), 1430–1452.

Paul, Hermann. 2002. *Deutsches Wörterbuch. Bedeutungsgeschichte und Aufbau unseres Wortschatzes*. 10., überarbeitete und erweiterte Auflage v. Helmut Henne, Heidrun Kämper, and Georg Objartel. Tübingen: Niemeyer.

Piirainen, Elisabeth. 2002. "'Landschaftlich', 'norddeutsch' oder 'berlinisch'? Zur Problematik diatopischer Markierungen von Idiomen". *Deutsch als Fremdsprache* 39. 36–40.

Polenz, Peter v. 1974. "Ideolektale und soziolektale Funktionen von Sprache". *Leuvense Bijdragen* 63. 97–112.

Schall, Sabine. 2004. "Forensische Linguistik". *Angewandte Linguistik*, ed. by Karlfried Knapp, Gerd Antos, Michael Becker-Mrotzek, Arnulf Deppermann, Susanne Göpferich, Joachim Grabowski, Michael Klemm and Claudia Villiger, Tübingen/Basel: Francke. 544–562.

Schmutz, Christian. 1999. "Unterschiede zwischen der Sprache von alten und jungen Leuten: bedauerlicher Verlust oder normales linguistisches Verhalten?" *Deutschfreiburg im Aufbruch. Festschrift zum 40. Jahrestag der Gründung der Deutschfreiburgischen Arbeitsgemeinschaft*. Freiburg (Schweiz). 130–140.

Siebenhaar, Beat. 2003. "Sprachwandel von Sprachgemeinschaften und Individuen". *Spracherwerb und Lebensalter*, ed. by Annelies Häcki Buhofer, unter Mitarbeit von Lorenz Hofer et al., Tübingen-Basel: Francke (Basler Studien zur deutschen Sprache und Literatur 83). 313–326.

Stötzel, Georg and Thorsten Eitz. 2003. *Zeitgeschichtliches Wörterbuch der deutschen Gegenwartssprache. Schlüsselwörter und Orientierungsvokabeln.* 2., erw. u. akt. Aufl. Hildesheim: Olms.

Thimm, Caja. 1996. "Sprache und Kommunikation im Alter: Plädoyer für eine gerontologische Linguistik". *Sprachreport* 1/1996. 4–5.

Thimm, Caja. 2000. *Alter – Sprache – Geschlecht. Sprach- und kommunikationswissenschaftliche Perspektiven auf das höhere Lebensalter.* Frankfurt-New York: Campus.

Thimm, Caja. 2002. "Generationsspezifische Wortschätze". *Lexikologie / Lexicology. Ein internationales Handbuch zur Natur und Struktur von Wörtern und Wortschätzen.* Vol. 1., ed. by A. Alan Cruse, Franz Hundsnurscher, Michael Job and Peter Rolf Lutzeier, Berlin-New York: De Gruyter (HSK 21.1), 880–888.

Tophinke, Doris. 2002. "Lebensgeschichte und Sprache. Zum Konzept der Sprachbiografie aus linguistischer Sicht". *Bulletin VALS-ASLA* 76. 1–14.

Tucholsky, Kurt. 1924. "Der Fall Knorke". *Gesammelte Werke* Vol. 3. 1921–1924. Reinbek: Rowohlt 1960, 471–473.

Wiegand, Herbert Ernst. 1981. "Pragmatische Informationen in neuhochdeutschen Wörterbüchern. Ein Beitrag zur praktischen Lexikologie". *Studien zur neuhochdeutschen Lexikographie I*, ed. by Herbert Ernst Wiegand, Hildesheim-New York: Olms (Germanistische Linguistik 3–4/79). 139–271.

Wolf, Norbert Richard. 2002. "Gibt es den sprachlichen Fingerabdruck? Oder: Was kann die Kriminalistik von der Sprachwissenschaft erwarten?" *Sprache und Recht.* ed. by Ulrike Haß-Zumkehr, Berlin-New York: de Gruyter (IDS-Jahrbuch 2001). 309–320.

Part 3

Organizing legal systems: The contribution of computational linguistics and artificial intelligence

Definition extraction from court decisions using computational linguistic technology

Stephan Walter

1. Introduction[1]

1.1 Definitions in legal texts

Two central kinds of knowledge contained in the statutes of code law systems are normative knowledge, connecting legal consequences to descriptions of certain facts and situations, and terminological knowledge, consisting in definitions of some of the concepts used in these descriptions (Valente and Breuker 1994).

Normative content is exemplified by (1), part of section 29 of the German Federal Water Act. The legal consequence consisting in the responsibility for the maintenance of waters is connected to the precondition of ownership of the respective waters:

(1) *Die Unterhaltung von Gewässern obliegt (…) den Eigentümern der Gewässer*

[(…) the owners are responsible for maintaining their waters (…)]

Terminological knowledge consists in definitions of concepts used to describe the sanctioned facts. For example, article 1 of the Federal Water Act captures a specific terminological sense of waters as follows:

---

1. The research described within this paper is carried out within the project CORTE funded by the German Science Foundation, DFG PI 154/10-1 (http://www.coli.uni-saarland.de/projects/corte/)

G. Grewendorf, M. Rathert (eds.): Formal Linguistics and Law, 183–223

(2) *(1) Dieses Gesetz gilt für folgende Gewässer:*
1. das ständig oder zeitweilig in Betten fließende oder stehende (..) Wasser

[This Act applies to the following waters:
1. permanently or temporarily flowing or standing (...) waters confined within a bed]

If the definitions contained in statutes would fully specify how the relevant concepts are to be applied, cases could be solved by mechanically checking which concepts apply, and then deriving the appropriate legal consequences by means of a logical conclusion.

However, such a simple procedure is never possible in reality. Discussions in court are in large parts devoted to pinning down whether certain concepts apply. The central arguments within these discussions are definitions or definition-like statements. Controversies arise because not all relevant concepts are defined within statutes, and because the terms used in legal definitions are often in need of clarification themselves. This is true for reasons of principle with evaluative concepts such as e.g. *significant* value. Such concepts cannot be captured by general descriptive definitions in advance of application. However, even relatively concrete descriptive concepts, such as *waters* in (2) often need to be supported by further definitions in courts' decisions. The definitions in (3) e.g. are quoted from a decision by the Higher Administrative Court of Hamburg. Sentence (3.1) fixes what generally counts as the *bed of a body of water* (a concept that is used in (2), but not defined in the Federal Water Act), and (3.2) states precisely how this definition is to be applied regarding the specific case of tubed ditches.

(3.1) *Unter einem Gewässerbett ist eine äußerlich erkennbare natürliche oder künstliche Begrenzung des Wassers in einer Eintiefung an der Erdoberfläche zu verstehen (vgl. BVerwG, Urt. v. 31.10.1975, BVerwGE Bd. 49 S. 293, 298; Beschl. v. 17.2.1969, Buchholz 445.4 § 1 WHG Nr. 3, m.w.N.).*

[A bed of a water is the discernible natural or artificial confined space of a water that is located below the surface of the earth.]

(3.2) *Von einem derartigen Bett kann u.a. dann nicht mehr gesprochen werden, wenn ein Graben vollständig verrohrt wird.*

[If a ditch is fully tubed, it cannot be called a bed of a water (...).]

Definitions in court decisions are generally open for later amendment or revision. As can be seen from the extensive amount of citation sources mentioned in (3.1), definitions are often re-used and remain binding beyond the case at hand. Easy access to definitions in decisions is thus of great importance to the legal practitioner. Judges need to know such definitions in order to achieve a uniform application of the law over longer periods of time, and lawyers may be provided with valuable arguments to make their clients' case. Finally, definition extraction is a prerequisite to building up an information system that allows concept-centered access to the interpretational knowledge spread over the tens of thousands of documents that are produced by courts every year.

Computational linguistic analysis helps answering this need. It enables efficient and accurate search methods for definition extraction in large document collections. Moreover it provides a structural level on which the extracted knowledge can be processed further in such a way that an information system can adequately answer the needs of its users.

1.2 Related work

Research on advanced information technology in the legal domain has up to now mostly been concerned with models for legal reasoning and with knowledge representation issues. One focus of interest has been legal ontologies. Most of the resources produced in this field are relatively small knowledge repositories that were hand-made by experts (for a summary of existing legal ontologies, cf. Valente 2005). However, it is evident that large legal knowledge-based applications will need automatic support for knowledge acquisition. This is especially true for large scale information access. Extensive conceptual indexation of just a fraction of all court decisions published in one year seems hardly possible without automatic methods.

Linguistic processing is generally regarded as one key technology for such purposes. However there has been relatively little research on the use of natural language processing in the legal domain (exceptions are Lame 2005; Saias and Quaresma 2005; and – to some degree – the European LOIS project (Dini et al. 2005)). This contrasts with the general picture in areas such as information/relation extraction, ontology learning, and question answering, where linguistically informed methods are well established. The techniques used there range from surface patterns (e.g. Soubbotin and Soubbotin 2001), over matching on phrase-chunked data (Hobbs et al.

1997; Hearst 1992) to full syntactic parsing as a pre-processing step (Gaizauskas et al 1995). By now, the focus of research in these fields has moved to generic models and methodologies for the acquisition of extraction rules based on linguistic structures (e.g. Stevenson and Greenwood 2006; Sudo et al. 2003). However, the mentioned tasks differ in important respects from the task of legal definition extraction that will be discussed in this paper:

- Many approaches in the above mentioned areas can rely on highly redundant information sources – in many cases the WWW (e.g. in Ravicahndran and Hovy 2002; Brill et al. 2001) – that help to deal with problems in the retrieval process. Redundancy as such may ease recall problems, and precision can be increased e.g. by trusting information better if it occurs more frequently. Such redundancy cannot be assumed for definitions in legal text. Pieces of information that occur only once when one specific case is solved can be of great importance as soon as a similar new case occurs.
- The typical extraction targets in information extraction and ontology learning are proper names, named entities, or short NPs, and relations between such items that are expressed using relatively unambiguous cue-phrases. No such restrictions apply for definition extraction. As will be discussed in section 3, definitions in our corpus are expressed by various, sometimes quite unspecific linguistic means. The definiens[2] is often a full subclause, and definienda are almost never proper names or named entities. Instead, they can be quite complex NPs including e.g. relative clauses.
- Question answering (q & a) systems use the question that is to be answered as the main source of information for the identification of relevant text passages (e.g. containing the definiendum specified in the question). For definitional q & a – studied mainly in connection with definition questions at several of the TREC-competitions (e.g. Xu et al 2004; Hildebrandt et al. 2004; Lin and Demner-Fushman 2005) – systems use additional features to identify answer candidates that might contain definitional information in a broad sense. In contrast, the ap-

2. We use the term *definiendum* to refer to the item that is defined, and the term definiens to denote the condition or description given to capture the meaning that is to be assigned to the definiendum

proach in this paper tries to identify explicit definitions in a narrower sense, but without looking for specific definienda.

The task of direct definition identification has been investigated up to now mainly for the domains of English technical documentation (e.g. Meyer 2001 and Pearson 1998; Storrer and Wellinghoff (2006) work with German text) and biomedical text (Klavans and Muresan 2001; Fahmi and Bouma 2006)). It will be argued in this paper that our application field poses special problems due to properties of German in general (such as its relatively flexible word order), and in particular due to the high degree of linguistic complexity in German legal language (see section 2.1).

1.3 Plan of the paper

In section 3, the corpus used for the research presented here is characterized. Moreover, statistical data on the characteristic syntactic complexity of German legal language are presented. Finally, the *Preds* parser (Braun 2003) is introduced. This parser is used as a pre-processing tool in our definition extraction system.

Section 4 discusses typical formulation patterns for definitions found in our corpus. In addition, a structural segmentation scheme is proposed. This scheme covers common subparts of many definitions and allows identifying the ways in which they are typically realized.

In section 5, it is shown how definition patterns are turned into extractor rules for a definition extraction system that processes parsed text. The section then evaluates three experiments with different sets of extractor rules and discusses the integration of machine learning techniques. A ranking function is acquired automatically and this improves the quality of extraction results. Finally, the topic of automatic acquisition of further extractor patterns is addressed.

Section 6 concludes and discusses prospects and problems for further processing stages setting up on a definition extraction system.

2. Corpus resources and parser

For the research that is discussed in this paper we use data provided by *juris GmbH*, Saarbrücken. *Juris* maintains a large collection of German court decisions. To serve as input for definition extraction, decision texts from this collection are parsed for topological structures and so called *partially resolved dependency structures* (*Preds*). *Preds* are predicate argument structures that employ default based underspecification to deal with attachment ambiguities. The first part of this section presents some characteristics of the corpus that we are using for our current experiments. The second part contains a description of the *Preds* parser (Braun 2003) and discusses some features and problems of parsing legal language.

2.1 Corpus

About 4 million cases are dealt with by German courts every year. The number of court decisions that are published in Germany every year may currently be estimated at about 30,000. A large (and increasing) portion of these are documented electronically e.g. by *juris GmbH* – their total collection comprises about 800,000 decisions, 27,939 of which were e.g. documented in 2004.

These numbers may seem small compared to the total number of 4 million cases. However, these 4 million cases include a large number of terminated legal proceedings that end for instance with an abandonment of action or lead to a settlement. Even with about 30,000 published decisions, the amounts of text involved are still enormous.

For our research purposes we currently have access to a corpus of 35,506 decisions. The corpus consists of all decisions documented by *juris* regarding environmental law in the years 1979 – 2001, all decisions with respect to administrative law from 1995, 1996 and 1997 as well as about 10,000 further decisions from other legal fields. An additional set of 40 decisions not belonging to any of these three collections was checked for definitions by three annotators in a pilot study (cf. section 3.1). Table 1 summarizes the contents of these four collections.[3] Although our corpus comprises only a fraction of the decisions documented by *juris*, it contains already a total of over 75 million tokens in more than 2 million sentences.

3. The environmental and the administrative law collection are not fully disjoint, about 1400 decisions occur in both of them. Some decisions in these two collections are documented in an abridged version of only a few sentences: however, about 65% are longer than 5 sentences. The Various-collection contains only full text documents that are in neither of the two other collections.

Table 1. Contents of corpora

Collection	Decisions	Total sentences	Total tokens	Tokens / Sentences in relevant parts
Envir. 1979–2001	9,226	568,437	18,164,024	14,342,888 / 418,691
Admin. 1995–1997	17,829	934,054	30,382,448	22,383,618 / 638,529
Various	9,884	875,478	26,615,327	21,335,022 / 655,186
Pilot study	40	4,799	162,207	127,151 /3,509

The work in this paper uses the pilot study subcorpus as a resource for heuristic orientation (mainly in section 4). The environmental law subcorpus provides the basis for a large scale evaluation in section 4.2; this subcorpus is split into test data and training data for the machine-learning experiments discussed in section 4.3

Not all parts of a court decision are equally relevant for the purpose of extracting definitions. Large passages written in (comparably) non-technical language are typically devoted to the description of the facts of the case. The judge separates these passages from the actual legal argumentation and gathers them in a section of their own under the standardized heading *Tatbestand.* The last column in Table 1 refers to the contents of all sections apart from the *Tatbestand,* which has also been excluded from consideration for the investigations discussed in this paper.

The documents in our corpus are plain text files. These are pre-processed by a module that recognizes document structure and extracts certain types of metadata (e.g. the reference number of each decision). All textual document parts except for the *Tatbestand* sections are then given to a sentence boundary recognizer and finally to the parser described in section 2.2. Up to now, all decisions in the pilot study, the environmental law and the administrative law collections have been parsed.

2.2 The *Preds* parser

2.2.1 Parser and target structures

Before the documents in our corpus are input to the definition extraction component that is described in section 3, they are parsed using the *Preds* parser. The *Preds* parser (*Preds* stands for *partially resolved dependency structure*) is a semantically-oriented parsing system that has been developed in the Saarbrücken Computational Linguistics Department within the project COLLATE. It was used there for information extraction from newspaper text (Fliedner 2004).

The *Preds* parser balances depth of linguistic analysis with robustness of the analysis process and is therefore able to provide relatively detailed linguistic information even for large amounts of syntactically complex text. The *Preds* format encodes semantic dependencies and modification relations within a sentence using abstract categories such as deep subject and deep object. In this way it provides a common normalized structure for various surface realizations of the same content (e.g. in active or passive voice). Representation formats such as *Preds* are particularly well suited for automatic information access in free text. On the one hand they can be calculated robustly and in reasonable processing time, e.g. by combining multiple shallow processors. On the other hand they abstract away from much of the surface variation in language that is not actually crucial for the core content. This provides a uniform input for subsequent information access components to act on, and e.g. allows the use of relatively few concise search patterns to retrieve a variety of different sentences that express the same type of information.

The *Preds* parser generates a semantic representation of the input by a cascade of analysis components. Starting with a topological analysis of the input sentence, it continues by applying a phrase chunker and a named entity recognizer to the contents of the topological fields. The resulting extended topological structure is transformed to the *Preds*, a dependency-based semantic representation, by a series of heuristic rules. The *Preds* parser returns an XML-tree that contains the semantic (*Preds*) structure together with the full linguistic information accumulated during the analysis process. Figure 1 shows the parse for the definition in example (4).

(4) *Bei einem Einfamilienreihenhaus liegt ein mangelhafter Schallschutz dann vor, wenn die Haustrennwand einschalig errichtet wurde (…) (OLG Stuttgart, 22.11.1995, 1 U 199/93, juris)*

[In a semi-detached house, a one-layered separating wall means insufficient noise insulation]

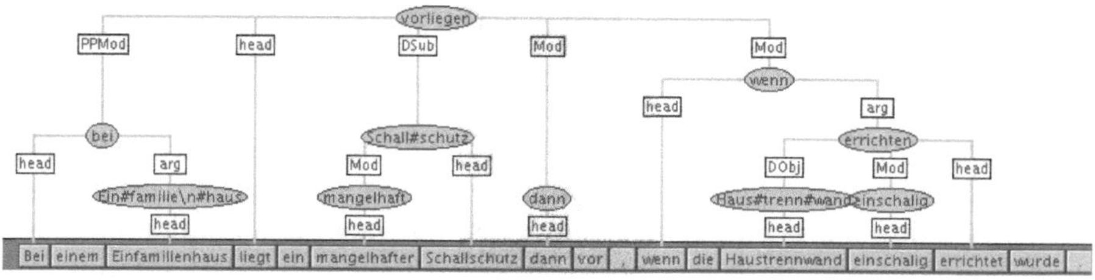

Figure 1. Grammatical structure for example (4)[4]

To deal with the problem of ambiguity, the *Preds* parser makes use of syntactic underspecification. It systematically prefers low attachment and marks the affected parts of the result as default-based. Similarly, default categories such as nominal argument are assigned when the parser finds a phrase and the head that it depends on, but does not recognize the type of the dependency. This increases robustness and efficiency of the parsing process because the parser does not need to pursue alternative analyses. Moreover, subsequent components (such as a definition extraction module) can access common parts of multiple readings without having to enumerate and search through all alternative representations (although it remains possible in principle to resolve ambiguities and enrich parses based on further information).

2.2.2 *Parser performance on legal text*

The linguistic complexity of legal text is much higher than in many other fields of language use, as indicated by the figures discussed in the previous section. It therefore cannot be taken for granted that a parser that has been developed for processing newspaper text will perform equally well on legal texts. Extreme sentence length alone gives rise to performance issues such as timeouts and resource problems with many parsing systems. Moreover, the potential for parser errors rises with syntactic complexity, when for instance more possibilities for wrong attachments become available with a higher number of embedding levels in a sentence.

Additionally, in order to process specialized language, parsers generally need to be able to deal with specific types of named entities that are typical

4. This figure (as well as figure 2) was generated using the SALSA-Tool (Burchardt et al. 2006).

of the respective area of specialization. The most frequent expressions of this kind in court decisions are *legal quotes*, i.e. references to statutes, other decisions or legal commentaries. Citation information is sometimes given parenthetically, but is frequently also integrated into the syntactic structure as a standard noun phrase. References in part conform to established schemes using abbreviations and numbers, but may also contain common language descriptions of e.g. documents and their parts. The reference in example (5) is part of a prepositional phrase and consists of a formal reference to a section of the Aliens act, which is coordinated with the common language description *der dazu erlassenen Anordnung (the issued directive)* using the (standardized) abbreviation *i.V.m.* (*in Verbindung mit* – in connection with)

(5) *Aufenthaltsbefugnis nach § 32 AuslG i.V.m. der dazu erlassenen Anordnung*

[Permit of residence according to § 32 AuslG in connection with the issued directive]

The *Preds* parser treats such *legal quotes* along with other named entities, but according to a specialized subgrammar. This grammar is a recursive-descent grammar describing various quotation schemes based on a gazetteer with full names and abbreviations of courts, codes and legal journals (currently more than 10,000 entries). Recall is relatively high for references to court decisions and sections of codes (87% of a test set of about 200 items were recognized correctly). References to commentaries are a lot harder to identify because they are much less regular and very often contain parts that are formulated in natural language.

In order to assess the general performance of the *Preds* parser, 100 sentences from two court decisions were annotated with dependency-triples (i.e. triples that contain headword, dependency type and dependent for each dependency in a sentence) by two annotators. A gold standard was then constructed by merging these two annotations. Of the 1839 dependency-triples in this gold standard, 1088 were recognized correctly by the *Preds* parser (a recall of about 59%) if underspecified representations were allowed to match freely with their correct resolutions. 611 of the 1,699 dependencies assumed by the *Preds* parser were wrong (a precision of 64%). This amounts to an F-score of about 61.5 %.[5]

These figures are not optimal. However, it is unlikely that better performance can be achieved by using other parsing systems without considerable additional efforts. To our knowledge, there is no other German parser that is able to process legal quote expressions at all, and this requirement is indispensable for parsing court decisions. Large coverage parsers moreover often employ statistical models and would need to be re-trained on annotated legal text to be used for our purposes, but no syntactically annotated corpora are available in this area. We tested the *Sleepy* statistical parser (Dubney (2005), trained on the *Tiger* corpus) and an LFG-parser with a German grammar (Dipper 2003; Maxwell and Kaplan 1991) developed in the framework of the Xerox Linguistic Environment on our pilot study data. Both systems were used out of the box, without any additional preprocessing to deal with legal quote expressions. *Sleepy* returned a parse for 2,453 of the 3,509 sentences, the LFG-system only for 1,025. The *Preds* parser is able to process 3,105 sentences.[6]

Because *Sleepy* and the LFG-system were in no way adapted to legal text, the reported figures are probably not a fair basis for comparison, and it may well be worth trying to supplement different parsing systems with legal-text specific processing-capabilities. Unfortunately, the legal quote-processing component of the *Preds* parser cannot readily be plugged into different systems. Adding similar functionality to other parsers would therefore probably require significant development work.

Manual inspection of wrong *Preds* parses and sentences without a parse suggests that also for this parser, incomplete or incorrect recognition of legal quotes is still a very frequent source of errors. The main reason for this is that unrecognized material from legal quotes is falsely integrated into the parse tree at later stages. We therefore assume that the *Preds* parser needs refinements in the legal-quote subgrammar of the named entity recognizer.

---

5. See footnote 7 below for an explanation of the terms *precision* and *recall*. F-scores combine precision and recall into one value.

6. I.e., *Preds* solved 87.5 % of the collection. With improvements in sentence boundary recognition, the proportion increases to 92%. Due to the large number of uncommon abbreviations and numbering methods, sentence boundary recognition is a non-trivial task in legal text. The rule-based general-purpose sentenizer that we use should best be supplemented by a data driven method as described in Kiss and Strunk (2006).

3. Analysis of definitions in our corpora

This section discusses a classification of typical linguistic definition patterns based on observations made on our pilot study corpus. The next section will then show how such linguistic patterns can be turned into extraction rules for a definition extraction system.

The concept of a definition is itself relatively hard to define. Most sentences can be seen as usage examples for the concepts that they contain, and thus as partly definitional. Moreover, the text of court decisions is inherently normative, backed by the authority of courts. Any specific usage of a concept by a court is therefore also a determination of its future usage. This power to define is regulated by the hierarchy of courts as well as the rules of legal interpretation. In legal philosophy, the view of law as *open texture* (Hart 1961) emphasizes the general importance of such continuous adaptation of concepts in use for the functioning of legal systems.

On the other hand, it is clear that not all sentences in a court decision that mention a particular concept are equally good search results for a user who is looking up a definition in a legal database. In order to be relevant from the user's point of view, a search result should be intended as a definition by the author, and it should warrant a transfer to the user's own case. In some cases, the author's intention can only be derived from a large context together with domain specific knowledge. It may for instance be necessary to know about the role of a statement in an argumentation to realize that it is a definition. In many cases, however, statements are marked as definitions by linguistic means, such as certain sentence predicates. If a statement is marked in this way, and is abstract and general or prototypical (these properties can for instance often be recognized from specific patterns of determiner use or certain adverbs), it is likely to provide useful general information about a concept. We will regard such statements as definitions in the narrow sense.

3.1 Annotation of the pilot study corpus

In order to assess the proportion and structures of linguistically marked definitions in legal text, we conducted an annotation study on 40 court decisions from various legal fields (the collection referred to above as pilot study). The full text of 20 of these decisions was examined and text passages with definitions were marked by three annotators (two computational linguists and one post-graduate law student). Based on this data, a simple

XML-based annotation scheme was devised and the full collection was annotated using this scheme.

The annotation scheme covers definitions that consist of one sentence or multiple sentences. Definitions are to be classified as *sure* or *unsure* according to the annotator's confidence in his decision. Inside definitions, occurrences of the defined term and elements indicating the presence of a definition (cf. 3.2) are marked. Additionally, each sentence within a definition is tagged as either CORE, ADDITION, or DEFINIENDUM according to its function. A CORE sentence has strictly definitional content. It must be self-contained to capture an essential feature of the defined concept. ADDITION-sentences in contrast depend on CORE information (either expressed in a sentence or left implicit) in various ways, for instance by providing elaborations. They are relatively poor sources of information on the definiendum if taken on their own, but may provide important details or clarifications. Example (6) illustrates the two functions:

(6.1) *Eine Rundfunksendung iSv UrhG AUT §§ 17, 59a liegt immer schon dann vor, wenn ein Werk mit Hilfe von Hertzschen Wellen innerhalb der Reichweite dieser Wellen jedem wahrnehmbar gemacht wird, der sich eines entsprechenden Empfangsgeräts bedient.*

[A broadcast in the meaning of UrhG AUT §§ 17, 59a is given if a piece of work is made perceivable by everyone who uses a receiver for Hertzian waves.]

(6.2) *Gleichgültig ist, ob die Sendung auch wirklich wahrgenommen wird; es genügt, daß die Möglichkeit hierzu geboten wird. (Oberster Gerichtshof Wien, 13.November 2001, AZ 4 Ob 182/01w, juris)*

[It does not matter whether the broadcast is actually perceived; the possibility to perceice it is sufficient.]

Sentence (6.1) is a CORE sentence. It states a sufficient condition for the application of the concept *Rundfunksendung* (*broadcast*). Sentence (6.2) is an ADDITION. It ponders and rejects a stricter condition and then refines the one given in (6.1).

The tag DEFINIENDUM is used to mark up sentences that do not actually contain definitional information, but mention a definiendum that is then referred to anaphorically in subsequent CORE or ADDITION sentences.

Within the 4,799 sentences of the 40 documents that were examined, a total of 123 definitions were found, only one of them in a *Tatbestand-*

section. Of the 123 found definitions, 83 are one sentence long, the other 40 range from two to five sentences.

87 definitions were marked as *sure*. All 87 sure definitions contain at least one CORE sentence (in two cases there are two CORE sentences). In three of the 36 *unsure* cases, no CORE sentence was marked. Since it is less clear in these cases if the given information is actually definitional at all, it is not surprising that some of these passages contain no part that provides CORE applicability conditions.

In seven cases the definiendum is not referred to at all in any of the CORE sentences, but is mentioned in a preceding sentence. In eight further cases, the definiendum is mentioned before the CORE sentence and then referred to anaphorically, twice by definite NPs containing the definiendum itself, otherwise by pronouns. In all other cases, the first occurrence of the definiendum is within a CORE sentence.

3.2 Indication of definitions

The definitions identified in our pilot study can be divided into two classes, according to the means used to mark them as definitions and to establish the relation between definiens and definiendum:

1. Predicate-based: The relation between definiens and definiendum is established by the clause-level predicate.
2. Paratactic: The definiens is somewhere in the environment of the definiendum, but is not related to it through a common clause level predicate.

Predicate based definitions form by far the larger class. Of the 123 definitions in our pilot study corpus, 94 contained a sentence with a predicate marking the definition. Only 31 definitions contained a parenthetical definitions sentence (two multi-sentence definitions included both types). The proportion remains almost the same if only CORE sentence and *sure* cases of definitions are considered.

In predicate-based definitions, the presence of a definition is indicated by the sentence predicate together with a certain pattern of complements and/or adjuncts. These complements and adjuncts then correspond to definiens, definiendum, and other structural definition subparts. For instance the verb *vorliegen* (to be present) is used to express a definition of its subject. The definiens is expressed either by a conditional clause or as a *bei*-PP with a relative clause, as in the following example (7):

(7) *Ein durch einen Unglücksfall verursachter öffentlicher Notstand liegt nur bei einem Gefahren- oder Schadensereignis vor, das die Allgemeinheit unmittelbar betrifft. (Verwaltungsgerichtshof Baden-Württemberg 1. Senat, 7.Dezember 1992, AZ 1 S 2079/92, juris)*

[A public state of emergency caused by an accident is given only due to a dangerous or damaging event that affects the general public directly.]

Certain predicative adjectives (such as *erforderlich* – required) as well as combinations of certain nouns with function verbs or the copula *sein* (e.g. *Voraussetzung* + *sein* – prerequisite + to be) may also be more or less reliable indicators of definitions.

The copula *sein* (be) itself frequently indicates a definition when coupled with a modified NP as a predicative noun. This large subgroup of predicate-based definitions (31 of the 94 predicate-based definitions observed in our pilot study were copula constructions) corresponds syntactically to the well known Aristotelian scheme of a *definition by proximate gender and specific difference.* In such sentences, the subject is typically the definiendum, the head noun of the predicative NP denotes a superclass of the definiendum, and the modifier (often a relative clause) within this NP specifies an additional property. An example of this pattern is the following sentence (8) that defines *Klärschlamm* (sewage mud) as a subconcept of substance with the specific property that it stems from the treatment of sewage water.

(8) *Klärschlamm iS der AbfKlärV ist diejenige Substanz, die bei der Behandlung von Abwasser in Abwasserbehandlungsanlagen anfällt. (Oberverwaltungsgericht Rheinland-Pfalz 7. Senat, 12.April 1991, AZ 7 B 10080/91, juris)*

[Sewage mud as understood in AbfKlärV is the substance which results from the treatment of sewage water in sewage water treatment plants.]

A number of verbs, nouns and adjectives quite reliably mark the presence of a definition in virtue of their standard meaning. Other items are not perfectly reliable as definition indicators. For instance, it is obvious that the verb *sein* (be) is frequently used as a predicate in contingent, non-definitional statements. In other cases, the predicate chosen for a definition is specific to the given definiendum, such as in (9):

(9) *Die in Art. 5 Abs. 1 Satz 2 GG verbürgte Pressefreiheit schützt die Eigenständigkeit der Presse von der Beschaffung der Information bis zur Verbreitung der Nachrichten und Meinungen. (BVerfG 1. Senat 1. Kammer, 13.September 2001, AZ 1 BvR 1398/01, juris)*

[The freedom of the press as established in Art. 5 Abs. 1 Satz 2 GG protects the autonomy of the press, starting from gathering information up to the distribution of news and opinions.]

The verb *schützen* (protect) can be used to state a definition in this case only because the concept *freedom of the press* is standardly defined through the purpose of the norms that are related to it. In most other cases, *schützen* does not indicate a definition. It may require significant legal background knowledge to decide with certainty whether a given sentence expresses a definition in such cases. Such knowledge is of course not available to an automatic definition extraction system. However, the presence of additional weak definition indicators such as certain cue words or patterns of determiner use may make an automatic decision possible even in such cases of doubt.

Paratactic definitions employ a range of linguistic and paralinguistic means to establish the connection between definiendum and definiens. For instance, either may be mentioned in brackets or as an apposition along with the other (often introduced by abbreviated formulaic phrases such as *sog. – so called*) as in the following example:

(10) *...Fluchtgründe, die erst mit oder nach Verlassen des Herkunftslandes begründet werden (sog. Nachfluchtgründe)...*

[... reasons for fleeing which are given while or after fleeing the country (so called post-fleeing reasons)]

The definiens may also be attached to the definiendum as a non-restrictive relative clause or as an *als* (*as*)-introduced noun phrase. In other cases a whole sentence functions as a definiens for a concept in the preceding sentence. This is the case in (11), where the entire second sentence provides the definiens for the definiendum *lacks need for legal protection.*

(11) *... fehlt der Beschwerde der Antragsgegnerin das Rechtsschutzbedürfnis. Sie kann ihre Rechtsstellung im Beschwerdeverfahren nicht mehr verbessern. (Bayerischer Verwaltungsgerichtshof München 22. Senat, 18.Juni 2002, AZ 22 CE 02.815, juris)*

[... the appeal of the defendant lacks need for legal protection. In the appellate procedure, she cannot improve her legal status.]

Paratactic definitions are generally less informative than predicate-based definitions about the relation that holds between definiendum and definiens. In (10), for instance, the definiendum can be substituted for the definiens, while the definiens in (11) states a sufficient condition. In other cases, the definiendum is a "shortcut" that can be used to refer to some situation or regulation described in the definiens, but is not simply substitutable for the definiens in all contexts. This is the case in (12), where the term *Drittstaatenregelung* is mentioned after a lengthy description of the contents of that regulation. However, the term cannot be used interchangeably with that description if only for syntactic reasons.

(12) *Auf das Asylrecht des Art. 16a Abs. 1 GG kann sich gemäß Art. 16a Abs. 2 Satz 1 GG, § 26a Abs. 1 Sätze 1 und 2 AsylVfG nicht berufen, wer aus einem Mitgliedstaat der Europäischen Gemeinschaften oder aus einem anderen Drittstaat einreist, in dem die Anwendung des Abkommens über die Rechtsstellung der Flüchtlinge und der Konvention zum Schutze der Rechtsstellung der Flüchtlinge und der Konvention zum Schutze der Menschenrechte und Grundfreiheiten sichergestellt ist (sog. Drittstaatenregelung). (Sächsisches Oberverwaltungsgericht 4. Senat, 28.August 2001, AZ A 4 B 4388/99, juris)*

[In accordance with Art. 16a (...) persons cannot appeal to the right of asylum (...) if they enter from a member state of the EC or from another state in which the application of the agreement over the legal status of refugees and the convention for the protection of human rights and fundamental freedoms is guaranteed (so-called third state rule).]

From the perspective of automated processing, paratactic definitions pose two further problems. Firstly, the means by which definiens and definiendum are connected are highly unspecific – the use of parentheses or nonrestrictive relative clauses for instance is in no way particular to definitions.

Secondly, there is no general way of identifying the text spans that correspond to the subparts of a given paratactic definition.

The observations made in our pilot study suggest that most paratactic definitions either group with (10), which could be recognized and processed using shallow methods such as regular-expression search and NP chunking, or would require significant semantic and legal knowledge for this purpose, such as (11) and (12). Our research therefore focuses on processing predicate-based definitions, a task for which syntactic-semantic structure provides an adequate level.

3.3 Structure of predicate-based definitions

Predicate-based definitions display a range of common structural elements that are connected to typical linguistic realizations. We will illustrate this with the example definition in (4), repeated below (with an interlinear translation):

(4) *[$_4$ Bei einem Einfamilienreihenhaus] [$_3$ liegt] ein [$_1$ mangelhafter Schallschutz] [$_3$ dann] [$_3$ vor, wenn] [$_2$ die Haustrennwand einschalig errichtet wurde].*

[[$_4$ In a semi-detached house] [$_1$ insufficient noise insulation] [$_3$ is given if] [$_2$ the separating wall is one-layered].]

This definition consists of:

1. The *definiendum*, i.e. the element that is defined (*unzureichender Schallschutz* – insufficient noise insulation).
2. The *definiens*, i.e. the element that fixes the meaning of the definiendum (*die Haustrennwand einschalig errichtet wurde* – the separating wall is one-layered).
3. A *connector*, indicating the relation between definiendum and definiens (*liegt ...dann ... vor, wenn, "is given if"*). Normally, the connector contains at least the predicate of the main clause, often together with further material (a subjunction, a relative pronoun, a determiner). It does not only indicate the presence of a definition, it also determines how definiens and definiendum are realized linguistically, and it often contains information about the type of definition (full, partial, by examples, etc.). A common pattern realizes the definiendum as the subject, and the definiens within a sub-

clause. Templates for combinations of connectors with variables for the definiendum and definiens slots will provide the basis for the primary search mechanism used in our definition extraction system.

Apart from the constitutive parts just introduced, the cited definition contains an optional element:

4. A qualification specifying a *domain area* of applicability, i.e. a restriction in terms of that part of reality that is referred to in the regulation (*Einfamilienreihenhäusern* – semi-detached houses).

The domain area is often specified by a PP introduced by *bei* as in the example. Further possibilities are other PPs or certain subclauses. Signal words may be particles (*dann* in the example), adverbs (e.g. *begrifflich* – conceptually) or transparent nominal constructions containing the definiendum (e.g. *der Begriff des...* – the concept of...).

Many definitions also contain further structural elements that are not present in example (3). For instance hedges such as certain adverbials or modal verbs modify the force, validity or degree of commitment to a definition. The *field of law* within which the given definition applies is often specified as a PP containing a formal reference to sections of statutes or simply the name of a statute, document, or even a complete legal field (e.g. *Umweltrecht* – environmental law). Citation information for definitions is standardly included in brackets as a reference to another verdict by date, court, and reference number, but may also occur as a full NP or PP.

As mentioned in section 3.2, many definitions can be analyzed according to the classical Aristotelian scheme of definition by *proximate gender and specific difference* In terminological research, such definitions are also called *formal* (e.g. Trimble 1985; Flowerdew 1992; Pearson 1998). The original requirements for definitions imposed by Aristotle are usually not met. The employed gender term may be very unspecific rather than the true proximate gender of the definiendum, and it is often hard to tell whether the given difference is actually *the* specific difference, or just one out of many ways of characterizing the definiendum. Regardless of these ontological problems, splitting the definiens of such definitions further into a superconcept of the definiendum, and a condition on that superconcept gives access to interesting taxonomical information. Certain connector verbs (in particular the copula *sein* (*be*)) are typical of definitions that clearly display this Aristotelian structure in their syntax. In the copula-based prototypical realization of this scheme (cf. example (8)), the predicative noun states the superconcept and a restrictive relative clause gives the condition. The condition is also sometimes specified by modifiers such as attributive adjectives or prepositional phrases.

Aristotelian definitions may also be 'hidden' in formulations that do not syntactically match the scheme just described. The superconcept may be expressed verbally, and the condition as an adverbial modifier, such as in (13).

(13) *Eine Beeinträchtigung des Naturhaushaltes und des Landschaftsbildes liegt immer dann vor, wenn Natur und Landschaft in einer Weise nachteilig verändert werden, die nach Art, Umfang oder Schwere nicht als völlig unwesentlich angesehen werden kann. (Verwaltungsgerichtshof Baden-Württemberg 7. Senat, 21. Mai 1980, AZ VII 1657/79, juris)*

[The ecosystem and the landscape are damaged whenever nature is adversely affected in a way which, according to kind, extent, or degree, cannot be regarded as completely insignificant.]

If this definition is reformulated by using the deverbal noun *Veränderung* instead of the verb *verändern* (*affect*), it fits the Aristotelian scheme without any further changes. In other cases, the superconcept is not specified at all; however it can either be supplemented from context or even be inferred from the sentence itself, such as in (14).

(14) *Danach liegt Massentierhaltung vor, wenn die Zahl von 250 Mastschweinen oder 150 Mastkälbern oder 150 Jungmastrindern überschritten wird. (Bayerischer Verwaltungsgerichtshof München 22. Senat, 13.Juni 1996, AZ 22 N 93.2863, juris)*

[Intensive animal husbandry is given if the number of 250 piglets or 150 calves or 150 young bulls is exceeded.]

This definition of the term *Massentierhaltung* (intensive animal husbandry) omits the superconcept *Tierhaltung* (animal husbandry). However, this superconcept can be derived easily because it is the base noun of the compound definiendum.

An automatic identification of superconcept and condition will generally only be possible if both parts are actually present in a sentence and are realized prototypically. Optional elements in definitions (such as *domain area* or *modification*) will be identifiable if they are expressed according to typical schemes. If such definition subparts can be identified, this information can be used at various later stages within a definition extraction system: First, to improve the definition search itself, e.g. to calculate a ranking on the results of the actual extraction process. Second, to transform search results into a structured resource, e.g. an ontology that contains concept-subconcept links between defined terms and records metadata on the validity of found definitions.

3.4 Defined parts of speech

All examples of predicate-based definitions given above contain nominal definienda. Obviously, other parts of speech would require different formulation patterns for their definition, because they could not fulfill the grammatical functions of nominals. In our pilot study, only one kind of predicate-based definition with non-nominal definienda occurred more than once. These were definitions in which adjectives were defined in their predicative use, such as in (15):

(15) *Sachdienlich ist eine Klageänderung in der Regel dann, wenn sie der endgültigen Ausräumung des sachlichen Streits zwischen den Beteiligten im laufenden Verfahren dient. (VG Berlin 1. Kammer, 4.Juli 2001, AZ 1 A 389.00, juris)*

[An amendment of a legal action is usually pertinent if it serves to put an end to the controversy between the parties of the ongoing proceedings.]

In order to determine if this observation reflects the general distribution of different parts of speech as definienda (respectively as heads of definienda) in legal text, we examined 640 terms from the *juris*-definition index, a small and fragmentary index that records defined expressions within a small portion of the decisions collected by *juris*. It turns out that the vast majority of terms are nominal. Table 2 summarizes our observations:

Table 2. Defined parts of speech in the juris definition index

POS of head of phrase	Frequency
Noun	617
Verb	4
Adjective	12
Adverb	7

A closer look at the 617 nominal index terms shows that 173 of the nominal heads are derived: 39 are nominalized infinitives, 129 are *–ung*-derivations from verbs and 9 are *–keit/–heit*-derived nominalizations of adjectives (not counting lexicalized derivations). This suggests that even if a term may have a non-nominal base form, its definition is likely to use a nominal derivation instead.

4. Definition extraction

4.1 Design and application of extraction patterns

In order to extract sentences from a corpus by formulation patterns like the ones discussed in the previous section, these patterns have to be transformed to a format that allows using them as executable queries. In our case, this means that identified patterns have to be re-formulated so that *Preds*-structures can be matched against them efficiently. The *Preds* parser has XML-structures as output. Specifying *Preds* fragments in terms of XPath-expressions therefore is an intuitive way of formulating search templates that are at the same time executable directly using off-the-shelf tools such as the GNU LibXML- and LibXSLT-libraries. This section introduces the XPath-based search template format used in our definition extraction system. It is shown how search templates are specified and applied.

The example in (4) instantiates the definition pattern *vorliegen + wenn-subclause*. The parse tree produced by the *Preds* parser for this example is displayed in figure 1. In the previous section we discussed the various structural subparts of the definition. Figure 2 illustrates how these subparts correspond to nodes in the *Preds* parse.

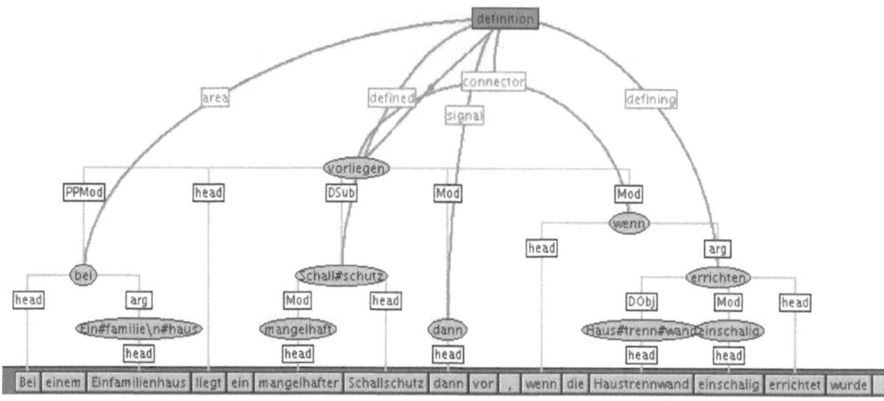

Figure 2. Structural analysis of the definition in (4)

To identify sentences such as (4) in our corpora, the XML-structures produced by the *Preds* parser for all sentences are first matched against the following XPath-expression:

```
sent[parse/Preds/descendant::word[@stem="vorliegen"
  and attrs/ind and not(attrs/past)
  and Mod[word[@stem="wenn" and @pos="subj"]
    |word[@pos="conj"]/arg/word[@stem="wenn"and pos="subj"]]
  and DSub]]
```

This expression selects all clause-level predicate nodes that have the stem *vorliegen* in indicative present tense, have a subject and are modified by a subclause introduced by the subjunction *wenn*, or by a conjunction of such subclauses.

Once such definition predicates have been identified, the nodes corresponding to the various structural elements can be addressed by paths starting from the predicate node. The top node of the definiendum will for instance be selected by the path `DSub/word`. Information about a subset of the definition parts discussed in 3.3 is added to the extracted structure by such additional path-expressions after successful retrieval.

In order to avoid unnecessary reduplication of elements that are common to different patterns, we do not specify extraction patterns using full XPath-expressions in practice. Instead we use a condensed pattern specification language. This language allows defining larger numbers of patterns by combining a number of separately specified common definition-bearing syntactic frames (such as the combination *subject and wenn-subclause*) and mappings (e.g. *subject-to-definiendum and wenn-subclause-to-definiens*) with lists of lemmata of potential definition predicates. This flexibility is especially helpful for development purposes, where many different patterns have to be specified and tested. Section 4.4 discusses the potential of a generate-and-test approach to semi-automatic pattern acquisition by exploring the full combinatorics of definition-bearing frames and lemmata.

Figure 3 illustrates how the *liegt vor*, *wenn*-pattern is represented using the condensed specification format, along with various other instantiations of the required predicate and the alternative syntactic frame "subject and *bei*-PP" (note that this frame is combined with a mapping that identifies a superconcept and a condition instead of an unanalyzed definiens):

```
<pattern>
 <key>vorliegen, bestehen, erforderlich</key>
  <frames>
     <frame id="DSub-Wenn">
        <mapping id="DSub:defined_cond:defining_1"/>
        <condition>INDPRES</condition>
     </frame>
     <frame id="DSub-PP:Rcl" args="PREP:bei">
        <mapping id=" DSub:defined_PP:superconcept_PPRCl:
         condition" args="PREP:bei"/>
        <condition>INDPRES</condition>
  </frame>
 </frames>
</pattern>
```

Figure 3. Extraction rule for *liegt vor*, *wenn*-definitions and others

Both syntactic frames referenced in this pattern specification do not contain the present tense and indicative mood attributes. These are specified as further conditions. Other conditions, for instance on the surface order of subject and subclause, can be specified in the same way. The condensed pattern specifications are then translated into collections of full XPaths and the actual matching of XPath-expressions on *Preds*-structures is carried out using generated XSLT-Scripts.

4.2 Evaluation

This section evaluates a series of extraction experiments. The precision[7] of a first experimental set of extractor patterns (extractor pattern set 1) was evaluated on a subcorpus of 6000 decisions from our environmental law corpus. Our pilot study corpus was then used to assess the performance of these patterns in terms of recall. After a detailed investigation of the recall problems identified in this experiment, an extended and refined set of patterns (extractor pattern set 2) was compiled. These patterns were again tested on the pilot study data and the environmental law corpus.

Both pattern sets were compiled based on expert knowledge (in co-operation with a trained jurist). Patterns 1 were designed with a focus on precise extraction and therefore incorporate a number of generic and pattern specific filtering rules (e.g. constraints on determiners and ordering of definition subparts, stopword lists). This approach turned out to be too restrictive. Pattern set 2 therefore not only contains further patterns based on observations from the pilot study data, but also does away with any hard-coded filtering mechanisms. Patterns 2 perform considerably better than patterns 1 in terms of recall. Not surprisingly, however, evaluation on the environmental law corpus revealed that this gain in recall means a loss in precision.

The rest of this section gives more detail on the evaluation results obtained for the two different pattern sets. The next section then shows how automatic classification techniques can be used to induce a ranking that improves the mentioned loss in precision.

---

7. Precision scores measure the proportion of true positives within the total results of a search. Recall scores compare the number of true positive search results to the total number of target items. A precision score of 1 for a search thus means that the result set consists only of target items, but says nothing about the number of target items that were not retrieved. A recall score of 1 indicates that all target items have been found, but the result set may contain additional irrelevant items.

4.2.1 Extractor pattern set 1

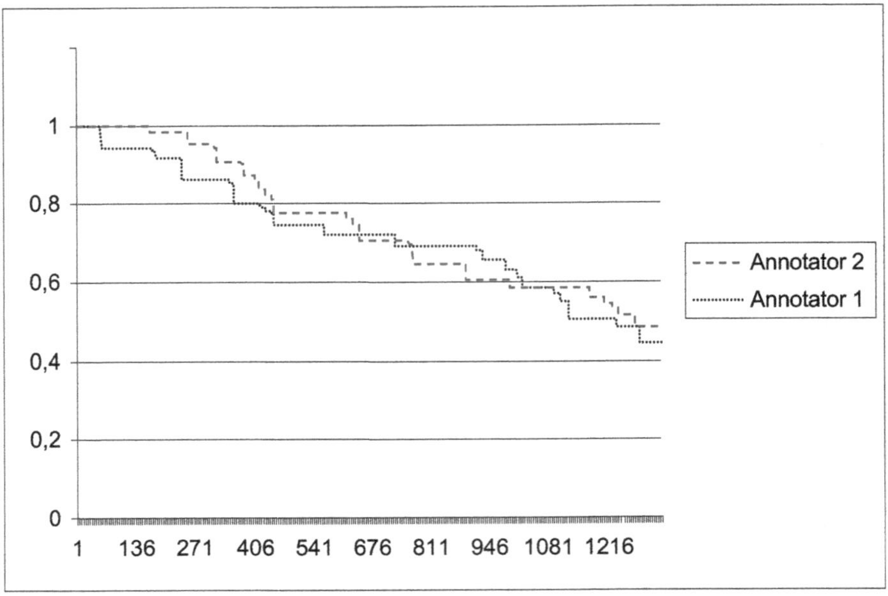

Figure 4. Precision scores for patterns 1 on environmental law corpus

Extractor pattern set 1 consists of 33 patterns. Walter and Pinkal (2006) contains a detailed discussion of evaluation results for these patterns to 6,000 decisions from our environmental law corpus (237,935 sentences, the subcorpus that had been parsed at that time). A total of 1,342 sentences were extracted in this experiment. A double annotation was performed on 492 sentences from this result set (the annotation was later extended to a total of 546 sentences) by one graduate law student and one computational linguist. The sentences to be annotated were selected randomly, but balanced over the various patterns. Annotation consisted in a *yes-no*-decision. As a rough guideline, the annotators were asked to state for each sentence whether it was likely to be useful for deciding about the application of the definiendum in a reasonable number of cases. The overall agreement of the annotators' judgements was relatively high in spite of the vagueness of this instruction, with κ=0.71 on the full 546 annotated sentences.[8]

8. Cohen's κ coefficient is a measure of inter-annotator agreement that also accounts for the probability of chance agreement. A value of 1 corresponds to full

Based on the annotated hits, precision estimates were calculated for each pattern. The precision estimates for the different patterns varied considerably. Figure 4 gives an overview of the estimated maximum precision achievable for an increasing number of retrieved hits. It is obtained by sorting all extraction results according to the precision estimate for their respective retrieving pattern, and then calculating the overall precision within each top-*n*-segment of this ordering.[9]

The median of the estimated precision for n retrieved hits (e.g. the precision at which half of all hits can be retrieved) is above 70% according to both annotators (71.9% according to annotator 1, 70.8% according to annotator 2).

4.2.2 Evaluation on the pilot study corpus

In a second experiment, we used our first extractor pattern set to extract definitions from our pilot study corpus and performed a detailed analysis of the reasons for the recall failures on that data. One obvious reason is the relatively small number of patterns in our extractor set 1. We were able to devise a number of further extractor patterns based on our observations in this experiment. Our observations further allowed us to correct errors and introduce generalizations within some patterns. Additionally, all filtering mechanisms were removed. The resulting pattern set 2 consists of 59 extractor patterns. While patterns 1 retrieve 27 of the total verified 93 predicate-based CORE definitions in the pilot study data, patterns 2 extract 42 of them.

---

agreement while a value ≤ 0 indicates that the agreement is no larger than would be expected by chance.

9. This also means that the precision values that can be taken from the diagram are estimates that are based on more data from left to right. The rightmost point corresponds to the total precision score for all of the annotated results and is thus the most reliable estimate.

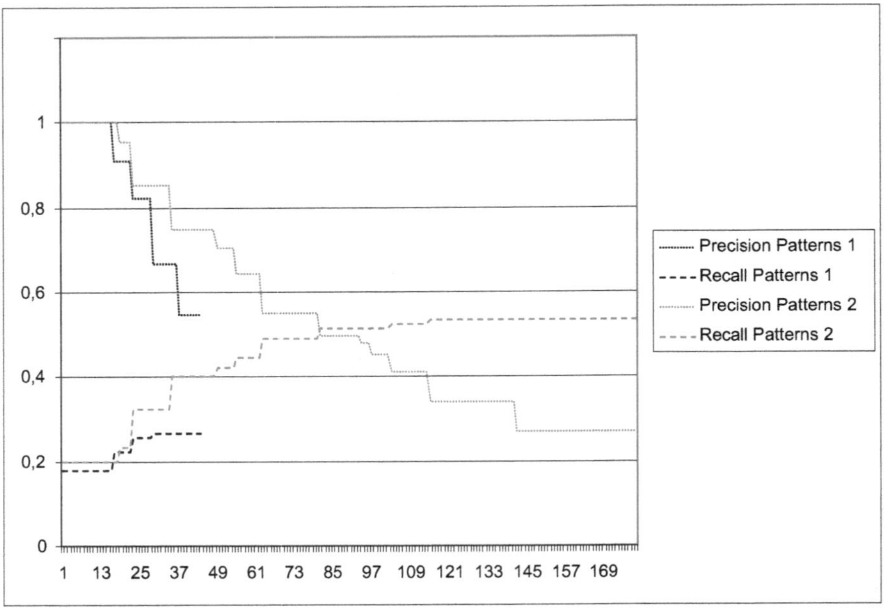

Figure 5. Precision and recall scores of both pattern sets on pilot study corpus

The second major reason for recall problems lies in insufficiencies of the linguistic pre-processing. A number of definitions would have matched one of the extractor patterns but could not be retrieved due to parser errors and misrecognized sentence boundaries. A closer investigation of these problems led to a series of improvements in all pre-processing steps, from better sentence boundary mark-up over additional named-entity recognition rules to enhancements in the actual *Preds*-construction process. After the corpus had been re-parsed using improved pre-processing modules, the number of definition sentences that were not found due to pre-processing errors was reduced from 36 to 26. However, pattern set 2 contains matching patterns for only six of the ten additional correct parses. A comparison of extractor pattern set 2 on the re-parsed corpus with patterns 1 on the old corpus version shows that recall scores were more than doubled. The diagram in figure 5 plots both recall and cumulative precision scores according to the scheme already introduced in connection with figure 4.

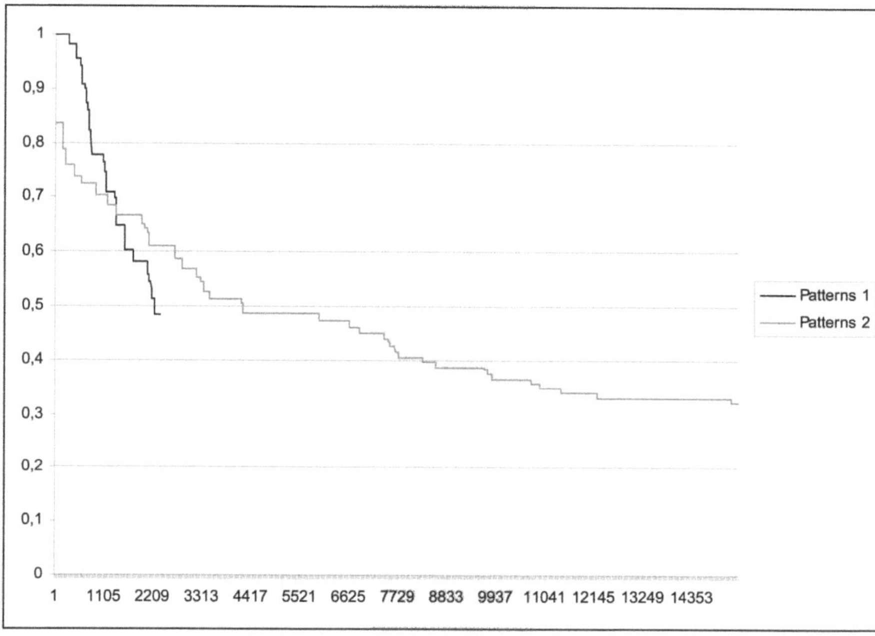

Figure 6. Precision scores of patterns 1 and 2 on full environmental law corpus

Pattern set 2 is consistently superior to patterns 1 also in terms of precision according to this evaluation. This is quite surprising, given the considerable advance in recall achieved by patterns 2 over patterns 1. We assume that the effect is incidental. A comparison of both pattern sets on the full environmental law corpus supports this assumption.

4.2.3 Extractor pattern set 2 on the full corpus

Figure 6 plots precision scores for extraction on our full environmental law corpus using patterns 1 and patterns 2 (without recall curves because we have no basis to assess recall scores on the full corpus).[10] The precision scores for pattern set 2 were calculated from a single (law student) annotator's judgments on a random selection (again balanced over the single patterns) of 3,816 hits. Of these 3,816 sentences, 219 were also among the

10. The values for patterns 1 are those labelled *annotator 2* in figure 4. The curve has been scaled up according to the full corpus size in order facilitate comparison.

ones judged by annotator 2 in our first experiment. The inter-annotator agreement on this overlapping segment was κ =0.62.

The precision scores for patterns 1 exceed those for patterns 2 around the first 1,400 hits and then drop below that line. The total yield of pattern set 2 is much higher than that of pattern set 1. The total number of sentences retrieved by patterns 1 is 2,364, compared to 15,389 sentences retrieved by patterns 2. The median of the precision achieved by patterns 1 is still slightly higher than that of patterns 2 on the same number of hits (0.71 compared to 0.68). However, while the precision score reduces considerably (to 0.48) for the total 2,364 hits retrievable by patterns 1, it remains relatively stable (at 0.61) for the same number of hits by patterns 2.

4.3 Ranking

The experiments with our first extractor pattern set have shown that high precision scores can be achieved for a small number of hits by supplementing predicate/frame-based extraction patterns with various strict filtering rules. The results have shown that this strictness leads to strong restrictions on recall. But abandoning filtering completely (as it has been done with our patterns 2) leads to higher recall at the price of less precision for smaller portions of hits. This section discusses an approach to post-processing that evaluates hits using various criteria instead of filtering them through a cascade of all-or-nothing decisions. These criteria are combined flexibly using automatically acquired weights. From this combination of criteria, a ranking can be constructed. This has the additional advantage that 'false negatives' (i.e. sentences that are in fact definitions but still match some filtering criterion and so would have been removed by strict filtering) remain accessible in principle on the lower ranks.

4.3.1 Features used for ranking

In order to evaluate retrieved sentences, they are turned into feature vectors encoding a number of properties that we intuitively observed to be typical of true or false positives identified by our search patterns. The values for these features are all easily determinable, mostly either from the surface string or from the *Preds*-structures of each hit that is being evaluated. They fall into the following categories:

- *structure*: Which structural parts of a definition could be identified (definiendum, definiens, superconcept and condition) and in which ordering do they stand? Did the search pattern occur in an embedded clause or at top level?
- *reference*: Does any of the identified subparts contain a definite NP or a pronoun? Another feature encodes whether the retrieved sentence contains references to features of the concrete case or situation. This is assessed by a list of words that usually establish such references (*klägerisch*, *vorliegend*, *hier*).
- *polarity*: Does the matched clause or any of the identified subparts contain negation?
- *lexicon*: We check for the occurrence of certain stop- and boost-words, both within the complete sentence and within the identified definition subparts.
- *terminology*: Features specifing tf-idf values[11] for the heads of the phrases that make up the structural definition subparts are given.

A further feature encodes potential definitions identified within a three-sentence window before the sentence that is being considered. Another feature specifies the length of the sentence in tokens.

Boost-words used within the lexical features are certain adverbs that are typical of (modified) definitions (e.g. *typischerweise* or *jedenfalls* – *typically* or *in any case*), and expressions that can be used to talk about meaning directly (e.g. *feature*, *concept*, *definitorial*). Additionally, we check whether a hit or its subparts contain a legal quote-construction (cf. section 2.2).

Potential stop-words have different origins. One list is based on the evaluation of about 1,000 sentences extracted by pattern set 2 from our administrative law corpus. It contains a hand-checked selection from those nouns and adjectives that occurred more often in hits that turned out to be no definitions than in ones that were true positives. Another list was completely hand-written based on subjective observations and intuitive assumptions. Both lists were then taken as seed in an extension process based on similarity of distribution in our environmental law corpus. They were filled

11. Tf-idf values are a standard measure in information retrieval. They assess the importance of a given term in its source document by considering its frequency in the document as well as its selectiveness for documents in the collection.

up from the 500 nouns and 500 adjectives that were most similar to one of the seed words according to cosine-distance of co-occurrence vectors.

4.3.2. Evaluation function

The evaluation score that is calculated for each hit is based on a linear combination of the described features. The coefficients used in this combination are determined by linear regression analysis (using the linear-regression classifier contained in the WEKA-tool suite (Witten and Frank 2005). We have conducted several experiments in which we have constructed a ranking from evaluation scores obtained in this way from the described features alone as well as with various additions. The 3,816 annotated extraction results of patterns 2 on the environmental law corpus (cf. 4.2) served as basis in these experiments. To allow for cross-validation, sentences were partitioned into training- and test-sets of about the same size in four different ways (randomly, but balanced over the various patterns), and all experiments were performed with all four partitions.

As *baseline*, all hits in the test set were ranked based only on the precision score of their retrieving pattern. The precision scores used in this setting were calculated only from the respective training sets.

The evaluation function in *setting 1* uses just the features described above. Thus, it has no access to the estimated precision of the retrieving pattern of the evaluated hit.

In *setting 2*, the estimated precision of the retrieving pattern (calculated on the training set) was taken as a further feature in the regression analysis.

Setting 3 employs an instance based classification algorithm, namely k-nearest neighbor (k-NN)-classification, implemented by the Timbl-package described in Daelemans et al. (2004). The classifier produces a *yes/no*-judgment for each hit using the features from setting 2. Hits are first sorted in two groups according to this classification and then ranked as in setting 2 within these groups.

Setting 4 introduces lexical comparison with the training material as a ranking criterion. This setting uses the features from setting 2 and two additional features. One contains the k-NN classification decision from setting 3, the other additional feature specifies information about lexical similarity. It holds the decision of the same instance-based classifier, but applied to lexical count vectors in place of the features from setting 2. The lexical count vector for a sentence records occurrence counts for all lemmata in that sentence. The classifiers' decisions were not used for pre-sorting in this setting. Instead, they were considered together with all other features in the regression analysis.

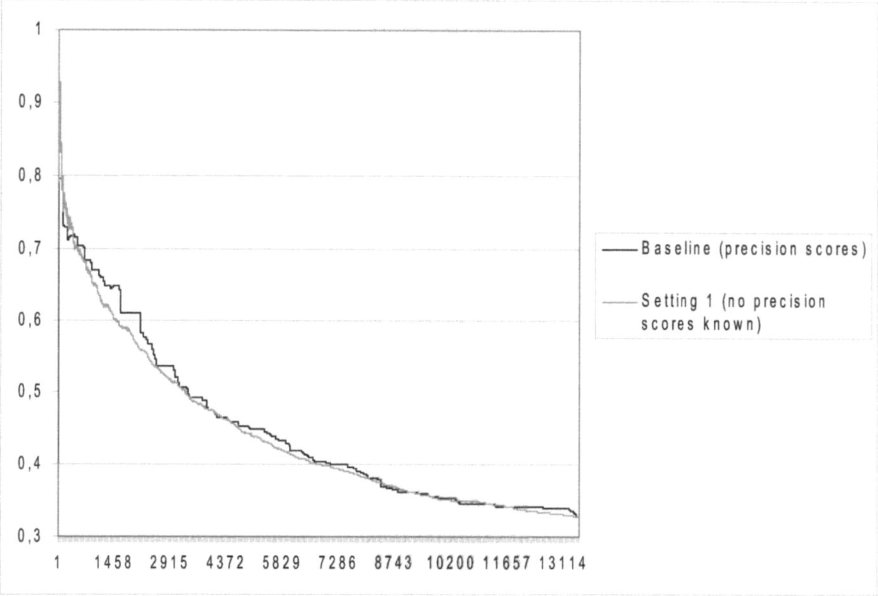

Figure 7. Comparison of rankings: baseline and setting 1

The diagrams in figures 7 and 8 show the precision scores for all top-*n* segments of the rankings produced by the described settings, averaged over the four test sets. The rankings were built by ordering all items in the respective test sets, but the precision scores are of course only based on the annotated hits. The values in the diagrams are thus again projected estimates and become more reliable from left to right with the increasing amount of underlying annotated data. The extreme peaks and drops of some of the curves within the top 50 segment are likely to be epiphenomena owed to a particular distribution of annotated hits. However, the tendencies displayed by the diagrams are similar if only annotated data is considered, and they mostly remain stable on the lower ranks, for which they are more reliable.

As can be seen in figure 7, setting 1 performs only slightly worse than the baseline. The features we have selected obviously say almost as much about the quality of a given search result as direct access to a precision estimate for the retrieving pattern. However, figure 8 shows that these two information sources are not independent. While the combination of precision estimates and other features explored in setting 2 does perform better than baseline, the improvement is only moderate.

A further slight improvement, especially on the first ranks, is reached by pre-sorting according to the k-NN-classification in setting 3. The precision reached on the first 1,182 hits (i.e. 50 % of the hits achieved by pattern set 1) in this setting is 70.2 %, thus close again to the performance of patterns 1 (where the median precision score was 70.8 % according to one annotator and 71.9 % according to the other).

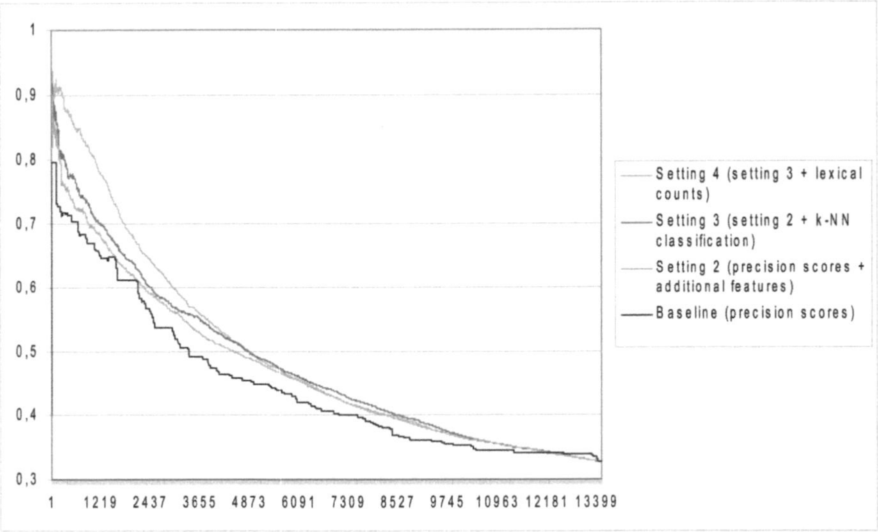

Figure 8. Comparison of rankings: baseline and settings 2, 3 and 4

A much larger gain finally comes with the inclusion of lexical similarity information in setting 4. The estimated precision for the top 1,182 hits in this setting is 78.3 %. This is not surprising. Setting 3 basically just introduced an additional way of using the same information as setting 2. With lexical count vectors, setting 4 in contrast has access to another source of information that is presumably independent of the features used in settings 2 and 3.

4.3.3 Contribution of engineered features

The relatively good performance of setting 1 (no access to precision estimates) suggests that the weights assigned to our hand selected features by the regression analysis do in fact reflect the importance of these features quite accurately. This in turn allows us to draw conclusions concerning typical linguistic features of definitions that are missed out by a strict focus on typical definition predicates and their syntactic environment.

Table 3 shows those features that were assigned the strongest positive respectively negative weights in setting 1, when using all annotated instances as training data. Some of the features used in our experiments are specific to definitions that introduce a superconcept, or can only be determined if the main subparts of a (candidate) definition could be identified. The training data was therefore portioned into three groups (*with superconcept, no superconcept* and *no subparts identified*) on which linear regression was performed separately. Table 3 reflects this categorization. In the categories *no superconcept* and *no subpart* there was only one feature that was given a negative weight.

Table 3. Features with strong positive or negative weights

with superconcept	no superconcept	no subparts
	positive	
definiendum precedes superconcept	definition is top level-clause	definition is top level-clause
legal quote in concept	definiendum is not a negated NP	definition contains no legal quote
definiendum precedes condition	definiendum is not a definite NP	definition is not negated at sentence level
definition is top level-clause	definition is not negated at sentence level	definition contains modifier
no nominal stopp-word as definiendum	definiendum is anaphoric	at least one hit within previous three sentences
	negative	
definition contains concrete case-stopword	definition contains concrete case-stopword	definition contains concrete case-stopword
concept contains no adjectival stop-word from hand-compiled list		
definition contains no condition		

These results largely conform to the expectations we had when selecting the respective features. References to the concrete case are avoided, and in fact sentences with such references are usually not general enough to qualify as definitions. Negations as well as embeddings are penalized. This presumably reflects the fact that such statements often assert the factual inapplicability of an assumed definition. The feature *hit within previous three sentences* was given positive weight in all categories (although it only occurs in the top five in the category *no* subparts). As our annotation pilot study suggests, there are sometimes accumulations of definitions, where e.g. one sentence introduces applicability conditions that are then developed further in the subsequent context. A further feature that was weighted positively in all three categories but does not figure in the top five is *sentence length in tokens*, suggesting that definitions are often particularly long sentences.

4.4 Pattern acquisition

The process of hand-writing patterns is very time consuming. This is especially true of the method of manual inspection of subcorpora in order to identify missed out definition instances and potential additional search patterns (as described in 4.2). This method is therefore almost by necessity limited to the consideration of relatively small corpus fragments as basis.

Standard techniques that are applied to avoid this bottleneck in information extraction are either direct learning of patterns from annotated training data, e.g. (Sonderland 1999; Snow et al. 2005), or pattern acquisition through bootstrapping from some initial extractor set such as in Riloff and Jones (1999). Neither of these techniques can be applied directly in our setting. The major problem for direct learning is that we do not have access to a large enough amount of training data. The annotated extraction results produced in the experiments described above are inadequate for this purpose, because all of them are instances of patterns that are already part of our collection. Bootstrapping approaches on the other hand rely on the identification of typical slot-fillers. These can then in turn be used to identify typical contexts that serve as new search patterns, which again extract further slot fillers. Various heuristics can be used to decide which fillers and patterns to keep and when to halt the bootstrapping cycle. Since the subparts of definitions are almost never proper names or named entities (such as the typical slot fillers in information extraction) but rather subclauses and complex NPs, the main problem for bootstrapping approaches in our domain is to find a suitable granularity of seed items. Full phrases are inadequate because they do not allow enough variability. The particular wording of a full phrase is unlikely to be shared by other definitions, and the phrase type more or less determines the syntactic frame in which it can occur. A reasonable solution is not to use full phrases as seed, but to select single seed words from these phrases according to structural criteria. We are currently experimenting with two semi-automatic approaches to pattern acquisition. Both make use of known and verified search results to identify extraction candidates that have been missed out so far. However, we provide more structure in the acquisition step than standard bootstrapping methods, and we assume that the automatic process will only suggest potential new extraction patterns, while manual inspection and evaluation steps will still be needed to select from these suggestions.

Our first approach is based on keywords from verified search results. We identify three words in each annotated definition via paths within the identified subparts. E.g. in definitions that do not introduce a superconcept, we choose the head of the definiendum as key 1, the predicate of the definiens as key 2 and the head of the subject or direct object of that predicate (whichever is present) as key 3. We then scan the corpus for sentences that contain one of these triples in its original hierarchical configuration. In each of the extracted sentences, we then identify the lowest common node above all three keys, together with the paths from this node to key 1 and key 2. The combination of this node and paths is then proposed as a new pattern.

For example, the sentence in (16.1) contributes the keywords *Bebauungszusammenhang*, *Bebauung*, and *zusammenhängend* (contiguous building area, building, and contiguous). These keywords retrieve sentence (16.2).

(16.1) *(...) erfordert der Bebauungszusammenhang nur eine tatsächlich aufeinanderfolgende, zusammenhängende Bebauung.*

[the building area requires only successive, contiguous buildings]

(16.2) *Der hierfür maßgebliche Bebauungszusammenhang reicht (nur) so weit, wie die zusammenhängende Bebauung den Eindruck der Geschlossenheit vermittelt (...).*
[the building area reaches (only) as far as contiguous buildings give the impression of cohesiveness]

The corresponding candidate pattern *subject+reichen* (reach), is highly specific for this keyword combination because the predicate *reichen* is collocationally associated with the subject. Thus, it cannot be a member of the extractor set. In our experiments, this approach has provided a small number of patterns that seem very plausible, but we have not yet evaluated their performance in the extraction task. A large amount of pattern candidates were either derived from wrong parses or were specific to particular keyword triples as seen in the example above.

Our second approach uses the flexibility of our condensed pattern specification language (see 4.1) to generate potential new extraction patterns. Each of these candidate patterns is then applied and its extractions are classified using k-NN classification based on the lexical count vectors of all known definition instances. For our current experiments with this approach we use a hand-compiled list of 62 potential definition-bearing predicates and 43 syntactic frames, yielding 2,666 extraction pattern candidates. These patterns extract a total of 72,208 sentences from our environmental law corpus. In a first experiment, we have used k-NN classification to judge the first twenty hits of each pattern candidate, and then sorted the pattern candidates according to the proportion of positive judgments on these instances. For most pattern candidates that were ranked best in this experiment, it seems indeed likely that they will frequently match in definitions, however they almost always have large overlap with some of our existing patterns. Often they have one syntactic element in common with an existing pattern, and specify an additional one for which it is hard to see what function it would have in a definition.

5. Conclusion and future work

We argued that definitions are an important element of legal texts and in particular of court decisions. We presented a corpus based survey of various realizations of definitions in such texts, provided a structural segmentation scheme for definitions and discussed a method of applying computational linguistic analysis techniques for their text-based extraction and automatic segmentation. We showed that a large number of definitions can in fact be extracted at high precision using this method, and that the quality of extraction results can be improved with an induced ranking. We also discussed methods for acquiring further extractor patterns.

The preliminary results seen in the previous section suggest, however, that pattern acquisition may not be the only important topic for improving the presented definition extraction system. A serious problem for the approach discussed in this paper is the negative influence of inaccuracies in linguistic pre-processing on the recall achievable by the extraction component. In the experiments with our pilot study corpus described in section 4.2, the number of recall failures that were due to parser errors remained relatively high even after several improvements in the pre-processing chain. It will surely be beneficial to put effort into further improvements of this processing stage.

6. References

Braun, Christian. 2003. "Parsing German text for syntacto-semantic structures". *Prospects and Advances in the Syntax/Semantics Interface, Lorraine-Saarland Workshop Series, Nancy, France.* 99–102.

Brill, Eric, Jimmy J. Lin, Michele Banko, Susan T. Dumais and Andrew Y. Ng. 2001. "Data-Intensive Question Answering". *Proceedings of TREC.*

Burchardt, Aljoscha, Katrin Erk, Anette Frank, Andrea Kowalski and Sebastian Padó. 2006. "SALTO – A Versatile Multi-Level Annotation Tool". *Proceedings of LREC 2006, Genoa, Italy.*

Daelemans, Walter, Jakob Zavrel, Ko van der Sloot and Antal van den Bosch. 2004. *TiMBL: Tilburg Memory Based Learner, version 5.1, Reference Guide.*

Dini, Luca, Doris Liebwald, Lauren Mommers, Wim Peters, Erich Schweighofer and Wim Voermans. 2005. "Cross-lingual Legal Information Retrieval using a WordNet Architecture". *Proceedings of ICAIL.* 163–167.

Dipper, Stefanie. 2003. *Implementing and Documenting Large-Scale Grammars – German LGF. Doctoral Dissertation, IMS.* Stuttgart: University of Stuttgart [Arbeitspapiere des Instituts für Maschinelle Sprachverarbeitung (AIMS)].

Dubey, Amit. 2005. *What to do when lexicalization fails: Parsing German with Suffix Analysis and Smoothing.* Ann Arbor, Michigan.

Fahmi, Ismail and Gosse Bouma. 2006. "Learning to Identify Definitions using Syntactic Features". *Proceedings of the Workshop of Learning Structured Information in Natural Language Applications, 11th Conference of the European Chapter of the Association for Computational Linguistics.*

Fliedner, Gerhard. 2004. "Deriving FrameNet Representations: Towards Meaning-Oriented Question Answering". *Proceedings of the International Conference on Applications of Natural Language to Information Systems (NLDB). Salford, UK* 3136. 64–75.

Flowerdew, John. 1992. "Definitions in Science Lectures". *Applied Linguistics* 13. 202–221.

Gaizauskas, Robert, Takahiro Wakao, Kevin Humphreys, Hamish Cunningham and Yorick Wilks. 1995. "Descriptions of the Lasie System as used for muc-6". *Proceedings of the Sixth Message Unterstanding Conference (MUC-6).*

Hart, Herbert L.A. 1961. *The Concept of Law*. London: Oxford University Press.

Hearst, Marti A. 1992. "Automatic Acquisition of Hyponyms from large Text Corpora". *Proceedings of the Fourteenth International Conference on Computational Linguistics, Nantes*. 539–545.

Hildebrandt, Wesley, Boris Katz and Jimmy J. Lin. 2004. "Answering Definition Questions using Multiple Knowlegde Sources". *Proceedings of HLT-NAACL*. 49–56.

Hobbs, Jerry, Doug Appelt, John Bear, David Israel, Megumi Kameyama, Mark Stickel and Mabry Tyson. 1997. "FASTUS: A Cascaded Finite-State Transducer for Extracting Information from Natural-Language Text". *Finite State Devices for Natural Language Processing*, ed. by E. Roche and Y. Schabes, Cambrige, MA: MIT Press.

Kiss, Tibor and Jan Strunk. 2006. "Unsupervised Multilingual Sentence Boundary Detection". *Computational Linguistics* 32. 485–525.

Klavans, Judith and Smaranda Muresan. 2001. "Evaluation of DEFINDER: A System to mine Definitions from Consumer-Orientated medical Text". *Proceedings of the 1st ACM/IEEE-CS Joint Conference on Digital Libaries (Roanoke, Virginia)*. 201–202.

Lame, Guiraude. 2005. "Using NLP Techniques to Identify Legal Ontology Components: Concepts and Relations". *Lecture Notes in Computer Science* 3369. 169–184.

Lin, Jimmy J. and Dina Demner-Fushman. 2005. "Authomatically Evaluating Answers to Definition Questions". *Proceedings of HLT/EMNLP*.

Maxwell, John T. and Ron M. Kaplan. 1991. "A Method of Disjunctive Constraint Satisfaction". *Current Issues in Parsing Technology*, ed. by M. Tomita, Dordrecht: Kluwer. 173–190.

Meyer, Ingrid. 2001. "Extracting Knowledge-Rich Contexts for Terminography". *Recent Advances in Computational Terminology*, ed. by D. Bourigault, C. Jacqemin and M.-C. L'Homme, Amsterdam/ Philadelphia: John Benjamins. 279–302.

Pearson, Jennifer. 1998. *Terms in Context*. Amsterdam/ Philadelphia: John Benjamins.

Ravichandran, Deepak and Eduard Hovy. 2002. "Learning Surface Text Patterns for a Question Answering System". *Proceedings of the 40th ACL Conference Philadelphia, PA.*

Riloff, Ellen and Rosie Jones. 1999. "Learning Dictionaries for Information Extraction Using Multi-level Boot-strapping". *Proceedings of AAAI-99*. 474–479.

Saias, José and Paulo Quaresma. 2005. "A Methodology to Create Legal Ontologies in a Logic Programming Information Retrieval System". *Lecture Notes in Computer Science* 3369. 185–200.

Snow, Rion, Daniel Jurafsky and Andrew Y. Ng. 2005. "Learning Syntactic Patterns for automatic Hypernym Discovery". *Proceedings of NIPS, Vancouver, Canada.*

Soderland, Stephen. 1999. "Learning information extraction rules for semi-structured and free text ". *Machine Learning* 34. 233–272.

Soubbotin, M. M. and S. M. Soubbotin. 2001. "Patterns of Potential Answer Expression as Clues to the Right Answers". *Tenth Text Retrieval Conference (TREC-10), Gaithersburg, MD.*

Stevenson, Mark and Mark A. Greenwood. 2006. "Comparing Information Extraction Pattern Models". *Proceedings of the ACL-2006 Workshop on Information Extraction Beyond the Document, Sydney, Australia.*

Storrer, Angelika and Sandra Wellinghoff. 2006. "Automated Detection and Annotation of Term Definitions in German Text Corpora". *Proceedings of LREC, Genoa, Italy.*

Sudo, Kiyoshi, Satoshi Sekine and Ralph Grishman. 2003. "An improved Extraction Pattern Representation Model for automatic IE Pattern Acquisition". *Proceedings of the 41st Annual Meeting on Association for Computational Linguistics* 1. 224–231.

Trimble, Louis. 1985. *English for Science and Technology. A Discourse Approach.* Cambridge: Cambridge University Press.

Valente, Andre. 2005. "Types and Roles of Legal Ontologies". *Lecture Notes in Computer Science* 3369. 65–76.

Valente, André and Joost Breuker. 1994. "A functional ontology of law". *Towards a global expert system in law*, ed. by G. Bargellini and S. Binazzi, Padua: CEDAM Publishers. 201–12.

Walter, Stephan and Manfred Pinkal. 2006. "Automatic Extraction of Definitions from German Court Decisions". *Proceedings of the ACL-2006 Workshop on Information Extraction Beyond the Document, Sydney, Australia.* 20–28.

Witten, Ian H. and Eibe Frank. 2005. *Data Mining: Practical Machine Learning Tools and Techniques*. San Francisco: Morgan Kaufmann.

Xu, Jinxi, Ralph Weischedel and Ana Licuanan. 2004. "Evaluation of an extraction-based approach to answering definitional questions". *Proceedings of the 27th annual international ACM SIGIR conference on Research and development in information retrieval, July 25–29, 2004, Sheffield, UK*

Making sense of legal texts

Emile de Maat, Radboud Winkels and Tom van Engers

1. Introduction

The Leibniz Center for Law is concerned with research and teaching in the area of Computer Science & Law, i.e. applying methods and tools from Computer Science, notably Artificial Intelligence, to the legal field to support legal practitioners and legal theory. Whatever the task we are supporting or problem we are trying to solve, we are always starting from and working with legal sources. In the end all legal activity is grounded in legal sources justifying it. These sources are meant to be read by humans and written in natural language. In order to build models and programs that are executed by machines, these sources need to be translated from natural languages to formal machine executable languages. Our core business is finding better ways to support this translation process; it is a time and effort consuming task, usually performed by knowledge engineers. Obviously this formalisation process requires interpretation at some point by human knowledge engineers with the aid of legal experts. We try to see how far we can get using automated translation. Natural language processing (NLP) techniques play an important role in this effort. Besides the fact that NLP may reduce time an effort, it serves other aims:

- We want to create a theory that explains how legal experts interpret legal source texts and give meaning to the expressions in those texts.
- We want to develop an inter-coder independent and repeatable procedure for translating the legal sources into formal representations. This will lead to more uniformity and consequently better maintainability of the systems that are based upon those formal representations.

The goal is to have a formal representation of the original source text that is as isomorphic as possible (Bench-Capon and Coenen 1992), i.e. a well defined correspondence of the knowledge base to the source texts. This will enhance traceability, i.e. it will be possible to exactly pinpoint to those parts

G. Grewendorf, M. Rathert (eds.): Formal Linguistics and Law, 225–255

of the formal representation that will change when the original source changes. It will be easier to explain the decisions made by systems based upon the formal representation and it facilitates the validation of the formal models by legal experts. Also when in practice problems arise with certain categories of cases it will be much easier to give feedback to the responsible authorities. The referential structure between the implementation (i.e. the source code of the supporting systems, the descriptions of the processes and procedures etc.) and the legal sources can be used to find out which parts of legal sources should be adapted to overcome the problems at hand.

The process of making sense of legal texts can be divided into three steps:

1. Structuring the legal source: In the past legal texts were hardly structured in a systematic way, i.e. every text was structured differently. Nowadays this is less of a problem, certainly for most national legislation that is sometimes even available in some XML format. We need structure to divide and conquer the problem of interpreting the meaning of the text and to provide justification of our models at the right grain size level (e.g. an article and not the entire law). We have used parsing techniques to detect structure in for instance legislation and produce XML tagged versions, but we consider those too trivial to discuss in this article.
2. Identifying the source and resolving references: Once the source is structured, we want to identify which legal source it actually is, of which type (legislation, case law or legal doctrine for instance) and resolve all references, both internally and to external other legal sources. We use parsing techniques to perform this task and will discuss the details in section 3.
3. Interpreting the meaning of the source: When we have a structured source with known identity and resolved references, we can dive into the meaning of actual clauses or provisions. This is the most challenging task where at some point human intervention is inevitable. In fact we propose to tackle this problem in two steps: (a) Use parsing techniques to suggest translations from single provisions to formal model fragments, and (b) integrate these model fragments into a single model representing the entire legal source. The first phase will be discussed in section 4 and 5. The second phase will not be discussed here, because it does not involve natural language techniques, but see e.g. Engers et al. (2001).

2. Building parsers: general method

In the projects described in this chapter, we extract information from legal text using a parser based on a context-free grammar. Context-free grammars are not the most suited tool to model natural languages, since they lack expressive power, but their flaws are compensated by their computational advantages which make them better suited for our purposes. Context-free grammars are usually simpler than other grammars, and parsing and compiling large pieces of source texts require less computer resources compared to context sensitive grammars.

An important reason for the lack of success of context-free grammars when dealing with natural languages is that natural languages are highly ambiguous and context-sensitive (Alblas and Nymeyer 1996). Normally, a problem arises when we try to parse a sentence like "The man walked to the woman with a limp." This sentence is ambiguous, since there are two different interpretations: the man has a limp, or the woman has a limp. Although a grammar can be constructed in such a way that such syntactically ambiguous sentences can be parsed, it will never be able to distinguish between the two different interpretations. Thus, we cannot create the right model (at best, we could create two models and have a human select the correct one).

However, we are able to use the context-free grammars to parse and translate legal sources. Syntactic ambiguity should not be a problem here: the text should be syntactically unambiguous[1], since this is a legal text, a law. We do not want any lawyers arguing that the sentence "You are not allowed to shoot anyone with a gun" means that you can shoot anyone who doesn't carry a gun. In general, laws are written to avoid such problems, and as such, we do not often encounter them. Also, a large part of the context has been established: we know that this is a legal text, and that the sentences need to be interpreted in that fashion. Of course, although a legal

---

1. Note that the legal text needs only be syntactically unambiguous. The grammatical structure of the sentence should be so that only one explanation is possible (or plausible). This does not mean that the legal text should be entirely unambiguous. It will always retain a certain degree of vagueness and ambiguity. However, this ambiguity is semantically in nature, and lies in the interpretation and meaning of the words, not in the interpretation of the structure of the sentence. For the application of the grammar and detecting the sentence structure, it does not matter if a term is vague. The (vague) words are not translated, but are retained in the model. The term is merely a label, and as long as it is used consistently throughout the text, it will not raise problems. The interpretation of the term remains with a judge.

source should be syntactically unambiguous, there may be ambiguity in a given legal source, and a context-free grammar cannot handle that correctly. We are not too concerned with these cases as they are very rare.

Another reason why context-free grammars are not as useful is that they can only be used when there are structures or patterns to follow. A parser can only recognize and accept structures that have been define beforehand. This can be fine for simpler structures, such as "an article should be followed by a noun", but it rapidly gets more confusing when you are dealing with more specific meanings that require specific words (instead of a generic "noun"). Natural language offers a huge amount of options to state (more or less) the same thing. These options can differ both in the words and in the structure used.

When dealing with a legal source, or more specific, when dealing with a law or regulation, this problem has been reduced by the legal drafters. Over the years, they have been standardizing the words and structures used for certain "legal statements".[2] For a lot of structures that may appear in a law, this standardization has left us with only a handful of options, instead of the many options that natural language offers.

Finally, interpreting the law is easier than interpreting most other natural language expressions as the law avoids the use of synonyms and descriptions. Instead, a law will usually introduce a term, define it and use it consistently throughout the text. Thus, several problems are avoided with respect to recognizing terms that refer to the same object.

2.1 Context-free grammars

A context-free grammar consist of a number of variables, production rules, terminal symbols, and a start symbol (see Sudkamp 1994). The terminal symbols are the actual words used in the legal source. The production rules are transformation rules that allow a variable to be rewritten to strings of other variables and terminals. Sentences can be derived by starting with a specific variable and then using a production rule to replace it with a new sequence of variables and terminals. The new variables are also replaced, until only terminals are left. If the grammar is correct, these resulting terminals form a correct sentence.

To parse a legal source, we will need such a grammar. We will assume that there is already a terminal from which a noun phrase can be derived.

2. Dutch Guidelines for Legal Drafting ("Aanwijzingen voor Regelgeving").

This terminal will be called NP. With that, it is easy to create rules for the main sentence types. For example, an 'application provision' has the following pattern (see 4.3):

<reference> [is van toepassing][3]
<reference> applies
or: *<reference> [is niet van toepassing]*
<reference> does not apply

This would lead to the following grammar rule (variables in capitals):

APPLICATION→ NP is van toepassing | NP is niet van toepassing

The other sentence patterns can be turned into a grammar rule in a similar fashion. Together they form the options for a sentence. A sentence consists of a main sentence, possibly accompanied by an explicit condition:

S → MAIN_SENTENCE
| EXPLICIT_CONDITION MAIN_SENTENCE
| MAIN_SENTENCE EXPLICIT_CONDITION

The main sentence can include a scope definition:

MAIN_SENTENCE → SCOPE_DEFINITION ACTUAL_MAIN
ACTUAL_MAIN

The actual main sentence can be a norm, definition, deeming provision, application provision, etc.:

ACTUAL_MAIN →NORM
| DEFINITION
| DEEMING
| APPLICATION
| ...

This transformation process leads to a non-deterministic grammar, which could be used by a computer application to determine whether or not a certain sentence is of the identified sentence types in a legal source.

3. Of course all examples are originally in Dutch, but we provide translations.

Often it will be desirable to extend a context-free grammar with attributes, whose values may be checked and/or changed every time a grammar rule is applied. In this way, these attributes are used to store information. They can be used to generate output, or to add restrictions to the grammar. This way the context-free grammar is extended with attribute grammar features.

3. Detecting references

A legal text is glued together by means of references. Its position in the complete legal framework is also made clear through references. This makes references an interesting subject to start the analysis of legal texts with. In the next paragraphs, we will discuss the patterns used for references from laws to other laws. These formats are not restricted to laws, however. In general, any formal legislative text will use the same format to refer to laws, as will commentaries[4]. In addition, as most legal sources follow a structure that is similar to laws, most references to such legal sources will also have a similar structure. With some extensions (mostly added labels, as explained below), the patterns presented here could also be applied to other legal documents.

Other legal documents, such as case law, are structured in a different way. References to those documents can usually be resolved in a similar manner, but this requires different patterns.

3.1 Structure of references

We distinguish four types of simple references.

1. The simplest structure is a reference by name, which consist of the name of the entity being referred to: "*Douanewet*" ("Customs Law"), "*Wet installaties Noordzee*" ("Law installations North Sea").
2. Next are the references comprised of label and number. These references are comprised of a label, such as *article* or *chapter* combined with

---

4. Though in the case of commentaries, the meaning of certain references may change. In a law (or other legal source), a reference to "article 1" means "article 1 of this law (or source)". In a commentary, it means "the article 1 we have been discussing earlier". This means that the such references are to be resolved in a different way.

a number (or letter, or some other designation). Examples of such references are "*artikel 1*" ("article 1") and "*afdeling 1A*" ("part 1A"). In the case of members or subparts that are numbered, the number may appear as an ordinal in front of the label, instead of a number following the label: "*eerste lid*" ("first member"). This ordinal numbering is hardly used above the level of article (i.e. in legislation no references to the "first section" or the "second chapter" will be found).

3. A variation of label and number are references comprised of a label, a number and/or a publication date (and sometimes a venue of publication). An example of such a reference is "*de wet van 13 april 1995*" ("the law of April 13th, 1995"). These patterns are usually somewhat more elaborate than label and number patterns, and may require certain additional keywords and other elements (such as brackets). While label and number patterns generally refer to parts of a document, references including publication information refer to a complete document.
4. Finally, there are the anaphors, indirect references, which often refer to an earlier reference: "*dat artikel*" ("that article"), "*deze wet*" ("this law") and "*het volgende artikel*" ("the next article"). These references can always be resolved to one of the former (label and number or name).

3.1.1 Complex references

The first type of complex reference is the multi valued reference. This is a label and number reference that includes several numbers, for example, "*artikel 9, 13 en 15*" ("article 9, 13 and 15"). Often, these numbers are represented as a range: "*artikel 13-18*" ("article 13-18"). These ranges can themselves be included in a list containing more numbers: "*artikelen 12, 14-18, 20, 22 and 24-26*" ("articles 12, 14-18, 20, 22 and 24-26").

Multi valued references can also be constructed using ordinals: "eerste en tweede lid" ("*first and second member*"). They differ from multiple simple references in that the label is not repeated, so both references need to be read as one to determine what is referenced. In a multi valued reference, the label may be plural (i.e. "articles" instead of "article", but this is not necessary).

The second type of complex reference is a multi-layered reference. This is a reference that consists of several simple references, which "navigate" through the structure of the target document. For example: "*Bankwet 1998, artikel 1, eerste lid*" ("Banking Law 1998, article 1, first member"). These references are ordered in one of three ways:

- Zooming in: the reference starts with the broadest part and ends with the narrowest part, as the example given above.
- Zooming out: the reference starts with the narrowest part and ends with the broadest part: "*lid 1, artikel 1, Bankwet 1998*" ("member 1, article 1, Banking Law 1998"). In this case, the parts may be connected through the word "*van*" ("of"): "*eerste lid van artikel 1 van de Bankwet 1998*" ("first member of article 1 of the Banking Law 1998").
- Zooming in, then zooming out: The reference starts at some (convenient) level in the target document, then "zooms in" and finally "zooms out" again: "*artikel 11a, tweede lid van de Consulaire Wet*" ("article 11a, second member, of the Consular Law"). The "zooming out" part usually consists of one step, sometimes two, but seldom more. A multi-layered reference can have a multi-valued reference as its lowest level. For example: "*lid 1-3 en 5 van artikel 5 van de Gaswet*" ("members 1-3 and 5 of article 5 of the Gaslaw"). When "zooming in", multi-valued references can occur on more levels, resulting in a more tree-like description: "*Gaswet, artikel 5, eerste tot en met derde en vijfde lid en 5a, tweede lid*". ("Gas law, article 5, first through third and fifth member, and 5a, second member")[5].

3.1.2 Special cases

A common exception to the structures presented above is the use of the word "*aanhef*" ("opening words"). This is used when an element in the text contains a list that is preceded by a description of the list, without which the list does not make sense. In these cases, the reference can be made to this description (the "opening words") and one or more of the list elements. For example: "*artikel 12, aanhef en onderdelen i en j*" ("article 12, opening words and parts i and j").

One special case is the exception to a range, for example: "*artikelen 1-12, uitgezonderd artikel 7*" ("articles 1-12, with the exception of article 7")[6]. An exception can also occur on different levels within the reference,

5. This reference gets rather confusing when instead of ordinals, numbers are used for the members as well, resulting in: "Gas law, article 5, member 1-3 and 5, and 5a, member 2" To minimise this confusion, it is common in these cases to use numbers for articles and ordinals for members.

6. Because of the possible existence of articles numbered for example 6a or 7.1, this reference is different from "articles 1-6 and 8-12".

with the higher level being the "range" from which the lower level is omitted: "article 1, with the exception of the second member". Here, article one represents (for example) the range "article 1, first member" through "article 1, fifth member".

Another special case is the use of the word "*telkens*" ("each time"), which is used to shorten a list when there is a series of references with lower level references, where the lower references have the same number. For example, when a reference is made to the first member of article 1, the first member of article 2 and the first member of article 4, the reference can be shortened to "*artikelen 1, 2 en 4, telkens het eerste lid*" ("articles 1 ,2 and 4, each time the first member").

So far we can classify references using two distinctions:

- Single layer or multilayered: does the reference refer to a single structure unit, or does it specify specific subparts of a unit?
- Single valued or multi valued: does the reference refer to one location, or to multiple locations?

A final distinction must be added that is important for resolving such references (see section 4). This distinction is whether the reference is complete or incomplete. A reference is complete if it includes information of the complete document (in these cases, the law) it refers to. It is incomplete if it does not include that information. Thus, "member 1, article 1, Banking Law 1998" is a complete reference, whereas "member 1, article 1" is an incomplete reference. This distinction has been made by (Palmirani et al. 2003) as well. They did a study on references in Italian legal texts. There, complete references were named "well-formed references" and incomplete "not well-formed references". Not well-formed references were named that way because they do not contain sufficient information to distinguish the document referred to (50% of their cases while 35% was well formed; in the remainder the reference could not be completely identified). As we shall see in section 3.2, this is not a problem for the way we parse legal texts.

3.2 Resolving references

After a reference has been found in a text, it should also be resolved, meaning that the identity of the document being referred to is determined. This identity will usually take the form of a Universal Resource Identifier (URI).

In Winkels et al. (2005), it is discussed that there are (at least) three different levels of reference to a specific regulation:

1. A reference to a work, referenced by its citation title (or date of publication, if no citation title exists).
2. A reference to a source. A source is a version of a work at a particular time.
3. A reference to a manifestation. A manifestation is a specific publication of a source. Two manifestations can differ in terms of, for example, medium, layout and comments.

References found in legislation always refer to a work; for case law and commentaries, references to sources can be found and in commentaries sometimes even to manifestations or sources that never came into operation.

As the URI for a specific document can be anything, the best way to resolve it is to have a *resolver* (such as an online database) or a similar resource to retrieve the correct ID. Based on such a resolver, constructing an URI for the work referenced is easy when the reference is a "complete" reference, that is, a reference that includes the name of the law that is being referred to. For example, if we have a reference to "*artikel 2, eerste lid, van de Destructiewet*" ("article 2, first member, of the Destruction law"), we can get the URI of the law ("*Destructiewet*") from our resolver.

After this, the URI for the precise location in the document must be found. When matching the reference to the regular expression, we will find that we need to be at article 2, member 1. An URI for this location can be constructed. The easiest and most universal approach would be to communicate with a *resolver*, a database of different URIs. Alternatively, if the URI methodology supports it, the URI can be constructed using the base URI and the information found. For example, within the 'Norme In Rete' project, it is prescribed that the identifier for "article 2" should be "art2", and that the complete identifier for article 2 of the Destruction law should be "#art2" appended to the URI for the Destruction law (see Spinosa 2001).

Things get a little bit more complicated if we do not have a complete reference. In that case, we do not have a name which points to a base document. Within the text of a law, however, such an incomplete reference usually means a reference within the current document. Thus, al that is needed is that we know the identity of the text that we are parsing, and we can resolve the reference in a way similar to the resolving of the complete reference. In some cases, this requires us to have information that is a bit broader than the identity of the current text. If there is only one member of an article that has subparts, then other members may refer to those subparts without referring to that member. Thus, within articles, we will need not only information on the identity of the member being parsed, but also information on the structure of the other members, if any.

In order to establish the identity of the text it will not always be sufficient that we can identity the law the text refers to. A reference to "the first member" means "the first member of this article of this law". In order to resolve this reference, we will need not only the name of law being parsed, but also the designation of the current article. This means that the input document for a reference parser should contain sufficient information on the structure of a document. It helps if this structure is already made explicit as in an XML document. (For example, our parser works on MetaLex documents, see Boer et al. 2002).

Another group of references that is somewhat harder to resolve are the anaphors. From the point of resolving the reference, the anaphors come in three groups. The first group are those references that refer to the current text[7]: "this article", "this law". Such references are easily resolved if the identity of the current location is known, as discussed above.

The second group of anaphors refers to an earlier point in the text, such as "the previous article". These can be resolved using structure information as well (though they require that the parser does not only know its current location, but also keeps a (limited) history).

Finally, there are those anaphors that refer to an earlier reference, for example "that article", referring not to the current article, but to an article that was earlier mentioned in the text. Usually, this is the most recent reference to an article in the text. In order to resolve these references, the parser keeps a history of the references found so far. This history can be limited to the current piece of text, since such anaphors will not cross the boundaries of (for example) different articles.

3.3 Putting it into practice

The Dutch Tax and Customs Administration (DCTA) is one of many organizations that has to deal with several collections of electronic legal data. Each of these collections comes from a different source and they usually

7. This applies only to laws and similar documents; in other documents, these references do not refer to the referring text itself.

differ in format. In case of the DCTA, the collections come from different publishers. In addition, they themselves produce legal data and enrich existing data, adding another collection.

Having so many different collections can lead to several problems. One of these problems comes from the fact that the links between the different electronic documents are confined to the collection the document belongs to, i.e. a document will never refer to a document outside its own collection. Also, not all references within a collection have been made explicit. This presents the user with a lot of work, as he will have to search through each collection separately to find all the information he needs.

To solve these problems, we have constructed a prototype parser based on most of the patterns presented in section 3.1 (de Maat et al 2006). Not included were the special cases for references containing exceptions to ranges and references constructed using "each time". This parser has been tested by applying it to six Dutch laws. These laws were selected randomly, with two additional requirements: we wanted to include one law written before 1900, and one between 1920 and 1949, since we expected that the references from these older laws, i.e. the language used to express them, would be different from modern laws.

The parser identified almost all references correctly and completely: 99% of the simple references and 95% of the complex references. The few misses were caused by missing labels, names or patterns from the grammar. The grammar can be corrected for this, and will be if those labels and patterns occur often enough. However, there may always remain some patterns that are too rare and/or complex to include.

There were a few false positives (four, compared to almost a thousand correctly identified references) False positives occurred when one of the labels (such as "article" or "member") is used in a different meaning, for example, when "the first member" does not refer to the first member of an article, but to the first member of a certain committee discussed in the text. These false positives may be identified when trying to resolve them, as there is seldom a complete reference that the anaphor refers to. For instance, a reference to "the first member" (of a committee) as indicated above, may be proven to be a false positive if the current article does not include any members. Another way to prevent false positives is to study the context in which the reference occurs. Most sentences in a law that refer follow one of a number of specific formats. However, more research into these formats must be done before anything can be said of the effectiveness of such an approach.

3.4 Classification of references

References from one legal (part of a) document to another (part) usually occur with a reason. We distinguish four major categories of references:

1. *Normative references*: Indicate how the norms in the two (parts of a) document(s) are related. One document may for instance use a reference to 'import' definitions from another source ("as meant in…").
2. *Meta-normative reference*: These are similar to normative references in that they indicate a relationship between to norms. However, instead of referring to what is described in the text referred to, the reference deals with the text itself. Usually, this is used to restrict the application of another norm. For example, a reference may limit the scope of application of some norms ("for the application of this article and others that rely on it…"), etc
3. *Delegating references*: Delegate some kind of competence from one (higher) set of norms to another (lower) set of norms. These references can be found in both directions. First, the delegating document refers to a (future) document that may implement specific norms ("Our Minister has the competence to issue further rules…"), next, this future document will, once it exists, refer to the delegating document (most of the time in the introduction, "by the power of…").
4. *Life cycle references*: Change the status of the document that is referred to. It concerns things like enactment, alterations and retractment of (parts of) law ("In <ref> the following changes will be made…").
5. *Informative references*: Refer to documents with additional, relevant information. These types of references also occur in non-legal texts. They are hardly ever used in legislative texts, but occur frequently in case law and legal commentaries, e.g. citations, examples and general references ("For example…", "See…").

Of these reference types, normative references and meta-normative references are necessary for the understanding of the law. Delegating references and life cycle references are more "administrative" in nature.

The most common normative references are:

– References to a description of some concept that is given in the text being referred to. These are usually indicated by the words "*bedoeld in*" ("meant in").

- References to some concept that has been explicitly named in the text being referred to. These are indicated by the words "*genoemd in*" ("named in"). It differs from the former type in that they refer to one specific concept instead of a group.
- References to the result or the outcome of a text, indicated by "as a result of". These are used when follow-up actions need to be defined.

There are also different types of meta-normative references:

- Scope definitions: these restrict the application of the referring text to those texts being referred to. Scope definitions are marked with the words "*voor de toepassing van*" ("for the application of").
- Application provisions: an application provision indicates that the text being referred to is (not) applicable. The words "*is van toepassing*" ("is applicable") indicate an application provision.
- Exceptions: these indicate that the referring text forms an exception to the text being referred to. An exception is marked by "*in uitzondering op*" ("in exception of"). Exceptions are implicit application provisions, as they indicate that the text being referred to is not applicable[8].

As these different categories of reference each have their own signal words, a reference parser can be extended to recognise the type of most references as well. If the text is being parsed to benefit the reader, providing him with links, then these links can also be categorised, so that a browser program handles different kind of references in a different way. If the text is being parsed in order to generate a model, than these types of references are very useful when trying to integrate several partial models (see 5.4).

4. Classification of sentences

Our research has led us to the conclusion that the number of different types of "provisions" used in legal texts is limited (Bolioli et al. 2002 claim the same). These types of provisions correspond to sentences in the legal text. For each provision, there are a number of sentence formats or patterns that

8. There is also an opposite of the exception, indicate by "notwithstanding", which indicate that the text being referred to *is* applicable. This reference is included as a clarification for the reader; the referring text could probably be seen as being in conflict with the text being referred to.

are used to describe it in the text. This means that sentences can be classified as to what provision they represent, by studying the format the sentence follows.

In the following paragraphs, the different types of sentences used to construct norms in a law[9] are discussed. Sentences regarding delegation and life cycle management are not included in this overview. Also missing are the sentences determining penalties and punishments. We have concentrated on those provisions that have most impact for citizens and companies addressed by the law. For an analysis of life cycle related provisions, see e.g. Bolioli et al. (2002) and Boer et al. (2004). These sentence types cover most laws, with the exception of modifying laws (which consist of mostly, if not only, life cycle management sentences) and the Penal Code (which has mostly sentence determining punishments).

Each of the sentence types described has its own set of signal words by which it can be recognized and thus classified. This list is not exhaustive; although we believe the most common signal words have been covered, other patterns and signal words may exist.

4.1 Definitions and type extensions

In a definition, a description is given of terms that are used in the legal source.

(1) *Income Tax Law 2001, article 2.1, 1st member*
Taxpayers for the income tax are natural persons who:
- live in the Netherlands (native taxpayers) or
- do not live in the Netherlands but do earn Dutch income. (foreign taxpayers).

(2) *Income Tax Law 2001, article 2.1, 2nd member*
Dutch income is income as meant in chapter 7.

Both these definitions use the verb “*zijn*” (“to be”). The basic format for a definition is:

---

9. Other legislative documents use the same types of sentences to construct norms. This means that though these patterns have mainly emerged from our study of laws, they can generally be applied to other legislative documents (such as decrees and decisions) as well.

<subject> [zijn|is] <definition>.
<subject> [are|is] <definition>.

In addition to the verb "*zijn*", the verb "*verstaan*" ("to understand") is also used, as is shown in the next example.

(3) *General Administrative Law, article 1:3, 3rd member*
By application is understood: a request, made by a stakeholder, to make a decision.

This sentence follows the format

[Onder] <subject> [wordt verstaan] <definition>.
[By] <subject> [is understood] <definition>.

In addition to definitions, there are type extensions. These are used to broaden or narrow a definition that has been given earlier.

(4) *Income Tax Law 2001, article 1.7, 1st member*
By annuity is also understood the claim on dividends insofar those dividends are related to an annuity.

The main format of a type extension uses the verb "*verstaan*":

Broaden:	*[Onder]*	*< term>*	*[wordt mede verstaan]*	*<new_term>.*
	[By]	<subject>	[is also understood]	<definition>.
Narrow:	*[Onder]*	*< term>*	*[wordt niet verstaan]*	*<new_term>.*
	[By]	<subject>	[is not understood]	<definition>.

For the example given above, the term is "annuity" and the new_term is "claim on dividends insofar those dividends are related to an annuity".

If the sentence contains a scope definition, the order in the sentence changes (reference is the scope definition):

<Reference> [wordt][mede][verstaan] [onder] < term> <new_term>.
<Reference> [wordt][niet][verstaan] [onder] < term> <new_term>.

In addition, the verb "*behoren*" is also used in type extensions:

(5) *Income Tax Law 2001, article 1.2, 4th member*
As wages are not considered those wages over which the taxes based on article 31 of the Income Taxes Law 1964 are owed by the employer, nor is any resulting advantage for the taxpayer.

The format for these sentences is:

Broaden:	*[Tot]*	*< term>*	*[behoort mede]*	*<new_term>.*
	[As]	<term>	[is also considered]	<new_term>.
Narrow:	*[Tot]*	*<term>*	*[behoort niet]*	*<new_term>.*
	[As]	<term>	[is not considered]	<new_term>.

Finally, two other verbs are used to denote type extensions. They are only used to broaden definitions, never to narrow them. These verbs are "*gelijkstellen*" ("to consider equal to") and "*aanmerken*":

(6) *Income Tax Law 2001, article 1.2, 4th member*
A person who lives permanently separated from his spouse is considered equal to an unmarried person for the application of this article.

(7) *Income Tax Law 2001, article 1.6*
For the application of this law and any regulations based thereon, the countries of the Kingdom of the Netherlands are considered to be separate entities.

The format for these sentences is:

<new_term>	*[wordt gelijkgesteld met]*	*<term>.*
<new_term>	is set to equal with	<term>.
<new_term>	*[wordt aangemerkt als]*	*<term>.*
<new_term>	is qualified as	<term>.

4.2 Deeming provisions

Deeming statements are sentences in which a given situation is said to be considered as if it where another situation. Thus, if situation A is deemed equal to situation B, then all rules that apply to situation B apply to situation A as well. In this way, definitions can be extended to cover certain special, exceptional situations.

(8) *Income Tax Law 2001, article 2.2, 1st member*
A person who stops residing in the Netherlands and who returns to reside the Netherlands within a year without having resided in a different power is deemed to have resided in the Netherlands during his absence.

All deeming provisions in the Dutch legal sources follow the same format:

<subject> [wordt] <denotation of time period> [geacht] <fiction>.
<subject> [is deemed to] <fiction> <denotation of time period> [geacht].

4.3 Application provisions

Application provisions (mentioned earlier in 3.4) are sentences that specify cases in which another article does (not) apply. In this way, existing definitions are broadened or narrowed for specific rules.

(9) *Bankruptcy Law, article 137g, 3rd member*
The fifth, sixth and seventh department do apply.

The general form of these sentences is:

<reference> [is van toepassing].
<reference> [applies].

Or, in the case of the text referred to does not apply:

<reference> [is niet van toepassing].
<reference> [does not apply].

4.4 Value assignment, change and comparison

A number of verbs are used to assign a value to a certain concept. The same verbs are also used to later change this value or to compare the value of the concept with another value.

(10) *Income Tax Law 2001, article 3, member 2.2*
Taxable wages are wages reduced with the employee's discount.

In addition to "*zijn*" ("to be"), another verb is used; values are also assigned using the verb "*bedragen*" ("to amount to"). This can be seen in the following sentences.

(11) *Income Tax Law 2001, article 2.12*
The tax on taxable income from considerable interest (section 4.1 and section 7.3, respectively) amounts to 25%.

(12) *Income Tax Law 2001, article 2.3, member 3*
The strike discount is equal to the profit meant in the first member, but amounts to no more then € 3630.

The value assignments have the following format:

<subject>	*[is|bedraagt]*	*<formula>.*
<subject>	[is|amounts to]	<formula>.
<subject>	*[wordt op <formula>]*	*gesteld.*
<subject>	[is set to]	<formula>.

The 'formula' in the presented format can take many different forms. It can be a concrete value (e.g. € 1000 or 20%), as well as some kind of calculation. Several constructions are possible, such as:

- *x vermeerderd met y* (*x* increased by *y*)
- *x verminderd met y* (*x* decreased by *y*)
- *maximaal x* (at most *x)*
- *minimaal x* (at least *x*)
- *som van x en y* (sum of *x* and *y*)

4.5 Norms

Norms give the actual rules that are presented in the legal sources. A norm is a statement to the effect that something ought to, ought not to, may or can be done (von Wright 1963).

(13) *Income Tax Law 2001, article 3.66, 1st*
If the nature of the business justifies this then the profit may be determined over a financial year that does not correspond with the calendar year.

In Dutch, some norms may be recognized by certain verbs or constructions in the sentence, such as "*kunnen*" ("can"), "*mogen*" ("may") and "*moeten*" ("must"). However, most sentences do not contain such clear indicators, such as the following:

(14) *Law on the Municipal Base Administrations, article 41, first member*
The data on guardianship are derived from the Guardianship Register.

These sentences imply something that will happen or is done; in other words, something that should be done. Therefore, it is a norm.

5. Automated modeling of sentences

The structure for main sentences, presented in the previous paragraphs, forms the basis for a parser that can generate models. There are several ways in which such a main sentence can be extended. To generate more complete models, the pattern list has to be expanded to include these additions. In the next sections, these additions are described.

5.1 Conditions

Most sentences in a law come accompanied by a subordinated clause that puts one or more limitations on the main clause it is attached to. There are two ways in which these limitations are present in the sentence: implicit and explicit. An explicit condition always starts with an "*indien*" ("if") or (in some cases) with its synonym "*voorzover*". In the subordinate clause there will be a subject, which will refer to an element in the main sentence.

(15) *Income Tax Law 2001, article 3.58, 2rd member*
If a house as meant in the second member becomes part of the property of a business of a person who belongs to the taxpayer's

household at the time of the taxpayer's decease then the market value of that house at that time is fixed at 60% of the house's value.

These subordinate sentences have the following structure:

[Indien] *<subject>* *<feature>*
[If] <subject> <feature>

An implicit condition is not announced with an "if". It is a subordinate clause that starts with "*die*" or "*dat*" ("that" or "which"). The sentence simply describes additional features of an element of the main clause.

(16) *Income Tax Law 2001, article 3.56, 1st member*
The taxpayer who is involved in a general transition concerning the splitting of a legal body is deemed to have sold his stocks and claims on the splitting legal body at the moment of the split.

The format of these sentences is:

[die] *<feature>*
[dat] *<feature>*
[who|which|that] *<feature>*

The who, which or that refers to the noun in the main sentence that precedes this subordinate clause; the feature belongs to that noun.

5.2 Exceptions and scope definitions

In paragraph 3.4, the different types of references have been described. The different categories of references differ in how and where they appear in sentences. Some of them form a crucial part of the main sentence, and correspond to a main sentence type. This is the case for the application provision, life cycle references and delegating references.

Normative references are usually attached to some concept (a noun phrase) and such are part of a noun phrase that in turn is part of a main sentence or a condition. The same is often true of those references that indicate the implementation of a delegation.

The remaining references often form some additional information to the main sentence, while not being a condition as described in paragraph 5.1.

This is the case for exceptions and scope definitions. They are placed in a separate subordinate clause, and as such are a separate extension to the main clause.

(17) *Telecommunications Law, article 11.5b, third member*
Contrary to the second member, the explicit consent of the person concerned is not required, if …

Exceptions follow the format:

[contrary to] *<reference>*
[in afwijking van] *<reference>*

The subordinate clause usually appears at the start of the sentence, but may also occur elsewhere in the sentence.

(18) *Income Tax Law 2001, article 3.76, 4th member*
For the application of this article, by profit is understood the accumulative amount of the profit that the taxpayer earns as an entrepreneur from one or more enterprises.

A scope definition follows the structure:

[for the application of] <reference>
[Voor toepassing van] <reference>

5.3 Putting it all together

Based on the observations for the elements of sentence, the model for legal sentences emerges that is depicted in figure 1. The dotted squares denote parts that need not be present. Thus, the model tells us the following:

- A sentence always consists of a main sentence, which may have been extended with a (explicit) condition or a scope definition.
- An explicit condition consists of the actual condition with possible a reference to another source that has been applied.
- Both a condition and a main sentence will contain at least one noun phrase.

- A noun phrase contains at least a main term, and possibly an implicit conditions and/or a reference.

Based on the structure outlined in figure 1, we can build a model of a sentence by splitting the sentence in its several subparts, build a model of each subpart and subsequently merge them into a single sentence model. To do this, we need not only grammar rules for the different language patterns, but some additional grammar rules for recognizing noun phrases and subordinate clauses.

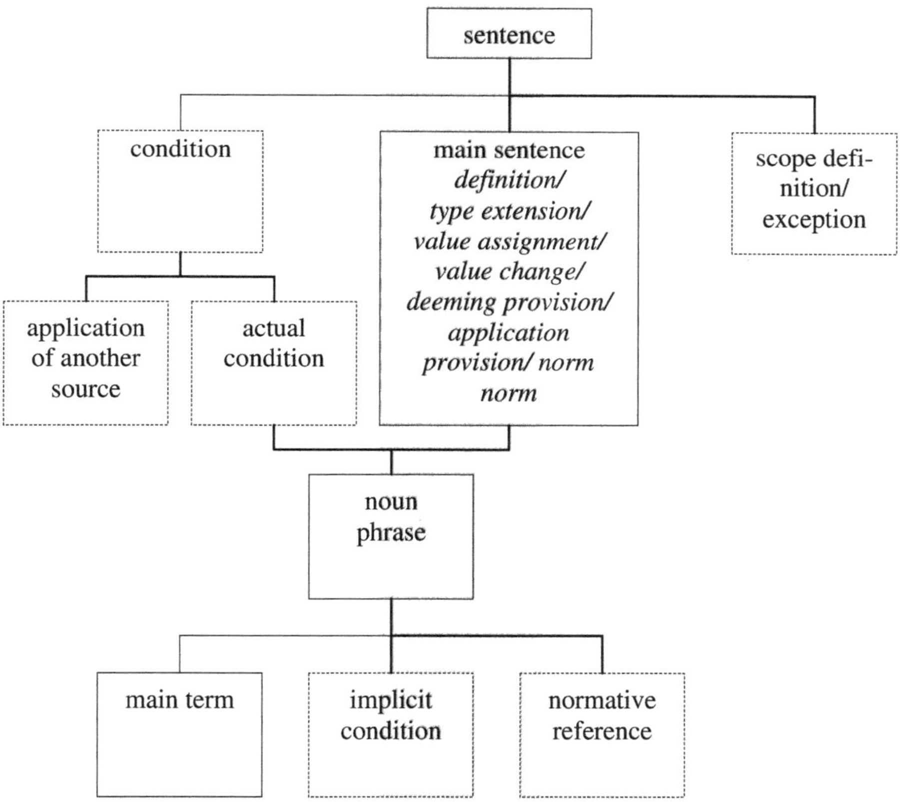

Figure 1. Model of legal sentences

5.4 Integrating sentence models

A final step that will have to be taken is the integration of the different models that have been constructed for the individual sentences. After all, they will rarely have a lot of meaning by themselves.

For the integration of the partial models into a more complete model, the text provides us with two clues: terms and references. If two sentences refer to the same concept, then (most often) they are connected through this concept. If a sentence refers to another location, it is connected to the sentences in that location in the manner defined by the type of reference.

5.5 Putting it into practice

The Dutch Tax and Customs Administration (DTCA) has conducted a research program called POWER (Program for an Ontology-based Working Environment for Rules and regulations), that aimed at developing a method and supporting tools for the whole chain of processes from legislation drafting to executing the law by government employees (van Engers et al. 2001). Within the POWER project, UML/OCL models were created of legal texts. These models would subsequently be used to build applications.

As part of the POWER project, a parser has been developed to support the automatic modeling of legislation (van Gog and van Engers 2001). This parser is called OPAL (Object-oriented Parsing and Analysis of Legislation). OPAL consists of a parser, two lexicons (generic Dutch and juridical Dutch), two grammars (Dutch and translation patterns), a category guesser which tries to identify the grammatical category of an unknown word and a model generator which translates the parsed source text into formal model components. A modeling interface is added to assist the knowledge engineer to adapt the generated model to suit his needs.

Within the POWER project OPAL is part of a production line. The input to OPAL is delivered by the JEWEL (Juridical Editor and Working Environment for Legislation drafting), an editor assisting in the drafting of legislation. JEWEL divides the text of the law in separate articles and delivers them to OPAL. The result of OPAL, the model components, is remodeled (manually) by the knowledge engineer to a knowledge model. The FORCE (Factory for Object-oriented Rule-base and Component-based Engineering) component generates a knowledge component from the knowledge model and process model. The interaction between these components is given in figure 2.

The OPAL parser is based on unification grammars that take into account not only the actual word but also on attributes of that word such as the grammatical category (noun, verb etc.) and person, number, gender etc. This information is obtained from two lexicons: A lexicon for the Dutch language and a lexicon with (mostly compound) juridical terms for example "exclusive or nearly exclusive" and "taxable income").

It is likely that the lexicons do not contain every word occurring in a given text. It is necessary though to find one or more suitable categories for an unknown word to be able to parse the sentence anyway. The category guesser tries to perform this task. It assigns a category (noun, verb, adjective or (cardinal) number) to each word encountered that is not in the vocabulary. These categories are assigned without looking at the context of the word. Any errors will not propagate, as the parser will ignore incorrect categories, because in those cases no grammar rules can be applied[10].

The core of the parser is formed by the two grammars. The first part is a grammar for the Dutch language. It does not aim to make a complete parsing of sentences. Instead, it recognizes phrases that are interesting for the modeling process (for example a noun phrase (NP)). The Dutch grammar used in OPAL is mainly based on the grammar presented in the book *Prisma Grammatica Nederlands* [Prisma Dutch Grammar] (Houët 1997).

The second part is a grammar of the fixed juridical constructs (translation patterns). An example of such a construct is "a house is considered an owned house", the translation pattern in this example is "<NP> is considered <NP>".

The actual parser is based on a bottom-up approach. This choice is based on the fact that OPAL focuses on the recognition of text fragments. This means that there is no starting symbol for the generation of complete sentences, so top-down is not possible. OPAL starts with the given sentence and words are put together to form text fragments by applying the applicable grammar rules

The algorithm used within OPAL is described in detail by James Allen (1995). Roughly said the parsing algorithm reads words from the given sentence consecutively and tries to combine a word with the (partly) recognized fragments up to this word. If for example a rule like NP → DETERMINER ADJECTIVE NOUN is part of the grammar and the words "the blue" are previously read, a noun is expected and when the next word is "bicycle" the aforementioned rule will be recognized.

10. This only functions correctly if the greater part of the words in the text is provided with a correct category, i.e. is contained in the lexicon.

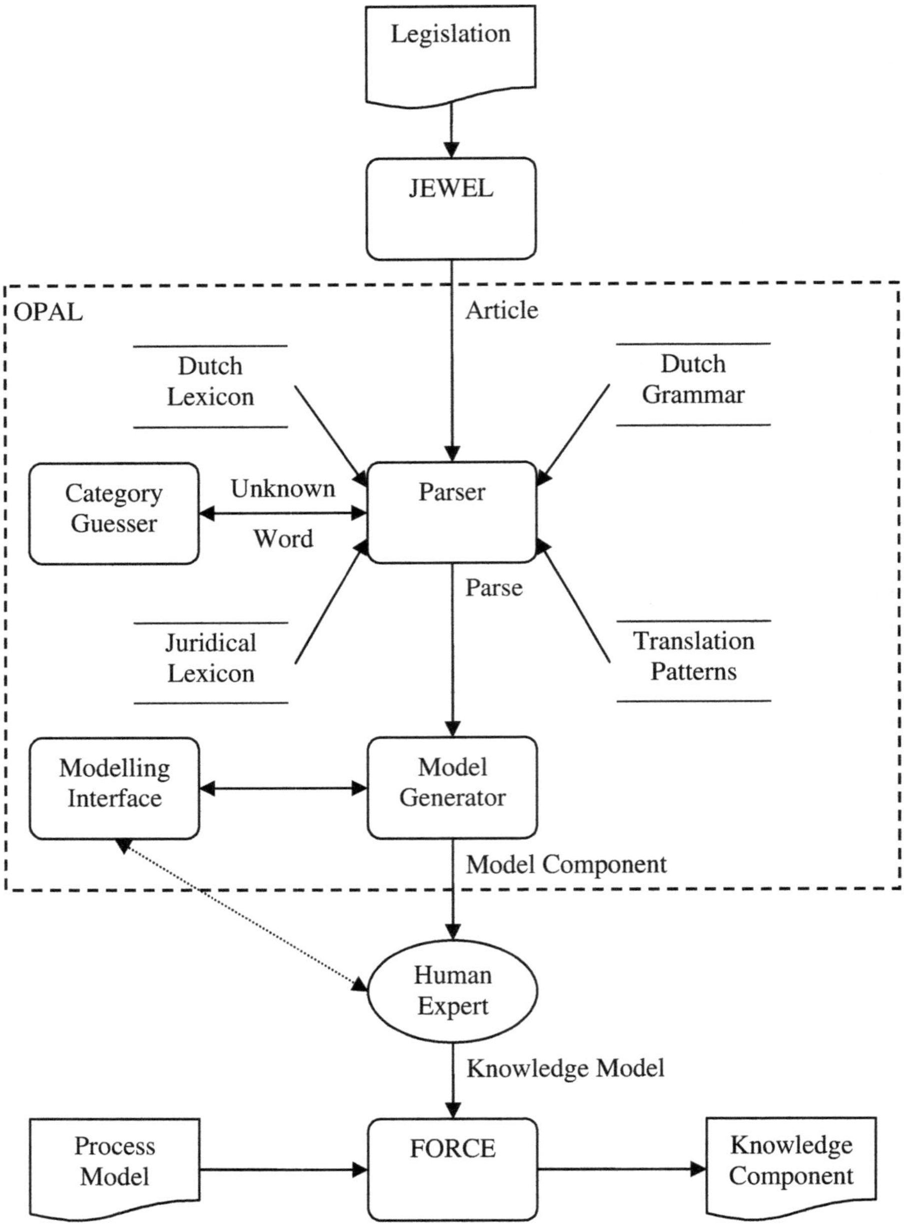

Figure 2. The OPAL architecture

To apply this algorithm within OPAL, two adaptations were needed. Firstly, the grammar of OPAL contains empty rules; these are rules where the right hand side of the rule is empty. The algorithm does not take this possibility in account. There are two solutions to this problem, changing the algorithm or removing the empty rules from the grammar. Within OPAL the last solution is chosen, because there is an algorithm to transform a grammar with empty rules into an equivalent grammar without empty rules. This algorithm is described by Thomas A. Sudkamp (1994).

Secondly, the original algorithm by Allen was not intended for a unification grammar. So, a unification mechanism had to be added to the parsing algorithm as well. This meant keeping track of additional information of symbols and for applying the unification during the execution of the parsing algorithm.

The parser will return different interpretations of the text. The final recognition consists of choosing the largest possible meaningful text fragment that is found (noun phrase, translation pattern etc.).

The parses found by the parser have to be translated into concepts of the formal specification language (UML). At the moment OPAL is restricted to modeling object types and attributes by using noun phrases and modeling the juridical translation patterns.

The translation is performed based on the feature structure found with the text fragment that needs to be modeled. This feature structure contains information about the semantics of the parse. The translation is done by the Model Generator component, and is performed in two steps.

First, any noun phrases found are translated. A noun phrase (in Dutch) is built around a noun (the core). Within OPAL the core is to be considered an indication for an object type. Extra words can occur before and after this noun. For example a determiner and adjectives can occur before the core, while prepositional phrases can occur after the core. These text fragments are usually a description of properties of the core and therefore give a clear indication of the attributes of the core.

In the noun phrase "the blue bicycle", the core is "bicycle". This can be viewed as an object type. The adjective "blue" is an indication of an attribute of bicycle. Usually, this would be modelled with an attribute colour. However, within POWER legislation is modelled and in legislation it is especially interesting to know whether a certain object type has a specific property or not. This leads to the idea that properties are logical values, so within POWER attributes are most of the time modelled as a Boolean. So the chosen method within OPAL is that OPAL takes the noun as the object type and models the additions to the core as Boolean attributes. The noun phrase "taxable income from owned house" would be modelled as in Table 1.

Table 1. POWER UML model: Taxable income from owned house

«type» *Income*
taxable: Boolean fromOwnedHouse: Boolean

Some extensions to the noun, like a prepositional phrase, can contain a noun phrase by itself. This requires that the translation process is recursive. Within OPAL this is done by creating an association between the current object type (from the noun) and the recursive object type. Take for example the noun phrase "the distance by bicycle". The core of this noun phrase is "distance". This is modeled by an object type distance. There is also a prepositional phrase "by bicycle", which contains the noun phrase "bicycle". This is modeled by an object type bicycle. An association is created between distance and bicycle with the role name "by".

The depth of the recursion is an important choice for the generation of the model. The modeling interface of OPAL gives the possibility to choose his depth. For example there are three levels of recursion in the noun phrase "the distance by bicycle", see figure 3.

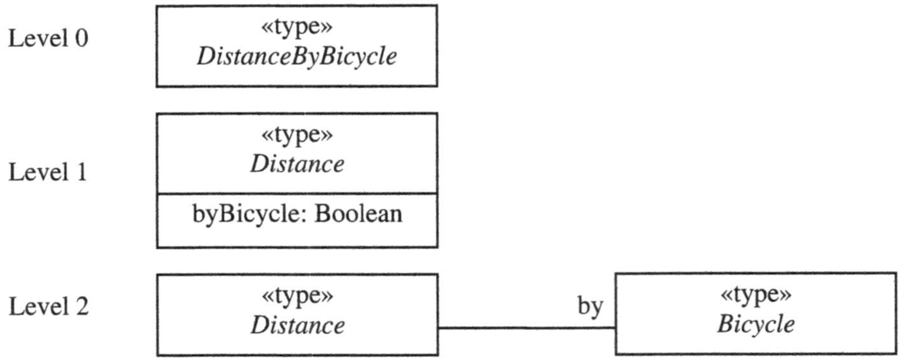

Figure 3. Levels of recursion

Through the Modeling Interface, a human expert can make changes to the model proposed by the Model Generator.

6. Conclusion

We have shown that with the relatively simple technique of parsers using context free grammars we can achieve useful results in mapping the natural language used in legal texts to formal models representing its meaning. This result can be explained by the somewhat restricted use of natural language in legal texts:

- Legal drafters tend to avoid syntactical ambiguity;
- They tend to use stereotypical phrases to denote the recurring items;
- They tend to use the same terms for a particular concept throughout a text.

Besides these advantages, we do not need to check whether sentences are grammatically correct; we assume they are.

We showed that a shallow parser based on a context free grammar can be used very effectively to find and resolve references in and between (parts of) legislation. Besides the parser, we ideally need a structured text and a way to uniquely identify laws (or other legal sources) and parts within it. The MetaLex XML interchange standard for legal sources, developed by the Leibniz Center for Law, is a good candidate for such a structure. Public authorities in the Netherlands have recently agreed on standard ways of uniquely identifying legal sources.

We have also shown that a context-free grammar can be used to support knowledge engineers in formalizing legal texts by suggesting interpretations of its meaning.

Next step is building a legislative editing environment that automatically structures the sources being edited, handles unique identifiers, referencing etc. In short, this development will make the parsing functionality described in this article superfluous, but not the analysis that led to the parser specifications. The same results will be used in specifying the editing environment in which for instance the sentence patterns will be used as building blocks for legal drafters.

The research explained in this chapter shows that we can improve the efficiency of the process of translating legal source texts into formal executable formal representations. This will enhance coder-independency and also helps to achieve to realize the earlier mentioned aims.

We are also a bit closer to our more fundamental quest, i.e. understanding what anchors a human reader of a legal text may use in order to grasp its meaning.

7. References

Alblas, Henk and Albert Nymeyer. 1996. *Practices and Principles of Compiler Building with C*. London: Prentice Hall.

Allen, James. 1995. *Natural Language Understanding*. Second Edition. Redwood City (CA). The Benjamin/Cummings Publishing Company Inc.

Bench-Capon, Trevor and Frans Coenen. 1992. "Isomorphism and legal knowledge based systems". *Artificial Intelligence and Law* Vol. 1 (1). 65–86.

Bolioli, Andrea, Luca Dini, Pietro Mercatali, and Francesco Romano. 2002. "For the Automated Mark-Up of Italian Legislative Texts in XML". *Legal Knowledge and Information Systems. Jurix 2002*, ed. by T. Bench-Capon et al., Amsterdam: IOS Press. 21–30

Boer, Alexander, Rinke Hoekstra, Radboud Winkels. 2002. "METALex: Legislation in XML". *Legal Knowledge and Information System. Jurix 2002*, ed. by T. Bench-Capon et al., Amsterdam: IOS Press. 1–10.

Boer, Alexander, Radboud Winkels, Tom van Engers and Rinke Hoekstra. 2004. "A Content Management System based on an Event-based Model of Version Management Information in Legislation". *Legal Knowledge and Information Systems. Jurix 2004*, ed. by T. Gordon, Amsterdam: IOS Press. 19–28.

de Maat, Emile, and Tom M. van Engers. 2003. "Mission impossible?: Automated norm analysis of legal texts". *Legal Knowledge and Information Systems, Jurix 2003*, ed. by D. Bourcier, Amsterdam: IOS Press. 143–144.

de Maat, Emile, Radboud Winkels, and Tom M. van Engers. 2006. "Automated Detection of Reference Structures in Law". *Legal Knowledge and Information Systems, Jurix 2006*, ed. by T. M. van Engers, Amsterdam: IOS Press. 41–50.

Engers, Tom M. van, Rik Gerrits, Margherita Boekenoogen, Erwin Glassée and Patries Kordelaar. 2001. POWER: "Using UML/OCL for Modelling Legislation – an application report". *Proceedings of the International Conference on Artificial Intelligence and Law*, ACM Press. 157–167.

Gog, Ron van, and Tom M. van Engers. 2001. "Modelling Legislation using Natural Language Processing". *Proceedings of the 2001 IEEE International Conference on Systems, Man, and Cybernetics.*

Houët, Henriëtte. 1997. *Prisma Grammatica Nederlands*. Utrecht: Het Spectrum.

Palmirani, Monica, Raffaella Brighi, and Matteo Massini. 2003. "Automated Extraction of Normative References in Legal Texts". *ICAIL-2003: Proceedings of the 9th International Conference on Artificial Intelligence and Law*, ed. by. G. Sartor, ACM Press. 105–106

Spinosa, Pier Luigi. 2001. "Identification of Legal Documents through URNs". *Proceedings of the Euroweb 2001 Conference "The Web in Public Administration"*, ed. by O. Signore and B. Hopgood, Pisa: Felici.

Sudkamp, Thomas A. 1994. *Languages and Machines*. Reading (MA): Addison-Wesley Publishing Company.

von Wright, Georg Henrik. 1963. *Norm and action: a logical enquiry*. London: Routledge & Kegan Paul.

Winkels, Radboud, Alexander Boer, Emile de Maat, Tom van Engers, Matthijs Breebaart, and Henri Melger. 2005. "Constructing a semantic network for legal content". *Proceedings of the Tenth International Conference on Artificial Intelligence and Law (ICAIL)*, ed. by A. Gardner, ACM Press. 125–140.

Interfacing between different legal systems using the examples of N-Lex and EUR-Lex

Doris Liebwald

1. Introduction

It is an interesting matter that since the classic "Handbook of Legal Information Retrieval" edited by Jon Bing was published in 1984[1], improvement in legal information retrieval has not seen any major advancement. Quite to the contrary, information overload and increased demand for cross-national and cross-lingual legal information have amplified the basic problems. The handbook already points out many of the shortcomings a lawyer typically has to struggle with when searching for relevant legal documents. Legal information retrieval systems still do not represent legal structural and conceptual knowledge, user friendliness regarding search strategies and input formats is lacking, and information about system functions and information content (completeness) is often not sufficient. Also, continuity, representation of time layers and consolidated versions are inadequate and different user situations and information needs are disregarded. Finding the correct search terms is a game of chance, language approximation is minimal and even simple linguistic tools are missing.

This paper will demonstrate and explain the typical shortcomings of legal information retrieval systems. Since the emphasis is on multilingual and cross-national information retrieval, the experimental prototype N-Lex, the new common access portal for national law, EUR-Lex, the gateway to EU law, and the N-Lex and EUR-Lex implemented EUROVOC thesaurus will serve as case study examples. These applications are maintained by the office for official publications of the EC and are freely available on the inter-

1. A revised version is freely available at http://www.lovdata.no/litt/hand/hand-1991-0.html.

G. Grewendorf, M. Rathert (eds.): Formal Linguistics and Law, 257–291

net.[2] Whereas EUR-Lex supplies legal texts produced by the EU institutions, N-Lex is a new attempt to provide a common gateway to national law of the EU member states. In its current state, N-Lex is an experimental prototype which is made publicly available on the internet for free test use. N-Lex is an ideal example to explain the specific requirements and information needs in multilingual and cross-national legal information retrieval.

1.1 Multilingualism and cultural diversity in EU-law

The EU currently embraces 27 member states and has 23 official languages[3]. Legislation and documents of major public importance or interest are produced in all official languages, but most of the institution's work is available in French and/or English only. Communication with the EU and its institutions by governments, civil servants, businesses and citizens may take place in any of the official languages. The national law of the member states is not translated into the official languages of the EU. Thus, it is very difficult for the EU institutions to watch, compare and correct implementation measures, and it is also very difficult for governments, businesses and citizens to locate relevant cross-national legal information.

Especially with regards to legal texts, multilingualism and the diversity of legal cultures pose intractable situations. Of course, EU legislation is translated into 23 languages, but the EU legal language and the specific concepts chosen do not correspond with the national legal language and concepts of the respective member state to a very high degree. Also, legal

---

2. See N-Lex at https://europa.eu.int/celexdev/natlex/, EUR-Lex at http://eur-lex.europa.eu/ and EUROVOC at http://eurovoc.europa.eu.

3. Many languages spoken in member states (e.g. Catalan, Welsh, Basque, Breton, Sardinian) do not have the official EU language status. Besides the 23 official languages, about 60 other indigenous and non-indigenous languages are spoken over the geographical area. English, French and German are the three strongest languages within the EU institutions. Within the EU, German is the most widely spoken mother tongue (18%), and English is the most commonly used language with over a half (51%) speaking it either as their mother tongue (13%) or as a foreign language (38%), cf. Eurobarometer (2006). The European Commission's Directorate-General for Translation, which is responsible for written text only (there exists also a Directorate-General for Interpretation), has a permanent staff of some 1.750 linguists and 600 support staff, and also uses freelance translators. This is the world's largest translation service.

practice and institutions differ. 27 member states interpret the same legal text, each influenced by its own political system, legal tradition, legal language and concepts, and overall legal view. Member states are required to implement EU legislation into their existing framework of national legislation, and these frameworks are congruent with each other to varying degrees. Within the EU, most countries belong to the civil law tradition, with the exceptions of Ireland and the United Kingdom. In some countries, the *"Länder"*, or states, have minor legislative importance, but this is not true for all countries, e.g. Germany, Austria, and Belgium. Even where the same language is used (e.g. Austria, Germany), the legal systems, their structures, hierarchies and legal terminologies differ. Therefore, one particular EU directive may be implemented in more than 27 different ways on the federal and the state level.[4] Not only terminology will differ, but also the exact meanings of the individual concepts. Furthermore, different national legal systems may organize and link the various concepts in different ways.

Lawyers use a very sophisticated technical legal language which differs from common language or other technical languages. The complexity of law demands an abstract, differentiating, economical, and functional technical language which is able to represent the structures and meanings in law. Even between and within various groups of legal experts, the concepts, document types, styles of writing and parlance vary, cf. Liebwald (2007). Each field of law forms its own specific concepts and structures, which all show significant differences in their semantics. This is also true within legislation, administration, justice and doctrine. Additionally, the law and the legal language are dynamic and consist of variable semantic spaces. There are, however, also syntactic differences. For example, contrary to common language the Austrian legal language has a strong tendency towards substantivization, compound words and the use of participle instead of subordinate clause.

The legal language abstracts away from facts and attaches very specific meanings to concepts. It specifies or reinterprets common language concepts, creates new specific concepts or adopts or adapts foreign concepts. These special forms of polysemy are exactly the reason why the distinction between "terms" and "concepts" is stressed by legal theory. However, this is still not fully acknowledged in legal information retrieval science. Legal

---

4. Contrary to EU regulations, directives are only binding on the member states (not directly applicable to citizens) and usually leave some leeway as to the exact rules to be adopted.

concepts are known as being open textured concepts, they feature a high degree of specialization and their various meanings and their interpretation strongly depends on the legal system and legal tradition they emanate from. Lawyers interpret legal concepts within the context and structure of the legal system they are accustomed to. Each legal language has typical national peculiarities, structural knowledge and differing legal systems in general. The legal languages of various states differ to varying degrees, and the EU legal language differs from the national legal languages of its member states.

The following example of the Data Privacy directive 95/46/EC shall illustrate linguistic and conceptual differences. The text of the Austrian Data Privacy Act[5] at first glance appears very similar to the German version of the directive. Nevertheless, a closer examination reveals many hidden linguistic differences and problems.

The definition of Art. 2 of the directive establishes three actors of the norm: the *"controller"*, the *"processor"* and the *"data subject"*. The concept *"controller"* is defined by the directive as the natural or legal person or any other body which alone or jointly with others determines the purposes and means of the processing of personal data. The German version of the directive translates *"controller"* into *"für die Verarbeitung Verantwortlicher"*, literally translated back into English: *"the one who is responsible for the processing"*. Yet, a phrase like *"the one who is responsible for the processing"* is not economic in use, a term like *"controller"* is much more functional. Therefore, the Austrian legislator replaced the name of the concept with *"Auftraggeber"*. This differs from the German Data Privacy Act[6] which uses *"verantwortliche Stelle"*, translated into English as *"responsible person or institution"*. The Austrian *"Auftraggeber"* is difficult and not easy to translate. The conventional and also the German common language meaning as well as the more general legal meaning of *"Auftraggeber"* is best translated as *"contracting agency"* or *"principal"*. The Austrian Purchase Contract Awards Act, for example, uses *"Auftraggeber"* in the sense of *"contracting authority"*. *"Auftraggeber"* in terms of the Data Privacy Act is misleading even in German. Austrian legal experts and data protec-

---

5. Datenschutzgesetz 2000 (DSG 2000), BGBl I 1999/165, last amended by BGBl I 2005/13.
6. Bundesdatenschutzgesetz (BDSG) of 14th January 2003, BGBl. I S. 66, last amended by BGBl. I S. 1970.

tion officers[7] meanwhile add information to yield the correct meaning *"the one who is responsible for data processing in terms of the Data Privacy Act"*. But lay persons still need clarification. However, the Data Privacy Act is not directed to experts only.

The *"processor"* or *"Auftragsverarbeiter"* of the directive, generally understood to be the person who processes data on behalf of the controller, is replaced in the Austrian Data Privacy Act by the term *"Dienstleister"* (literally: *"service provider"*). The German Data Privacy Act refers to the concept *"processor"* in the sense of the directive by adding *"im Auftrag"* (literally: *"by order of"*) or using *"Auftragnehmer"* (literally: *"contractor"* or *"supplier"*).

The third actor of the directive is the *"data subject"*, in the German version the *"betroffene Person"* (literally: *"person concerned"*). This corresponds to the concept *"Betroffener"* (short for *"person concerned"*) in terms of the Austrian and the German Data Privacy Acts.

Upon closer examination, however, not only the wording, but also the specific meanings differ. Lesmo et al. (2005) describe the same problem giving some English/Italian examples. Furthermore, they introduce an example of the diversity of meanings using the concept *"in clear and comprehensible manner"* taken from the directive on Distance Contracts 97/7/EC. Lesmo et al. (2005) compare the information conditions a distance seller has to fulfill to provide a distance contract in clear and comprehensible manner under the U.K. (*"clear and comprehensible"*), the German (*"klar und verständlich"*) and the Italian (*"chiaro e comprensibile"*) legal system. Finally, they point out that the main criteria for a *"clear and comprehensible manner"* vary in all cases. The German *"klar und verständlich"* refers to three different concepts: 1) the form or the writing of the information must be clear and legible (*"Gestaltung der Information"*); 2) the information must be intelligible for the consumer (*"Formulierung der Information"*); and 3) the language of the information must be that of

7. In terms of the Privacy directive, a *"data protection official"* corresponds to a *"Datenschutzbeauftragter"*. The Austrian Data Privacy Act did not establish an obligatory *"Datenschutzbeauftragten"*. Therefore, the concept does not appear in the text of the Austrian Privacy Act, but the institution does exist. The German Privacy Act differentiates between a *"Bundesbeauftragter für den Datenschutz und die Informationsfreiheit"* in a similar but broader sense like in the directive, and a *"Datenschutzbeauftragter der Deutschen Welle"*. *Deutsche Welle* is a German international broadcaster. The tasks and the quality of the Austrian and the German institutions differ.

the consumer (*"Sprache der Information"*). The Italian judiciary focuses primarily on the more formal concepts 1 and 3 and less on concept 2. In England, the main focus is on concept 2. Also, the Austrian legislator included the phrase *"klar and verständlich"* into the Consumer Protection Act, but additionally refers to the technical means: *"The information ... shall be supplied to the consumer in a clear and understandable manner that is suitable for the means of distance communication used. Its commercial purpose shall be unequivocally recognizable."*[8] Austrian Doctrine and justice emphasize timeliness, comprehensibility (unambiguity) and easy traceability of information.

These problems are, however, not limited to legislative texts. The following example taken from Austrian doctrine shall illustrate the different semantic spaces of national interpretations of decisions of the European Court of Justice (ECJ): Schacherreiter (2006) analyzed two written statements from both a German and an English expert regarding the ECJ case Owusu vs. Jackson[9] C-218/02 of 1st March 2005.[10] The ECJ had to deal with the applicability of the English *forum non conveniens* principle in the area of European procedural law. The conclusions of the two experts are absolutely contrary: while the German expert (civil law) considers the findings of the ECJ indicatory and generally applicable, the English expert (common law) cannot detect a new general rule, he rather considers the ruling of the ECJ an exception of the general rule, justified by very specific circumstances and facts.

One directive and many different terms, notations and concepts which led to different meanings of EU-concepts on the one hand, and conflicting interpretations of ECJ case law on the other hand. The challenge of legal knowledge management systems which intend to cover legal information from different nations or to address different legal systems is clearly not

8. The original wording of § 5c Abs 2 KSchG: "Die in Abs. 1 genannten Informationen müssen dem Verbraucher klar und verständlich in einer dem verwendeten Fernkommunikationsmittel angepassten Art und Weise erteilt werden. Ihr geschäftlicher Zweck muss unzweideutig erkennbar sein."
9. There is another peculiarity with regard to the Austrian legal system. Due to reasons of privacy, Austrian court judgments are made anonymous before publication. Therefore, Austrian doctrine does not refer to the parties to name important judgments, but to striking facts.
10. To demonstrate the diversity of possible references: Andrew Owusu v. N. B. Jackson, Judgment of the Court (Grand Chamber) of 1 March 2005, Case C-281/02, European Court reports 2005 Page I-01383, CELEX number 62002J0281.

only multilingualism. Such a system must also take into account the different legal systems and structures as well as the conceptual discrepancies and the differing user needs and user behavior. Additionally, the law and the legal language are dynamic, therefore a legal information system must be flexible enough to handle and represent changes in the law as well as in the meanings of concepts, caused by new statutes, amendments or case law.

1.2 Lawyer's needs in legal information retrieval

The lawyer's needs in legal information retrieval are in fact very specific. The key issues are authenticity, reliability, timeliness, completeness and continuity of content, powerful but easy to use search capabilities, flexibility, presentation of structural and conceptual knowledge, consideration of differing user groups and their specific needs, and last but not least a clear documentation and useful help-tools, cf. Wahlgren (1999), Liebwald (2003).

Luuk Matthijssen (Matthijssen 1995; Matthijssen 1999) describes four theoretical limitations of legal information retrieval: (1) the fact that the index of a database only partially describes its information contents, (2) the imperfect description of an information need by the query formulation, (3) the rough heuristics and tight closed world assumption of the matching function, and (4) the presence of the conceptual gap: the discrepancy between users' views of the subject matter of the stored documents in the context of their professional setting and the reduced formal view on these subjects as presented by information retrieval systems. Legal practitioners have to translate their information need – which they have in mind in the form of legal questions and concepts – into a query, which must be put in technical database terms.

A legal practitioner applies conceptual thinking and legal structural knowledge gained through long-term training. A legal information system should therefore represent those structures and concepts to minimize the conceptual gap. Cross-references between texts and document types are very important utilities for lawyers. These references may also link different time layers and are more complex than they might appear at first glance. To some extent, they represent the legal structural knowledge. In practice, lawyers use printed legal commentaries and subject-classified case law directories, which describe explicit legal knowledge. Legal commentaries are written by legal experts, have a long tradition and are widely accepted. They integrate all the explicit knowledge of a specific legal domain or specific code and provide exact references to the source documents. For the time being, legal commentaries are still the most advanced form of legal knowledge representation.

Therefore it is not sufficient to google the law and to provide some proximity result sets. A simple law-google will not take important legal elements like amendments, temporal and geographical limits, coverage, authenticity, legal basis etc into account. In most cases, lawyers need accurate information. Furthermore, Google does not use formal semantics and is not an example of a semantic web; rather, it is based on a statistical approach and designed to enable general information search. Research in text analysis has clearly shown that structure, style and wording of legal documents significantly differ from general information sources like newspaper articles or information sites, cf. Moens et al. (1997), Moens and Dumortier (1998). The content of a newspaper article is usually given by one or more striking keywords in the title and in the first sentences, and these keywords are repeated in the article. This is not true for legal documents. In terms of automatic text analysis, it is easier to calculate the similarity of facts than the similarity of the legal questions posed. A judge's decision may take various approaches into account, but the quintessence may appear very late in the text and there is no reason to repeat it. The judge does not use the exact wording of a norm she/he refers to. On the other hand, legal texts offer typical document structures such as title, scope, document number, decision date or date of enactment/annulment, facts, findings, grounds, legal proposition etc., which offer a base for semantic annotation. This does not mean that statistical approaches are unfeasible for legal information retrieval, but they have to be adapted to legal texts and enriched by meta-data and semantic information, cf. Liebwald (2008).

2. Case studies: N-Lex, EUR-Lex and the EUROVOC thesaurus

2.1 A short introduction to the EUROVOC thesaurus

The EUROVOC thesaurus,[11] which is used in various applications, is also integrated in N-Lex and EUR-Lex. EUROVOC is a multilingual and mul-

---

11. EUROVOC is maintained by the EC Publications Office and available at http://eurovoc.europa.eu. The site also offers a subject-oriented or alphabetical version of

tidisciplinary thesaurus and was originally built for processing the documentary information of the EU institutions. It offers a controlled set of vocabulary covering 21 wide-ranging fields, more than 20 languages and more than 6,500 concepts for each language of which about 500 are top terms, and with a maximum depth of 8 levels. EUROVOC comprises more than 6,650 reciprocal hierarchical relationships (broader term BT/narrower term NT), and 3,600 reciprocal associative relationships of various kinds (related term RT). With regard to equivalence relationship, the numbers of non-descriptors (used for UF/USE) and scope notes vary from language to language. Some descriptors are accompanied by scope notes (SN). Scope notes contain either a short definition or guidance how to use the descriptor when indexing documents and formulating queries. The 21 fields of the first level split up into some 130 micro-thesauri. All descriptors are accompanied by a reference to a micro-thesaurus (MT).[12]

EUROVOC, however, contains "European" concepts, with a certain emphasis on parliamentary activities. It is an effective tool to index (European) documentary resources and to retrieve documents indexed by this means, but its general usability in full text or cross-national retrieval is limited.

2.2 The experimental N-Lex project

N-Lex is an attempt of the EC Publications Office to provide a common gateway to national law of the EU member states. It is an experimental system, put online for test-use in April 2006. N-Lex allows users to search the official national legal databases of 22 member states using a single, uniform N-Lex search screen. The idea behind N-Lex is to allow easier access to diverse national legal databases by offering one single access point.

A user may choose the source country and then fill in one or more input fields. This query put to N-Lex is forwarded unaltered to the input form of the respective national database. In the next step, N-Lex presents the original result set or result document of the actual national database in its own main frame. Therefore, N-Lex has to tackle four main obstacles: (1) multi-

---

Eurovoc 4.2 in pdf format for download and basic information on the structure and development of the thesaurus.

12. EUROVOC has been compiled in accordance with ISO 2788-1986 and ISO 5964-1985.

lingualism, (2) diverse national legal systems, (3) the recall from 22 different technical systems, and finally (4) the various user groups and their particular information needs.

2.2.1 Multilingualism

The user may choose her/his preferred language in the search form, the language bar offers 20 languages. For example, a user may choose the Austrian database but select her/his native language for display of the search mask and to show help and some general information. However, a user lacking sufficient language abilities will not be able to formulate an adequate query or assess the retrieved documents. The national databases provide their legal documents and corresponding meta-data in the respective national language(s). It is a long term goal to have all the national legal documents translated into all 23 official languages of the EU. However, such automatic translations of legal documents lack authenticity and might be erroneous. The EUROVOC thesaurus, which is implemented to translate search terms, is not very helpful since it uses European terminology and does not provide any additional linguistic support.

2.2.2 Diverse legal systems

Information on the respective national databases (link *"general information"*) is poor, and the user is left with many questions regarding completeness, authenticity and timeliness of the content, the document hierarchies, the document types and their structure, and the relationship between documents.

The consultation of the Austrian RIS database[13] per N-Lex shall demonstrate the shortcomings. A user might at first take a look at the *"general information"* to check the content and completeness of the Austrian database. The *"general information"* site will tell the user that the Austrian Legal Information System RIS contains federal and provincial law gazettes, federal law, provincial law, municipal law, case law of various courts, deci-

---

13. The RIS database is the legal information system of the Republic of Austria operated by the Austrian Federal Chancellery. It is available at http://www.ris.bka.gv.at/. The section *"Austrian laws"* even provides a few nonofficial English translations of statutes.

sions of various administrative tribunals, etc. If the user is satisfied by this information, she/he might move on to the search mask. Unfortunately, the user would then miss the sentence *"N-Lex allows users to search the consolidated Federal legislation of Austria"* somewhere in the middle of the text. This would inform the user that not all of the content of the Austrian RIS database is accessible via N-Lex. But what does *"consolidated Federal legislation"* exactly mean? And is the database complete with regard to federal legislation? Is state law of minor importance? What about previous documentation and timeliness?

Consolidated versions are, however, not the authentic versions. Authentic versions are available in the federal law gazette only[14], which is a sub-database of RIS and not accessible through N-Lex. Austrian federal statutes as well as later amendments are published in the electronic federal law gazette. Amendments contain only those elements of the statute which have changed. To determine the actual wording of a statute at a specific point in time one has to put together the original statute (*"Stammgesetz"*) and all relevant amendments. This is a cumbersome task, therefore the RIS database generously provides consolidated versions. These consolidated versions incorporate all amendments, but they are not binding, may eventually not be up to date and there is no liability for correctness. To be able to provide consolidated versions and also versions at other specific points in time, the Austrian RIS database does not store complete statutes, but each article of a statute separately. The result list therefore displays not titles of statutes, but single articles of statutes. Without this additional information, the result set will be incomprehensible for the user, especially since "zero-articles" also exist. "Zero articles" contain some basic information about a statute such as entry into force, legal basis and a list of the amendments.

On the way to a relevant result document the user may encounter another problem. The N-Lex system allows the user to restrict the search to a specific document type. But the selection provided in the help-text is German and there are no further explanations, e.g. on the quality or hierarchy of the document types. In general the Austrian legal theory distinguishes between abstract general norms addressed to the general public (e.g. constitutional law, statutes, regulations), and individual, specific norms addressed to individuals (e.g. courts decisions, administrative rulings). The distinction

14. From 2004 onwards, the legally binding Austrian federal law gazette is published in RIS only (authentic electronic federal law gazette at http://www.ris.bka.gv.at/). See Engeljehringer and Schefbeck (2006).

between public and private law is still a fundamental structural element of the entire legal system. Furthermore, the Austrian legal system is based on the traditional "hierarchy of norms" (*"Stufenbau der Rechtsordnung"*) which was developed by Hans Kelsen and Adolf Merkel and is accompanied by specific abrogation and precedence rules. Law is created at different levels, at state, federal and municipal level, whereby, contrary to the German system, state law and federal law have the same rank. Various bodies establish these different types of norms.[15]

Finally, a user unfamiliar with the respective legal system and legal language will not be able to evaluate the retrieved result documents and thus make use of the legal information. The user will lack knowledge concerning the context of legal documents. Additionally, information is in fact incomplete. State law is not of minor importance in Austria, but is missing in N-Lex. Even in civil law systems the law is not simply reduced to (federal) legislation. For interpretation of the law it may be necessary to refer to preparatory work, case law, administrative decisions and doctrine. The integration of case law or the establishment of an "N-Curia" would be preferable, but be an even more challenging task. Yet, the interlinking of ECJ and national case law is in a fledgling stage.

The EULEGIS (European Legal Information in a Structured Form) research project, which took place from 1999 to 2001, already identified the critical points related to the merger of different national legal databases.[16] EULEGIS aimed to offer a consistent user interface to retrieve legal information created in different legal systems and at different levels. Information on the context of legal documents was given by graphical data models. The prototype offered three different views: an actor view, a process view, and a legal information source view. The models were abstract and simplified and therefore not perfect, but helpful, cf. Lyytikäinen et al. (2000a), and Lyytikäinen et al. (2000b). The results of EULEGIS have never been commercialized but were available for the EUR-Lex and N-Lex projects. The follow-up work within RASKE2[17] focused, however, on Finnish and European law and on legislative standards.

15. For further details see Hausmaninger (2003).

16. The EULEGIS project involved nine partners from six European countries under Finnish coordination and was part of the Telematics Application Programme of the European Commission. An overview on the EULEGIS reports is available at http://www.it.jyu.fi/raske/publications.html.

17. RASKE2, Methods for the Integration of Systems and Services in e-Government, 2003-2006. See http://www.it.jyu.fi/raske/.

2.2.3 N-Lex and EUROVOC

The implementation of the EUROVOC thesaurus in the experimental N-Lex application clearly demonstrates the limits of such thesauri for free text and cross lingual information retrieval. Within N-Lex, EUROVOC is intended to support full text search capabilities. National legal documents (legal documents produced by the member states) are generally not linked to EUROVOC descriptors. Therefore, a corresponding keyword search cannot be established. Users may either browse EUROVOC and select a suitable descriptor in the target language or search for a descriptor in her/his preferred language and ask for the translation into the target language.

Due to the fact that EUROVOC uses European terminology, it is not convenient to search or to index national legal documents, even if those texts are partially based on European input requirements. Each member state has its own legal tradition, legal system and legal terminology. A national indexer would in many cases choose different descriptors based on national legal traditions and interpret EUROVOC descriptors in a different way. Additionally, EUROVOC descriptors do not necessarily appear in the relevant national legal texts. On the contrary, more specific concepts, variants of concepts and specific national legal language terms are used within national codes and case law. Moreover, EUROVOC appears to be based to some extent on literal translations not indicating the exact implied meaning. European as well as literally translated concepts usually do not correspond to the terms and phrases a national user of a legal database would use naturally.

For example, the German concept *"Datenschutz"* is a prominent concept in German and Austrian law, but is not covered by EUROVOC. Austrian and German lawyers will connect a specific concept regarding the protection of personal data processed by electronic means to the term *"Datenschutz"*. On the other hand, EUROVOC offers the English concept *"data-processing law"* for the German translation *"Datenrecht"*. What is *"Datenrecht"*? A test search revealed that *"Datenrecht"* is never used in Austrian or German legislation. EUROVOC also offers the concept *"personal data"* and the German translation *"persönliche Daten"*. The Austrian legal language as well as the Data Privacy directive use the concept *"personenbezogene Daten"*. Searching the Austrian law with the search term *"persönliche Daten"* will retrieve result documents, but not the relevant ones. It will mainly retrieve those texts containing the terms *"persönliche"* and *"Daten"* beyond the meaning of *"personenbezogene Daten"*. Incidentally, specific concepts such as the three actors of the Data Privacy directive, the "controller", the "third party", and the "data subject" as mentioned in the example in chapter 1.1., are not included by EUROVOC.

Once the N-Lex user has chosen a fitting EUROVOC descriptor, the system sends the search question to the corresponding national databases. Most of these national databases execute a simple string search. Specific technical parlance, morphological changes, derivations, compounds, synonyms, polysems, etc. are therefore not taken into account.[18] Only those documents containing exactly the same character string are sent back to the user. EUROVOC offers, for example, the English concept *"protection of communications"* and the corresponding German concept *"Brief-, Post- und Fernmeldegeheimnis"*. This string is never used in Austrian legislation, even though the concept does exist. Searching the German law delivers 22 hits.

This accumulation of shortcomings produces incomplete result sets with low-recall or even empty result sets. Using EUROVOC in the way in which it is implemented in N-Lex wrongly assumes that all agents use exactly the same wording to state the same thing and that the same terms always have the same meaning.

2.2.4 Diverse technical systems

N-Lex currently provides one unified search screen for 22 different technical systems. Queries are forwarded to the respective national database, and the actual result set or documents are displayed in the N-Lex main frame.

The N-Lex search mask offers only a few input fields (full text search, search in document titles, document type, document number, date of document), some of which may or may not function depending on the country selected. The input field for document numbers is not available for many countries, and where it is active, the necessary input format is not clear. In the help section, N-Lex advises against using the date/time span field, *"as it is ... liable to produce zero responses"*. In fact, the results retrieved by using the date-field are not comprehensible, at least regarding searches for Austrian legal documents. Document numbers and date/time-span are,

---

18. There are of course language and provider dependent differences (additional functions offered by the corresponding national provider will influence/better the result set).

however, of vital importance and in many cases even essential criteria for the identification of legal documents.

The original input forms of the national legal databases offer more sophisticated search fields and search functions. Their search screens are not only adapted to the national legal systems, the national document structure, and the national language(s), but also to the features and abilities of the respective technical system. Even search functions most typically used for legal information retrieval may have been implemented in very different ways. In the national systems, digital information is available in different formats and comes along with country specific meta-data. A simple, unified search mask covering all of these different legal and technical systems nullifies many of the country specific functionalities, meta-data, and textual information.

A query put to N-Lex is forwarded unaltered to the actual national database. The user is given absolutely no information on the technical functioning of the corresponding national systems, which influences the appropriateness of a search. Most of the national databases do either a simple string search or a type of automatic stemming. In a string search, the search string put forward by the user is matched exactly, character by character, with the respective index. Stemming is used to expand a query to morphological word variations. Without some basic information on the functioning of the system in the background and about necessary input formats, the user is left alone with a trial and error game. Inconsistencies and heterogeneity have already proven difficult within one specific legal system. Users are in general not aware of the consequences of an inadequate query and therefore not able to adapt their query.

Now back to the Austrian RIS database in N-Lex. The RIS system does string matching. Through N-Lex, search strings may be compared either to the title or to the full text of federal statutes. The field *"document number"* does not work, the field *"date of document"* retrieves unreliable results. Furthermore, there is a field *"document type"* and a German list of the document types allowed. The user will eventually find out that it is not possible to restrict the search to document types which include the special character "ä" in their name. Perhaps the user will try a full text search without any further restriction. The help entry tells the user: *"The search terms must be entered in French, with or without accents. Do not enter nouns and adjectives in the plural, or use conjugated forms of verbs; the targeted search engine will find a word in all its various forms."* This is of course completely false. Search terms must be entered in German and the targeted search engine will not find word variants but execute an exact string matching. The font size of the retrieved result documents is much too small and hardly readable, increasing the font size using corresponding browser functions entails that the fonts of the other frames of N-Lex also become resized, overlap and do not fit to the screen anymore.

Assuming the user has German language skills and some knowledge of the Austrian legal systems, she/he enters exactly the string *"Strafgesetzbuch"* or *"StGB"* into the field *"title"*. The result list will display 385 documents (50 documents per page), because the statute is split up in its articles. Maybe the user is lucky to know the relevant article number, in this case she/he can scroll and browse, a respective search field does not exist. Otherwise the user may either go back to the search form and try to restrict the search by adding keywords like *"Mord"* (*"murder"*) to retrieve a specific article, or click all 385 documents. Contrary to the original database RIS, N-Lex does not support the building of a consolidated version, therefore it is not possible for the user to display a statute as a whole document. N-Lex indeed displays the link *"Geltende Fassung"* in the blue bar on top of the document retrieved from the RIS system, but this link does not, as it does within RIS, retrieve the consolidated version.

The example perfectly illustrates the multitude of difficulties for a unification of different technical systems, which differ in functionality, user interfaces, content, structures, document types and languages. Additionally, the national technical systems may change. Expert knowledge is needed about the local national databases and the local legal systems, advanced technical skills and some enthusiasm for accuracy in detail as well as a lot of manual and intellectual work to make a cross-national legal information retrieval system work properly. National retrieval systems also represent a specific national legal system from the technical point of view. They are not built coincidentally; there are reasons why they are as they are. The knowledge about the differences must be accepted and implemented as far as feasible.

2.2.5 Diverse user groups

The user target group of N-Lex is not clear and the user's perspective is widely ignored, except the language choice for the search screen. N-Lex will, however, not solve real life questions of persons subject to the law. A family migrating to another EU member state and searching for information regarding taxes, social insurance, childcare, etc. does not consult N-Lex. The semantic spaces of laypersons differ significantly from the semantic spaces of the lawmaker or legal expert. Usually they will not be able to retrieve relevant bills from legal databases or be able to identify the relevant articles therein. They will not understand the original text of a bill or the legal language, and they will need some complementary explanations in their common language. It is even more unlikely that citizens will understand the concepts, structure and language of a foreign legal system. Citizens need citizen-tailored texts and will appreciate supplementary information such as the responsible departments, contact data or references to further appropriate services. N-Lex gives citizens the impression of a common legal culture, which does not exist in reality.

N-Lex is restricted to legislative texts on the federal level but does not reflect the entire national legal systems. Nevertheless, it may be useful for EU institutions and some national documentary and legislative services. N-Lex presupposes an expert user who knows what she/he is looking for and already has specific information available, for example the title of a statute or some striking keywords. A more advanced search is hardly conceivable. However, N-Lex could serve as a basis for a more advanced system monitoring national implementation measures.

2.2.6 Final remarks on N-Lex

On its welcome page, N-Lex states: *"The search possibilities and the results are completely dependent on the national sites, which explains the differences in the availability of search criteria and in the presentation and scope of results."* The examples above clearly falsify this statement. N-Lex reduces the capabilities as well as the contents of the national databases. Dubious input formats, insufficient information on search strategies, structures and content will misguide the user and lead to inappropriate queries. Regarding the N-Lex system, the general principle that authenticity is directly related to the closeness to the original source is true.

In its current state, N-Lex displays many deficiencies and considers differences in the national legal and technical systems inadequately. However, it is still in the experimental phase and some points of criticisms might become obsolete at a later time. At least, it offers a single access point and has provided a first test that can be studied and improved upon.

2.3 EUR-Lex

EUR-Lex, the gateway to EU law which is the result of the merger of CELEX and old EUR-Lex in 2002,[19] provides direct and free access to EU law. EUR-Lex contains the legal texts of the EU institutions published in the Official Journal, and the European Court Reports in all official EU languages. All language versions are authentic versions. Article 13 (1) of regulation 1049/2001/EC defines which documents have to be published in the Official Journal. However, the exact extent of the documentation in terms of completeness (full text/references only, covered document types, etc.) and continuity (backward documentation, topicality, etc.) in the numerous document types and different languages is unclear to most users.

Contrary to N-Lex, EUR-Lex focuses on EU law. Nevertheless, that does not mean that EUR-Lex must not consider the diversity of national legal systems and the diversity of national document structures, document types and formats. Users are caught up in national legal language, conceptual thinking and search strategies and have to draw correct relations from European to corresponding national law and vice versa.

2.3.1 The EUR-Lex search functions

EUR-Lex offers two search interfaces: a simple search function with many sub-search masks as well as an advanced search function, available since August 2006.

---

19. CELEX has a long tradition as the key database offering European Community law. The work on CELEX started as early as 1967 and since 1971 it has been available for internal use. In 1980 CELEX was opened against a fee also to external users. For the CELEX history see e.g. Bernet (2006), and Düro (2006). In 1998 a new databank, EUR-Lex, was established with the intention of providing the Official Journal on a daily basis. Subsequently, EUR-Lex has been enhanced, improved and gradually expanded to the CELEX content. Since 2002, EUR-Lex has been available on the internet free of charge. By the end of 2004, CELEX and its less functional but free of charge counterpart EUR-Lex were replaced with a new version of EUR-LEX. Primarily the interface and the alignment of the language versions changed, the basic database structure remained. See Berteloot and Cruz (2006), and Liebwald (2005).

2.3.1.1 The EUR-Lex advanced search

The new Java applet based advanced search, which relies on the old CELEX tool Expert 4, is indeed a powerful search tool. It integrates a wide range of Boolean operators and allows exploitation of the extensive field structure of the database. Nevertheless, it is in no way a comprehensive and timely tool. The applets work rather slowly and appear to be experimental. Just as in the old CELEX it is likely that the user will have serious problems with respect to incompatibility and firewall blocking. To benefit from the advanced search function the user is expected to have a deep understanding of the underlying data structure. The database covers about 100 different document types, all of which are marked with a specific identification code, and more than 100 different possible fields, allowing a very detailed structuring of documents. The search tool is targeted to information experts, e.g. documentalists, information intermediaries or EU staff, and especially to those who are familiar with the old CELEX Expert Search Version 4 and the structure and the content of the database. A typical legal expert who does not use the search tool on a very regular basis will have trouble with the formulation of a query. The engineering of more advanced search screens is left to commercial hosts. Here an example of a fairly easy query taken from the Expert Search Quick Start Guide:[20]

> *(Title = equal treatment NOT wom?n) NOT Type_Sector = 9 AND Date_of_document >= 2006/11/01*

According to this query, the system will search for documents which contain the phrase *"equal treatment"* (exact string matching), but not the terms *"woman"* or *"women"* in the title, furthermore documents of the sector 9, which are parliamentary questions, will be excluded, and the search will be restricted to documents issued on 1st November 2006 or later. A search field assistant and a descriptor lexicon support the user in the selection of appropriate fields and descriptors.

---

20. The Expert Search Quick Start Guide 11/2006 is available at http://eurlex.europa.eu/en/tools/help_advanced.pdf (in English only). However, the 23 pages guide is indeed a Quick Start Guide, the full exploitation of the advanced search tool requires more detailed reference information. The old 131 pages CELEX Expert Search Guide from 2001 is not available for free download any more.

2.3.1.2 The EUR-Lex simple search

Considering the huge amount of documents the simple search function is not sufficiently powerful. Simple search allows a direct search of document numbers or publication references as well as a direct search with search terms, date or time span, the author, classification headers (directory of community legislation, case law directory), subject matter, or EUROVOC-keywords. The search can also be restricted to a specific category (treaties, legislation, preparatory acts, case law, parliamentary questions), which offers another direct search in the next step (search terms, date, author, kind of procedure, etc.). The organization and classification of documents as well as the legal terminology, however, do not correspond to the usage of national practitioners. The directory of community legislation in force, for example, is based on the structure of the EC Treaty.

The keyword search within simple search does not allow many term combinations. It allows only reduced Boolean logic without the proximity of field operators. Bracket terms cannot be used either. The form provides two fields to be connected by the Boolean AND (*"WITH"*) and a third field which represents the Boolean NOT (*"EXCEPT"*). The search term can be a single word or a string of words (phrase). This means that only two words can be connected by a conjunction (Boolean AND). Should the user enter more than one word in a field, a phrase search will be conducted to produce the exact string as a result. A disjunction (Boolean OR) can be achieved by using a comma between the terms. Furthermore, an asterisk for truncation and a question mark as a wildcard to replace one single character can be used. Both symbols may only be used in the middle or at the end of the string, not at the beginning.

As far as free text searching is concerned, the limited functionalities of the simple search are most obvious. EUR-Lex contains a huge amount of documents. According to the EUR-Lex FAQ (point 2.2.) *"it includes some 400,000 references in several languages, 1,400,000 texts in total*[21]*. An average of 15,000 documents are added each year."* Therefore a simple search usually retrieves much too large result sets, except in those cases

21. According to Berteloot and Cruz (2006): 1.800.000 documents in total, 410.000 bibliographical notices, and some 12.000 new documentary units each year. A search in EUR-Lex in the English versions of secondary legislation retrieves that 2936 regulations, 317 directives and 1353 decisions (each inclusive corrigenda; the search was not restricted to legislation still in force) were published in 2006.

where the user has the correct reference number or title available. Even the use of *google* or another internet search engine to retrieve a correct title, a reference number or proper keywords or phrases of a legislative or court document, which can be used for a search in EUR-Lex, is not a bad approach. The more powerful advanced search is not an acceptable alternative for most users. There is still a real need for a more powerful but more easily manageable search function, especially for specific groups of expert users.

Contrary to the old EUR-Lex version, the user may either search the full text or alternatively restrict the simple search to document titles with the advantage of a more precise result – provided that the user has striking title-keywords or the title available. EU directives or regulations usually have "meaningful" titles, but those titles are unsuitable for general use.[22] Therefore national legal languages create abbreviations. E.g. the directive *95/46/EC of the European Parliament and of the Council of 24 October 1995 on the protection of individuals with regard to the processing of personal data and on the free movement of such data* is better known as *"Data Privacy directive"*[23], in Austrian or German legal language as *"Datenschutzrichtlinie"*. Neither *"privacy"* nor *"Datenschutz"* appear in the titles, the term *"data"* respectively *"Daten"* appears too frequently for an adequate search. The simple search function allows for the conjunction of two terms only, thus a full-text search will retrieve result sets that are too large. With regards to the Data Privacy directive, Austrian users often fail on a very simple linguistic problem; because the term *"Datenschutzrichtlinie"* does not exist, they try the phrase or conjunction "personenbezogene

---

22. The Swiss Chancellor Annemarie Huber-Hotz presented in a speech in 2000 a much more impressive example of an "meaningful" title: The *Commission regulation (EC) No 2592/1999 of 8 December 1999 amending regulation (EC) No 1826/1999 amending regulation (EC) No 929/1999 imposing provisional anti-dumping and countervailing duties on imports of farmed Atlantic salmon originating in Norway with regard to certain exporters, imposing provisional anti-dumping and countervailing duties on imports of such salmon with regard to certain exporters, amending decision 97/634/EC accepting undertakings offered in connection with the anti-dumping and anti-subsidies proceedings concerning imports of such salmon and amending Council regulation (EC) No 772/1999 imposing definitive anti-dumping and countervailing duties on imports of such salmon (OJ L 315, 9.12.1999, p. 17–25).* Quoted in Herberger (2004).

23. Also: *"directive on the Protection of Personal Data"* or *"Data Protection directive"*, both of which are less problematically in terms of information retrieval.

(AND) Daten" or "persönliche (AND) Daten". However, the exact string of the German title is "personenbezogene*r* Daten"[24] Of course, simple truncation would help, but the users do not expect or recognize this genitive/plural problem.

The deficiencies are even more apparent when a keyword search in ECJ case law is conducted. Once a national lawyer obtained a reference number from a relevant judgment, e.g. from a national law review or bulletin, she/he will perhaps try to retrieve the original decision. Regardless of the crucial importance of the decisions of the ECJ and the Court of First Instance for interpretation of the law and the harmonization of the law of the member states, the use of EUR-Lex as general information pool is rather unusual.

2.3.1.3 EUR-Lex and EUROVOC

One of the main issues is European terminology; users must simply learn "euro-jargon" by experience. Legislative documents in EUR-Lex[25] are indexed according to EUROVOC, and the first level of the simple-search allows a keyword search restricted to those EUROVOC-descriptors. However, EUR-Lex contains a huge amount of documents and only the upper levels of EUROVOC may be selected from the simple search classification schema. Therefore, the use of EUROVOC-descriptors usually results in a set of a few hundred, sometimes even of a few thousand documents. This is contrary to the use of EUROVOC within N-Lex. Of course, the system allows the user to refine the search by adding additional keywords, by selecting the document type or the date/time span. Alternatively the user can use the trial and error method and guess and enter various EUROVOC descriptors from a deeper level or use the advanced search descriptor lexicon. Once at least two letters are entered into the lexicon, an index-assistant may be started which suggests descriptors neighboring the letter combination entered. The index assistant does not exploit the EUROVOC structure to provide, for example, related terms. Admittedly, most of these choices as-

---

24. Richtlinie … zum Schutz natürlicher Personen bei der Verarbeitung personenbezogener Daten und zum freien Datenverkehr.

25. The ECJ case law (sector 6) is, however, not indexed by EUROVOC descriptors, but by the case law directory code. According to the Quick Start Guide coverage is not exhaustive, but generally includes all documents in force on 1 January 1995.

sume additional knowledge about the document or about EUROVOC, which might not be available at this stage, or simply do not reduce the amount of result documents to a manageable number.

2.3.2 Multilingualism

One of the most difficult requirements EUR-Lex has to meet is that of multilingualism, cf. Berteloot and Cruz (2006), and Düro (2006). EUR-Lex offers different language versions for all the official languages of the EU, but one has to be aware that the linguistic coverage is greater for the four languages (Dutch, French, German, Italian) of the founding member states. The French database was the first to be developed and opened to the public. For the other languages only translations of the legislation in force at the time of the accession of the country in question and the texts adopted after this date are available.[26]

A language choice bar on the top of the page allows a result list or a result document to be easily replaced by another language version (if available). Furthermore it is possible, for example, to choose the English search screen but to use German keywords for the search (to achieve this DE must be chosen for German in the pull down menu of the simple search form). In this case the system will produce an English result list of those (English) documents which in their German version contain the entered keywords. Additionally the system offers a bilingual display of documents in the form of two language versions of the same document presented in columns.

Registered users may define a linguistic profile in order to set the preferred languages. The user may choose a main language and determine those languages in which she/he wishes to receive documents not available in the main language. Registration is free.

However, the Expert Search Quick Start Guide exists in English only and the Simple Search Guide in English, French and German. The text of the help entry for the *"First-time user"* is available in English and French only.

---

26. There are only provisional texts available for the new member states Bulgaria and Romania yet.

2.3.3 The additional value of EUR-Lex: bibliographic notices

The heart of EUR-Lex is a bibliographic notice provided for each document. Not only does it offer the basic data of the document such as dates, author, classification, procedure, etc., but it also contains information on the relationship between documents: legal basis, amendments, cited instruments, case law affecting the relevant act, etc. The notice also allows the retrieval of all documents based on or mentioning the result document. In most cases hyperlinks allow direct access of the cited documents. With regards to legislation, a direct link to the respective site on the decision making process (OEIL) is offered for more recent directives and regulations. Also (non-official) consolidated versions are sometimes available, but are not always up to date. Concerning ECJ judgments, hints on some relevant doctrine are provided.

A very important element is the notice on national implementation measures of directives. This notice is somewhat hidden in between the other bibliographic data. Clicking on this notice (*"MNE"*) reveals a list of corresponding national provisions as communicated by the member states. The list usually provides the title(s) of the implementation measure(s) in the respective national language and a document reference, but no active link to the source document.

With a view to EUR-Lex it seems to be common that there are just no explicit, complete, updated and standardized recordings of the implementation measures available, the MNE-entries are inconsistent, incomplete and not up-to-date. Regarding the implementation measures, there are multiple problematic situations with respect to the identification of the relevant national sources, which need to be resolved in a consistent way. The ideal situation in which one specific directive corresponds to exactly one national statue is rare. Additionally, the directory of community legislation is based on the structure of the EC Treaty and does not correspond to national classifications. Eventually there is no implementation measure necessary, because national (federal and/or state) law already covers the requirements set by the respective directive. It is also possible that the directive requires the amendment of a vast number of national statutes on different levels. It is possible that some parts are already sufficiently regulated, while others are not. Or there exist additional national provisions related to the subject but not directly considered by the respective directive.

The notice on national implementation measures could provide a basis for a more sophisticated interface between European law and national implementation measures. At any rate, it would be a laborious but feasible task to enhance the quality of the information and to build a connection to the source documents. To copy an appropriate phrase from a respective entry in the EUR-Lex bibliographic notice on implementation measures and to paste it into the N-Lex search template should already work.

At one time there was work on a EULEX III project conducted by the EU IDA organization (Interchange of Data between Administrations) in cooperation with the European Commission and the Publications Office.[27] Also the Commission Communication Better Monitoring of the Application of Community Law[28] referred to this project. EULEX III aimed at networking national databases to allow electronic communication of transposition measures by interconnecting the national official databases through a single portal for access to Community law. Whereas EUR-Lex contains hints to national measures transposing Community instruments, EULEX III envisaged giving access to full text of national implementing measures. Electronic communication of implementation measures should have made access to Community law and monitoring of conformity easier. Yet, it seems that the project was put on hold sometime in 2003 and priority was given to N-Lex. A project like EULEX III is not only labor intensive and costly, but also relies on the cooperation of the member states. Admittedly, the benefit of the European institutions would prevail.

2.3.4 EUR-Lex: A database for lay citizens and expert users?

Who benefits from EUR-Lex? According to the EU-pages, citizens are the main target users. EUR-Lex was created to make Europe more transparent and to bring it closer to its citizens. The EU is estimated to embrace about 495,000,000 inhabitants[29], EUR-Lex registers about 38,000,000 visits a year[30]. The outcome of this is one visit per citizen every 13 years. Indeed, not many citizens make the effort to read these almost incomprehensible

---

27. See the EULEX III progress reports published by the Council of the EU, Doc. 8055/03 of 22nd May 2003, and 9825/05 of 6th June 2005. The preparatory work (EULEX I) started in 1995.
28. COM/2002/725 final. See also Nurcombe (2003: 39–55) (transcription of a speech by Albrecht Berger: EULEX Project: Access to the Texts of National Measures Implementing Community directives).
29. See EUROSTAT: Population and Social Conditions 41/2007.
30. According to Berteloot and Cruz (2006): 170,000 visits per working day and 38.000.000 visits per year.

directives. Usually they do not know that EUR-Lex exists at all and if a specific rule they have to comply with results from European or solely from national legal sources. Furthermore national politicians and media have some tendency to ascribe failures to mandatory EU rules and prosperities to national policies. The existence of the ECJ is well known and appreciated but out of reach for the average citizen. In general lay citizens search neither for ECJ nor for national case law.

The original texts of Community legislation are, however, not understandable to most lay citizens. To make the law more easily accessible for the persons subject to the law is an ambitious goal, but from point of view of a lay person, it is not sufficient to simplify access to the law and then the presentation of the original legal texts. The sole presentation of complex Community legislation does not make legislative texts more comprehensible to citizens, and the law is not accessible in the sense of the principle of access to the law if the people it is intended to address do not understand the texts. Moreover, it is arguable that EUR-Lex in fact provides easy access. In the rare cases lay citizens indeed use a legal database, they will use other concepts than legal experts or the lawmaker,[31] will have other questions, and will have other information needs. Citizens primarily need citizen-tailored texts and issue-related information.

The main users of EUR-Lex are the EU related institutions and national legal experts or at least persons experienced with legal texts and the EU system and with some skills in legal information retrieval. A basic legal knowledge is indispensable. But even experts are shy of using European law resources. An example is given by Marc van Opinjen, who reports from the Netherlands the successful embedding of CELEX in the judge's IT workplace within the Eurinfra-programme. The project was disposed by the Dutch Minister of Justice, who acknowledged the reproach that there is an urgent need to strengthen the Community-law knowledge infrastructure of the judiciary and started in 2000. Judges had only limited knowledge, and interest in, Community law. Just pointing them to the European sources on the EU websites was considered insufficient and the incorporation of

31. Significantly there is a "*plain language guide to Eurojargon*" available in 20 languages at the Europe-server (http://europa.eu/abc/eurojargon/index_en.htm). According to this site the guide was developed because euro-jargon can be very confusing to the general public. The language guide and the attached glossary contain in sum about 300 concepts and short descriptions, but the concepts are not linked to further information and the descriptions do not solve real life questions.

CELEX into the Dutch Porta Iuris, the legal knowledge portal on the intranet of the Dutch judiciary, which already integrated legal sources from various suppliers, offered the additional advantage of making legal dependencies more easily clear. In any case, the Eurinfra-programme was successful, EU law is now integrated in daily practice and interest was raised at the policy level, cf. van Opinjen (2006) and Prechal et al. (2005).

2.3.5 The (expert) user's perspective[32]

Too much time has to be spent to find out the relevant functions and to understand the system's structure as well as to identify the precise content. The simple search functionality is limited, and the advanced search function hardly manageable. The various search strategies and search forms, the database structure, the diverse collections, document types and available formats irritate many users. Information about EUR-Lex is scattered and fragmented, and the user has the confusing choice between "Sitemap", "Help", "FAQ", a Simple Search Guide (to be downloaded in five separate PDF files), an Expert Search Guide (which is valid for the *"advanced search"* function) and a newsletter.

It is indicative that the Institute for European Studies (IES), Vrije Universiteit Brussel,[33] presented an e-learning project on the better use and understanding of EUR-Lex and other European information sources to be integrated in the existing IES e-learning programs on EU Law and related topics.[34] That idea clearly shows that European information sources are far from being easy and self-explanatory, even for experts. A subscription-based e-learning tool to train the use of the Europe-Server and EUR-Lex is necessary to make use of the free information sources. Nevertheless, the project is commendable since consideration of legal information retrieval in law curricula is in general rather poor.

Also the author herself gained considerable experience in teaching legal information retrieval to students as well as to practitioners and professionals and therefore knows very well the problems facing a typical user. Teaching legal information retrieval is sometimes nearly as cumbersome as

32. See also Hudson (2006).
33. See http://ies.be and http://www.vub.ac.be.
34. This project was presented by Ruben Lombaert and Frederique Lambrecht at the JURIX EU-Info-Workshop ("Integration of EUR-Lex in e-Training Environments"), Brussels, December 2005.

building the ideal information retrieval system. A typical lawyer is not very interested in technical material and Boolean logic, and lawyers are generally not known for their IT skills. In the words of Michael Lloyd: "... *the lawyer does not wish to learn how his car works; he wishes to drive it*" (Lloyd 1986: 23). To teach the EUR-Lex advanced search function to lawyers would be wasted time and frustrate the scholars. Lawyers expect an uncomplicated system which accurately and precisely retrieves the relevant documents and usually capitulate easily when facing difficulties with the system. Of course, what users believe is relevant differs and depends inter alia on individual experience, the individual case, and the intention of the information request. For lack of technical knowledge on how information retrieval and the actual system works, users are not able to assess the reasons why their query retrieved "dubious" or "zero" results. This makes a determined effort to reformulate an inadequate query impossible.

Concerning European law and EUR-Lex there are also comprehensibility problems, especially in regards to database and document structure, document types including document numbers, the systematics of concepts, the complexity of the decision making process and the production process of texts, and the relationship between European documents and between European and national legal acts. Also the classification systems, which are especially the directory of legislation in force, the case law directory code, the subject matter index, and the EUROVOC descriptors, are closed books for most users.

Furthermore users dislike changes and strain under the diversity of legal databases they have to launch. One or two for doctrine, the library catalogue, another database for legislation, preparatory work or case law, and then a database tailored to a specific field of law or an internally system, and finally various European information sources. All of them feature different functions, show different structures and require different search strategies and operators. The learning curve for each new system is difficult. Nevertheless, the minimizing of the number of interfaces and the engineering of inflexible, confusing and hardly manageable mammoth-databases is not what users have in mind. Yet, users are also confused by the overlapping content of different EU law resources. This is especially true for EUR-Lex and CVRIA[35] on the one hand, and EUR-Lex, PreLex[36],

35. The CVRIA site and its case law databases are available at http://curia.europa.eu.
36. PreLex is available at http://ec.europa.eu/prelex/.

and OEIL[37] on the other hand.[38] This problem is amplified by the fact that the precise contents of the various databases are unclear to the users.

CVRIA is the homepage of the ECJ. Dependent on the specific information request, the use of CVRIA collections might be more advisable than to search documents of the ECJ, the Court of First Instance and the Civil Service Tribunal per EUR-Lex. It provides additional information on case law, like an alphabetical table of subject matter, a digest of the case law or references to published legal literature,[39] and in comparison to EUR-Lex a more advanced search form for its CVRIA case law collection. However, case law documentation in the CVRIA database starts with 17th June 1997, for earlier cases the user has to switch to EUR-Lex.

PreLex is the database on inter-institutional procedures of the European Commission and follows the major stages of the decision-making process between the Commission and the other institutions. It provides also those documents, which are not published in the Official Journal and a more advanced, user-friendly and stable interface. OEIL is the legislative observatory of the European Parliament and provides information and files regarding the legislative process from point of view of the Parliament. The use of OEIL needs some training, but it provides appropriate search strategies and an extensive documentation of the legislative history.[40]

2.3.6 Final remarks on EUR-Lex and the forgotten studies of Lloyd and Svoboda

This is the opportune place to refer to two past studies on behalf of the European Communities: the study *"Users of Legal Information Systems in Europe"* of Werner R. Svoboda, which was completed in 1977 and published in 1981, and the study *"Legal Databases in Europe: User Attitudes*

---

37. OEIL is available at http://www.europarl.europa.eu/oeil/.

38. Austrians are often additionally confused by the fact, that the RIS database of the Austrian Chancellery also provides a German "EUR-Lex/CELEX" version. The so-called RIS-CELEX shows the typical RIS interface and is adapted to the search habits of the RIS users.

39. Those registers are available in French only.

40. Also the document registers of the European Parliament, the European Council and the European Commission are relevant information sources in the legal field. The site http://europa.eu:80/documents/registers/index_en.htm provides an overview on the document registers.

and Supplier Strategies" of Michael Lloyd, which was carried out in 1985 and published in 1986. While the studies are nearly 30 years old and no longer completely valid, Svoboda (1981) ascertained that there existed altogether around 1 million retrievable legal full-text documents and about $2.1x10^9$ source characters (predominantly summaries) in the EC countries. Nevertheless, a lot of findings and statements are still of vital importance.

Both studies highlight the complexity of legal databases and the fact that only few of the facilities of a legal database are in practice used by most users. Search strategies should be few and simple in nature, Lloyd additionally criticizes the "computerese" flavor of the interrogation language. The interrogation language, which at that time had some similarity to the modern EUR-Lex advanced search, is too abbreviated and contains too many codes and special symbols. Furthermore both studies point out the need for improved training in general and in law schools, and disapprove of the usefulness of help facilities and the insufficiency of documentation as well as the poor user-friendliness in general. Lloyd ascertains that users need to access a database at least once or twice a week to be able to use it confidently and effectively and attributes the low level of use of databases to uncertainty over the detailed contents of the database and perceived inconsistency in the contents. Both studies emphasize the importance of the user's perspective and spent much effort on detailed analysis of different users needs and user behavior, cf. Bing (1984). Svoboda additionally states that utopian goals should be secondary to more modest/realistic objectives and that there must be very substantial reason for the adoption of any system changes which affect the user interface. Furthermore, *"one can only aim for constant improvement and not expect to attain absolute perfection."* With regard to CELEX, Lloyd already pointed out: *"a legal database should be able to offer answers to questions formulated according to the local national legal tradition."*

Yet, EUR-Lex has to handle much more information, languages and queries, and users are more discerning today. EUR-Lex is manageable and a great help for those who are familiar with the structure of the database and the peculiarities of the technical system as well as with the European legal system and language. Legal information retrieval is a learning process and this must be communicated to the users in a motivating way. Nonetheless, becoming accustomed to the system and "to drive the car" could be easier, and there is space and hopefully also the willingness for constant improvement.

2.4 Final remarks on EUROVOC

The correct conclusion is not that EUROVOC is generally a bad thesaurus of low quality but that it is being used for purposes other than originally intended and has not been adapted to such uses.[41] For the reasonable use in EUR-Lex and especially in N-Lex, EUROVOC has to be supplemented by national legal language concepts. For this reasons a merger of EUROVOC and LOIS or the integration of LOIS into N-Lex has already been taken into account. LOIS (Lexical ontologies for legal information sharing)[42] is a multilingual and linguistically motivated legal thesaurus with natural language definitions of legal terms based on the Princeton WordNet and the EuroWordNet technology[43]. It was developed as a general legal ontology and built independently of a specific application system for the purpose of facilitating multilingual legal information retrieval. With respect to the feasibility of a merger of EUROVOC and LOIS, this approach might be a disadvantage. Structure and techniques of EUROVOC and LOIS differ; they were originally engineered for deviant use cases. Furthermore LOIS definitions are based inter alia to some extent on the U.S. Princeton WordNet 1.6, which might differ from European legal language(s), and on legal definitions extracted from different language versions of EU directives, cf. Dini et al. (2005). Corresponding national legal concepts or legal definitions (*implemented_as* relations) have to be linked and integrated manually. This is feasible for a specific field of law, but considering the dynamics of the law and the huge amount of European and national rules in the 27 member states on a general basis, it is almost impossible or at least very expensive. However, LOIS provides a solid basis that can be studied and improved upon. An integration of EUROVOC into LOIS or at least an alignment is possible and dependent on the use case also promising, but will not resolve the dilemma of conceptual differences across the various national legal systems on its own. Nonetheless, national legal concepts, which do not only differ in terms, but also in meanings and systematics, have to be considered and attached adequately.

---

41. More successful was e.g. the test use of EUROVOC for calculating document similarity for European texts. See Steinberger et al. (2002).
42. LOIS was developed across six European languages (Italian, English, German, Czech, Portuguese, Dutch) within a two-year *e*Content research project 2004-2006. See the LOIS homepage at http://www.loisproject.org/ and Schweighofer and Liebwald (2007). A demonstrator is available at http://search.elois.biz/.
43. See http://wordnet.princeton.edu/ and http://www.illc.uva.nl/EuroWordNet/.

3. Conclusions and next steps

The development of advanced and user-friendly legal information retrieval systems covering different information sources has proven a cumbersome and difficult task. Users' needs in legal information retrieval are often disregarded or not sufficiently communicated to the engineer. In recent years, a new trend from simple full text and keyword search to more sophisticated semantic querying became apparent in legal information retrieval research. This new and promising development, which is characterized by the predominant keywords XML, ontologies and semantic nets or Web 2.0, may entail significant improvement as well in legal information search. Computational linguistics, markup languages, knowledge based methods and semantic representation provide instruments which may facilitate the step from text documentation to content representation. But also modern semantic tools will not, however, work properly if they do not consider the general shortcomings of legal information retrieval and the very specific information needs of lawyers.

With regards to information retrieval systems like EUR-Lex and N-Lex, ontologies could be deployed to support the organization and structuring of information, the integration and interoperation of different technical systems, and, mostly important, for semantic indexing and search. However, multilingual ontologies covering the whole legal system of the EU as well as those of the 27 member states cannot be built manually. Though, the use of natural language processing (NLP) methods to automatically extract and relate concepts of legal text (e.g. norms) for the purpose of ontology engineering is limited, because on the one hand legal terminology differs across nations, and on the other hand NLP cannot sufficiently consider the various meanings of linguistically equal concepts. Relationships between concepts are neither obvious nor easily available and can only be set by human experts. A continuous cross-reference system encompassing all relevant sources is not easy to establish for just one specific legal system, much less across the entire EU and all the local legal systems. Nevertheless, hybrid systems combining statistical and semantic approaches seem most promising for semantic indexing and search, ideally supplemented by agreement on approximation of meta-data. Drafting common European legislative XML standards to be shared by all EU member states will, however, face similar problems that arose within the N-Lex: the diversity of legal cultures and corresponding legal practices, cf. Biagioli et al. (2007).

Additional work must be spent on providing citizen-tailored information and citizen-tailored access to such information, e.g. the semantic translation of the citizen's queries or specific question answering systems. The approach to develop one combined system that serves experts and citizens is perhaps too ambitious and idealistic; such a system runs the risk of being a confusing compromise.

4. References

Bernet, Hélène. 2006. "Les racines: Histoire de CELEX, de 1963 à 1986". *25 Years of European Law Online*. Luxembourg: The Office for Official Publications of the European Communities. 11–23.

Berteloot, Pascale and Manuela Cruz. 2006. "From CELEX and EUR-Lex towards the New EUR-Lex". *25 Years of European Law Online*. Luxembourg: The Office for Official Publications of the European Communities. 36–47.

Biagioli, Carlo, Enrico Francesconi and Giovanni Sarto (eds). 2007. *Proceedings of the V Legislative XML Workshop (Florence 2006)*. Florence: European Press Academic Publishing.

Bing, Jon (ed.). 1984. *Handbook of Legal Information Retrieval*. New York: Elsevier.

Dini, Luca, Doris Liebwald, Lauren Mommers, Wim Peters, Erich Schweighofer and Wim Voermans. 2005. "Cross-lingual Legal Information Retrieval using a WordNet Architecture". *Proceedings of ICAIL*. 163–167.

Düro, Michael. 2006. "CELEX Grows Up: History of CELEX from 1987 to 2003". *25 Years of European Law Online*. Luxembourg: The Office for Official Publications of the European Communities. 25–35.

Engeljehringer, Wolfgang and Günther Schefbeck. 2006. *The E-Law Project in Austria: Electronic Support of Law Making*. Vienna: Republik Österreich, Parlamentsdirektion (available at http://www.parlinkom.gv.at/portal/page?_pageid=895,81000&_dad=portal&_schema=PORTAL).

Hausmaninger, Herbert 2003. *The Austrian Legal System*. Vienna: Manz.

Herberger, Maximilian. 2004. "Die Rede von der Verständlichkeit des Rechts in den Zeiten des Internets im Internet: Eine Collage". *Recht verstehen. Verständlichkeit, Missverständlichkeit und Unverständlichkeit von Recht*, ed. by K.D. Lerch, Berlin-New York: Walter de Gruyter. 185–192.

Hudson, Grace. 2006. "The EU's Legal Information Service: A User' s Perspective". *25 Years of European Law Online*. Luxembourg: The Office for Official Publications of the European Communities. 60–71.

Lesmo, Leonardo, Guido Boella, Michele Graziadei, Alessandro Mazzei and Piercarlo. Rossi. 2005. "The next EUR-Lex: What Should Be Done for the Needs of Lawyers Belonging to Different National Legal Systems?". *Proceedings of the JURIX 2005 EU-Info Workshop*. Brussels (available at http://www.di.unito.it/~guido/PS/jurixWorkshopPaper.pdf).

Liebwald, Doris. 2003. *Evaluierung juristischer Datenbanken (Evaluation of Legal Databases)*. Vienna: Verlag Österreich.

Liebwald, Doris. 2005. "An Evaluation of 'New EUR-Lex': All Tasks Achieved and All Problems Solved?". *MR-Int (European Media, IP & IT Law Review)* 3/2005. 156–160.

Liebwald, Doris. 2007. "Semantic Spaces and Multilingualism in the Law: The Challenge of Legal Knowledge Management". *Proceedings of the ICAIL 2007 LOAIT Workshop*. 131–148.

Liebwald, Doris. 2008. "Auf dem Weg zum Begriff: Vom Rechtswort zur Rechtsontologie – Automatisierte Verfahren zur semantischen Erschließung von Texten". *Wort/Bild/Zeichen – Beiträge zur Semiotik im Recht*, ed. by H. Speer, Heidelberger Akademie der Wissenschaften.

Lloyd, Michael G. 1986. *Legal Databases in Europe: User Attitudes and Supplier Strategies*. Amsterdam-New York: Elsevier.

Lyytikäinen, Virpi , Pasi Tiitinen and Airi Salminen. 2000a. "Challenges for European Legal Information Retrieval". *Proceedings of the IFIP 8.5 Working Conference on Advances in Electronic Government*, ed. by F. Galindo and G. Quirchmayer, Universidad de Zaragoza. 121–132.

Lyytikäinen, Virpi. 2000b. "Graphical Information Models as Interfaces for Web Document Repositories". *Proceedings of the AVI 2000, Palermo, Italy, May 23–26*, ed. by V. Di Gesù, S. Levialdi and L. Tarantino, New York: ACM Press. 261–265.

Matthijssen, Luuk. 1995. "An Intelligent Interface for Legal Databases". *Proceedings of the ICAiL 1995*, New York: ACM Press. 114–122.

Matthijssen, Luuk. 1999. *Interfacing Between Lawyers and Computers: An Architecture for Knowledge-Based Interfaces to Legal Databases*. The Hague: Kluwer Law International.

Moens, Marie-Francine and Jos Dumortier. 1998. "Automatic Abstracting of Magazine Articles: The Creation of 'Highlight' Abstracts". *Proceedings of the SIGIR 1998*, New York: ACM Press. 359–360.

Moens, Marie-Francine, Caroline Uyttendaele and Jos Dumortier. 1997. "Abstracting of Legal Cases: The SALOMON Experience". *Proceedings of the ICAIL 1997*, New York: ACM Press. 114–122.

Nurcombe, Valerie J. (ed.). 2003. *Accessing EU documents: new initiatives and developments from the EU institutions: a one day seminar with EIA (London, June 2003)*. London: SCOOP.

Prechal, Sacha, Ronald H. van Ooik, Jan H. Jans and Kamiel J.M. Mortelmans. 2005. *Europeanisatoin of the Law: Consequences for the Dutch Judiciary. Research Memoranda* 2–2005. Den Haag: Raad voor de rechtspraak. (available at http://www.rechtspraak.nl/Gerechten/RvdR/Publicaties/Research+memoranda.htm).

Schacherreiter, Judith. 2006. "Legal Culture und europäische Harmonisierung". *Juridikum* 1/2006. 17–21.

Schweighofer, Erich and Doris Liebwald. 2007. "Advanced Lexical Ontologies and Hybrid Knowledge Based Systems: First Steps to a Dynamic Legal Electronic Commentary". *AI & Law Journal* 15.

Steinberger, Ralf, Bruno Pouliquen and Johan Hagman. 2002. "Cross-lingual Document Similarity Calculation Using the Multilingual Thesaurus EUROVOC (Proceedings of the CICLing 2002)". *Lecture Notes in Computer Science* 2276/2002. 415–424.

Svoboda, Werner R. 1981. *Users of Legal Information Systems in Europe. A Case Study*. München: J. Schweitzer Verlag.

van Opinjen, Marc. 2006. "CELEX embedded: Joint Access to National and Legal Sources.". *25 Years of European Law Online*. Luxembourg: The Office for Official Publications of the European Communities. 73–81.

Wahlgren, Peter. 1999. *The Quest for Law: Law Libraries and Legal Information Management of the Future*. Stockholm: Jure AB.

The LOIS project and beyond

Erich Schweighofer[*]

1. Introduction

Web2.0 (or semantic metadata) ideas are getting stronger attention in law. This should play the role of a catalyser for the journey from predominant syntactic to semantic knowledge representations. The success of projects providing public legal information on the web did not satisfy the need for an easier access to law for the citizen. Legal semantic metadata as some form of describing the sources of a legal system (Visser and Bench Capon 1999) may support search engines in this endeavour.

In civil law, the term *legal system* refers to the body of rules in a territory; in common law, the equivalent term is jurisdiction, the power of courts for application of law in a geographic area. The "law", the statutory and constitutional enactments and court rulings, e.g. the body of principles, norms, standards and rules form the basis of legal knowledge representations. This task of the discipline of computers and law (legal informatics) focuses on the knowledge of a legal order and its proper representations in a computer-usable way, either in legal databases (legal information systems) or legal knowledge systems (legal expert systems) (Schweighofer 1999). In a legal database, legal rules are stored as a structured collection of records or data for information retrieval. In a knowledge system, information and knowledge is represented for computer applications in order to simulate human intelligence.

Whereas the object – the law – is the same, the quality of the knowledge representation is quite different. Legal databases are mostly limited to

[*] On leave; working for the European Commission in Brussels. The author acknowledges the support of Doris Liebwald for helpful comments on an earlier version of the paper and the research assistance of Anton Geist. This paper is based on earlier articles and conference contributions on the LOIS project. Further thanks are due to the anonymous reviewers for their critical and helpful comments.

G. Grewendorf, M. Rathert (eds.): Formal Linguistics and Law, 293–311

syntactic representation. Legal knowledge systems contain highly sophisticated knowledge bases aiming at supporting and replacing human legal reasoning. The syntactic approach smoothed the way to the huge legal databases with the complete coverage of today. A semantic knowledge system proved to be too much of a challenge for legal applications; a lot of research has still to be done.

From a citizen's point of view, the situation remains disappointing. Legal databases are now standard in many legal systems, freely accessible and provide invaluable support for accessing legal norms with powerful search engines but citizens cannot cope with this mass of information and complex vocabulary. Knowledge systems that are easier to use are only available in very specific sectors. Therefore, an improvement of this situation is pressing and the key to it may be legal language.

Legal language has always played a major role in legal thinking and reasoning. In legal documentation, thesauri and classifications have been used for a long time and were added as some sort of meta knowledge in the legal database. The catchword of ontologies, in both computer science and information science a formal representation of a domain as a set of concepts with relations (similar, related, or opposite meanings), adds the advantages of computer-usability together with a more sophisticated data set to the old concept of thesauri. More limited representations, e.g. word lists with definitions and relations, are called lexical ontologies.

The main task of the EU-funded e-Content LOIS project (Lexical Ontologies for legal Information Sharing) was the building of a multi-lingual legal WordNet for the purpose of facilitating legal information retrieval. Thesaurus and lexical ontologies research was used to develop a cross-linguistic ontology with 5000 thesaurus entries in seven languages in order to improve cross-linguistic legal information retrieval. This approach could face the problem of lack of knowledge of a certain language that prevents users from formulating queries, and thus from finding relevant results but also provide some support to lawyers having to cope with the EU's linguistic challenge of 23 official languages.

2. Law and language

Law is closely related to language as this body of regulatory knowledge must be communicated from the lawmaker to the citizens (Rathert 2006; Tiscornia 2006). Vocabulary of lexical items not necessarily restricted to the legal domain are partly associated with specific semantic meaning due to the ontological structuring of a conceptual model of a legal domain with legal concepts. The practice of lawmakers and courts has been arbitrary and legal vocabularies remain difficult and complex. Legal vocabularies contain open-textured terms, are inherently dynamic, and the norms in which legal terms are used are syntactically ambiguous. This allows for contradictions to arise from judicial problem solving. A legal 'language', consisting of a complex structure of concepts, forms an abstraction from the text corpus as represented in legal databases. Such legal structural knowledge does not only contain interpretations of the meaning of legal terms, but also shows the (supposed) logical and conceptual structure.

This assessment is confirmed by many statistical analyses of legal sources. It is well known that statistical tools for ranking do not sufficiently work in legal databases. On the web or in news databases, statistical word distribution provides support for information filtering and classification. In law, results are interesting but not at all satisfying (Schweighofer et al. 2002). On the web, redundancy of knowledge is a measure of importance. In law, the distribution of redundancy is arbitrary and not at all linked to importance. Norms do not (or should not) have any redundancy whereas court decisions contain much redundancy. The relevant ruling or reasoning may be a short paragraph or even only a sentence in a very long legal document.

Bridging the gap between legal text archives and legal structural knowledge is the principal task of studying the law, and the key challenge in legal information retrieval and knowledge representation.

The LOIS project tried to take this fact into account and developed a lexical ontology in the legal domain allowing not only cross-linguistic information retrieval but also making a step towards establishing a more advanced linguistic knowledge base in an advanced structure. Quite evident, the focus of the project was on information filtering and not on information understanding as this would require a much more extended knowledge representation.

3. Potential for information retrieval

Results of queries in legal databases are often too disappointing. It is easy to get some information but 100% recall of relevant knowledge remains a challenge also for experienced searchers.

One main reason lies in the conceptual gap of information retrieval: The syntactic representation provides not knowledge but information hints.

Semantic support for legal information retrieval has gained importance over the years after having been neglected in the 1990ies (Schweighofer

1998). As the other pressing problems of the 1990ies have been solved – bad coverage, difficult interface and quality problems – the vocabulary question plays the central role now. It should be noted that the situation is worsening with the growth of the legal databases.

Thus, legal databases have to offer support for deep linguistic knowledge for their users, e.g. information on vocabulary, synonyms, homonyms, polisems, topics, subtopics, etc. Luuk Matthijssen (Matthijssen 1999) has identified this problem as the conceptual gap: the discrepancy between the users' view on the subject matter of the stored documents in the context of their professional setting and the reduced formal view on these subjects as presented by information retrieval systems. Legal practitioners have to translate their information needs - which they have in mind in the form of legal concepts - into a query, which must be put in technical database terms. Matthijssen's solution, the special interface, proved to be too costly to implement for today's huge legal databases.

Legal research but also database applications address this linguistic problem. For the Norwegian jurisdiction (here two versions of the same language are used, Bokmål and Nynorsk), a special method called "conceptual text retrieval" was developed and is still successfully used. Queries are described by a term class called "conceptor" consisting of a class of words representing the same idea (Harvold and Bing 1977). For the homonym problem, a contextual approach for analysis of different meanings was developed in the KONTERM projects (Schweighofer 1999). The method proved quite successful but not sufficiently appropriate for practical application in huge legal databases in the technological environment of the 1990ies. Legal databases like Westlaw (Turtle 1995) have also included natural search functions taking advantage of linguistic knowledge.

4. Representations of knowledge on legal language

Many possibilities exist for the representation of legal knowledge; however, an optimal solution has not emerged yet. Important questions like the number of term entries, the depth of content and relationships have not found a convincing answer yet.

4.1 Ontologies

Ontologies (Gruber 1993) constitute an explicit formal specification of a common conceptualization with term hierarchies, relations and attributes that make it possible to reuse this knowledge for automated applications. The formalization must be on the one hand sufficiently powerful with regard to the knowledge representation, on the other hand it must offer functionalities for automation as well as tools to be produced automatically (see Hirst 2004 for lexically based ontologies).

In law, two ontologies are required: A world ontology for understanding the facts and a legal domain ontology for structuring the legal knowledge. Any ontology describing the world and its knowledge can be regarded as a world ontology. The term as such corresponds with facts of a legal case: state of things, actions performed, events. Lawyers have to understand – with the help of experts – as much as possible of the world and its facts in order to handle legal governance properly. Thesauri or lexical ontologies may mix both ontologies but at a later stage a strict differentiation is needed for the purpose of legal subsumption.

4.2 Thesauri and lexical ontology

A thesaurus for indexing contains a list of every important term in a given domain of knowledge and a set of related terms for each of these terms (Wikipedia 2007; ISO 2788, 1986). A lexical ontology builds up from this basis with works on glossaries and dictionaries, extends the relations and makes this knowledge computer-usable in order to allow intelligent applications. Lexical ontologies provide this formalised description of a domain that can be understood and re-used by a knowledge system. In law, no particular distinction between world knowledge and domain knowledge is needed at this step.

4.3 Semantic web

The semantic web can be considered as an extension to the current web in providing a common framework that allows data to be shared and reused.[1] According to Tim Berners-Lee, the semantic web is "not a separate web but

1. Website: http://www.w3.org/2001/sw/.

an extension of the current one, in which information is given well-defined meaning, better enabling computers and people to work in cooperation" (Berners-Lee et al. 2001). Information available on the web is semantically tagged and linked using the technologies of Resource Description Framework (RDF), XML and URIs. This layer model (Koivunen and Miller 2002) is based on XML (schema, name spaces) that offers a structuring of documents and data at the syntactic level. The next level forms RDF (schema) using the syntax of XML and providing clear rules for the production of meta-data. RDF describes resources by attributes. The RDF attributes are defined as a valid vocabulary by the RDF schema forming also classes and class hierarchies. The next layer may be a logical one, an inference machine (see for ideas of AI & Law on the semantic web, Benjamins et al. 2005). In 2004, the W3C has published, besides RDF, the Web Ontology Language (OWL) for the development of sets of terms called ontologies that can be used for supporting advanced web search, software agents and knowledge management.

Besides establishing the framework, the web has so far not been changed to a semantic representation and offered a broad high-level structuring of knowledge.

In law, the semantic web constitutes a tool for a representation of domain knowledge but has so far also not been implemented.

4.4 WordNet technologies

WordNet is an online lexical reference system that is an initiative of the linguist George Miller. It has been developed and is being maintained by the Cognitive Science Laboratory at Princeton University (Miller et al. 1990, Fellbaum 1998)[2]. Its design is inspired by current psycholinguistic theories of human lexical memory. It encodes conceptual relationships between terms by arranging them in a hierarchical structure. Words (nouns, verbs, adjectives and adverbs) and their short definitions are grouped into synonym sets (synsets), each representing a specific lexical concept. The synsets are linked by a set of different semantic relations (mainly synonymy/antonymy, hyponymy/hyperonymy, meronymy and morphological relations to reduce word forms). WordNet aims at supporting automatic text analysis and AI applications and at providing an intuitively useable en-

2. Website: http://wordnet.princeton.edu/.

hanced dictionary. The database of the current version 2.0 contains about 150,000 words organized in 115,000 synsets for 200,000 word-sense pairs.

The WordNet technology primarily aims at linguistic support. As concepts are defined with natural language terms, no semantic definitions exist in a formal language. The definitions remain vague from a legal point of view. It is also evident that re-use for automatic reasoning support is limited, cf. Fensel (2004: 6–7).

The motivation of the EuroWordNet (EWN)[3] was the support of mono- and cross-linguistic information retrieval. Based on the Princeton WordNet technology, lexica for eight European languages were developed and connected by an inter-lingual index (ILI) (Vossen 1993). Within the EWN, the structure of the WordNet was supplemented with additional semantic-lexical relations and three top-level categories. The top level offers 63 semantic distinctions grouped into 3 types of entities. They can be accessed by the ILI and form the common semantic framework for all European languages. The work on EWN was finished in 1999 but its framework has been continued by the Global WordNet Association, which builds on the results of Princeton WordNet and EWN and provides a worldwide platform for discussing, sharing and interconnecting WordNets.[4]

A standard conversion of the Princeton WordNet to RDF/OWL has been developed under the auspices of the W3C (Assem et al. 2006).

4.5 Cyc

The aim of the Cyc project is to provide automated applications with a knowledge base of formally represented "common sense": real world knowledge that can provide a basis for additional knowledge to be gathered and interpreted automatically (Lenat 1995). At present, over three million facts and rules have been formally represented in the Cyc knowledge base using CycL, Cyc's formal representation language.[5]

The huge potential of the Cyc knowledge is still under investigation. Applications currently available or in development are integration of heterogeneous databases or intelligent search. In the list of potential applications proposed by the Cyc project, law is not mentioned; semantic data mining may be close to the proposed development of an electronic commentary. However, no experiments are reported in this direction so far.

3. The documentation is available at www.illc.uva.nl/EuroWordNet/docs.html.
4. Further related projects are e.g. EUROTERM, MEANING, BalkaNet or SUMO.
5. Website: http://www.cyc.com/cyc.

4.6 Legal ontologies

Ontologies in law have some particularities due to the legal domain and its language. This legal text corpus is not inherently structured and a formal taxonomy does not exist. Legal structuring as such is done by lawyers, in their minds, and is presented and made explicit in their argumentations and writings. As a product of this process, a legal commentary is considered as the highest level of this endeavour. The understanding of logic remains also quite different from the formal logic of computer science: its open legal concepts, inherent dynamics of law, system models and syntactic ambiguities provide strong impediments to formalisation.

The challenge for legal ontologies is bridging this gap between formal logic required for automated legal applications and the classical logic of jurisprudence. Legal ontologies could function as the missing link between the AI & law and the theory of law. The lack of a sufficient number of explicit specifications of knowledge could thus be solved.

The motivations for the creation of legal ontologies are evident: common use of knowledge, examination of a knowledge base, knowledge acquisition, representation and reuse of knowledge up to the needs of software engineering (Bench-Capon and Visser 1997).

After important preliminary work (e.g. McCarty 1989; Hafner 1978 or Stamper 1991), the frame-based ontology FBO (van Kralingen 1995, Visser 1995) as well as the functional ontology FOLaw (Valente 1995) achieved some prominence. Both were formalized with the description language ONTOLINGUA (Gruber 1993) and represent a rather epistemic approach.

The FBO is designed as a general and re-usable legal ontology, which offers three classes of model primitives, whereby for each unit a frame structure with all relevant attributes is defined. The types of frames are norm, action and concept.

The aim of FOLaw is the organization and interconnection of legal knowledge, in particular with regard to conceptual information retrieval. It contains six basic categories: normative knowledge, meta-legal knowledge, world knowledge, responsibility knowledge, reactive knowledge and creative knowledge. FOLaw has been used in follow-up projects. The central difficulty of the FOLaw proved to be the modelling of the world knowledge. The knowledge gained from FOLaw was used in the project E-Court and in the development of a core legal ontology, LRI-Core (Breuker and Hoekstra 2004).

4.7 Conceptual analysis by semi-automatic text analysis

Automatic text analysis and conceptual indexing provides support in two areas: finding concepts based on corpora-based analysis or linking text corpora to knowledge bases (see e.g. the projects KONTERM (Schweighofer 1999; Schweighofer et al. 2002), SALOMON (Moens et al. 1997), FLEXICON (Smith et al. 1995), SMILE (Brüninghaus and Ashley 2001), SUM (Hachey and Grover 2004) or Support Vector Machines (Gonçalves and Quaresma 2005)). Existing techniques – TFxIDF vector document representation and feature extraction – have proven their feasibility and potential to structure, classify and describe huge amounts of legal text corpora, in particular if intellectual improvement is done. However, scaling-up, e.g. deeper investigation on a larger text corpus and use of a more advanced ontology has not yet been achieved.

On the one hand, ontologies may offer a solution for the structuring of extracted information. Legal databases could be transformed into a semantic representation by semi-automatic means into logical sentences or as process diagrams, conceptual structures or relationships (e.g. AustLII[6], SiteSeer[7]). This semantic representation would not be perfect but provide an easier access to the legal database.

On the other hand, semi-automatic lexical analysis provides support for word sense disambiguation or definitions. In the LOIS project, this tool was used for extracting multi-lingual definitions from the database EUR-Lex.

5. The LOIS project

The main task of the LOIS project (2004-2006) was the development and connection of a WordNet with concepts in seven European languages, based on the EuroWordNet (EWN) framework. Using this framework assured compatibility of the LOIS WordNets with EWN, and allowed them to function as an extension of EWN for the legal domain. Ten partners from six European countries (seven universities/research centres and three enterprises) participated in this project. Within the approved project duration of 24 months, around 5000 synsets were localized for each language involved. The LOIS project primarily aimed at providing easier access to European legal databases for legal experts as well as for laymen. Further research was envisaged on improved techniques for information retrieval, on providing

6. Website: http://www.austlii.edu.au/.
7. http://citeseer.ist.psu.edu/cs.

document standards (common XML standard for the representation of legal documents), on the commercial use of public sector information, on show-case applications for test and demonstration purposes, and on product placement for integration of the result into commercial applications.

5.1 LOIS WordNets

To reach this goal, WordNets of six different languages (Italian, Dutch, Portuguese, German, Czech, English; later on, French was added) were localized and - according to the archetype EWN - cross-linked through an unstructured inter-lingual index (ILI).

Underlying the present research is a model of linking concepts from different legal systems in various languages. This model is based on the following assumptions. First, the meaning of legal terms is for the greater part established in authoritative legal documents. These documents consist of legislation, case law or doctrine (insofar as these document types are considered to be authoritative within a certain jurisdiction). Such legal documents contain terms, some of which are explicitly defined, whereas the meaning of other ones is established on the basis of everyday or contextual use. For explicit definitions, assembling definition elements is relatively easy, especially in continental law, where many of such elements are codified. Sometimes, additional elements have to be assembled from other sources; e.g., different parts of legislation, and discussions in authoritative case law or doctrine. A term with an assigned meaning (either a legal definition, or an everyday or contextual definition) is a *concept*. Thus, legal documents contain terms, and terms refer to concepts, which on their turn are constructed from definitions or definition parts found in legal documents.

With respect to building the LOIS WordNet, especially the definition techniques were useful: generalizations (definitions by general descriptions), specifications (definitions by listing the elements that constitute a concept) and recursive definitions (definitions by listing along the lines of a decreasing set of elements constituting the concept) can be used as glosses for the corresponding terms, abbreviations can be used as synonyms for terms. As to the first and second definition techniques, they merely provide an indication that, instead of an explicit legal definition, the implicit lexical definition should be used. The third definition technique provides an indication that the scope of a definition is extended to a different legislative document; this information can be used in establishing the correct use of WordNet synsets in specific contexts.

The composition of the LOIS WordNet presented challenges for both *defining* legal concepts and for *linking* concepts from those legal systems. First, explicit definitions ought to be given to represent legal concepts in a certain language, and those definitions should be linked to each other in meaningful ways. Second, representations of comparable legal concepts from different languages should be linked to each other in order to create the possibility of cross-linguistic information retrieval. So, for instance, the German legal term 'Eigentum' should be defined, and be linked to (hierarchically) related English legal terms (property), and to comparable terms in other languages (again, if any). In the German "Begriffsjurisprudenz" (concept jurisprudence) a best practice example for such work can be found that is also illustrative for the challenge of such an endeavour (see references in Schweighofer 1999:30 ff.).

In a context of cross-linguistic information retrieval, the links between terms in different languages have to be established on the basis of their meaning. The deviations that exist between lexical meanings and legal meanings pose additional difficulties for this linking activity. First, differences between lexical meanings and legal meanings have to be made explicit. Second, legal meanings are defined relative to a legal system. Definitions of terms contain other terms that can have lexical or legal meanings that are quite different from similar terms in different languages.

Legal terms or concepts with explicit definitions by the lawmaker or the highest courts were the easiest cases. Such definitions could be automatically extracted. It has to be mentioned that such legal terms are context-sensitive, e.g. the meaning is limited to that legal domain. Other concepts are based on general or special meaning in the particular legal context.

The existing Italian legal WordNet 'JurWordNet' (JWN), which was developed as an extension of the Italian part of EWN, provided the basis for the LOIS lexical database (the first module of the LOIS database). Before the start of manual localization, an automatic intersection of the 1695 synsets of the Italian JWN with EuroDicAutom was made. Subsequently, a mapping was created between the English result list of 579 literals and the Princeton WordNet 1.6. The WordNet structures of the different WordNets have been established analogously to the Italian JWN.

The legislative database (the second module of the LOIS database) is based on legal definitions extracted from EU sources and, for the subdomain of consumer protection law, also from the national implementations and other relevant national provisions. For this purpose, a tool was developed to extract legal definitions from European directives (Dini et al. 2005). Definitions of different language versions were automatically connected and national implementation measures could be added manually.

As a result of the distinction of a lexical database and a legislative database, two different types of concepts are represented within LOIS: *lexical concepts*, designated by terms and the lexical meanings assigned to them, and *legal concepts*, designated by terms and their definitions from legal documents.

Regarding language internal relations, primarily, the lexical relations synonymy/antonymy and the taxonomic relations hyponymy/hyperonymy were used. Equivalence relations between synsets in each language were made explicit in the ILI, whereas each synset in monolingual WordNets had – either directly or indirectly by related synsets – at least one equivalence relation with an ILI-record. For demonstration purposes, the subdomain of consumer protection law had been further structured with other WordNet relations.

Figure 1 shows a schematic presentation of the modular LOIS architecture, with the Italian legal database (IT) as example. The main LOIS module is the National Legal WordNet. This is composed of lexical and legal concepts. The first type consists of lexical concept representations. The second type covers legal terminology. These occur in national legislation, and therefore, they are part of the National Legal WN (NC2 in figure 1), and in EU legislation, in which case they are, because of their pan-European character, part of the National Legal WN on the one hand, and the ILI on the other (NC1 in figure 1). Each National Legal WordNet concept representation has a number of information fields associated with it. These provide information on, e.g., language, orthography, definition and associated field of law. Any of these National Legal WordNet concept representations presented in language specific synsets (LSS in figure 1 below) of the corresponding EWN language components that were linked to these synsets by means of plug-in relations.

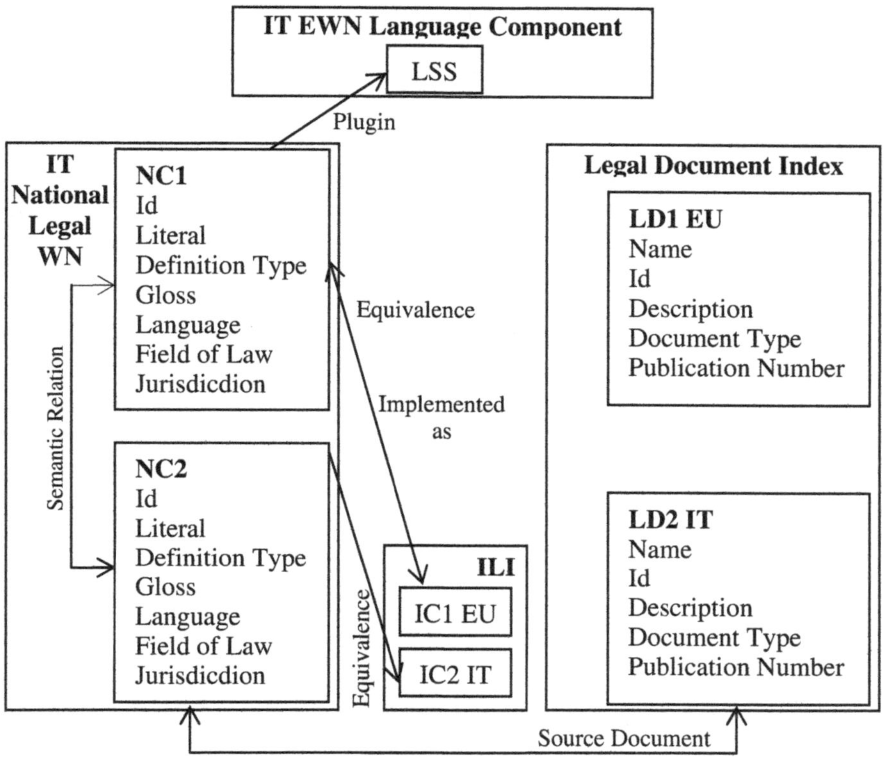

Figure 1. The LOIS database lay-out

All National Legal WordNet concept representations are linked into the Inter-Lingual-Index by means of equivalence relations. Furthermore, an 'implemented as' relation has been introduced to indicate the link between EU concept representations and their nation-specific implementations. The Legal Document Index contains keys into national and European legislative texts in which the legal terms are explicitly used and defined. It was envisaged to establish a consolidated legislative database, comprising current (thus, no historical) versions of statutes. Each legal document (LD in figure 1) had a number of information slots associated with it that further specify its nature. The main information was provided by the CELEX document number that is taken from the EUR-Lex database for EU documents, and local categorizations for national documents.

Overall, the LOIS architecture allows users to investigate a wide range of legal issues, such as the following:

- multiple meanings of terms, due to different legislative sources (for instance, a legislative text amending a definition is considered as introducing a new sense of the concept);
- differences between definitions of concepts in EU and national legislation through the *implemented_as* relation;
- comparisons of national legal systems;
- lexical definitions of concepts, if no terminological definition is given;
- comparisons between common language meaning and terminological legal meaning through available plug-in links.

Two types of relations among legal concepts were distinguished: structural and content relations. Structural relations reflect actual systemic connections between legal concepts; content relations reflect similarities or differences among the meanings of legal concepts. A structural relation that can be used in the current model is the *implemented_as* relation, providing a reference relation between a definition in a Community directive and a definition in a national legislative document. Content relations were taken from standard WordNet relations (especially hyperonymy and hyponymy).

In easy cases, such a legal interrelationship already exists like in European Community legislation, in public international law treaties or in some multi-lingual jurisdictions (e.g. Belgium). Here, multi-lingual legal texts exist that are authoritative and thus deemed to be authentic.

In the standard situation, conceptual structures are different and a legal interrelationship requires some term sense disambiguation.

These problems arise quite often in the transposition of EU law. Transpositions should, of course, remain within the preconditions set by the directive. As Member States can either choose to implement definitions of directives literally, or they can opt for a different definition or refer explicitly or implicitly to existing definitions in the legal system. The implementation relation does not say anything about the way in which a concept is implemented; it only says *that* a concept has been implemented. The implementation relation can be complemented by a relation stating the nature of the link between the original concept and the implemented concept(s). Transposition of EU law was thus classified as equivalence relation (identity could be established), near equivalence relation (definitions are almost identical), narrower term (the national concept has a more specific definition than the Community concept) or broader term (the national concept has a more general definition than the Community concept).

In difficult cases, the relationship has to be established by the lawyer and might later be subject to judicial review by the European Court of Justice. These cases were not sufficiently dealt with in the LOIS database.

Most definitions are very fine examples of lexical definitions but do not sufficiently distinguish different meanings and thus different legal consequences.

The Vienna University group has done some experimental research on this question in distinguishing between the different terms for the same meaning or different meanings for the same term in the German and Austrian legal systems. This proved to be difficult and time-consuming. A detailed study of different legal conceptual structures was required in order to achieve the necessary quality. Thus, only a small selection of terms has been specified.

5.2 Successes and shortcomings of the LOIS project

Each legal lexical ontology has to show quality, accuracy and suitability for practise. The LOIS project proved that thesaurus work is a good start for achieving the required comprehensiveness of legal ontologies in proposing an easier start with a lexical ontology. Thesaurus entries and definitions are hard work but a lot of that can be automated or taken from other works like dictionaries or glossaries. Thus, a good lexical ontology integrating all different endeavours in a legal system has two advantages: a quite complete thesaurus of legal systems and the availability of this thesaurus for automation.

Cross-linguistic and conceptual interrelationship could not be developed to the degree of quality a lawyer needs. These relationships were good for the purpose of legal information retrieval as giving only information hints. However, an automated legal application would require more depth and accuracy of the lexical ontology.

The improvement of legal information retrieval was tested only on a small project and the conclusions are therefore only tentative. The benefit for accessing foreign legal systems was evident. Customary selection of relevant and non-relevant documents was sufficient for some results; but obviously, the better the quality of the lexical ontology, the less work in selecting relevant documents had to be done.

No strong consensus was established in the project group if more synsets would improve the thesaurus. In my view, the number was not sufficient. Taking into account the number of thesaurus entries required for just describing the content of a book, about 10,000 concepts should be represented, not considering additional concepts for world knowledge. However, that would also mean a more difficult linking of the various national synsets or a more stochastic approach.

6. Beyond LOIS

The next obvious step of the LOIS project would be the deepening and broadening of the thesaurus in order to extend the number of thesaurus entries to about 10,000. Further, the linking should be substantially improved.

With about 10,000 thesaurus entries, equivalence relations between terms in different languages and jurisdictions will be much more difficult to establish. The methodology would change, too. The core set of descriptors – the LOIS thesaurus – will be enlarged with those methods, e.g. checking text books, commentaries etc. for proper thesaurus entries. Then, an approach of computational linguistics and legal concept research should be implemented. In order to include as much as possible of linguistic knowledge, a corpus-based approach is proposed. The use of the various terms should be checked against a representative text corpus in order to grasp the various meanings of the term (e.g. KONTERM method). In law, particular focus would be also given to the special term use by different organisations (e.g. lawmaker, courts, authors etc.).

Only on the basis of a well-developed concept system the next step could be implemented: the building of taxonomies, classes and association types and the possibility of linking and equating concepts and definitions in different material contexts and languages for the development of a multilingual ontology. Further, a distinction between world knowledge and legal domain knowledge should be then established.

7. Conclusions and future work

For building the LOIS thesaurus, traditional lexical ontology techniques were used. Legal theory was taken into account as much as possible. The LOIS WorldNet consists of both lexical and legal definitions. With this approach, cross-lingual information could be attained both on a more general, lexical level, and on a more specific, legal level. Lexical definitions could be translated manually on the basis of the original lexically oriented JurWordNet and its English translation. Legal definitions could be based on the authoritative language versions of all European regulations and directives. This offers the possibility of introducing an equivalence relation between legal concepts in different languages. An equivalence relation (for identical concepts from directives) and a near-equivalence relation (for related lexically defined concepts) would establish links between concepts in different languages. If no equivalence or near-equivalence relation was present, analogous hierarchical structures could help finding relations between terms in different languages, for instance by comparative law research. The LOIS project proved that this approach has its advantages but also limitations. A corpus-based approach should be tried.

For the next phase of the project we propose an approach combining methods of legal theory, terminology and computational linguistics. The LOIS thesaurus should be checked against a representative text corpus in the various languages in order to detect the various meanings in different situations and organisations. Then, better equivalence relations should be established.

Such an enlarged and improved thesaurus would not only be a support for legal work, e.g. help for cross-linguistic information retrieval or first information on a legal system, but also an invaluable tool for translators and interpreters.

8. References

Assem, Marc van, Gangemi, A. and Schreiber, G. (eds.). 2006. "RDF/OWL Representation of WordNet, Technical Report", *W3C Working Draft*, freely available at: http://www.w3.org/TR/2006/WD-wordnet-rdf-20060619/.

Bench-Capon, Trevor J. M. and Visser, Pepijn R. S. 1997. "Ontologies in Legal Information Systems: The Need for Explicit Specifications of Domain Conceptualisations". *Proceedings of the 6th ICAIL* (Melbourne, Victoria, AU, 1997). , New York: ACM Press. 132–141.

Benjamins, Richard, Pompeu Casanovas, Joost Breuker and Aldo Gagem. 2005 "Law and the Semantic Web, an Introduction". *Law and the Semantic Web.* ed. by Richard V. Benjamins, Pompeu Casanovas, Joost Breuker and Aldo Gangemi, Berlin-Heidelberg: Springer, 1–17.

Berners-Lee, Tim, James Hendler and Ora Lassila. 2001. "The Semantic Web". *Scientific American* 284, New York: Scientific American Inc. 34–43.

Breuker, Joost and Rinke Hoekstra. 2004. "DIRECT: Ontology-based Discovery of Responsibility and Causality in Legal Case Descriptions". *Proceedings of the 17th JURIX* (Berlin, DE, 2004). Amsterdam: IOS Press. 59–68.

Brüninghaus, Stefanie and Kevin D. Ashley. 2001. "Improving the Representation of Legal Case Texts with Information extraction Methods". *Proceedings of the 8th ICAIL* (St. Louis, MO, 2001). New York: ACM Press. 42–51

Dini, Luca, Doris Liebwald, Lauren Mommers, Wim Peters, Erich Schweighofer and Wim Voermans 2005. "Cross-lingual information retrieval using a WordNet architecture". *Proceedings of the 10th ICAIL* (Bologna, IT, 2005), New York: ACM Press. 163–167

Fellbaum, Christiane (ed.) 1998. *WordNet: An Electronic Lexical Database*. Cambridge: MIT Press.

Fensel, Dieter. 2004. *Ontologies: A Silver Bullet for Knowledge Management and electronic Commerce* (2nd Ed.). Berlin: Springer.

Gonçalves, Teresa. and Paulo Quaresma. 2005. "Is linguistic information relevant for the classification of legal texts?" *Proceedings of the 10th ICAIL* (Bologna, Italy, 2005). New York: ACM Press. 168–176.

Gruber, Thomas R. 1993. "A Translation Approach to Portable Ontology Specifications", *Knowledge Acquisition* 5/2, London et al.: Academic Press. 199–220.

Hachey, Ben and Claire Grover. 2004. "A rhetorical status classifier for legal text summarisation". *Proceedings of the ACL-04 Text Summarization Branches Out Workshop* (Barcelona, ES), 35–42.

Hafner, Carole D. 1978. *An Information Retrieval System Based on a Computer Model of Legal Knowledge*. Ph.D Thesis, Ann Arbor: UNI Research Press

Harvold, Tryve and Jon Bing. 1977. *Legal Decisions and Information Systems*. Oslo: Universitetsforlaget.

Hirst, Graeme. 2004. "Ontology and the Lexicon". *Handbook on Ontologies*. ed. by Steffen Staab and Rudi Studer, Berlin-Heidelberg: Springer. 210–229.

Koivunen, Marja-Riitta and Eric Miller. 2002. "W3C Semantic Web Activity". *Proceedings of the Semantic Web Kick-off Seminar* (Helsinki, FI, 2001). Helsinki: HIIT Publications. 27–43, freely available at www.w3.org/2001/12/semweb-fin/ w3csw.

Kralingen, Robert W. van. 1995. *Frame-based Conceptual Models of Staute Law*. Ph.D. Thesis, The Hague: University of Leiden.

Lenat, Douglas B. 1995. "Cyc: a Large-Scale Investment in Knowledge Infrastructure". *Communications of the ACM* 38 (11), 33–38.

Matthijssen, Luuk. 1999. *Interfacing between Lawyers and Computers: An Architecture for Knowledge-based Interfaces to Legal Databases*, The Hague et al.: Kluwer Law International.

McCarty, L. Thorne 1989. "A Language for Legal Discourse: I. Basic Features". *Proceedings of the 2nd ICAIL* (Vancouver, BC, Canada, 1989). New York: ACM Press. 180–189.

Miller, George A., Richard Beckwith, Christiane Fellbaum, Derek Gross, and Katherine Miller. 1990. "Five Papers on WordNet", *CSL Report* 43, Princeton University: Cognitive Science Laboratory ftp://ftp.cogsci.prince ton.edu/pub/wordnet/5papers.ps.

Moens, Marie-Francine, Caroline Uyttendaele and Jos Dumortier. 1997. "Abstracting of Legal Cases: The SALOMON Experience". *Proceedings of the 6th ICAIL* (Melbourne, Victoria, Australia, 1997). New York: ACM Press. 114–122.

Rathert, Monika. 2006. *Sprache und Recht*. Heidelberg: Universitätsverlag Winter.

Schweighofer, Erich. 1998. "The Revolution in Legal Information Retrieval or: The Empire Strikes Back", *Proc Conf The Law in the Information Society*, Firence, December 1998, republished: *Journal of Law and Information Technology* 1999, http://www.law.warwick.ac.uk/jilt/99-1/schweigh.html.

Schweighofer, Erich. 1999. *Legal Knowledge Representation, Automatic Text Analysis in Public International and European Law*, The Hague: Kluwer Law International. [Law and Electronic Commerce, Volume 7]

Schweighofer, Erich et al. 2002. "Improvement of Vector Representation of Legal Documents with Legal Ontologies". *Proceedings of the 5th BIS* (Poznan, PL, 2002). Poznan: Poznan University of Economics Press.

Smith, John Charles, Daphne Gelbart, Keith Maccrimmon, Bruce Atherton, John Mcclean, Michelle Shinehoft and Lincoln Quintana. 1995. "Artificial Intelligence and Legal Discourse: The Flexlaw Legal Text Management System". *Artificial Intelligence and Law* 3/1–2, Dordrecht et al.: Kluwer. 55–95.

Stamper, Ronald K. 1991. "The Role of Semantics in Legal Expert Systems and Legal Reasoning". *Ratio Juris* 4/2. Oxford: Blackwell Publishing. 219–244.

Tiscornia, Daniela. 2006. "The Lois Project: Lexical Ontologies for Legal Information Sharing", ed. by Carlo Biagioli, Enrico Francesconi and Giovanni Sator, *Proceedings of the V. Legislative XML Workshop*, Firence: European Press Academic.

Turtle, Howard. 1995. "Text Retrieval in the Legal World", *Artificial Intelligence and Law* 3/1-2, 5–54.

Valente, André. 1995. *Legal knowledge engineering: A modelling approach*. Amsterdam: IOS Press.

Visser Pepijn R. S., Bench-Capon, Trevor J. M. 1999. "Ontologies in the Design of Legal Knowledge Systems, towards a Library of Legal Domain Ontologies", *Proceedings of Jurix* 99, Leuven.

Visser, Pepijn R. S. 1995. *Knowledge Specification for Multiple Legal Tasks: A Case Study of the Interaction Problem in the Legal Domain*. The Hague: Kluwer Law International [Computer Law Series 17].

Vossen, P. (ed.) 1993. "EuroWordNet General Document" (LE2-4003, LE4-8328). Final Document (3th Ed.), freely available at: www.illc.uva.nl/EuroWord Net/docs.html.

Part 4

Multilingualism and the law: The contribution of translation studies

Multilingualism in the European Union Status quo and perspectives: The reference language model

Karin Luttermann

1. Introduction*

The Bible explains multilingualism with the building of the tower of Babel. God had mankind speak in different languages, so they could not communicate any longer and therefore could not finish the tower.[1] Today, we speak of the "Language Babel of Brussels". Should this lead to the failure of the linguistic integration of Europe? The legal basis emphasizes unity in diversity.[2] This means that EU language law is positioned in an inevitable field of tension: To preserve the national identity of each member state and meet the requirements of everyday communication.[3]

In practice, the limits of the translation services, in the final instance also their costs, are remarkable. The Community authorities and independent European institutions such as the Trademark Office[4] (Alicante) and the Court of Auditors already reduce the general use of official and working

---

* "Now the whole earth had one language and few words. (…) And the LORD said: "Behold, they are one people, and they have all one language (…). Come, let us go down, and there confuse their language, that they may not understand one another's speech." So the LORD scattered them abroad from there over the face of all the earth." (Genesis 11, 1–8)

1. Cf. Trabant (2006: 20–21). Legal state of August 2006.

2. "Unity in diversity" is the motto of the European Union; cf. Löffler (2006: 52). Cf. also Art. 6 paragraph 3 Treaty on European Union [TEU], Art. 151 Treaty establishing the European Community (TEC), Art. 22 Charter of Fundamental Rights.

3. Cf. Oppermann (2001: 2668).

4. The languages of the office are German, English, French, Spanish and Italian; cf. European Court of Justice (ECJ), decision of September 9, 2003, Case C-361/01 P, Coll. 2003, I-08283, margin no. 7 – Kik.

G. Grewendorf, M. Rathert (eds.): Formal Linguistics and Law, 315–338

languages to a great degree, in order to be able to work efficiently. For instance, the European Court of Justice makes nearly exclusive use of French. Babel needs to be transcended. In the long run, the European Union is unthinkable without a working language regulation. The solution of the language question is *the* task of our time.[5]

In statistics: Since the extension eastwards in May 2004, the European Union comprises 25 states with more than 450 million inhabitants, 20 working languages and 380 language combinations. In 2007 Gaelic was granted official language status, and Bulgaria and Rumania are to join the European Union.[6] This means that there will even be 23 official languages and 506 combinations.[7] Is this situation still manageable? – The extension and the perspectives of joining the European Union (particularly Croatia is keen to become an EU member) demand a reform of the regulations in order to make the Community fit for the future.

The central part of this paper deals with the reference language model (section 8), which takes maximal account of cultural identities. It is developed from a legal-linguistic perspective and is founded on the mother tongue basis, the jurisdiction of the European Court of Justice, the necessary legal certainty (sections 4 to 6) and in contradistinction to conventional language models (section 7); prior to that, the different types of languages (section 2) and historical stages of language regime (section 3) will be treated.

2. Language law of the European Union

2.1 Differentiation of language types

European law is multilingual. This entails numerous language regulations regarding the protection and distribution of languages (so-called material language law)[8] as well as procedural questions (so-called formal language

5. George Pompidou considers the language problem to be "the most important of our epoch"; cf. Spiegel 1971 (24): 100.
6. Europeans and languages. Special Note Eurobarometer (2006: 1, fn. 1).
7. The calculation is based on the formula n x (n-1), n being the number of official languages.
8. E.g., the European Union may take educational measures in order to promote multilingualism (Art. 126 TEC).

law). Formal language law distinguishes between treaty languages, official languages, working languages and languages of a case.

2.2 Treaty languages

Treaty languages are of prime importance for the interpretation of the Constituting Treaty of the European Union. They are regulated by primary law in Treaty establishing the European Community (TEC) Article 314 (ex Article 248). This first denotes the original text in German, French, Italian and Dutch (Sentence 1). The wording of each version is authentic (Sentence 2). This regulation was extended in the respective accession documents to the official languages of the joining member states.

According to the accession treaties the principle of equality also applies to: Danish, English, Estonian, Finnish, Gaelic, Greek, Latvian, Lithuanian, Maltese, Polish, Portuguese, Swedish, Slovakian, Slovene, Spanish, Czech and Hungarian. Thus the treaty is valid in 21 treaty languages.[9]

2.3 Official languages

Official languages are those languages used externally by the Community organs. They are mentioned in the derived law in Regulation no. 1/58 for ruling about the institutional use of the languages.[10] Under Article 1, Regulation no. 1/58 all treaty languages are also official languages, except Gaelic. At the moment there are 20 official languages: Danish, German, English, Estonian, Finnish, French, Greek, Italian, Latvian, Lithuanian, Maltese, Dutch, Polish, Portuguese, Swedish, Slovakian, Slovene, Spanish, Czech and Hungarian.

---

9. In the official languages of the 25 member states: Belgium, Denmark, Germany, England, Estonia, Finland, France, Greece, Ireland, Italy, Latvia, Lithuania, Luxembourg, Malta, Netherlands, Austria, Poland, Portugal, Sweden, Slovakia, Slovenia, Spain, Czech Republic, Hungary and Cyprus. It is erroneously supposed that the text versions are always identical in meaning (Art. 33 paragraph 3 Vienna Agreement on the Right of Treaties); see subparagraph V.3.

10. Council Regulation no. 1 of April 15, 1958 regarding ruling on the language question for the European Economic Community. In: Official Journal EC no. 17 of October 6, 1958, p. 385–386; last modified through Act of Accession 2003 of April 16, 2003. In: Official Journal EU no. L 236 of September 23, 2003, p. 33.

Regulations and documents of general validity have to be written down in these languages and published in the Official Journal (Articles 4 and 5, Regulation no. 1/58); the respective language version is concurrent with the versions in other languages. In the same vein, collections of decisions of European jurisdiction must be published in all official languages. Furthermore, a member state may address a document to a Community organ in one of the official languages and demand an answer in this language (Article 2, Regulation no. 1/58). An organ must answer a member state in the language of this state (Article 3, Regulation no. 1/58).

2.4 Working languages

Working languages are certain languages in which the Community organs work internally and in communicating with one another. They are also set down in the Council Regulation. Article 1, Regulation no. 1/58 treats the working languages on a par with the official languages (see subparagraph 2.3). It is only regarding details that the Community organs can decide for themselves within the autonomy of their own rules of procedure (Article 6 Regulation no. 1/58).[11]

In practice, the languages are no longer treated in identical fashion.[12] For instance, the Commission has officially determined that all internal documents must be published in German, English and French.[13] But even this regulation is not always adhered to; at first contact, commission staff regularly only use English or French. In the internal procedure manual of the Commission, German is not determined as the third working language.

Mention should also be made of the language debate which flared up in July 1999 under Finnish Council Presidency regarding German as a working language in the informal meetings of the Council of Ministers besides English, French and Finnish (as the language of the presiding state) due to lacking translation capacities. It was not until Germany and Austria boycotted three meetings that interpreting also took place in German. The following Swedish Presidency refused to use German in the expert meetings

---

11. In their Rules of Procedure they may determine details on the use of languages (Art. 6 Regulation no. 1/58).
12. Further examples on the limiting of languages in C. and K. Luttermann (2004: 1003).
13. Protocol statement of September 1, 1993. In: EG-Nachrichten no. 34 of September 6, 1993, p. 4.

below the level of ministers and finally limited the interpreting services to English only, in agreement with most member states.

2.5 Languages of a case

Languages of a case denote the respective language used in legal proceedings before the European Court of Justice. They are determined separately in the Rules of Procedure (see Article 290 TEC, Article 7 Regulation no. 1/58).[14] Article 29 § 1 of the Rules of Procedure of the European Court of Justice (ECJ) determines that all official languages and Gaelic can be languages of a case. This also applies to the Court of First Instance founded in 1989 (Articles 35-37 Rules of Procedure of the Court of First Instance). Gaelic is admitted before the European Court due to the constitutional principle of obtaining a hearing, although it is not an official language or a working language of the Community organs.

In general, the plaintiff has the privilege of language choice and may choose one of the 21 languages as the language of his case (Article 29 § 2 Rules of Procedure of the ECJ). This language then dominates all the stages of the court case. The parties have to submit their documents in it. The closing arguments and the sentence are binding only in the language of the case, not also in the other official languages (Article 31 Rules of Procedure of the ECJ). This means that the European Court is the only Community organ in which procedures are not legally binding on a multilingual level.

The sentence must be published in the official collection of the Court in all official languages (Article 30 § 2 Rules of Procedure of the ECJ). Due to this and to the fact that French is always the internal working language, the bulk of translation is considerable: Everything first practically has to be translated from French (working language) into the respective language of the case and then into all the other EU languages.

14. Rules of Procedure of the ECJ of June 19, 1991. In: Official Journal EC no. L 176 of July 4, 1991, p. 7; codified version, Official Journal EU no. C 193 of August 14, 2003, p. 3.

3. Historical development of the language regime

3.1 Language power

Right from the outset, the language question proved to be politically highly explosive. It is at the same time a question of power: Execution of power through language use or non-use! Whoever has the word, can effectuate more, exert greater influence and has the final say (see subparagraphs 3.2, 3.3). Among the founding states of the European Coal and Steel Community, it is particularly Germany and France who argue about the linguistic claim to leadership. The monolingual approach favoured by France[15], in which the French language dominates, is not able to prevail over the multilingual approach (complete equality of German, French, Italian and Dutch).

Today, the former rivals are partners and support each other in linguistic matters. In June 2000 they set up a "Joint German-French language directive". According to this, the leaders of the German and French delegations jointly appeal to the Presidency, if problems occur at informal meetings regarding interpreting, in order to find a satisfactory solution.[16] This cooperation is also termed „German-French declaration of solidarity“[17] or "language alliance between France and Germany"[18]. – Now to the linguistic beginnings.

3.2 Founding treaties

When the Netherlands, Belgium, Italy and Luxembourg join Germany and France to sign the Paris Treaty for the foundation of the European Coal and Steel Community on April 18, 1951 a discussion ensues regarding the language question. French becomes the only authentic language in the European Coal and Steel Community (see Treaty for the foundation of the European Coal and Steel Community, Article 100). By contrast, the other text versions in German, Italian and Dutch are regarded as translations of the French original text. The founding states cannot agree on four equal treaty languages.

---

15. Cf. Haarmann (1973: 122).
16. Message to the Secretary's Office of the Standing Conference of European Ministers of Education of July 25, 2000.
17. Petry (2004: 46).
18. Ammon (2004: 29).

There is also disagreement on language use for the organs of the Community, so that the official languages, working languages and languages of a case are thus initially not regulated. From the wording of the Treaty of the Coal and Steel Community, France deduces linguistic predominance for itself, which, however, is disputed by the other countries. In July 1952, an interim commission achieves an agreement saying that all four official languages of the six member states are at the same time binding languages of the Community organs.

In contrast to the European Coal and Steel Community (ECSC) Treaty, the Rome Treaties for the foundation of the European Economic Community and the European Atomic Energy Community of March 25, 1957 make provisions for an egalitarian rather than a preferential language use in the European Economic and Atomic Energy Community. According to Article 314 TEC (ex Article 248), all official languages of the founding states are authentic languages of the founding treaties.

On the basis of Article 290 TEC (ex Article 217), the Council issued Regulation no. 1 on April 15th, 1958 for regulating the language question for the Community organs. It is the first Regulation ever. It declares German, French, Italian and Dutch to be official languages and working languages on the level of Community law. The language charter of the European Union[19] is adapted to the increased number of languages, which resulted from several extensions of the Community (see Table 1), while remaining untouched in principle.

3.3 Follow-up treaties

The follow-up treaties confirm the language regime of the European Economic and Atomic Energy Community. For our purposes it is interesting that according to the Treaty on European Union, signed on February 7, 1992 in Maastricht, the member states intend to cooperate with each other intergovernmentally not only in the areas of the economy and currency, foreign and security policy, jurisdiction and home policy, but also on the *cultural* level: "DESIRING to deepen the solidarity between their peoples while respecting their history, their culture and their traditions" (preamble of the Treaty on European Union (TEU)).

19. www.europa-digital.de/aktuell/dossier/sprachen/sprache1.sthml of June 2005.

They assure that they will cooperate on a basis of solidarity by maintaining their "national identity" (Article 6 paragraph 3 TEU). These declarations of intent give a new dimension to the cooperation that had up to that point been of a mainly economic nature. They make the languages of the member states come clearly into focus. The languages have a special identity-forming function. The identification of the nations is to a large degree based on languages: European identity is "synonymous with the co-existence of the old developed cultures and thus also with the languages."[20]

Their cultures indisputably also include the languages of the member states. Though this is not explicitly stated in the preamble of the EC Treaty, it is expressed in Article 151 TEC (ex Article 128), which was newly introduced through the Union Treaty. According to paragraphs 1 and 4 the Community aims to preserve the "diversity of its cultures" and "its common cultural heritage". The Charter of Fundamental Rights of the European Union, which was proclaimed on the 7th December 2000 in Nice, explicitly includes the language. Its Article 22 demands respect for "the diversity of cultures, religions and languages".

The Treaty of Amsterdam signed on October 2, 1997 regarding the modification of the Treaty on European Union, the Treaties establishing the European Community as well as some connected legal acts, contains further specifications for the consolidation of the authentic languages as a cultural component. Thus, Article 314 Sentence 2 TEC specifies that the treaty texts of the non-founding members are equal versions ("Pursuant to the Accession Treaties, the Danish, English, Finnish, Greek, Irish, Portuguese, Swedish and Spanish versions of this treaty shall also be authentic.").

A new second paragraph in Article 53 TEU (ex Article S) emphasizes that according to the Treaty of Accession of 1994 Finnish and Swedish are also binding treaty languages. Paragraph 3, inserted into Article 21 TEC through the Amsterdam Treaty, enables every Union citizen to apply to the Community organs in one of the treaty languages. An answer must be given in the same language. In this way, Gaelic is placed on a par with the other official languages "through the back door"[21], as it were. At the European Court of Justice, Gaelic has already been admitted as language of a case (see subparagraph 2.5). The Court shapes European law and sets standards for the use of the mother tongue.

20. Born and Schütte (1995: 46).
21. Schübel-Pfister (2004: 58).

Table 1. Statistical data

Number of member states	Effective date of the Treaties of Accession of the member states[22]	Number of official languages	Number of language combinations
6	1957 - European Economic Community (EEC): Belgium, Germany, France, Italy, Luxembourg, Netherlands	4	12
9	1973 - EC – extension to the North: Denmark, Great Britain, Ireland	6	30
10	1981- EC – extension to the South: Greece	7	42
12	1986 - EC – extension to the South: Portugal, Spain	9	72
15	1995 - EU: Finland, Austria, Sweden	11	110
25	2004 - EU: Estonia, Latvia, Lithuania, Malta, Poland, Slovakia, Slovenia, Czech Republic, Hungary, Cyprus	20	380

4. European Court of Justice

4.1 Function

The European Court of Justice is a Community organ (Article 7 paragraph 1 TEC). It makes sure that European law is observed and the treaties are interpreted correctly and applied in a uniform way (Article 220 paragraph 1 TEC). This means that it has the function of the highest instance of jurisdiction within the European integration process. The Court can determine that a member state has violated its duties according to the treaties and that a Community organ has acted in an unlawful way.

National courts can suspend cases and apply to the European Court regarding questions of interpretation of state-internal relevant Community

22. Cf. Weidenfeld (2006: 20–22).

law and regarding the validity of legal acts of the Community organs (Article 234 TEC, ex Article 177). The "dialogue of judges"[23] is the procedurally most important connection between European Community law and national legal systems.

4.2 Maintaining the law

The judges of the European Court are the keepers of Community law. It is their task to ensure that the law "in the interpretation and application of this Treaty" is observed (Article 220 paragraph 1 TEC). This leads to the question: "Maintaining the law" in what language? For Europe has no uniform language. Nobody speaks European. Community law is formulated multilingually, the equality of all treaty languages is given (multilingual authenticity; cf. Article 314 TEC, Article 53 TEU).

The mission of Article 220 paragraph 1 TEC itself is expressed in all treaty languages. Further provisions for dealing with multilingual text versions are lacking. The legislator leaves open the question as to how the principle of the equality of all authentic languages should be applied in interpretation. In consequence, the answer must be: "Maintaining the law" in all (official) languages! This answer determines the approach.

4.3 Methods of interpretation

Article 220 paragraph 1 TEC gives prime position to interpretation within jurisdiction. The primary legal acts (treaties) and the secondary laws created by the organs (regulations, directives, recommendations) are to be interpreted in an equally binding way. Their sense is to be made "to speak"[24] with a view to legal application. However, there is no legal basis for the interpretation of multilingual texts. That is why European jurisdiction must be taken account of, which makes important statements regarding questions of interpretation in "remarkable clarity".[25]

Methodologically, the European Court of Justice takes recourse to the traditional criteria of grammatical, historical, systematic and teleological interpretations. They are shaped with a specific dimension, which is usually

23. Geiger (2004) Art. 234 TEC margin no. 1.
24. Larenz and Canaris (1995: 26, 133–134).
25. C. Luttermann (1999: 403).

termed "interpretation in conformity with European law"[26]. Basically, it is a comparison of legal terminologies.

4.4 Comparison of legal terminologies

At the beginning of any interpretation of a Community-law norm there is the comparison of its different linguistic versions. For, according to the express formulation of the European Court of Justice, there is "the requirement of a uniform interpretation of the language versions".[27] Suspending a decision of the Hamburg Higher Administrative Court, the German Federal Constitutional Court has determined the European interpretation method alone is to be applied for Community law and for German norms influenced by Community law.[28] Whoever applies the law must deal with all language versions.

As the languages are equal, they must also be given equal status in the process of interpretation. This means that interpretation according to the actual wording applied in monolingual law is extended to the requirement for multilingual analysis. The decision of the European Court of Justice is not based on one language version alone, rather, all binding texts are examined and considered. If there are any divergences, the "regulation in question is [to be interpreted] according to general systematics and the purpose of the regulation to which it belongs".[29] The purpose can be found mainly in the preamble.

Factually, legal comparison is closely connected with this language comparison. Law – national as well as supranational – takes effect only in language. The jurist Ernst Forsthoff (1940: 1) speaks of a "connection going to the essence" between language and law. Language structures determine the structure and contents of legal norms. It is true, they are "not an inescapable prison for the mind", but they do create a "strong current ef-

26. C. Luttermann.(2003), cf. Federal Supreme Court, Neue Juristische Wochenschrift (NJW) 1993, 1595 (III a).
27. ECJ, decision of February 2, 1989, Case 186/87, Coll. 1989, 195; C. Luttermann (1999: 404); ECJ, Europäische Zeitschrift für Wirtschaftsrecht (EuZW) 1999, 154 margin no. 26 – Codan.
28. Federal Constitutional Court (FCC), NJW 2001, 1267.
29. ECJ, EuZW 1999, 154 margin no. 26 – Codan. See also ECJ, Coll. 1995, I-4291 = EuZW 1996, 181 margin no. 28 – Rockfon; ECJ, Coll. 1996, I-5403 margin no. 28 = EuZW 1998, 352 L – Kraaijeveld.

fect"[30] for legal thinking. In the European Union, many languages and legal-cultural influences meet.

This must be taken into consideration, and it definitely makes more difficult the process of interpreting the terms of a regulation of Community law autonomously, i.e. independently of the regulations of the member states. European law is characterized by the fact that the sense of terms of European law "lies somewhere between or above the [21] equal EU texts" and "is not readily deducible from a common understanding of the national legal systems."[31] This leads to the question: How are rules of law to be conveyed to the Union citizens?

5. Legal practice

5.1 Communication in the mother tongue

The European comparison of legal terminologies is the central task for the legal harmonization in the member states. This principle applies in general, the mother tongue being in the centre of attention. The language regime of equal intelligibility in the European Union mirrors the idea of the mother tongue. This is considered to be the respective main language of a member state; from this usually follows the status of "treaty language" and "official language" (see Article 53 TEU, Article 314 TEC, subparagraphs 2.2, 2.3).

The access to the mother tongue is founded on legal central aspects. The Union citizens have rights and duties (e.g. the right to freedom of movement, the right to vote, the right to petition, the right to information and the duty to observe the law). At the same time, it is matter of the acceptance of norms and economic participation on the market.[32] To this end they have to act on Community law basis in their language, gain a hearing and be able to recognize legal norms.

Being able to use one's own language with the organs of the Community is a fundamental right. This, it is true, is not stated in any European catalogue of fundamental rights.[33] But it is formed in legal acts and through further legal development by the European Court of Justice. According to

30. Großfeld (1984: 4).
31. Kjaer (2002: 129).
32. For the introduction of international standards for the rendering of accounts, a respective version in the mother tongue is also required.
33. Cf. Pfeil (1999: 146–147).

Article 6 paragraph 1 TEU, respect for the fundamental rights and human rights, including the mother tongue, is obligatory for the European Union. Article 21 of the Charter of Fundamental Rights of the European Union prohibits discrimination on the grounds of language.

The right to one's own language is further guaranteed by Article 41 paragraph 4 of the Charter of Fundamental Rights and Article 21 paragraph 3 TEC. On these grounds, every Union citizen has the right to apply to the organs of the Union (e.g., European Parliament, European Commission, European Court of Justice) as well as the European Ombudsman in one of the treaty languages and to receive an answer in the same language. The German Federal Constitutional Court also ruled as a condition of the Union treaty, "that the citizen who is entitled to vote should be able to communicate in his own language with the sovereign power whose subject he is".[34] Being an independent member of the community, he is not to be degraded to the object of governmental action. The European Court of Justice has formulated some basic principles regarding this point in Bickel and Franz.[35]

5.2 Bickel and Franz

According to Article 8 Regulation no. 1/58 the member states of the European Union may determine more than one language to be their official languages. This enables certain parts of the population and minorities, such as the Flemish and the Walloons in Belgium, the Germans in Danish Northern Schleswig or the South Tyrolese in Italy, to use their mother tongue officially when dealing with authorities and courts. In the case at hand, the issue was whether Austrian and German citizens also have the right to their mother tongue before a criminal court in the Italian city of Bolzano.

The truck driver Bickel was Austrian; the pretore in Bolzano took criminal proceedings against him due to drunken driving. The tourist Franz had German nationality; he was carrying a prohibited kind of knife with him on entering Italy. Both defendants did not know Italian and thus applied for German to be the language of their respective case. The criminal court refused and demanded Italian – despite the fact that German speakers

34. FCC, decision of October 12, 1993 – 2 BvR 2134/92 and 2159/92 = Juristenzeitung 1993, 1100, 1104.

35. ECJ, decision of November 24, 1998, Case C-274/96, Coll. 1998, I-7637 = Europäische Grundrechtezeitschrift (EuGRZ) 1998, 591 pp.

living in South Tyrol have the right to use the German language when dealing with Italian authorities. Relevant to these cases within European law were the prohibition of discrimination (Article 12 TEC, ex Article 6), freedom of movement (Article 18 TEC, ex Article 8a) and free services (Article 49 TEC, ex Article 59).

The European Court of Justice granted the Austrian Bickel and the German Franz the right to communicate in German. For, thus the ruling, it is contrary to European law to restrict court cases in the German language in South Tyrol to the protection of ethnic-cultural minorities. Linking linguistic legal rights to territorial conditions (place of abode; here German-speaking Italian citizens living in South Tyrol) is an act of discrimination. As a consequence, every Union citizen (Article 17 TEC) may in principle demand being able to deal with the administrative and legal authorities of a member state like the citizens of this state; persons in a situation regulated by community law are not allowed to be treated "unequally" with regard to the use of the languages sued therein.[36]

In general, the issue is according equal status (see Article 293 TEC), which the European Court of Justice makes explicit reference to in subparagraph 2 of its tenor. Incidentally, in this case before the European Court, the language of the case was Italian, the working language French, while the advocate general pleaded in English.

4.3 Givane

The European Court of Justice confirms its ruling; essentially – in the sense of the authenticity of each language version – in favour of the mother tongue. One single language version of a multilingual Community-law text cannot, thus the Court, override all other language versions. Rather, the principle of uniform interpretation requires interpreting the community regulations "according to the will of their author and the purpose followed by him particularly in the light also of the versions in all the other languages" (currently in 20 official languages), even if two language versions differ from all the others.[37]

36. ECJ, decsion of November 24, 1998, Case C-274/96, Coll. 1998, I-7637, margin no. 16 = EuGRZ 1998, 591.
37. ECJ, decision of November 20, 2001, Case C-268/99, Coll. 2001, I-8615, margin no. 47 – Jany.

The protection of rights and opportunities for the Union citizens is of particular importance in the domain of language.[38] They are the addressees and must basically be able to recognize, understand and rely on norms without the help of translators and interpreters. This is laid down in Guideline 1 of the "Joint practical manual for persons involved in the drafting of legislation" of the legal services of Parliament, Council and Commission.[39] But claim and reality do not always coincide, as studies on linguistic divergences before the European Court of Justice show.[40] Rather, the possibility remains that a norm is interpreted against its wording in one or more languages.

In the case Givane[41] the Court had to decide whether the wife of the deceased Portuguese and her three children could live in the United Kingdom for an unlimited period of time or whether they had to leave the country; wife and children had Indian nationality. Article 3 paragraph 2 Regulation (EEC) no. 1251/70 demands a continuous minimum stay of two years for this. However, the member states interpret these constituent facts in different ways. The majority believes that the period of two years must extend until death. Accordingly, the German version says "seit mindestens zwei Jahren", the French "depuis au moins 2 années" and the Italian "da almeno due anni". In contrast, other countries prefer not to link the stay with the time of death.

The Danish text formulates "i mindst 2 aar", the English "for at least two years", the Portuguese "pelo menos 2 anos", the Swedish "under minst tva ar" and the Spanish "un minimo de dos anos". By comparison of legal terminologies, the Court of Justice came to the conclusion that the death of the employee must be directly preceded by the stay in the host country. This only is demanded by the term freedom of movement of employees (Article 39 paragraph 1 TEC) and the protection of family life; recognizing other periods of stay in the past would have required an explicit determination of time.

38. ECJ, decision of July 11, 1985, Case 137/84, Coll. 1985, 2681, margin no. 11 – Mutsch.
39. European Commission (2003: 10).
40. Cf. Braselmann (1992: 59); Loehr (1998: 55); Schübel-Pfister (2004: 168).
41. ECJ, decision of January 9, 2003, Case C-257/00, Coll. 2003, I-345, margin no. 36.

6. Pleading from the official language babel

These findings underpin the need for reform. Due to a lack of uniform provisions for a functional language regulation in the European Union, legal texts may differ from each other. This results in communication problems in legal transactions. The present legal status being the way it is, diverging language versions are taken out on the Union citizen. In doubt, it is he who must make sure whether there are any differences between the multilingual Community-law text versions, of what nature these differences are, and to what degree they might influence the legal consequences. He cannot really – as is the case in national law – rely on the version in his mother tongue; a comparison of the legal terminology of all text versions is always necessary (see subparagraph 4.4).

First and foremost, however, he has to be made aware of this problem. This is probably not widely known among the EU citizens yet. From this viewpoint, the multilingual authenticity is a great factor of uncertainty and endangers legal security in the member states. Hardly anybody is able to master twenty or more languages considered to be authentic;[42] this has lead to the European Union becoming dependent on a gigantic language and translation service in Brussels and Luxembourg.

What is actually needed, however, is an intercultural language model directed towards understanding, which preserves diversity for the people while at the same time promoting unity for transnational traffic. It must be able to secure uniform jurisdiction, translation and control of execution in Community law. The comparison of legal terminologies established by the European Court of Justice shows the way. This is the point at which the new reference language model sets in (see section 8) and in which it differs from conventional models.

7. Excursion: Conventional language models

The linguistic regime of the European Union is currently subject to criticism. As shown (subparagraphs 5.2, 5.3 and section 6), there is a lack of legal security for Union citizens. Further points of criticism include weak areas in implementation (quality, costs, time) and the fact that legal practice

42. According to legend, Mithridates, king of Pontos, was a language genius; cf. Trabant (2006: 9–10, 116–121).

already employs the official languages and the working languages in a reduced number (section 1, subparagraph 2.4). Officially, however, multilingualism and language equality are propagated: This, so the critics say, means we are lying to ourselves![43] The extension of the Union to 27 members within the coming years would actually necessitate a reform of the language regime of the first Regulation of 1958:[44] "Without any doubt this task was ignored right from the start."[45] – But what could a legally sound new regulation look like? Including how many and which languages?

For years different suggestions for reform – ranging from a lingua franca to reduced multilingualism – have been in progress. From this spectrum, let us mention the one-language models: English (English is the official language of the United Nations and the only language that is present worldwide.[46]), Latin (The Vatican is the only state in the world with the official language Latin.[47]) and Esperanto (Esperanto is the most successful and most widespread artificial language.[48]), as well as the multilanguage models[49]: Three-language model (German, English, French), differentiated three-language model (the languages mentioned; English is sole working language), five-language model (the languages mentioned as well as Italian and Spanish), Danish model (prohibition of native language) and market model[50] (with a selection of standard languages).

The models aim at making the work of the Community organs more efficient (particularly on the level of the working languages) and at achieving smooth communication. In principle, this is very commendable. However, the disadvantage is that institutional multilingualism, an important element of democracy for the European Union, is reduced towards "one" unidimensionally. This automatically evokes the resistance of individual member states (especially those whose national language does not have official or working language status). The sociolinguist Ulrich Ammon (2006: 334-335) believes measures for achieving acceptance should primarily include money ("a financial component") and "regulations". Can language reforms

43. Sturm (2002: 315).
44. Oppermann (2001: 2667).
45. Ehlich (1999: 318); cf. also section 3.
46. Cf. Wu (2005: 75–76).
47. Cf. Frankfurter Allgemeine Zeitung of November 3, 2006, p. 36.
48. Cf. Wu (2005: 142).
49. Overview in Sturm (2002: 318).
50. On this see Petry (2004: 48–50); presentation by Minister of State Hans Martin Bury in the German Bundestag on May 22, 2003; Bundestagsdrucksache 15/330.

thus be purchased? – In the following, we will pursue a different path with the reference language model.

8. Reference language model for the EU language law

8.1 Reference languages and mother tongues

In order to reform the language regime of the European Union in a manageable way, a reference language model is developed.[51] This is a system consisting of reference languages and mother tongues. The basic idea is the following: In a first step, the European legal acts are translated at all levels (treaty, official, working languages and languages of a case; see section 2) authentically into two reference languages. This necessitates translation right from the start, which is methodologically the means for intercultural communication and Community-law understanding.

In practice, the European translation service has to phrase every European legal act in both reference languages. They are set off in a supranational dimension from the other official languages. Legal and linguistic questions in the interpretation of European law must be solved comparatively between the two reference languages in a way which is binding for the whole Union. This bilingualism as a point of reference is extended by the mother tongue. In the tradition of the nation states this is regularly the main language of a member state.[52] For the Union citizens are to be able to communicate with the Community organs and have access to the legal acts and all information in their mother tongue.

The member states have to take the responsibility for making sure of this. They have to prepare one text version of a European legal act; for the private legal domain, the relevant text is Article 20 paragraph 2 of the Directive on the harmonisation of transparency requirements.[53] For the necessary translation, the text versions of the European reference languages serve as a standard. One of the reference languages must always be used as a

51. Cf. C. and K. Luttermann (2004: 1008–1010).
52. ECJ, decision of October 6, 1982, Case 283/81, Coll. 1982, 3415, margin no. 18–19 – Cilfit.
53. See Directive 2004/109/EC of December 15, 2004 on the harmonisation of transparency requirements in relation to information about issuers whose securities are admitted to trading on a regulated market and amending Directive 2001/34/EC. In: Official Journal no. L 390 of December 31, 2004, p. 38–57.

standard (unit of reference). This means that in this case also the constitutional comparative principle of native and foreign language takes effect (see subparagraph 4.4). The authenticity of the (native) languages results from the agreement with the two reference languages.

8.2 Legitimization by the European Court of Justice

In actual fact, the system of reference languages and mother tongues has already been legitimized by the European Court of Justice. As a rule, it publishes its decisions in all official languages. But this does not create linguistic equality of the different text versions. The only version which is finally binding is the judgement version in the language of the case in hand (Article 31 Rules of Procedure of the ECJ; see subparagraph 2.5). According to the Rules of Procedure of the ECJ, the plaintiff generally has the right to select freely the language of his case before the European Court of Justice from the admitted official languages (Article 29 § 2 Rules of Procedure of the ECJ).

The organs do not have the privilege of language choice, as they are able to cover all languages due to the language services. Which language decides in a binding way for which legal question (see Article 220 paragraph 1 TEC), is thus a matter of pure coincidence; the comparison of legal terminologies basically secures this procedure (see subparagraphs 4.3, 4.4), but not necessarily in outcome. The reference language model methodologically also proceeds from the comparison of legal terminologies: on a supranational level between the reference languages and in relation to the member states between reference languages and mother tongues (see subparagraph 8.1).

Here also the following point must be taken into account: Not every language spoken in the respective member state is necessarily an official language of the European Union; at the same time, the range of selectable languages is limited. Only the reference languages are of equal standing. This means that a language version which agrees with the reference languages regarding contents has the status of authenticity without being able to be a reference language. For it is only from the reference languages that translations may be made into the target languages. Through translation on the basis of comparing legal terminologies, the reference languages, as well as the reference languages and mother tongues, can test each other mutually.

8.3 Selection of the reference languages

In contrast to conventional language models (see section 7), the reference language model is guided by the democratic majority principle in the selection of the reference languages. In practice, it is incidentally already employed in the organs of the Community, where the use of official and working languages sometimes greatly deviates from the legal foundations. The European Court of Justice regards the approach to limit the selection of languages "to those languages which are most widely known in the European Union" as "appropriate and adequate".[54]

Applying the majority criterion, five languages clearly stand out from the 21 treaty languages and languages of a case, and the 20 official and working languages in the European Union:[55] German is the mother tongue of 18% of the EU population, English and Italian of 13% each, French of 12%, and Spanish of 9%. Out of the number of the member states who joined in 2004, only Polish comes up to the Spanish share (however, regarding the absolute number of speakers, Polish ranks 5% points behind Spanish).

From this it is clear that German has to be one of the reference languages in the new language model. The question remains as to which other language besides German (for the time being keeping to two favoured reference languages[56]) can be determined according to the majority principle? With 38%, English is the most wide-spread foreign language in the Union. All in all, even 51% speak it (as native and foreign language). The share of the Union citizens for whom French is foreign language is 14%; merely 6% have any knowledge of Spanish and 3% of Italian.

German and English both belong to the Germanic language family (with Danish, Dutch and Swedish). This may at first glance seem to be disadvantageous. However, the Baltic (Latvian, Lithuanian), Finno-Ugric (Estonian, Finnish, Hungarian), Greek (Greek), Italic (French, Italian, Portuguese,

---

54. ECJ, decision of September 9, 2003, Case C-361/01 P, Coll. 2003, I-08283, margin no. 94 – Kik.

55. Europeans and languages. Special Note Eurobarometer (2006: 4). See also the study before the extension to the East by Eurobarometer (on www.europa.eu.int under "Languages in Europe" [Date: 16.2.2004]. Detailed report in: INRA (Europe) – European Coordination Office, Europeans and languages (Eurobarometer 54 Special Note, February 2001).

56. For further reference languages the genetic affiliation to a language family may be an additional criterion for selection.

Spanish), Semitic (Maltese) and Slavic (Polish, Slovakian, Slovene, Czech) languages remain present without any restrictions in legal communication. Available through the right of the Union citizen to use his own language when dealing with European institutions (see Article 21 paragraph 3 TEC, Article 2 Regulation no. 1/58); in principle through the systematic inclusion of the mother tongue(s) of a member state.

The translation of Community law into its official language(s) takes legal effect accordingly when it is in agreement with the reference languages. In addition, German represents Continental law, whereas English covers Case law. In this way, the reference language model preserves the cultural language diversity with the system of reference languages and mother tongues, while at the same time maintaining uniform jurisdiction in Europe by taking into consideration two legal systems with different roots.

Table 2. Speaker numbers

EU languages spoken most[57]	Mother tongue	Foreign language	Total share
German	18 %	14 %	32 %
English	13 %	38 %	51 %
French	12 %	14 %	26 %
Italian	13 %	3 %	16 %
Spanish	9 %	6 %	15 %
Polish	9 %	1 %	10 %

9. Resumé and prospects

Multilingualism is necessary in the European Union. It is a high cultural asset and must be preserved. However, communication of the Union citizens with the Community organs requires uniform standards guaranteeing legal security and peaceful cooperation in a healthy economy. The reference language model presented here provides a suitable method: Basically, two reference languages form the uniform standard for European law through a comparison of legal terminologies, which is accordingly trans-

57. Europeans and languages. Special Note Eurobarometer (2006: 4). See also Europeans and languages. Eurobarometer (2005: 5, 7) with minor divergences. According to the English version, German is even second most common foreign language before French, due to the extension to the east.

lated into the official languages of the member states. This makes it mandatory that the population as well as the institutions of the European Union have mother tongue access to Community law.

The comparison of legal terminologies is always also a comparison of cultures, thereby opening up the possibility to experience and understand foreign ways. Let us therefore regard multilingualism as a chance for shaping the rich heritage of this continent precisely by the act of translation for the European family. It was Valéry Giscard d'Estaing who said: "Being a member of a family does not prevent anyone from at the same time remaining an individual. Being a member of the European Union does not prevent anyone from remaining a citizen of his own country."[58]

10. References

Ammon, Ulrich. 2004. "Stand, Möglichkeiten und Grenzen deutscher Sprachenpolitik". *Die deutsche Sprache in der Europäischen Union. Rolle und Chancen aus rechts- und sprachwissenschaftlicher Sicht*, ed. by Christian Lohse, Rainer Arnold, and Albrecht Greule, Baden-Baden: Nomos Verlagsgesellschaft. 19–31.

Ammon, Ulrich. 2006. "Language conflicts in the European Union. On finding a politically acceptable and practicable solution for EU institutions that satisfies diverging interests". *International Journal of Applied Linguistics* 16. 319–338.

Born, Joachim and Wilfried Schütte. 1995. *Eurotexte. Textarbeit in einer Institution der EG*. Tübingen: Gunter Narr Verlag.

Braselmann, Petra. 1992. "Übernationales Recht und Mehrsprachigkeit. Linguistische Überlegungen zu Sprachproblemen in EuGH-Urteilen". *Europarecht* 1. 55–74.

Ehlich, Konrad. 1999. "Der deutsche Weg und die europäische Schiene – einsprachig oder mehrsprachig?" *Deutsch lernen* 4. 311–325.

European Commission (ed.) 2003. *Gemeinsamer Leitfaden des Europäischen Parlaments, des Rates und der Kommission für Personen, die in den Gemeinschaftsorganen an der Abfassung von Rechtstexten mitwirken.* [Joint practical manual for persons involved in the drafting of legislation within the Community institutions]. Bundesanzeiger Verlag GmbH.

Eurobarometer 2005. *Europeans and languages*. Special Eurobarometer. 237-Wave 63.4 – TNS Opinion & Social. Edited by the European Commission http://europa.eu.int/comm/public_opinion/archives/ebs/ebs_237.en.pdf.

58. In: Weidenfeld (2006: 17).

Forsthoff, Ernst. 1940. *Recht und Sprache. Prolegomena zu einer richterlichen Hermeneutik*. Halle: Max Niemeyer Verlag.

Geiger, Rudolf. 2004. *EUV/EGV. Vertrag über die Europäische Union und Vertrag zur Gründung der Europäischen Gemeinschaft. Vol. 4*. München: Verlag C. H. Beck.

Großfeld, Bernhard. 1984. "Sprache und Recht". *Juristenzeitung* 1. 1–6.

Haarmann, Harald. 1973. *Grundfragen der Sprachenregelung in den Staaten der Europäischen Gemeinschaft*. Hamburg: Fundament-Verlag Dr. Sasse & Co.

Kjaer, Anne Lise. 2002. "'Eurospeak' – 'Eurotexte' – 'Eurobegriffe': Zur Pluralität von Sprachen und Rechten bei der Produktion und Rezeption gemeinschaftsrechtlicher Texte". *Juristische Fachsprache. Kongressberichte des 12th European Symposium on Language for Special Purposes, Brixen/Bressanone 1999*, ed. by Lars Eriksen and Karin Luttermann, Münster: LIT Verlag. 115–131.

Larenz, Karl and Claus-Wilhelm Canaris. 1995. *Methodenlehre der Rechtswissenschaft*. 3rd edition. Berlin: Verlag C. H. Beck.

Loehr, Kerstin. 1998. *Mehrsprachigkeitsprobleme in der Europäischen Union. Eine empirische und theoretische Analyse aus sprachwissenschaftlicher Perspektive*. Frankfurt am Main: Peter Lang.

Löffler, Klaus (ed.) 2006. *Europa 2006. Wissen, verstehen, mitreden*. Berlin: Europäisches Parlament, Informationsbüro für Deutschland.

Luttermann, Claus. 1999. "Rechtssprachenvergleich in der Europäischen Union. Ein Lehrbuchfall: EuGH, EuZW 1999, 154 – Codan". *Europäische Zeitschrift für Wirtschaftsrecht (EuZW)* 13. 401–404.

Luttermann, Claus. 2003. "Einführung: Das Bilanzrecht der Aktiengesellschaft – deutsches, europäisches und internationales Recht", *Münchener Kommentar zum Aktiengesetz*, ed. by Kropf, Bruno and Johannes Semler, München: Verlag C. H. Beck and Verlag Franz Vahlen. 263–349.

Luttermann, Claus and Karin Luttermann. 2004. "Ein Sprachenrecht für die Europäische Union". *Juristenzeitung* 20. 1002–1010.

Oppermann, Thomas. 2001. "Reform der EU-Sprachenregelung?" *Neue Juristische Wochenschrift* 37. 2663–2668.

Petry, Uwe. 2004. "Deutsche Sprachpolitik in der Europäischen Union". *Die deutsche Sprache in der Europäischen Union. Rolle und Chancen aus rechts- und sprachwissenschaftlicher Sicht*, ed. by Christian Lohse, Rainer Arnold and Albrecht Greule, Baden-Baden: Nomos Verlagsgesellschaft. 43–50.

Pfeil, Werner. 1999. "Ein Grundrecht auf die eigene Rechtssprache im Gemeinschaftsrecht?" *Recht und Übersetzen*, ed. by Gerard-René de Groot, and Reiner Schulze, Baden-Baden: Nomos Verlagsgesellschaft. 125–147.

Schübel-Pfister, Isabel. 2004. *Sprache und Gemeinschaftsrecht. Die Auslegung der mehrsprachig verbindlichen Rechtstexte durch den Europäischen Gerichtshof*. Berlin: Duncker & Humblot.

Sturm, Fritz. 2002. "Europäisches Organisations- und Verfassungsrecht. Lingua Latina fundamentum et salus Europae". *The European legal forum* 6. 313–320.

Trabant, Jürgen. 2006. *Europäisches Sprachdenken. Von Platon bis Wittgenstein.* München: Verlag C. H. Beck.

Weidenfeld, Werner. 2006. *Die Europäische Verfassung verstehen.* Gütersloh: Verlag Bertelsmann Stiftung.

Wu, Huiping. 2005. *Das Sprachenregime der Institutionen der Europäischen Union zwischen Grundsatz und Effizienz. Eine neue Sichtweise in der institutionellen Sprachenfrage Europas.* Frankfurt am Main: Peter Lang.

Drafting and interpretation of EU law – paradoxes of legal multilingualism

Agnieszka Doczekalska

1. Introduction

The existence of multilingual law is paradoxical. On the one hand, no two languages are identical (Nida [1964] 2000: 126). Syntax and the systems of inflection (morphology) vary from language to language. Moreover, the semantic domain of a word in one language very rarely overlaps exactly with the semantic domain of its closest equivalent in another language, not to mention words that are untranslatable. Hence, if "there can be no absolute correspondence between languages" (Nida 2000: 126), two and especially more than two language versions of the same text cannot be identical and some, at least, slight divergences are inevitable. On the other hand, the semantic equivalence of all the authentic language versions of a legal act is the main presumption of legal multilingualism and the prerequisite of the existence and functioning of multilingual law. In other words, all language versions of a legal act should have the same meaning. The law of the European Union expressed in twenty-three and soon possibly in more languages is an interesting example of such a paradox.[1] This paper aims to describe and explain the paradoxes of EU legal multilingualism, which particularly emerge in the drafting and interpretation process.[2] Before the paradoxes are

---

1. At present, according to the several times amended *Council Regulation No 1* of 15 April 1958 (hereinafter Regulation No 1/1958) determining the languages to be used by the Community, the official languages of EC institutions are the following (in alphabetical order): Bulgarian, Czech, Danish, Dutch, English, Estonian, Finnish, French, German, Greek, Hungarian, Irish, Italian, Latvian, Lithuanian, Maltese, Polish, Portuguese, Romanian, Slovak, Slovene, Spanish, and Swedish. The extension of a number of official languages is probable due to the next planned enlargements by Croatia and Turkey which are candidate states.
2. The term the 'European Union' (EU) is used to denote the organization created in 1992 by the *Treaty on the European Union* (TEU) and founded on the three Communities (i.e. the European Economic Community (EEC) renamed by the

G. Grewendorf, M. Rathert (eds.): Formal Linguistics and Law, 339–370

indicated and described, an overview on the characteristics of and reasons for EU legal multilingualism is provided.

2. EU linguistic diversity and the principle of equal authenticity – characteristics, rationale and the basis of EU multilingualism

In his *Consideration on Representative Government* [1861] (1972), John Stuart Mill states that a culturally and linguistically unified nation is required in order to create a unified polity. As noted by Peter A. Kraus (2004: 303), Mill's opinion is still strong in contemporary thinking. As regards the European Union, Kraus refers to work by Dieter Grimm, according to whom the greatest obstacle to Europeanisation and functioning of democratic system within the EU is language, namely, the linguistic diversity that is reflected in EU multilingualism (Grimm 1995: 295-296).

Notwithstanding such opinions, the European Union is founded on 'unity in diversity'[3] or – in other words – actual European unity is based on diversity[4] – a diversity of cultures, customs, beliefs as well as languages. In reference to the European Union, Walter Hallstein regards cultural diversity

TEU to the European Community (EC), the European Coal and Steel Community (ECSC) and Euroatom), which form nowadays Pillar I of the EU. However, since mainly Pillar I (so-called EC Pillar) produces legally binding acts, my analysis focuses on EC law and legal multilingualism. As far as the legal basis of multilingualism in the II (i.e. Common Foreign and Security Policy) and III Pillars (i.e. Judicial Cooperation in Criminal Matters) of the EU is concerned, Article 28 and 41 of the *Treaty on European Union* states that the language regime will be that of the Community (Pillar I) in the fields of Common Foreign and Security Policy (Article 28) and Judicial Cooperation in Criminal Matters (Article 41). Moreover, *Declaration 29 on the Use of Languages in the Field of the Common Foreign and Security Policy annex to Final Act of the Treaty on European Union* provides that the use of languages shall be in accordance with the rules of the European Communities (Pillar I). Consequently, it is plausible to speak about EU multilingualism that embraces language regime in all the three Pillars.

3. See Article I-8 of *Treaty establishing a Constitution for Europe* providing that the motto of the Union shall be: 'United in diversity' (Official Journal of the European Union (OJ) of 16.12.2004 C 310/13).

4. See European Parliament Resolution on cultural cooperation in the European Union, OJ (2002) C72E/142; see also McDonald (1996: 47).

as a value, especially when it is translated into integral multilingualism[5] expressed by the equality of Member States' national languages (quoted in Savidan 2004: 333). Linguistic diversity is thus viewed as an essential element of the European identity and as an important factor of European integration (Brackeniers 1995: 91). The European Union cannot therefore build its unity without taking linguistic diversity into account (Fenet 2001: 235).

The most important feature of EU linguistic diversity is the equality between EU official languages. Multilingualism understood as the equal coexistence of official and national languages of Member States (MS) "represents the recognition of the identity and equality of all Member States, regardless of their economic power and the extent to which their languages are spoken" (Moratinos Johnston 2000: 59). It should, however, be borne in mind that EU multilingualism does not represent all the languages spoken in Member States,[6] since not all the official languages of Member States are recognised as official languages of EU institutions.[7]

As a general rule, the official language of a Member State is an official language of the EU institutions. However, national official languages of Member States do not automatically become official languages of the EU. Firstly, a state, before it joins the European Union, makes a request to the EU that its national official language be an official language of the Union (Laighin (2004)).[8] Then, the status of the language within the EU is debated during the accession negotiation. In practice, if the language has an official status within the territory of the state and does not share it with another language, it becomes an official and working language of the EU. If more than one official language is recognised within the state, not all of them

5. Integral multilingualism of EU institutions is the policy granting official and working status to all Member State official languages and conferring to EU citizens the right to choose the language before EU institutions.
6. Nevertheless, the EU takes measures to promote minority languages or lesser-used-languages. This subject is, however, much beyond the scope of this paper.
7. For instance, Irish gained the status of EU official language in 2007 although Ireland became a Member State in 1973. Nowadays, the example of the Member State's official language that has not become EU official language is Turkish that is along with Greek official language of Cyprus but not official language within the EU.
8. For instance, before the accession Ireland did not request Irish – recognised as a first official language of Ireland – to become an official language of EC institutions, and due to Agreement of 1971 between Ireland and the Community, Irish had a status of 'Treaty language'. Irish became EU official language in 1 January 2007 on the request of the Irish Government tabled in November 2004.

necessarily become EU official languages. The state is obliged to express whether it wants all, some or only one of its official languages to obtain the status of official and working language of the EU (Article 8 of Regulation 1/1958),[9] and the agreement on the EU official language(s) is included in the Act of Accession. Finally, the Council unanimously confers the status of EU official language on the official language of a Member State.[10] This is followed by the amendment of Council Regulation 1/1958.[11]

In order to better reflect the variety of languages spoken in the European Union, the Council enacted the Conclusion of 13 June 2005 on the official use of additional languages within the Council and possibly other Institutions and bodies of the European Union,[12] which relates to "(...) languages other than the languages referred to in Council Regulation No 1/1958 whose status is recognised by the Constitution of a Member State on all or part of its territory or the use of which as a national language is authorised by law" (par.1). The Council does not, however, automatically grant this special status to all the languages described in paragraph 1. It is necessary to conclude an administrative arrangement between the Council and the Member State which requests that its language(s) be granted the status of additional languages.[13] On the basis of such an arrangement the Council will authorise the official use of the language (par. 4).

---

9. Usually, if one of the official languages of the state is already official and working language of the EU due to its official and working language status in another Member State, the other languages do not attain this status in the EU (Milian-Massana (2002)). Example of this rule is Turkish (see *supra note* 6) that is along with Greek official language of Cyprus that become a Member State in 2004. Since Greek has been already official language of the EU due to Greece accession in 1981, Turkish did not become official language of the EU. The exception of this rule is a of Maltese (the official language of Malta) that became the official and working language of the EU although Malta recognises also English as its official language. English has been EC official language since 1973 due to accession of the United Kingdom and Ireland to the Community.

10. Council competence provided in Article 290 (ex-article 217) of the *Treaty establishing the European Community* (consolidated version OJ C 325/148 of 24.12.2002). Cf. Article III-433 of the *Treaty establishing a Constitution for Europe* (OJ C 310/184 of 16.12.2004).

11. See *supra note* 1.

12. OJ C 148/1, 18.6.2005.

13. If other EU institutions follow the Council, the arrangement could be concluded with other than Council institution or body. However official use of the languages will be authorised by the Council according to point 4 of Conclusion that is in accordance with Article 290 of *EC Treaty*, see *supra note* 9.

At the time of writing this paper (January 2007) the agreement[14] has been concluded with Spain and conferred the status of additional languages[15] on Basque, Catalan and Galician.

The additional languages, to which the arrangement refers, can be officially used within the EU. This means that, firstly, acts adopted in co-decision by the European Parliament and the Council are translated into additional languages (par. 5(a)). Unlike the official language versions, such a certificate translation is not the authentic version of a legal act. Therefore, it does not participate in the meaning of an act and consequently cannot be referred to for the purposes of judicial interpretation. Secondly, additional languages can be used in speeches at a meeting in the Council (par. 5(b)). Finally, citizens can send communications to an EU institution or body in an additional language and receive the reply in this language and in the official language of the Member State (par. 5(c)). All costs of languages services or other direct and indirect costs connected with the implementation of the arrangement are covered by the Member State (par. 5).

The change of status of the Irish language and conferment of official status on Maltese, as well as creation of a new category of additional languages within the EU, demonstrates that official and legal multilingualism is not reduced; on the contrary, it is constantly extended. From a legal standpoint, the main reason for the preservation of EU legal multilingualism and equality of language versions is the fact that the law of the EU is in some cases directly applicable (i.e., takes effect within the MS, without any need for national authorities to incorporate or implement) or has a direct effect[16] (i.e., provides rights and obligations to individuals enforceable in national courts).[17] For this reason, citizens should be able to understand – i.e., should have access in the language that they understand – all acts that affect them and which they can invoke before a court (Moratinos Johnston

---

14. See: Administrative Arrangement between the Kingdom of Spain and the Council of the European Union of 17.02.2006, No 2006/C 40/02.

15. Apart from the term 'additional languages', there are other terms used to denote these languages in the context of its use in the EU such as: 'official less-used languages' (MERCATOR/Eurolang (2005)) or 'semi-official languages' (Athanassiou 2006: 16).

16. The principle of direct effect was established by the ECJ in the Case *Van Gend en Loos v Nederlandse Tariefcommissie*, C-26/62, 5 February 1963, ECR 1; see also *Costa v Enel*, C-6/64, 15 July 1964, ECR 585.

17. For further details on direct applicability and direct effect, see int. al. Pescatore (1983: 155-177); Winter (1972: 425-438).

2000: 26). This is why EU legislation needs to be formulated in all official languages.

Furthermore, EU multilingualism is considered as a democratic right of the peoples of Europe to their own language (Phillipson 2003: 129-131). Such a democratic right includes the possibility of participating in the EU decision-making process and the possibility of communicating in the citizens' own language with the authorities they are subject to. Consequently, citizens should have the possibility to be elected to the European Parliament irrespective of their knowledge of languages and they should also be able to speak their own language during Parliament sessions. Moreover, all citizens should be able to communicate with EU institutions in the official language of their choice.[18] Accordingly, it can be stated that the democratic right to multilingualism can be converted into the right to monolingualism, namely the right for a citizen to remain monolingual (Phillipson 2003: 129-131).[19]

Official multilingualism not only guarantees the citizens of the European Union access to European law, but is also essential for a uniform application of EU law in Member States. However, in order to achieve such uniformity, it is not enough to enact law in all the official languages. Moreover, all the official language versions of a legal instrument have to be equally authentic; in other words, they have to be equally valid and have the same legal effect (Wagner et al. 2002: 4). As a result, all the authentic versions create a single legal instrument, which is presumed to have the same meaning in all the official languages, and therefore none of the versions can prevail for interpretation purposes. These requirements and presumptions are reflected in the principle of equal authenticity of all the official language versions of a legal instrument.

This principle forms the basis of the EU multilingual legal order. However, the aforementioned Council Regulation 1/1958 does not directly state

---

18. Cf. Article 41 of the *Charter of Fundamental Rights of the European Union* (OJ of 18.12.2000 C364/01) and Article II-101 (4) of the *Treaty establishing a Constitution for Europe* (OJ of 16.12.2004 C310/13).

19. Nevertheless the EU promotes linguistic diversity also by encouraging to language learning. See Communication from the Commission to the Council, the European Parliament, the European Economic and Social Committee and the Committee of the Regions. A New Framework Strategy for Multilingualism, 22.11.2005, COM (2005) 596; see also Communication from the Commission to the Council, the European Parliament, the Economic and Social Committee and the Committee of the Regions. Promoting Language Learning and Linguistic Diversity: an Action Plan 2004 – 2006, 24.07.2003, COM (2003: 449).

that all official language versions of a legal act are equally authentic.[20] Nevertheless, such conclusion follows from Article 1 of the Regulation, providing what official and working languages of the Community are, and from Article 4, stating that regulations and other documents of general application shall be drafted in all the official languages.[21] According to Desemont and Ansay (1995: 11), the term 'official languages' means not only that legal texts are published in these languages but also that all official language versions are considered equally authentic. Moreover, the principle of equal authenticity has been directly expressed and confirmed several times in the case law of the European Court of Justice and of the Court of First Instance, as well as in the opinions of the Advocates General. The Court stated that the different language versions are all equally authentic and that an interpretation of a provision of Community law involves a comparison of the different language versions.[22]

---

20. In EC documents, the term 'authentic language' can come across. For instance, the *Rules of Procedure of the European Commission* provide the definition of 'authentic languages' for the purposes of these Rules. According to Article 17 (5) of the Rules "'authentic languages' means all the official languages of the Communities, (...), in the case of instruments of general application, and the language or languages of those to whom they are addressed, in other cases" (OJ L 347/87 of 30.12.2005).
21. The principle of equal authenticity is very often laid down directly; for instance, in case of bilingual Canada, section 18 of the *Canadian Charter of Rights and Freedoms*, 1982 provides that English and French versions of the statutes are equally authoritative; see also the case of Hong Kong, Part II A, section 10B(1)(2) of the *Interpretation and General Clauses Ordinance*. The principle of equal authenticity has been also directly stated in international law in Article 33 on interpretation of treaties authenticated in two or more languages of *Vienna Convention on the Law of Treaties* of 1969 (United Nations, Treaty Series, vol. 1155: 331).
22. See the following judgments of the ECJ: judgement of 6 October 1982 in Case 283/81 Srl CILFIT [1982] ECR 3415, par. 18; judgment of 24 October 1996 in Case C-72/95 Aannemersbedrijf P.K. Kraaijeveld BV e.a. *v* Gedeputeerde Staten van Zuid-Holland [1996] ECR I-05403, par. 25 and 28; judgment of 17 July 1997 in Case C-219/95 P Ferriere Nord SpA *v* Commission of the European Communities [1997] ECR I-04411, par. 12; judgment of 17 December 1998 in Case C-236/97 Skatteministeriet *v* Aktieselskabet Forsikrinsselskabet Codan [1998] ECR I-08679, par. 25; see as well the judgements of the CFI: judgement of 6 April 1995 in Case T-143/89 Ferriere Nord SpA *v* Commission of the European Communities [1995] ECR II-00917, par. 31; judgment of 6 October 2005 in joined Cases T-22/02 and T-23/02 Sumitomo Chemical Co. Ltd and Sumika Fine Chemicals Co. Ltd *v* Commission, [2005] ECR II-04065, par. 42.

Unlike secondary legislation, in the case of which Council Regulation 1/1958 determines the languages of the legal instruments, each treaty indicates what languages it was drafted in. Furthermore, the final provisions of treaties directly express the principle of equal authenticity for the treaty. For instance, it follows from the provisions of Article 314 of the *Treaty establishing the European Community*,[23] Article 53 of the *Treaty on European Union*,[24] Article 13 of the *Treaty of Nice*,[25] and Article IV-448 of the *Treaty establishing a Constitution for Europe*[26] that the treaties have been drawn up in a single original in the official languages and that the texts in each of these languages are equally authentic. It should be borne in mind that treaties have a character of international agreements concluded between Member States and as such they are the subject to the *Vienna Convention on the Law of Treaties* of 1969.[27] That is, final provisions of treaties that lay down the equal authenticity of language versions are in accordance with Article 33 of the Convention, which regulates the interpretation of treaties that are authenticated in two or more languages (par.1 and 3).

The requirement of equality between EU languages and the practical difficulties in an equal use of all these languages at the same time lead to the diversity paradox explained in the next section.

3. Paradox of diversity – use of languages in EC institutions

The first paradox analysed in the paper does not stem directly from the phenomenon of multilingual law but rather from the linguistically diverse communication in EU institutions. This paradox – denoted as the diversity paradox – has been indicated by Anthony Pym (2001), who noted that during multilingual communication within institutions of international and supranational organisations, two contradictory tendencies can be observed at the same time. The first tendency is the growth of an international *lingua franca*, which should result in a decrease of linguistic diversity. The second is an increase in the use of translation, which should cause greater linguistic diversity. The two tendencies leading to these contradictory effects – i.e.,

23. Consolidated text in *OJ C 321E/180 of 29 December 2006.*
24. Consolidated text in OJ *C 321E/35 of 29 December 2006.*
25. OJ C 80/43 of 10 March 2001.
26. OJ C 310/191 of 16 December 2004.
27. United Nations, Treaty Series, vol. 1155: 331. It should be kept in mind that not all Member States ratified the Vienna Convention.

the growth and decrease of linguistic diversity – are also examined in the institutions of the EU, which is regarded by Pym as an extreme case because of the great number of possible language combinations, which can emerge during communication.[28] Pym examines the paradox not only in the reference to multilingual legal instruments but in a broader perspective. This section, however, is limited only to the explanation of the diversity paradox in the context of EU legal multilingualism and language use in Community institutions, especially during legal drafting process.

Pym considers the development of a *lingua franca* as a reason explaining the reduction in language diversity and the increase in translation as a reason for growth of language diversity. In order to explain the diversity paradox in the context of a legal and official multilingualism, it is the linguistic diversity that should be regarded as a reason for the two contradictory tendencies. In other words, the analysis of the diversity paradox does not start from the observation of the development of the *lingua franca* and translation increase but from the statement that linguistic diversity and legal multilingualism in the European Union are inevitable because of political and legal reasons explained in the previous section. Even if EU linguistic diversity does not represent a real variety of languages in Europe, there are still twenty three official languages which have at the same time the status of working languages (Article 1 of Regulation 1/1958). Although there are postulates to reduce EU multilingualism (cf. Moratinos Johnston 2000: 55-59), practice demonstrates that the diversity of official and working languages is growing, usually due to the accessions of new Member States.[29]

Hence, EU linguistic diversity and especially the number of languages in which legal instruments are authenticated cannot be reduced. However, on the other hand, it is equally not possible to use all the twenty-three languages at the same time for communicating or drafting a legal instrument. Therefore one or two languages are usually applied, which results in the development of a *lingua franca* or rather several *linguae francae*. Nevertheless, in order to preserve the equality between official languages required by official and legal multilingualism, interpretation and translation into other languages must be provided. Thus, even if some official and working languages are used more often than others (with the consequent

28. Nowadays in the EU of 23 official languages, according to the formula n(n-1) – proposed by Pym – where 'n' is the number of official languages, there are 506 language combinations.

29. The exemption of this rule is the case of Irish explained at length in the previous section.

development of a *lingua franca*), thanks to translation into all the other languages, the linguistic diversity provided by law is not reduced in practice. Accordingly, it is this great linguistic diversity that brings about the two tendencies which create the diversity paradox.

Pym explains the diversity paradox by reference to the distinction between communication inside the institutions (within their professional interculture) and communication beyond the institutions (between interculture within institutions and "the relative monocultures whose languages are accorded official status"). In the case of the first type of communication, for practical reasons, one or two languages only are used. Consequently, a *lingua franca* develops. With the second type of communication, the use of all official languages is necessary and therefore translation has to be applied. According to Pym, this explains why the growth of a *lingua franca* is compatible with the increase in translation.

EU languages have the status of both official and working languages. The latter can be defined "as those used between institutions, within institutions and during internal meetings convened by the institutions" (Labrie (1993: 82), after Gazzola (2002)). Accordingly, the first type of communication – characterised by the growth of a *lingua franca* – is held in working languages. By contrast, the official languages defined as "those used in communications between the institutions and the outside world" (Labrie (1993: 82)) are applied in the second type of communication recognised by Pym.

Although some authors analysing EU multilingualism propose the definitions of official and working languages and distinguish between these two concepts (Labrie (1993: 82), Pieters (2004: 39-45)), Regulation 1/1958 granting official and working status to EU languages does not define the two terms. Moreover, it stems from Article 1 of Regulation that official and working languages are the same. Therefore, the concept of official and working languages is regarded as a unitary one (Pujadas (2004)). The question on the difference between official and working languages was investigated by the Council due to the parliamentary inquiry.[30] The Council declared that neither the EC Treaty nor Regulation 1/1958 gives any answer to this question. Hence the matter should be solved by each institution in accordance with Regulation 1/1958 and under its own responsibility. Additionally, the Commission, while replying to parliamentary questions on the use of languages in EC institutions, states constantly that "according to

30. Written question no 1576/79 by Mr Patterson to the Council; OJ C 150, 18.06.1980: 17; see Šarčević (2002: 240-241).

Council Regulation No 1/58 all the official languages are also working languages (Article 1), and everybody is therefore fully entitled to use them interchangeably in the institutions."[31]

It seems that the Regulation provides an ideal solution – the same rights for both official and working languages to all EU languages (Phillipson (2003: 118)). In practice, however, only a limited number of languages is used within the institutions. Such a possibility is foreseen in Article 6 of Regulation, authorising the institutions to "stipulate in their rules of procedure which of the languages are to be used in specific cases."[32] Official languages are used as working languages to a different extent in the various EC institutions, which all apply Article 6 and establish the internal language regime in their rules of procedure. In order to illustrate the language use in EC institutions, the Parliament, the Council, and the Commission – the three institutions involved in legislative drafting – are taken into consideration in the following paragraphs.

Full multilingualism is observed within the European Parliament where the use of all the official languages is required in its works. Rule 138 of the Rules of Procedure[33] provides that all documents of the Parliament should be drawn up in the official languages (par.1). Moreover, the use of all the official languages is foreseen at all formal meetings of the Parliament and its components, where all Members can use the official language of their choice and their speeches must be simultaneously interpreted into the other official languages (par.2). Although it has occasionally been considered to limit the number of languages used by the Parliament,[34] all such suggestions have been rejected. Contrary to these proposals, the Committee on Rules of Procedure stated in its Resolution of 1982 that "any limitation of

31. Answer to Oral Question no 53 by Alfredo Antoniozzi (H-0159/05) on the subject of the use of Italian in the EU institutions; cf. Commission answers to Written Question E-3124/03 by Mrs Muscardini (UEN) and Written Question E-2111/04 by Mrs Reynaud.

32. This provision does not apply to the language regime of the Court of Justice that is obliged to lay down the languages to be used in the proceedings of the Court in its rules of procedure (Article 7).

33. Rules of Procedure of the European Parliament, OJ L 44 of 15 February 2005.

34. For instance, in 1978 Renée van Hoof proposed the "asymmetric system" that would allow Members of Parliament to make speeches in their own language while speeches would be interpreted only into the two dominant languages, namely, French and English (Coulmas (1991: 7), Morationos Johnston (2000: 26), Wright (2000: 166)). The Podestà committee proposed in 2001 that a single working language should be used in the works of the Parliament (Phillipson (2003: 136)).

the number of languages used by the European Parliament would interfere with the democratic nature of Parliament".[35] The Committee also confirmed the rule of absolute equality between the official languages "whether used actively or passively, in writing or orally, at all meetings of Parliament and its bodies" in the same Resolution.[36] Moreover, the Committee admitted that each citizen has the right to stand for Parliament and be elected regardless of his or her linguistic ability (Wright (2000: 166)).[37] In practice, certainly, not all languages are used at the Parliament's informal meetings (Coulmas (1991: 7), Wilson (2003: 4-6)). Truchot (2003: 102) notes that "the lower you get in the hierarchy or the less formal the meetings are, the less multilingualism is guaranteed". This statement is also true in the case of other institutions, as the following example of the Council illustrates.

The Council of the European Union also makes attempts to respect full multilingualism in its work. In accordance with Article 14 of Council's Rules of Procedure,[38] the Council deliberates and takes decisions on the basis of documents drafted in all the official and working languages (par. 1). However, in case of urgency, the Council acting unanimously can decide to work on the documents although they are not available in all the languages (par. 1). If the text of any proposed amendment is not drawn up in such of the languages referred to in par. 1, any member of the Council may oppose discussion (par. 2). As far as the adoption of a legal instrument is concerned, if the text of such an instrument is not available in all the official languages, the Council can debate the substance of an instrument and come to a political agreement on that substance (Pujadas (2004)); hence, it can informally adopt an instrument without waiting for versions in all the official languages (Huntington (1991:331), Tabory (1980: 24)). However, an instrument can be formally adopted only when all its official language versions are ready and have been reviewed by jurist linguists (Huntington (1991:331), Pujadas (2004), Tabory (1980: 24)). The language regime of oral communication depends on the level at which meetings are organised. Namely, during meetings of the Council of Ministers, the representatives of

---

35. Resolution on the multilingualism of the European Community, *OJ C 292 of 08.11.1982: 0096*, available at http://www.ciemen.org/mercator/UE19-GB.htm
36. *Supra note* 34.
37. On the arguments for the preservation of the principle of equality languages in the Parliament, see the Nyborg report of 1982 and the Galle report of 1994. On further details see int. al.: Coulmas (1991), Wilson (2003).
38. Council Decision of 22 March 2004 adopting the Council's Rules of Procedures OJ L 106 of 15.04.2004.

the Member States may speak in a language of their choice and interpretation into the other languages is provided. The COREPER, on the other hand, works only in French, English and German (Fenet (2001: 247) and Sabino (1999: 163)). The language regime of Council working groups and preparatory bodies is based on the request-and-pay system introduced in May 2004 due to the enlargement. According to this system, Member States, which partially pay for interpretation, decide whether they need interpretation and for which languages.

The Commission respects the principle that languages are equal as official and working languages.[39] However, for operational reasons, the number of languages used in internal meetings is limited. Consequently, some languages are used more often than the others. Although the Commission made no arrangements as to the preference for one or more particular languages in internal communication, it is admitted that the most widely used languages in the Commission are English, French and to lesser extent German (Athanassiou (2006: 20)).[40] Hence, as far as oral communication is concerned, the Commission applies the limited language regime. However, texts that are to be sent officially to other institutions and those that are to be published in the Official Journal have to be drawn up in all the official languages. Since it is not possible to draft simultaneously in 23 languages, a text is drafted in one language (usually English or French, or sometimes German) and then translated into the others. Moreover, English, French and German are those languages in which documents have to be provided before they can be adopted at the meeting of the Commission. They are denoted as 'procedural languages'. The versions in the official but 'non–procedural' languages have to be produced, but for a later deadline, usually 48 hours after the meeting (Wagner et al. (2002: 10)).

This short analysis of the language regime in the three institutions demonstrates that although, according to Article 1 of Regulation, all the official languages are working languages, often – especially in informal oral communication – only a few of them are used. Therefore, a distinction between working languages *de iure* (i.e., the working languages listed in Article 1 of the Regulation) and working languages *de facto* or internal working languages (i.e., those actually used in the institutions) is made.[41] Pujadas

39. See the answers to the parliamentary questions indicated in *supra note* 30.
40. The choice of one of these languages depends often on custom and the policy being dealt with (Athanassiou (2006: 20, ftn. 80)).
41. The following terms are used in the meaning of '*de facto* working languages': vehicular languages (Truchot (2001) or 'langues véhiculaires' in Heusse (1999:

(2004) rightly notes that "while the concept of official and working languages is, *de jure*, a unitary concept, in some cases it is *de facto* split into two different concepts: those languages strictly used for external communication [...] and those used for internal use (internal working languages)." The latter, i.e., *de facto* working languages can develop – as explained by Pym – into *lingua franca*.

This distinction between *de iure* and *de facto* working languages demonstrates that "the equality of all official languages is only formally proclaimed but not implemented in all cases" (Pujadas (2004)). The basis for such inequality can already be noted in Article 6 of Regulation 1/1958, which gives the possibility to Community institutions to stipulate "which of the languages are to be used in specific cases" (Ammon (2006: 321)). This contradiction between a legal requirement of equality between all EU languages and the practice of unequal language use can be regarded as the source of the diversity paradox.

However, it should be noted that when the language regime in EU institutions is examined, languages that are required for oral communication should be distinguished from those that are demanded for written documents. In the case of oral communication, the number of applied languages is often limited, especially during informal meetings of preparatory bodies. These languages are internal *de facto* working languages and those of them used the most often (like English and French) become *linguae francae*. On the other hand, most of documents, especially those that are a basis for the drafting of a legal instrument (e.g., proposal, amendments), have to be available in all the official and working languages. Hence, the documents are discussed in a limited number of languages but they are produced (often by means of translation) in all the official and working languages. Consequently, a full multilingualism of legal documents is achieved and linguistic equality is preserved as far as drafting process resulting in a multilingual legal instrument is concerned.

After the analysis of the general use of languages in the institutions and the explanation of the diversity paradox, the next section examines in more details the use of languages and of translation in the drafting of a multilingual legal instrument.

---

204)), in-house languages, administrative languages (Phillipson (2003: 118)), unofficial working language (Tabory (1980: 26) while talking about French as a working language of the ECJ).

4. Paradoxes of translation – drafting of EC law

Due to the high number of EU official languages, which has been expanded several times, translation is used to draft EU law. However, when the normative requirements of legal multilingualism, stemming from the principle of equal authenticity, are confronted with the practice of translation, two paradoxical situations can be identified. The first relates to the general question of the possibility of translation, especially to the dubious possibility of rendering exactly the same meaning in two or more languages. This translation paradox, generally acknowledged in translation theory, is significant for legal multilingualism, which requires that all authentic language versions of a single legal instrument have the same meaning, even though it seems to be virtually impossible to acquire identical meaning in two or more languages. The second translation paradox can be identified directly within the context of EU legal multilingualism, and relates to the principle of equal authenticity and the theory of original texts. These both require that all authentic texts be regarded as originals, whereas, in practice, the majority of them are prepared by means of translation. Both paradoxes of translation are analysed and explained in the present section.

The first paradox of translation can be acknowledged even without reference to legal translation or to methods of drafting law in many languages. As mentioned in the introduction, no two languages are identical; consequently, a perfect and exact translation is impossible. Some authors even assume that translation is generally impossible (see Benjamin (1923), Petrey (1984: 87) quoted in Fram-Cohen (1985)). At the same time, translation is carried out even in domains that demand precise translation, as in the case of legal translation. Michelle Fram-Cohen (1985) acknowledges that translation is impossible in theory but possible in practice, and she describes this as the paradox of translation. In her view, the translation paradox stems from the fact that linguistic translation theories concentrate on the differences between languages that make translation impossible. The author instead intends to focus on the features that are common to all languages, and that facilitate translation. The following two paragraphs demonstrate – on the basis of Fram-Cohen's observations on the possibility of translation – that the same meaning of all language versions of a legal act can be attainable, especially if the characteristics of the EU multilingual legal system are taken into consideration.

One of the difficulties in translating is the lack of a word in one language designating an existing concept in another language. However, concepts have their referents in reality; therefore, even if a word designating the concept does not exist in one language, it can be conveyed in translation by means of a neologism or descriptive phrase. It is common practice in the case of EU legal multilingualism to create new terms in EU official languages to denote the legal concepts that are characteristic for EU legal system. It should be borne in mind that the official languages of the EC are also official languages in the Member States and are used for drafting national legal acts. Although the Community law is applied, in some cases even directly, in Member States, the EC legal system is autonomous and has its own legal terminology. That is, terms used in EC legislation have their own specific meaning that differs from the meaning of the legal terminology used in Member States. Hence, in order to avoid confusion, when EC law is drafted, legal terms that are too closely linked to national legal systems should be avoided.[42] This guideline is in compliance with the case law of the European Court of Justice, which stated in the CILFIT case that "(…) Community law uses terminology which is peculiar to it. Furthermore, it must be emphasized that legal concepts do not necessarily have the same meaning in Community law and in the law of the various Member States".[43] In other words, if the meaning of Community legal terms was derived from the national legal systems of Member States, the uniform application of EC law would not be possible. In several of its judgments, the ECJ confirmed that EC legal terms cannot be defined by reference to the laws of the Member States because the terms have their own independent meaning in Community law, which has to be interpreted taking into consideration all the language versions of the legal act in question.[44]

Another difficulty for translation noted by Fram-Cohen is the result of the lack of equivalence between words and concepts, in the sense that one word can have more than one meaning in the same language and consequently represent more than one concept, whereas in another language there are different words for each of those concepts. This situation should not

42. Cf. guideline 5.3.2 of the Joint Practical Guide of the European Parliament, the Council and the Commission for persons involved in the drafting of legislation within the Community institutions. The English version of the Joint Practical Guide is available at http://europa.eu/eur-lex/en/about/techleg/ guide/pdf/en.pdf.

43. Case 283/81 Srl CILFIT and Lanificio di Gavardo SpA v Ministry of Health; [1982] ECR 3415.

44. See for example the Case C-449/93 *Rockfon A/S* v *Specialarbejderforbundet i Danmark*, [1995] ECR I-4291, par. 25; Case C-373/00 *Adolf Truly GmbH* v *Bestattung Wien GmbH*, [2003] ECR I-1931, par. 30, 40, 45; Case C-498/03 *Kingscrest Associates Ltd and Montecello Ltd* v *Commissioners of Customs and Excise*, [2005] ECR I-4427, par. 27.

occur in the case of the EU, since all the official languages of the EU share the same system of reference, i.e., the signs in each language refer to the same objects (see Šarčević (2000: 15, 230 –231)), or in other words, the term in all languages refers to the same concept. However, in order to achieve a full equivalence and coherence between the different language versions, the standardization of terminology in official languages is necessary.

Another paradox related to translation can be observed with regard to EU multilingual drafting methods. In order to preserve actual equality between the authentic language versions of a legal act, laws should be co-drafted simultaneously in all the languages.[45] It is not, however, possible to apply such a method in a legal system like that of the European Union, which comprises twenty-three official languages. Therefore the language versions of EU legal acts are often prepared by means of translation. At the same time, the term 'translation', which implies inferiority, cannot be used in reference to the language versions of a legal act that are considered as equally authentic due to the principle of equal authenticity. This view is confirmed by the theory of original texts, which presumes that none of the authentic texts can have a status of translation; or, in other words, that all of them are regarded as 'originals' regardless of the way in which they were drafted (Šarčević (2000: 20, 64)). This situation creates a paradox that Renato Correia, a translator at the European Parliament, has described with regard to the EU, as follows: "In practice, Community law is inconceivable *without* translation, whereas in strictly legal terms Community law is inconceivable *with* it" (2003: 41).

In order to verify the paradoxical character of Correia's statement, the meaning of equal authenticity should be carefully analysed. According to Emma Wagner, a former head of the Translation Service Department at the European Commission, the principle of equal authenticity is "a feat of legal magic which defies all logic but is nevertheless necessary, to safeguard linguistic equality" (2000: 2). She notes that in accordance with dictionary definitions of the terms 'original' and 'authentic', only one object can be original and authentic. Therefore the presumption of 'multiple authenticity'

45. Such a method excluding translation from a drafting process has been established and successfully developed in bilingual Canada where, at the federal level, legislation is co-drafted simultaneously in two languages. For further details on co-drafting in Canada, see esp. *Guide to Making Federal Acts and Regulations/Lois et règlements, l'essentiel* (Government of Canada, Privy Council Office 2001), see also *inter alia* Wood (1996: 66-77) and Šarčević (2005: 277-292).

and 'equivalent originals' stemming from the principle of equal authenticity and theory of original texts is a legal fiction (Wagner (2000: 2) and 2001: 67). Wagner bases her observation on Article 314 of the *Treaty establishing the European Community* which provides the principle of equal authenticity for the Treaty in the following way:

> This Treaty, drawn up in a single original in the Dutch, French, German, and Italian languages, all four texts being *equally authentic*, shall be deposited in the archives of the Government of the Italian Republic, which shall transmit a certified copy to each of the Governments of the other signatory States.
> Pursuant to the Accession Treaties, the Czech, Danish, English, Estonian, Finnish, Greek, Hungarian, Irish, Latvian, Lithuanian, Maltese, Polish, Portuguese, Slovak, Slovenian, Spanish and Swedish versions of this Treaty shall also be *authentic*.[46] (emphasis added)

Since other treaties comprise the corresponding provision laying down the principle of equal authenticity,[47] it suffices to base the analysis on Article 314. The English version of the Article speaks about a single original version expressed, although, primarily in four and finally in twenty-three languages,[48] and provides that all the language versions are equally authentic. In order to discover the meaning of the term 'authentic', not only English but also other authentic language versions of the Treaty should be taken into consideration. The phrase 'being equally authentic' is of special interest. The principle of equal authenticity is formulated in the same way and the exact equivalent of the term 'authentic' is used in most of the language versions.[49] Nevertheless, the French, Italian and German versions shed light on the meaning of the term 'authentic'. Although there is the word 'authentique' in French language and 'autentico' in Italian, the phrase 'being equally authentic' is rendered in French as 'faisant également foi'[50] and in

46. Consolidated text in OJ *C 321E/180 of 29 December 2006.*
47. On the principle of equal authenticity in treaties, see section 2 of this paper.
48. Since 1 January, 2007 Bulgarian and Romanian were added to the list.
49. Cf. for instance, the following equivalents of 'equally authentic': 'igualmente auténticos' (ES), 'gelijkelijk authentiek' (NL), 'na równi autentyczne' (PL), 'rovnako autentické' (SL).
50. It is, however, possible to use the French term 'authentique' in the sense of 'faisant également foi'; for instance, cf. authentic French text of Article 85 of *Vienna Convention on the Law of Treaties* providing that "L'original de la présente Convention, dont les textes anglais, chinois, espagnol, français et russe sont *égale-*

Italian as "facenti ugualmente fede' that means 'equally legally binding and valid'.[51] The French expression 'faire foi' can also be translated into English as 'authentic version'.[52] German also comprises the word 'authentisch'. However, the German version of Article 314 applies the expression 'gleichermaßen verbindlich'. The first dictionary meaning of the German term 'verbindlich' is not 'authentic' but 'authoritative', followed by 'binding' as the second meaning. The use of the German term 'verbindlich' in the meaning of 'authoritative' is in accordance with Article 33 of Vienna Convention, stating that a treaty is equally authoritative in all languages in which a treaty has been authenticated.[53] Moreover, the comparison of the meaning of the principle of equal authenticity in other multilingual legal systems, such as bilingual Canada[54] or Hong Kong,[55] confirms that the

---

ment authentiques, sera déposé auprès du Secrétaire general des Nations Unies" (emphasis added).

51. Cf. the Portuguese version of Article 314 using the phrase '*fazendo fé qualquer* dos quatro textos' (emphasis added).

52. For instance *Le Grand Dictionnaire Terminologique*, available at the website of the Office québécois de la langue française http://www.granddictionnaire.com, proposes English term 'authentic version' as equivalents of French expression 'faire foi'.

53. Cf. the French version of Article 33, which is along with Chinese, English, Russian and Spanish, the authentic text of Vienna Convention. The French text of par. 1 of Article 33 applies the expression 'faire foi' (cf. "Lorsqu'un traité a été authentifié en deux ou plusieurs langues, son texte *fait foi* dans chacune de ces langues, (...)." [emphasis added]). The Spanish authentic text of par. 1 of Article 33 of Vienna Convention uses the phrase close to the French 'faire également foi'; cf. "Cuando un tratado haya sido autenticado en dos o más idiomas, el texto *hará igualmente fe* en cada idioma, (...)" (emphasis added), whereas the Spanish authentic version of article 314 of EC Treaty applies the phrase similar to English 'equally authentic'; cf. "(...), cuyos cuatro textos son *igualmente auténticos*, (...)" (emphesis added). The German version is not analysed, since Vienna Convention is not authentic in that language.

54. It is interesting to compare English and French version of Section 18 the *Canadian Charter of Rights and Freedoms*, 1982. The English text states simply that English and French language versions are equally authoritative; cf. "The statutes, records and journals of Parliament shall be printed and published in English and French and *both language versions are equally authoritative*" (emphasis added), whereas French version provides the principle of equal authenticity in more descriptive way; cf. "Les lois, les archives, les comptes rendus et les procès-verbaux du Parlement sont imprimés et publiés en français et en anglais, *les deux versions des lois ayant également force de loi et celles des autres documents ayant même*

principle requires language versions to be considered as equally authoritative.

Hence, this short analysis of the term 'authentic' in Article 314 of EC Treaty and the comparison of various language versions of that provision demonstrates that the term 'authentic' does not express the standard dictionary meaning of 'genuine' or 'not copied' but is used in the sense of 'authoritative' and conveys the meaning of 'legally valid', 'legally binding' or 'having legal force' rather than of 'original'. Consequently, 'multiple authenticity' – described by Wagner as a legal fiction – means that several authenticated language versions have the same legal force. Certainly, then, it is improper to use the term 'translation' in reference to equally authentic language versions. However, it should be taken into consideration that they are not equally authentic when they are drafted but when they become legally binding as a result of their authentication. Thus, the principle of equal authenticity requires authenticated language versions to have the same legal force, in other words, in order to be regarded as equally authentic. This means that the principle of equal authenticity does not refer to the language versions of a legal instrument that is being drafted.[56] Accordingly, it can be stated that, from a legal standpoint, it is not the way of creating language versions that is important but their authentication (Sullivan (2004: 1006)). Language versions are authenticated when a legal instrument is enacted or adopted by a proper body. It is also possible for a language version which

---

valeur" (emphasis added). Accordingly, this comparison reveals that language versions that are equally authoritative have the same force of law.

55. Cf. *supra note* 20.

56. For instance, the English text of the *Treaty establishing the European Economic Community*, that has been authenticated, was the fifth English version of this Treaty. The four English versions have been prepared before Great Britain joined the EC and none of them is authentic either can be referred to for interpretation purposes. Some of the four English translations were published. On the cover of one of publications (H.M. Stationery Office 1962, code-number L 59-130) there is the notice: "This translation has been prepared for the convenience of Parliament and the public. *It must not be treated as an official or an authentic text.* Readers are reminded that the official and authentic text of the Treaty exist only in the French, German, Italian and Dutch languages. (…)" [emphasis added]. Authenticated English text of the EEC Treaty has been prepared by the Working Party on the Authentic English Text and completed in April 1971. Only this version has been published in the Official Journal and it is the only English version of the EC Treaty that is equally authentic with other language version of that Treaty. See Akehurst (1972: 20-32); Bowyer (1972: 439-455); Maas (1968-1969: 205-209).

did not exist when the instrument was enacted to be declared authentic through legislation (Sullivan (2004: fn. 102)).[57] All the same, it should be pointed out that language versions become authentic, due to their enactment or adoption, when the drafting process is completed.[58] Accordingly, the method of their drafting does not matter for their authentication and legal force as long as they are authenticated in the prescribed way.

In the light of this analysis, especially if the process of drafting is distinguished from the authentication of language versions, Correia's statement seems less paradoxical. Equally valid language versions of a legal instrument, even if actually translated, cannot be regarded as translations after their authentication, but they need not be called originals – before authentication – during their drafting process. Translation is usually considered as a substitution of one language for another, whereas, after authentication, the authenticated language versions do not replace each other but they coexist. Consequently, in the case of EU legal instruments, it is not translation but multilingualism in the sense of the co-presence of twenty-three EU official language versions.

According to Correia, Community law is, in practice, inconceivable without translation. However, if the practice of drafting Community law in many languages is examined, it has to be affirmed that this drafting process is not based on pure translation, but is rather a multilingual legal drafting with some elements of translation.[59] The aim of the drafting, in the case of EU law, is to produce all the language versions of a legal instrument in the same communicative situation comprising the same space (the EU) and the same addressees (EU citizens), whereas, in the case of traditional translation, a source text produced in the primary communicative situation is substituted for a target text produced in the secondary communicative situation (cf. Schäffner 1998: 83). Moreover, as far as translation is concerned, texts

57. Sometimes a language version does not even exist when a legal act is adopted. Such a situation takes place also within the European Union after each enlargement, when the number of official languages is expanded. It is a case of so-called subsequent translation (Šarčević (2000: 92-93) and (2002: 239-272)).

58. It is usual and proper situation. However, sometimes due to practical or technical difficulties, a text in one of official language(s) cannot be submitted before the adoption.

59. The following analysis refers only to the preparation of the authentic language versions of a legal instrument during legislative process within EU institutions, not to the preparation of new language versions of *acquis communautaire* by candidate states before the accession. The latter is a pure translation of final authenticated language versions of legal instruments already adopted.

in source and target languages are not usually produced at the same time, whereas all the EU official languages are present during an EU legal drafting. It should also be borne in mind that it is not only the final version of an instrument that is translated but that translation is used during the whole multi-stages process of drafting. Accordingly, all the languages participate in the drafting process at all its stages. For instance, although a proposal for a legal instrument is first drafted only in one language (usually in English or French), before it is submitted to the Council, it has to be translated into all the official languages by the Commission translation service.

The presence of all the official languages and, especially, the equality between them is evident during the revision of the multilingual drafts carried out by lawyer-linguists in all institutions participating in the legislative process, and at various stages of this process. First of all, all language versions of a draft are taken into consideration during revision, and moreover, it is possible to change the 'original' version as a result of the revision. This is precisely what differs the revision of a 'translation' during multilingual drafting from a revision in the classical translation process when only translated text can be changed. Indeed, the term 'co-drafting' has been used by Tito Gallas (2001: 90) and Manuela Guggeis (Gallas and Guggeis (2005: 499)) to describe the revision process where all the language versions are compared and in the case of discrepancies, changes can be introduced also into an 'original version' (a 'basic text' in Council terminology; cf. Piris (2004)). The same term 'co-drafting' is used in reference to the Canadian drafting method at the federal level, where two language versions are simultaneously co-drafted without any translation elements.

Another particularity of the EU production of multilingual law that brings this process closer to drafting than to translation is the role played by translators and linguists in the production of the various language versions of a legal act. Some authors commenting this process postulate a change in the perception of translators' roles in the EU legal drafting process viewing them as more creative than in classical translation (cf. Correia (2003: 43); Šarčević (1998) and (2000)). Others even state that translators and linguists are entrusted with a role which is actually equal to that of a drafter of legislation (cf. Agius).

Language versions of a legal text – from a Commission proposal to the signature by the legislative authorities – undergo many linguistic changes and permutations of translation. Moreover, language versions can influence each other, e.g., divergence between versions that have been translated can result from a badly drafted 'original' that has to be changed during revision. As a result, it is difficult to assert on which language a single provision of a legal act has been based on or influenced by. A provision (an expression or a term) can, for example, be changed during the legislation process, for instance by an amendment that is proposed in a language different from that in which the provision has been originally drafted. Moreover, during the revision, the 'original' version can be changed because it has been poorly drafted. This uncertainty about the language from which a provision originates makes it very difficult to distinguish between original and translated language versions. Hence, not only from a legal standpoint but also in practice, it can be difficult, especially at the micro-level of analysis, to distinguish translations from originals. However, this should guarantee equality between the authentic language versions of a legal instrument not only due to legal presumptions or fictions but also due to practice of EU multilingual legal drafting.

Undoubtedly, as stated by Correia, "in strictly legal terms Community law is inconceivable with [translation]". It is also true that Community law, in practice, is not conceivable without some elements of translation. However, in the case of drafting of multilingual Community law, we do not deal with classical translation but with techniques that ensure equality of the languages throughout a multilingual drafting process, as the above analysis attempts to prove.

The next section aims at explaining what the requirement of the same meaning for all the authentic language versions of a legal instrument means and whether all language versions conveying the same meaning should be taken into consideration for interpretation purposes.

5. Paradox of identicalness – interpretation of EC law

Not only the drafting but also the interpretation of multilingual law is a very challenging task, and can reveal paradoxical situations. The principle of equal authenticity presumes that all the authenticated language versions of a legal instrument contribute to the meaning of the instrument (Šarčević (2000: 64)). As a result, all the equally authentic versions should be taken into consideration when a legal instrument is interpreted. This requirement also guarantees that EC law is uniformly applied. On the other hand, as explained above, one of the reasons for legal and official multilingualism is the right of the citizen to his own language, i.e., the right to monolingualism. Hence, the question arises here whether a citizen can rely only on one version drawn up in his mother tongue and, if not, whether and how the right to monolingualism and to legal certainty is preserved.

It should be taken into consideration that the principle of equal authenticity not only requires that all the language versions be consulted but is also based on the presumption that all of them have the same meaning. It is paradoxical that the language versions of a legal instrument, which are presumed to have identical meaning, must all be considered and compared in order to find out the meaning of the legal instrument. If all the language versions have the same meaning, is it not enough to consult only one of them? Then the paradoxical situation – in which, on the one hand, multilingualism provides a citizen with the right to his own language, and, on the other, requires him to read all the language versions in order to apply Community law – could be explained.

In order to analyse this paradox of identicalness, one should firstly understand who is required to compare all the language versions in order to ascertain the meaning of the provision in question. Then the reasons why the consideration of all the language versions is demanded should be explained.

The European Court of Justice and the Court of First Instance in settled case law, as well as the Advocates General[60] in their opinions, frequently underline the need to compare all the official language versions for interpretation purposes. The ECJ already in 1969 stated in the judgement to Case 29/69 Erich Stauder v City of Ulm that owing to uniform application and according to uniform interpretation, it is impossible to consider one version of the text in isolation. On the contrary, Community law should be interpreted in the light of the versions in all the official languages.[61] Corre-

60. For instance, see opinion of Advocate General Alber delivered on 16 May 2002 in Case C-257/00 Nani Givane and Others v Secretary of State for the Home Department [2003] ECR I-345 who in par. 29 states that "[i]n accordance with the settled case-law of the Court, Community Regulations must be interpreted uniformly in the light of the versions existing in the other official languages"; or opinion of Advocate General Stix-Hackl delivered on 10 May 2005 in Case C-247/04 Transport Maatschappij Traffic BV v Staatssecretaris van Economische Zaken [2005] (not published in ECR at the moment of writing the paper) who in par. 17 asserts that "[t]he interpretation of a provision of Community law involves a comparison of all of the different language versions"; the same confirms Advocate General Leger in opinion delivered on 13 November 2003 in Case C-371/02 Bjornekulla Fruktindustrier AB v Procordia Food AB[2004] ECR I-5791.

61. See par. 3 of the judgment of the Court of 12 November 1969 in Case 29/69 Erich Stauder v City of Ulm [1969] ECR 419. *Cf.* as well par. 1 and 3 of ECJ judgment of 12 July 1979 in Case 9/79 Koschniske v Raad van Arbeid [1979] ECR 2717.

spondingly, in the CILFIT case (283/81) the ECJ indicated that since "Community legislation is drafted in several languages and that the different language versions are all equally authentic[, a]n interpretation of a provision of Community law thus involves a comparison of the different language versions" (par. 18).[62] The Court of the First Instance also respects the need to compare various language versions for interpretation purposes.[63]

This brief overview of ECJ and CFI case law demonstrates that in order to interpret an EC legal instrument, all its authentic language versions have to be taken into consideration by the European Courts. However, EC law is not only interpreted by the ECJ and CFI but also by the national courts of the Member States, especially when a legal instrument (like, e.g., a regulation) is directly applied in the MS. It is practically impossible for a national court to fulfil the requirement of comparison of all – at present – the 23 authentic language versions of an interpreted legal instrument. Therefore, a national judge in fact usually consults and relies on only one version in his language (Van Calster (1997: 390-391)). Only if the consulted language version is ambiguous or obscure, does a judge also take into account other language versions (Šarčević (2002: 259)), although usually not all twenty-

62. The Case 283/81 Srl CILFIT and Lanificio di Gavardo SpA v Ministry of Health [1982] ECR 3415. The ECJ expressed the necessity of comparison of all official language version in order to guarantee uniform interpretation and application of multilingual Community law not only in CILFIT but also in several cases; for example following cases can be mentioned: judgment of 27 March 1990 in Case C-372/88 Cricket St Thomas v Milk Marketing Board of England and Wales [1990] ECR I-1345, par. 19; judgment of 17 October 1996 in Case C-64/95 Konservenfabrik Lubella Friedrich Buker GmbH and Co. KG v Hauptzollamt Cottbus [1996] ECR I-5105, par. 17; Case C-296/95 The Queen v Commissioners of Customs and Excise, ex parte EMU Tabac SARL, The Man in Black Ltd, John Cunningham [1998] ECR I-1605, par. 5; judgment of 24 October 1996 in Case C-72/95 Aannemersbedrijf P.K. Kraaijeveld BV e.a. v Gedeputeerde Staten van Zuid-Holland [1996] ECR I-5403, par. 1, 28; judgment of 14 September 1999 in Case C-375/97 General Motors Corporation v Yplon SA. [1999] ECR I-5421, par. 22; judgment of 14 September 2000 in Case C-384/98 D. v W [2000] ECR I-6795, par. 16; judgment of 26 May 2005 in Case C-498/03 Kingscrest Associates Ltd and Montecello Ltd v Commissioners of Customs and Excise [2005] ECR I-4427, par. 26.

63. For instance, the CFI repeated the statement of the ECJ expressed in Erich Stauder v City of Ulm and in CILFIT Case in its judgment of 6 October 2005 in joined cases T-22/02 and T-23/02 Sumitomo Chemical Co. Ltd and Sumika Fine Chemicals Co. Ltd v Commission of the European Communities, [2005] ECR II-04065, par. 46 and par. 42 respectively.

three versions. This observation is consistent with the opinions of some Advocate Generals who state that the judgement in CILFIT should not be regarded as requiring the national courts to compare all the authentic versions of an interpreted instrument. That would involve, in words of one AG, "a disproportionate effort on the part of the national courts"[64] and would put "a practically intolerable burden on the national courts"[65].

If the consideration of all the authentic versions of a legal instrument is not required for interpretation purposes from the national courts, it is obvious that EU citizens can also rely only on the version in their mother tongues. Why then does the ECJ in CILFIT and other judgements underline the need to compare all the authentic language versions?

Even if it seems paradoxical, both the presumption of identical meaning of all the authentic language versions and the requirement of the comparison of all the language versions in order to discover the meaning of a legal provision are necessary to preserve and guarantee the equal authenticity of the language versions. All the authentic language versions have to be taken into consideration for interpretation purposes because they are equal and have the same legal effect. This has been explained by Advocate General Stix-Hackl in the opinion of 10 May 2005 in Case C-247/04 as follows: "[t]he interpretation of a provision of Community law involves a comparison of all of the different language versions thereof, as Community law provisions are equally binding in all the different language versions". Advocate General Tizzano explains the ECJ statement in the CILFIT case in the same way. According to Tizzano, when the ECJ in the CILFIT judgement noted that the "interpretation of a provision of Community law [...] involves a comparison of the different language versions", the Court wanted the national courts to "bear in mind that the provision in question produces the same legal effects in all those versions".[66]

The aim of the presumption of identical meaning is also to assure the equality between the authentic language versions. In other words, if all the language versions have the same meaning, none of them can prevail for

64. Opinion of Advocate General Jacobs delivered on 10 July 1997 in Case C-338/95 Wiener S.I. GmbH v Hauptzollamt Emmerich[1997] ECR I-06495, par. 65.
65. Opinion of Advocate General Stix-Hackl delivered on 12 April 2005 in Case C-495/03 Intermodal Transports BV v Staatssecretaris van Financiën [2005] ECR I-08151, par. 99.
66. Opinion of Advocate General Tizzano delivered on 21 February 2002 in Case C-99/00 Criminal proceedings v Kenny Roland Lyckeskog [2002] ECR I-04839, par. 75.

interpretation purposes, just as none of them can be rejected. Certainly, if there are divergences between the language versions, the interpretation can favour some of them, but those versions are preferred not because of preferences to these language versions but because they better cohere with the court's interpretation based on interpretative methods (cf. Sullivan (2004: 1010)). This is especially so with an interpretation that takes into consideration the purpose and general scheme of the rules of which the provision in question forms a part (the teleological and systematic approach).[67]

Accordingly, it seems that the guarantee of the right to a citizen's own language is not the objective of the presumption of the same meaning of all official language versions. However, the requirement of the examination of all the language versions, which seemed to be in the contradiction to citizens' rights, guarantees legal certainty for EU citizens. As already explained, Community law can be directly applicable in the Member States; it is therefore very important, especially in the light of the rule *ignorantia iuris nocet*, that the citizen has access to the law in his own language. It is often emphasized that multilingualism ensures legal certainty (Gazzola (2002)). Legal certainty can be achieved, however, only if the law binds all citizens in the same way; in other words, only if the law is applied uniformly in all the Member States. In order to achieve a uniform application of Community law, the law has to be interpreted in a uniform way. Consequently, all language versions should contribute to the meaning of the legal act (Šarčević (2000: 64)) and ought to be considered for interpretation purposes. As noted by Roderick A. Macdonald, "(…) citizens have a legitimate expectation of being able to understand the law that is applicable to them. But this argument [for enacting the law in many languages] simply exhausts itself in multilingual societies" (1997: 138, note 71) and it "rests primarily on symbolic and not on instrumental grounds" (1997: 138, note 71).

Ruth Sullivan provides the explanation of this paradox by making reference to bilingual Canada. In her opinion, "the primary purpose of bilingual

67. Cf. opinion of Advocate General Jacobs (supra note 63) who notes that "[i]n fact the very existence of many language versions is a further reason for not adopting an excessively literal approach to the interpretation of Community provisions, and for putting greater weight on the context and general scheme of the provisions and on their object and purpose". See as well par. 14 of judgment in Case 30/77 Regina v. Bouchereau [1977] ECR 1999, to which the ECJ has been referred several times, e.g., in Case 100/84 Commission of the European Union v United Kingdom of Great Britain and Northern Ireland [1985] ECR 1169, par. 17

legislation is not to facilitate unilingual access to the law, but to build community" (2004: 1008). This explanation can also be appropriate for EC multilingualism, which makes possible the creation of a Community based on diversity.

6. Conclusion

The paper demonstrates that the paradoxes of legal multilingualism appear when the practice of production and application of multilingual law is confronted with legal requirements and presumptions stemming from the principle of equal authenticity. These paradoxes result, however, from a superficial understanding of the concept of official and legal multilingualism and the principle of equal authenticity. The above analyses attempted to demonstrate that legal requirements and the practice of legal multilingualism are more congruent than may appear at first glance. The insight into the drafting process and application of multilingual law and the thorough comprehension of the principle of equal authenticity should reveal that contradictions creating paradoxes seem to be, to large extent, just ostensible.

7. References

Agius, Peter. "Aspects of Interpretation of Multilingual 'Acquis Communautaire'". *Paper published at the intranet of the Council Legal Service.*

Akehurst, M. 1972. "Preparing the Authentic English Text of the EEC Treaty". *An Introduction to the Law of the European Economic Community*, ed. by B. A. Wortley, Manchester: Manchester University Press. 20–31.

Ammon, Ulrich. 2006. "Language conflicts in the European Union. On finding a politically acceptable and practicable solution for EU institutions that satisfies diverging interests". *International Journal of Applied Linguistics* 16 (3). 319–338.

Athanassiou, Phoebus. 2006. "The Application of Multilingualism in the European Union Context". *Legal Working Paper Series* 2, February 2006, European Central Bank, available at http://www.ecb.int or from the Social Science Research Network electronic library at http://ssrn.com/abstract_id =886048.

Benjamin, Walter. 1923. "Die Aufgabe des Übersetzers". Preface to German translation of Baudelaire's *Tableaux parisiens*, Heidelberg, pp. xi ff., English translation by H. Zohn. *Theories of translation: an anthology of essays from Dryden to Derrida*, ed. by R. Schulte and J. Biguenet, Chicago-London: University of Chicago Press. 71–82.

Brackeniers, Eduard. 1995. "Le multilinguisme dans la Communauté européenne". *Terminologie et traduction* 1. 91–96.
Bowyer, John. 1972. "Englishing Community Law". *Common Market Law Review* 9 (4). 439–455.
Correia, Renato. 2003. "Translation of EU Legal Texts". *Crossing Barriers and Bridging Cultures. The Challenges of Multilingual Translation for the European Union*, ed. by A. Tosi, Clevedon-Buffalo-Toronto-Sydney: Multilingual Matters Ltd. 38–44.
Coulmas, Florian. 1991. "European Integration and the idea of the national language. Ideological roots and economic consequences". *A Language Policy for the European Union: prospect and quandaries* (Contributions to the sociology of language; 61), ed. by F. Coulmas, Berlin-New York: Mouton de Gruyter. 1–43.
Dessemont, François and Tuğrul Ansay. 1995. *Introduction to Swiss Law*. The Hague-Boston-London: Kluwer Law International.
Fenet, Alain. 2001. "Diversité linguistique et construction européenne". *Revue trimestrielle de droit européen* 37 (2). 235–269.
Fram-Cohen, Michelle. 1985. "Reality, Language, Translation: What Makes Translation Possible", *paper presented in the American Translators Association Conference in Miami in 1985*, available at http://enlightenment.supersaturated.com/essays/text/michelleframcohen//possibilityoftranslation.html.
Gallas, Tito. 2001. "Evaluation in EC Legislation. Statute" Law Revue 22. 83–95.
Gallas, Tito and Manuela Guggeis. 2005. "La traduction juridique dans l'expérience des juristes-linguistes du Conseil de l'Union européenne". *Jurilinguistique: entre langues et droits – Jurilinguistics: Between Law and Language*, ed. by J.-C. Gémar and N. Kasirer, Montréal: Les Édition Thémis, Bruxelles: Les Édition juridiques Bruylant. 491–503.
Gazzola, Michele. 2002. "Revised summary of La relazione fra costi economici e costi politici del multilinguismo nell'Unione europea". *Tesi di Laurea.*, ed. by Luigi Bocconi. Milan: Università Commerciale. Available at: http://www.uemilano.it/multilinguismo/multilinguismo_unione _europea_en.htm.
Government of Canada, Privy Council Office. 2001. *Guide to Making Federal Acts and Regulations/Lois et règlements, l'essentiel* 2nd edition. English version available at http://www.pco-bcp.gc.ca/docs/Publications/legislation/lmg_e.pdf, last visited January 2006.
Grimm, Dieter. 1995. "Does Europe Need a Constitution?". *European Law Journal* 1 (3). 282–302.
Heusse, Marie-Pascale. 1999. "Le multilinguisme ou le défi cache de l'Union européenne". *Revue du Marché et de l'Union européenne* 426. 202–207.
Huntington, Robert. 1991. "European Unity and the Tower of Babel". *Boston University International Law Journal* 9. 321—348.
Kraus, Peter A. 2004. "Between Mill and Hallstein. Cultural diversity as a challenge to European integration". *Cultural diversity versus Economic Soli-*

darity. Is There a Tension? How Must it be Resolved?, ed. by P. Van Parijs, Bruxelles: Deboeck University Press. 299–314.

Labrie, Normand. 1993. *La Construction linguistique de la Communauté européenne.* Paris: Honoré Champion Éditeur.

Laighin, Pádraig Breandán Ó. 2004. "Towards the Recognition of Irish as an Official Working Language of the European Union". *Brief presented to the National Forum on Europe, Dublin Castle*, January 8, 2004.

Maas, H. H. 1968-1969. "The English Version of the Treaty of Rome". *Common Market Law Review* 6. 205–209.

Macdonald, Roderick A. 1997. "Legal Bilingualism". *McGill Law Journal/Revue de droit de McGill* 42. 119–168.

McDonald, M. 1996. "Unity in Diversities: Some Tensions in the Construction of Europe". *Social Anthropology* 4. 47–60.

MERCATOR/Eurolang. 2005. "The European Council of Ministers decides on Linguistics Minorities", *MERCATOR, linguistic rights and legislation* www. http://www.ciemen.org/mercator/notis.cfm?lg=.

Milian-Massana, Antoni. 2002. "The Principle of Language Equality in European Union Institutions and in Community Law: Myth or Reality?". *Revista de Llengua i Dret* 38.

Mill, John Stuart. [1861] 1972. "Consideration on Representative Government", *John Stuart Mill: Utilitarianism. Liberty. Representative Government*, ed. by H. C. Acton. London: Dent. 187–428.

Moratinos Johnston, Sofía. 2000. "Multilingualism and EU Enlargement". *Terminologie et traduction* 3. 20–70.

Nida, Eugene A. [1964] 2000. "Principles of correspondence". *The Translation Studies Reader*, ed. by L. Venuti, London and New York: Routledge. 126–140.

Petrey, Sandy. 1984. "Must History Be Lost in Translation?". *Translation Perspectives*, ed. by M. G. Rose, Binghamton: National Resource Center for Translation and Interpretation. 86–93.

Pescatore, Pierre. 1983. "The Doctrine of Direct Effect: An Infant Disease of Community Law". *European Law Review* 8 (3). 155–177.

Phillipson, Robert. 2003. *English-Only Europe? Challenging Language Policy.* London and New York: Routledge.

Pieters, Danny. 2004. "Vers un régime linguistique diversifié mais coherent pour l'Union européenne". *Langues et Union européenne: colloque du 6 novembre 2003 à l'Assemblée nationale française*, ed. by P. Sabourin, Bruxelles: Bruylant. 37–49.

Piris, Jean-Claude. 2004. "Union européenne: comment rédiger une legislation de qualité dans 20 languages et pour 25 États members?" The French version of the paper submitted for the Conference "The Sir William Dale Memorial Lecture", London, 8 November 2004.

Pujadas, Bernat. 2004. "The rules governing the languages of the European Union: which languages and to what extent? A practical guide". *Dossier of the*

Mercator Linguistic Rights and Legislation Centre 17, available at www.ciemen.org/mercator/butlletins/60-48.htm - 73k.

Pym, Anthony. 2001. "Translation and International Institutions. Explaining the Diversity Paradox". *Paper presented to the workshop "Translation and Institutions" at the conference Language Study in Europe at the Turn of the Millenium*, Societas Linguistica Europea, Katholieka Universiteit Leuven. 28–31.

Sabino, Amadeu Lopes. 1999. "Les langues dans l'Union européenne ejeux, pratiques et perspectives". *Revue trimestrielle de droit européen* 35 (2). 160–169.

Savidan, Patrick. 2004. "Multiculturalism and Economic Solidarity. A Social Democratic Challenge for the European Union. Comments on Kraus and Pagano". *Cultural diversity versus Economic Solidarity. Is There a Tension ? How Must it be Resolved ?*, ed. by P. Van Parijs, Bruxelles: Deboeck University Press. 331–347.

Schäffner, Cristina. 1998. "Parallel Texts in Translation. In Unity or Diversity?" *Current trends in Translation Studies*, ed. by L. Bowker, M. Cronin, D. Kenny and J. Pearson, Manchester: Saint Jerome Publishing. 83–90.

Sullivan, Ruth. 2004. "The Challenges of Interpreting Multilingual, Multijural Legislation". *Brooklyn Journal of International Law* 29. 986–1066.

Šarčević, Susan. 1998. "Creativity in legal translation: how much is too much?". *Translation in Context. Selected Contributions from the EST Congress, Granada 1998*, ed. by A. Chesterman, N. G. San Salvador and Y. Gambier, Amsterdam-Philadelphia: John Benjamins Publishing. 281–292.

Šarčević, Susan. 2000. *New Approach to Legal Translation.* The Hague: Kluwer Law International.

Šarčević, Susan. 2002. "Problems of interpretation in an enlarged European Union". *L'interprétation des textes juridiques rédigés dans plus d'une langue: [Colloque organisé à Turin en 2000] / par l'Institut subalpin pour l'analyse et l'enseignement droit des activités transnationales (ISAIDAT)*, ed. by R. Sacco , Torino-Paris: L'Harmattan. 239–272.

Tabory, Mala. 1980. *Multilingualism in International Law and Institutions.* Alphen ann den Rijn: Sijthoff & Noordhoff.

Truchot, Claude. 2003. "Languages and supranationality in Europe: The linguistic influence of the European Union". *Languages in a Globalising World*, ed. by J. Maurais and M. A. Morris, Cambridge: Cambridge University Press. 99–110.

Van Calster, Geert. 1997. "The EU's Tower of Babel – The Interpretation by the European Court of Justice of Equally Authentic Texts Drafted in more than one Official Language". *Yearbook of European Law* 17, ed. by A. Barav and D. A. Wyatt, Oxford: Clarendon Press. 363–393.

Wagner, Emma. 2000. "Translation of Multilingual Instruments in the EU". Available at portal 'Europa', Translation and drafting aids in the European Union languages, http://ec.europa.eu/translation/reading/articles/pdf/2000_tp_wagner.pdf.

Wagner, Emma. 2001. "Translation of Multilingual Instruments in the European Union". *Legal Translation. Preparation for Accession to the European Union*, ed. by S. Šarčević, Rijeka: Faculty of Law, University of Rijeka. 65–74.

Wagner Emma, Bech, S. and Martínez, J. M. 2002. *Translating for the European Union Institution.* Manchester-Northampton: St. Jerome Publishing.

Wilson, Barry. 2003. "The Translation Service in the European Parliament". *Crossing Barriers and Bridging Cultures: The Challenges of Multilingual Translation for the European Union*, ed. by A. Tosi, Clevedon-Buffalo-Toronto-Sydney: Multilingual Matters Ltd. 1–7.

Winter, J.A. 1972. "Direct Applicability and Direct Effect – Two Distinct and Different Concepts in Community Law". *Common Market Law Review*, 9 (4). 425–438.

Wright, Sue. 2000. *Community and Communication: The Role of Language in Nation State Building and European Integration.* Clevedon-Buffalo-Toronto-Sydney: Multilingual Matters Ltd.

Wood, Michael J.B. 1996. "Drafting Bilingual Legislation in Canada: Examples of Beneficial Cross-Pollination between the Two Language Versions". *Statute Law Review* 17 (1). 66–77.

Multilingual law drafting in Switzerland

Andreas Lötscher

1. Introduction

This paper deals with the conditions and problems of multilingual law drafting in Switzerland. It concentrates on the problems on the federal level, leaving aside questions of multilingualism in the cantons.

Multilingual law drafting involves several problem areas which belong to different disciplines. Some of them are political, others linguistic. Therefore, law drafting within the conditions of multilingualism can be analysed from very different angles – language rights in a multilingual state, language of law and jurilinguistics, specificities of political language, contrastive linguistics. Ultimately, it is an interdisciplinary field of research.

However, it also is an everyday practice aiming at producing texts that primarily have to follow practical requirements, i.e. to formulate regulations that fulfil specific political or administrative purposes. Examining the practical problems can demonstrate how extralinguistic factors influence linguistic work in this particular area. Therefore, it may shed as much light on the problem of multilingual law drafting as a purely linguistic analysis.

Each state has its particular political and juridical situation and legislative traditions. Accordingly, the problems and practices of multilingual law drafting have developed in individual ways in different countries. Apart from Switzerland, there are only a few other multilingual states and institutions that have established forms of multilingual legislation, like Canada, Belgium and the European Union (EU). The case closest to Switzerland is Canada, which has, however, other traditions of laws and legislation, with a mixture of civil and common law. Not surprisingly, the EU with its unique political and linguistic structure and with its (currently) twenty-five member states and twenty official languages, has developed its own special informal and formal procedures in negotiating and elaborating enactments.[1]

1. Cf. Born and Schütte (1995), Flückiger (2005), Gallas (2001), Guggeis and Gallas (2005).

G. Grewendorf, M. Rathert (eds.): Formal Linguistics and Law, 371–400

One might even ask whether in a strict sense the EU has procedures of multilingual law drafting at all, since acts are often drafted in one or two languages only (English and French). Later, they get translated into the other languages, and the texts that will eventually get published are equally valid in all the official languages.

Switzerland is a unique case, both in its policies of multilingualism and in its traditions of legislation and legal language. Therefore, it seems worth to have a closer look at it, as in Switzerland, due to its tradition of direct democracy and having a multitude of language minorities, a rather high degree of consciousness of the problems of multilingualism has been developed. The necessity of a good quality of the language of laws has resulted in specific methods of quality assurance. Thus, Switzerland may represent a prototypical case for demonstrating the general problems.

2. The legal basis of multilingualism: National languages and official languages in the Swiss confederation

The choice of languages in which laws are published is directly affected by the linguistic situation in a country – at least if a state takes into account the real linguistic situation of its citizens. Switzerland is a classic example of a state with a multilingual population. Politically and legally, this is reflected in article 4 and 70 of the constitution of the Swiss Confederation. In these two articles, a difference is made between 'national languages' and 'official languages'. Article 4 enumerates the four national languages in a more programmatic sense, as a part of the national identity:

(1) *Art. 4 Landessprachen*
Die Landessprachen sind Deutsch, Französisch, Italienisch und Rätoromanisch.

Art. 4 National Languages
The national languages are German, French, Italian, and Romansh.

On the other hand, article 70, the so-called Sprachenartikel' ('language article'), defines the official languages in a more specific sense. Official languages are the languages which the government and the administration have to use for their official documents. Moreover, this article sets out the principles of language policies in Switzerland, which are intended to ensure a peaceful cohabitation of the different linguistic groups. Article 70 is the factual basis for legislation and measures of the confederation in the area of national languages:

(2) *Art. 70 Sprachen*

[1] Die Amtssprachen des Bundes sind Deutsch, Französisch und Italienisch. Im Verkehr mit Personen rätoromanischer Sprache ist auch das Rätoromanische Amtssprache des Bundes.

[2] Die Kantone bestimmen ihre Amtssprachen. Um das Einvernehmen zwischen den Sprachgemeinschaften zu wahren, achten sie auf die herkömmliche sprachliche Zusammensetzung der Gebiete und nehmen Rücksicht auf die angestammten sprachlichen Minderheiten.

[3] Bund und Kantone fördern die Verständigung und den Austausch zwischen den Sprachgemeinschaften.

[4] Der Bund unterstützt die mehrsprachigen Kantone bei der Erfüllung ihrer besonderen Aufgaben.

[5] Der Bund unterstützt Maßnahmen der Kantone Graubünden und Tessin zur Erhaltung und Förderung der rätoromanischen und der italienischen Sprache.

Art. 70 Languages

[1] The official languages of the Confederation are German, French, and Italian. Romansh shall be an official language for communicating with persons of Romansh language.

[2] The Cantons shall designate their official languages. In order to preserve harmony between linguistic communities, they shall respect the traditional territorial distribution of languages, and take into account the indigenous linguistic minorities.

[3] The Confederation and the Cantons shall encourage understanding and exchange between the linguistic communities.

[4] The Confederation shall support the plurilingual Cantons in the fulfilment of their particular tasks.

[5] The Confederation shall support the measures taken by the by the Cantons of Grisons and Ticino to maintain and to promote Romansh and Italian.

Although article 4 suggests that there are four official languages, the Swiss Confederation is not a four-language, but only a 'three-and-a-half-language' state, since the status of Romansh as an official language is restricted. While German, French and Italian are official languages in a general way, Romansh has official status only in interactions between the confederation and persons of Romansh language.

Article 70 points out the problems of Swiss multilingualism with regard to official languages. The political construction of Switzerland implies a multitude of layers and relationships among the entities on these layers – confederation, cantons, municipalities, linguistic regions – and multilingualism leads to several problems on each of those levels. However, the plurality of national languages is not the whole story. As a result of a long tradition of immigration from different regions of Europe and other continents, many more languages than the four official ones are spoken in Switzerland. In order to inform the people who are affected by laws and regulations – with regard to school education, social security, unemployment insurance, health and accident insurance and other sectors of life regulated by laws – the official institutions have to use many more languages than only the official ones. This is usually not a matter of legal regulations, but rather a problem of practical enforcement of legal regulations.

For official documents such as laws and similar texts, it is neither possible nor useful to make allowance for all languages that are possibly used in the population and in the economy. For such texts, only the official languages defined in article 70 are authoritative and officially acknowledged. Articles 14 and 15 of the 'Publikationsgesetz' (publication law) implement article 70 alinea 1 of the constitution for the choice of languages in the publication of official documents, especially for the 'Bundesblatt' (Official Federal Gazette), the 'Amtliche Sammlung des Bundesrechts (AS)' (Official Compilation of Federal Legislation) and the 'Systematische Sammlung des Bundesrechts (SR)' (the Classified Compilation of Federal Law) and determine that all official documents are to be published simultaneously in all official languages. The publication law thereby follows the 'three-and-a-half'-language system of the constitution. An essential point is that for legislative enactments, i.e. the constitution, laws, decrees and ordinances, all three versions in the official languages German, French and Italian are equally authentic and binding. It is implied that the principle of equality is also valid for accompanying texts such as 'messages' (explanatory and justifying documents of the Federal Government accompanying a draft submitted to the Federal Assembly for adoption):

(3) Bundesgesetz über die Sammlungen des Bundesrechts und das Bundesblatt (Publikationsgesetz) (SR 170.512)

German

Art. 14 Veröffentlichung in den Amtssprachen

[1] Die Veröffentlichung erfolgt gleichzeitig in den Amtssprachen Deutsch, Französisch und Italienisch. Bei Erlassen sind die drei Fassungen in gleicher Weise verbindlich.

[2] Der Bundesrat kann bestimmen, dass Texte, die nur mit Titel sowie Fundstelle oder Bezugsquelle veröffentlicht werden, nicht in allen drei Amtssprachen veröffentlicht werden oder dass auf eine Übersetzung in die Amtssprachen verzichtet wird, wenn:

a. die in diesen Texten enthaltenen Bestimmungen die Betroffenen nicht unmittelbar verpflichten; oder
b. die Betroffenen diese Texte ausschliesslich in der Originalsprache benützen.

[3] Die Bundeskanzlei kann bestimmen, dass Beschlüsse und Mitteilungen der Bundesverwaltung sowie von Organisationen und Personen des öffentlichen oder des privaten Rechts nach Artikel 13 Absatz 2 nur in der Amtssprache des betroffenen Sprachgebietes veröffentlicht werden, sofern sie von ausschliesslich lokaler Bedeutung sind.

Art. 15 Veröffentlichung in rätoromanischer Sprache

Erlasse des Bundes von besonderer Tragweite werden als Einzelausgaben in rätoromanischer Sprache veröffentlicht. Die Bundeskanzlei bestimmt diese Erlasse nach Rücksprache mit der Standeskanzlei des Kantons Graubünden.

English

Federal Act on the Compilations of Federal Legislation and the Federal Gazette (Publication Act)

Art. 14 Publication in the official languages

[1] Publication is effected simultaneously in the official languages German, French and Italian. In the case of legislation, the three versions are equally binding.

[2] The Federal Council may decide that texts that are only published as a title with a reference or source will not be published in all three official languages or that a translation into the official languages will be dispensed with if:

a. the provisions contained in these texts do not immediately bind the persons concerned; or
b. the persons concerned use the texts only in their original language.

> [3] The Federal Chancellery may decide that decisions and communications from the Federal Administration and from organisations and persons under public or private law in accordance with Article 13 paragraph 2 are published only in the official language of the persons concerned, provided these are solely of local significance.
>
> *Art. 15 Publication in Romans*h
> Federal enactments of particular significance are published as individual editions in Romansh. The Federal Chancellery decides which enactments are to be published in consultation with the Cantonal Chancellery of the Canton of Graubünden.

In defining the different versions as equally authentic and valid, the confederation relieves itself from a number of linguistic and juridical problems concerning multilingual publications. Politically, this provision is also a means of assuring the equal linguistic rights of the different linguistic communities. At the same time, in obeying this principle, the confederation has to guarantee special linguistic qualities of its official publications. If each single version is obliging and applicable as an authentic version without recourse to another version, then every single version should reliably convey exactly the same content. Each version should be able to be read and used independently.

3. Problems of linguistic equivalence in the multilingual constitution

Considering the notorious or alleged incomparability of languages, the presumption that linguistically different versions of laws are equal contains a certain potential of conflicts and risks.[2] However, this is the case less often than one might expect. Nevertheless, there are cases that raise conflicts, which can lead to more fundamental reflections on problems of drafting and translating laws.

For example, a couple of years ago, article 120 of the new constitution caused some turmoil and discussions among experts: In the German version, the constitution contains the formulation 'Würde der Kreatur' ('dignity of the creation'), while the corresponding expression in French is 'intégrité des organismes vivants' ('integrity of living organisms'):

---

2. For a sceptical view see Côté (2005)

(4) Schweizerische Bundesverfassung
German
Art. 120 Gentechnologie im Außerhumanbereich
[1] ...
[2] Der Bund erlässt Vorschriften über den Umgang mit Keim- und Erbgut von Tieren, Pflanzen und anderen Organismen. Er trägt dabei *der Würde der Kreatur* sowie der Sicherheit von Mensch, Tier und Umwelt Rechnung und schützt die genetische Vielfalt der Tier- und Pflanzenarten.

French
Art. 120 Génie génétique dans le domaine non humain
[1] ...
[2] La Confédération légifère sur l'utilisation du patrimoine germinal et génétique des animaux, des végétaux et des autres organismes. Ce faisant, elle respecte *l'intégrité des organismes vivants* et la sécurité de l'être humain, de l'animal et de l'environnement et protège la diversité génétique des espèces animales et végétales.

At first sight, the two wordings seem to have a rather different content. Such a difference could have serious consequences on the constitution and its implementation in laws. It turns out that in the present case, the difference does not pose any difficult problems. However, it is an interesting question what reasons could have caused such a difference, and what the semantic differences and the similarities of the two versions are. From a historical point of view, the German formulation 'Würde der Kreatur' is prior to the French version, as it was part of the previous constitution, which has been replaced by the new constitution in 1999. In the course of the interpretation and application of this provision on genetic engineering, it turned out that it is very difficult to determine in a legally clear way what could be meant by 'Würde der Kreatur'. The German version itself poses certain semantic problems, which are even more difficult to resolve as both 'Würde' and 'Kreatur' are expressions that have a long, entangled history of philosophical and even religions discussions and at the same time do not match very well.[3] Possibly, in the final revision of the text of the new constitution, the French speaking revision committee had the impression that following the German version word-for-word – i.e. 'dignité de la creature'

3. Questions of interpretation of this provision are discussed in Prätorius and Saladin (1996).

– would not be an appropriate formulation for the constitution, both for the more philosophical reason that 'dignité' is a rather problematic concept for applying it to 'creature' and that it is preferably replaced by a more neutral 'intégrité', and for the more linguistic reason that in French 'creature' can have a rather negative connotation. A careful linguistic analysis of the semantic content of both versions within the linguistic context reveals that both wordings have the same implications with regard to practical implementation in an official text.[4] The difference in wording does not cause differences in the juridical application. In this case, this may be the felicitous result of a careful reflection of all implications of the different possible formulations.

Another, less felicitous, but also less spectacular instance of a terminological incongruity can be found in article 87 of the constitution in the pair 'Seilbahnen' and 'téléphériques'.

(5) Schweizerische Bundesverfassung
Art. 87 Eisenbahnen und weitere Verkehrsträger*
Die Gesetzgebung über den Eisenbahnverkehr, die *Seilbahnen*, die Schifffahrt sowie über die Luft- und Raumfahrt ist Sache des Bundes.

Art. 87 Transports
La législation sur le transport ferroviaire, les *téléphériques*, la navigation, l'aviation et la navigation spatiale relève de la compétence de la Confédération.

Whereas 'Seilbahnen' includes all types of transport means carried or pulled by cables (aerial ropeway, cable car, cable railway, cableway, funicular railway, etc.), the french 'téléfériques' only means 'cableways', suspended from a cable. But the term is used differently in German and French. Apparently, while drafting the texts, the French drafters intended to give a formally parallel enumeration of means of transport and did not notice that the German expression 'Seilbahnen' does not correspond to one single French expression. Instead, they only associated the prototypical, most frequent type of 'Seilbahnen'.

Such problem cases are rare, though. Nevertheless, the examples show that equivalence in content and appropriateness in linguistic form do not come together easily all the time – for various reasons. Equivalent expres-

4. For a discussion of the problem cf. Lötscher (2000).

sions need to be found when drafting multilingual texts. Sometimes it is impossible to find a wording that is completely parallel in all languages. This makes it necessary to use different wordings, which makes it difficult sometimes to interpret the texts formally. At first sight, it might escape the drafters' attention that two apparently parallel formulations are in fact not fully equivalent. The ideal of perfect parallelism both on the level of surface form and content is difficult to achieve.[5]

4. Multilingual laws and law interpretation by the Federal Supreme Court

For the Federal Supreme Court, the equivalence of the various versions of a provision in different languages is relevant, too.[6] In principle, any of the different versions can be taken as the basis of a decision, depending on the language in which the case is proceeded. Occasionally, the court also uses all three different versions as a means for deciding on the interpretation of a provision. In this respect, different situations and decision procedures can be observed.

First, comparing the wording of different versions can help clarifying the interpretation that is to be disputed in one single language. In one case, the court decided that the congruence in content among the three versions in the different languages had 'einen hohen Indizienwert' (had a high value as a circumstantial evidence) for a given interpretation of the wording in one language. (K 8/99).[7] In this case it was doubted by the representatives of a health assurance company that Art. 27 of the Krankenversicherungsgesetz (SR 832)[8] (Health insurance law) obliged the assurance to pay for the treatment of any 'Geburtsgebrechen' (congenital deformity) as would be the case with a normal sickness:

5. See also section 8 below.
6. For an exposition of the general problems see Schubarth (2001), for an analysis of particular cases see Burr (2000). A Canadian view on the problems is given in Bastarach (2005).
7. Decisions of the Federal Supreme Court are accessible in the internet via www.bger.ch.
8. The text of Swiss laws in the "Systematische Sammlung des Bundesrechts (SR)" (the Classified Compilation of Federal Law) is accessible in the internet via www.admin.ch

(6) Bundesgesetz über die Krankenversicherung – Loi fédérale sur l'assurance-maladie (SR 832.10)

German
Art. 27 Geburtsgebrechen
Die obligatorische Krankenpflegeversicherung übernimmt bei Geburtsgebrechen (Art. 3 Abs. 2 ATSG), die nicht durch die Invalidenversicherung gedeckt sind, die Kosten für die gleichen Leistungen wie bei Krankheit.

French
Art. 27 Infirmité congénitale
En cas d'infirmité congénitale (art. 3, al. 2, LPGA) non couverte par l'assurance-invalidité, l'assurance obligatoire des soins prend en charge les coûts des mêmes prestations qu'en cas de maladie.

Italian
Art. 27 Infermità congenite
Per le infermità congenite (art. 3 cpv. 2 LPGA) che non sono coperte dall'assicurazione per l'invalidità, l'assicurazione obbligatoria delle cure medico-sanitarie assume gli stessi costi delle prestazioni in caso di malattia.

A comparison of all three versions shows no difference in the possible interpretation among the versions. From this, the court concluded that there was no justification to doubt the interpretation of one of the versions.

Comparing the wording in the different languages can also help to clarify the interpretation of sentences that are grammatically ambiguous in one language. In the following example it is not clear whether the German 'in der Regel' ('as a rule') has in its scope only 'monatlich' or both 'monatlich und zum voraus' ('monthly and in advance'); in a strictly grammatical view, both interpretations are possible:

(7) Bundesgesetz über die Alters- und Hinterlassenenversicherung – Loi fédérale sur l'assurance-vieillesse et survivants (SR 831.10), Art. 44 in der Fassung vom 4. Okt. 1968

German
Art. 44 Auszahlung der Renten und Hilflosenentschädigungen
[1] Die Renten und Hilflosenentschädigungen werden in der Regel monatlich und zum voraus ausbezahlt

French
[1] Les rentes et les allocation pour impotents sont payées, en règle générale, mensuellement et d'avance.

Italian
[1] Di regola le rendite e gli assegni per grandi invalidi sono pagati in anticipo mese per mese.
(I 302/00 Vr)

In contrast, in the French and the Italian version, it is quite clear that 'en règle générale' or 'di regola' covers both terms, i.e. 'mensuellement et d'avance' or 'in anticipo mese per mese' respectively.

There is a third type of cases, in which the tenor of the different versions differs substantially depending on the language. According to the federal court, in those cases the equivalence of all three versions has to be assumed a priori, and no particular version may be preferred. In order to determine which of the different meanings has to be applied – or which version will be preferred – the court has to resort to other elements of interpretation. They can look for example into the sense and purpose of a provision in its context, take into account the deliberation of the parliament or consider the explanation the federal government added to the particular passage in its 'message' to the parliament. An example is the following regulation:

(8) Bundesgesetz über die Alters- und Hinterlassenenversicherung – Loi fédérale sur l'assurance-vieillesse et survivants (SR 831.10), *Art. 29^{septies}* al. 1

German
[1] Versicherte, welche im gemeinsamen Haushalt Verwandte in auf- oder absteigender Linie oder Geschwister *mit einem Anspruch auf eine Hilflosenentschädigung der AHV oder der IV* für mindestens mittlere Hilflosigkeit betreuen, haben Anspruch auf Anrechnung einer Betreuungsgutschrift. ...

French
[1] Les assurés qui prennent en charge des parents de ligne ascendante ou descendante ainsi que des frères et sœurs *au bénéfice d'une allocation de l'AVS ou de l'AI pour impotent* de degré moyen au moins et avec lesquels ils font ménage commun, peuvent prétendre à une bonification pour tâches d'assistance. ...

Italian
[1] Gli assicurati che si occupano di parenti di linea ascendente o discendente nonché di fratelli e sorelle *che beneficiano di un assegno dell'AVS o dell'AI per grandi invalidi*, con un'invalidità almeno di grado medio, e che vivono in comunione domestica con essi, hanno diritto ad un accredito per compiti assistenziali. … .

The difference in this provision lies in the fact that according to the German wording, persons are entitled to receive 'Betreuungsgutschriften' (old age insurance credits for the caretaking of disabled persons) if they take care of persons that are entitled to receive 'Hilflosenentschädigung' (indemnity for severely disabled persons). The French and the Italian version, on the other hand, say that such persons are only entitled to receive these 'Betreuungsgutschriften' if they take care of persons that actually receive the 'Hilflosenentschädigung'. The court stated, 'dass die Materialien sowie der Sinn und Zweck der Bestimmung die auf dem deutschen Wortlaut des Art. 29^{septies} abs.1 1. Satz AHVG basierende Auslegung stützen'. ('the explanatory documents of the federal government and the debates in the parliament as well as the purpose of the provision in the whole context support an interpretation that bases on the German wording'). This case was decided in favour of the tenor of the German version, and the decision was based on general considerations about the purpose of the regulation in its context.

Another case of discrepancy between the German and Italian and the French version was decided in favour of the French version. The decision was based on an analysis of the evolution of the text in parliamentary deliberations. The court stated that the French version had the original and appropriate tenor, because the original German version of the draft was closer to the French one. It had been revised by a parliamentary committee only shortly before being adopted by the Parliament for stylistic reasons, i.e. to make the wording more easily understandable, and not by legislative intent. By this time, it went unnoticed that the stylistic correction changed the tenor of the provision. The change was applied on the Italian version, too.

(9) Zivilgesetzbuch (ZGB) – Code civil (SR 210), Art. 519

German
Art. 519
[1] Eine Verfügung von Todes wegen wird auf erhobene Klage für ungültig erklärt:

a. wenn …
[2] Die Ungültigkeitsklage kann von jedermann erhoben werden, der *als Erbe oder Bedachter ein Interesse daran hat*, dass die Verfügung für ungültig erklärt werde.

French
Art. 519
[1] Les dispositions pour cause de mort peuvent être annulées:
a. lorsque …
[2] L'action peut être intentée *par tout héritier ou légataire intéressé*.

Italian
Art. 519
[1] La disposizione a causa di morte può essere giudizialmente annullata:
a. se …
[2] L'azione di nullità può essere proposta da chiunque *come erede o legatario abbia interesse a* far annullare la disposizione.

The difference is subtle, but important. The German version says that a person who has an interest in the annullment of a last will (due to their position as an heir or beneficiary) can pursue the annullment legally. In contrast, the French version says that any heir or beneficiary (not only those who have an interest in the annullment) can take action and pursue the annullment.

With regard to the methods they apply when interpreting laws, the Swiss Supreme Court generally takes a pragmatic attitude. They use traditional categories of interpretation – grammatical interpretation, systematic interpretation, historical-genetic interpretation, teleological interpretation – and combine them in order to achieve the best possible results. The fact that regulations come in three languages does not in itself constitute a fifth dimension of interpretational methods. It rather adds some additional guide lines to the argumentation. Discrepancies between the different versions shed light to the problems of interpretation that might otherwise remain unnoticed; they help constituting a 'second order grammatical interpretation' (Burr 2000: 189).

Eventually, the interpretation of regulations may be different in different languages (Côté 2005), but this does not necessarily result in confusion. It helps, as a first step, to indicate problems of interpretation that might have gone unnoticed if the text had been written in one single language only. As a second step, the multilinguality enriches interpretation and helps to understand more precisely the tenor of a wording of the law.

5. Multilingual drafting: 'corédaction' / 'co-drafting'

Textual discrepancies between different language versions are of course inappropriate and should be prevented. It is necessary to work carefully when drafting law texts in order to guarantee consistent content among the different linguistic versions. This cannot be achieved by individual efforts alone; it has to be supported by institutionalized procedures. The Swiss federal administration has developed procedures for law drafting that aim at preventing textual discrepancies.

The administration is understood to be multilingual, i.e. all three languages are accepted as possible means of communication – internally and in contact with the citizens. All drafts for official documents have to be prepared in all three official languages before they are submitted for adoption. Still, the individual persons in the administration are usually not fully bilingual. The majority (about two thirds) are of German mother tongue, a minority is French speaking, and an even smaller minority is Italian speaking. All of them are expected to know at least one other official language passively or actively to some degree. Nevertheless, in most cases, the mother tongue is used when drafting texts.

This means that the first draft of most texts is written in one language only; in most cases this is German. Larger texts with a plurality of authors are sometimes mixtures of two or three languages. Consequently, one of the versions in a multilingual text is usually the result of a translation.

Two specialists of different languages cooperating in order to draft a bilingual text would be an exception. For more important texts, such as law drafts, there is an intermediary stage of revision and text control within the administration that has to assure that all texts are coherent, clear and precise and obey the requirements of good legal texts. This task is attributed to the 'verwaltungsinterne Redaktionskommission / commission interne de rédaction' ('internal committee of the administration of text revision'). They also have to make sure that all versions are identical in content.

The committee is composed by two linguists and two jurists, one of German and French language in each group. The working method of this committee is called 'co-redaction' ('co-drafting').[9] The text versions in the two languages are discussed in parallel, both for content and expression. The committee treats the French and German version as equivalent, irrespective of the language in which the text had been composed originally. The committee does not prefer or adapt one version to the other on the grounds that it is a translation. Rather, in case of discrepancies or insufficiencies, it seeks to develop two good versions, corresponding to each other in content, being as close to the other as possible but also as precise, clear and stylistically appropriate as possible. It happens sometimes that a version that has originally grown out of a translation represents the content of a provision more adequately than the 'original' version and gives inspiration for improvement of the the first version.

Incidentally, careful text control and revision in 'co-redaction' is not only an important way to assure the equivalence of German and French versions. It also helps to improve the texts as such, as it helps detecting text problems that have nothing to do with problems of linguistic equivalence of different versions. The revision committee is free to submit any proposition and remark on the text, including observations on substantial loopholes and textual or logical inconsistencies.

6. Multilingual law drafting and traditions of law drafting

6.1 General principles of law drafting

The legal language of any country with some political tradition develops over decades into an ensemble of patterns and formulation procedures where every new formulation or type of provision has to be fitted in. This is true as much for unilingual as for multilingual law drafting. This affects not only terminology, but also involves general conceptions with respect to drafting laws as texts. Since Eugen Huber's Civil Code (1907), simplicity, clarity and conciseness are the principles followed in the same way in Switzerland for legislation in all languages. Swiss laws stand out because of their greater simplicity in comparison with almost all other countries.[10]

---

9. "Co-drafting" takes its origins in Canada. On the methods of co-drafting in Canada and Switzerland cf. Caussignac (1995), Labelle (2000), Albrecht (2001), Bertagnollo (2005), Šarcevic (2005).
10. For the stylistic ideals of Eugen Huber's language of the Swiss Civil code compared to the German Bürgerlichen Gesetzbuch see Oplatka-Steinlin (1971).

This implies, at the same time, that formulations in each language should follow the same general drafting principles. In Swiss laws, divergences between different versions, as they can be found in Canadian laws, are unthinkable. In Canada two fundamentally different legal traditions (common law and civil law) are to be combined and, consequently, co-drafting bears a greater risk of leading to different versions:[11]

(10) The Minister may revoke the approval of security rules, either at the request of the operator or otherwise.

L'approbation est revocable.

The ideal of formulating regulations in a language as close to non-juridical language as possible is – at least in principle – followed in Swiss law drafting. This implies that each version should follow the natural rules of its language, and no version should slavishly follow the structure of another language. Thus, in detail, the different versions of a disposition regularly show stylistic and grammatical differences:

(11) Swiss Civil Code (SR 220), *Art. 17*

German
Handlungsunfähig sind die Personen, die nicht urteilsfähig, oder die unmündig oder entmündigt sind.

French
Les personnes incapables de discernement, les mineurs et les interdits n'ont pas l'exercice des droits civils.

This stylistic freedom in detail can only be realised on the basis of the common principles of simplicity and conciseness. Simplicity and clarity simplify the task of finding parallel formulations in all versions. In traditions where completeness in detail is more important than simplicity and reliance on context, such as in common law, or where diplomatic and technical styles of formulations are followed (as in EU legislation) it is much more difficult to achieve naturalness and linguistic equivalence. [12]

11. Example taken from Šarcevic (2005: 283).

12. On the problem of formulating a disposition within three different legal systems see Gémar (2001, 21f.)

6.2 Common helvetisms in Swiss legal language

In spite of the many structural and lexical differences between German, French and Italian, and as a result of the long history of multilingual legislation, the Swiss legal language has developed a great number of fixed formulations for particular types of provisions. Although they may differ in detail, there are fixed analogies between the wordings in the particular languages. This concerns standard formulations as the following:

(12) German
- a. Der Bundesrat regelt die Einzelheiten.
- b. Das Departement vollzieht diese Verordnung
- c. Aufhebung bisherigen Rechts
- d. Dieses Gesetz untersteht dem fakultativen Referendum.

French
- a. Le Conseil fédéral règle les modalités.
- b. Le département est chargé de l'exécution de la présente ordonnance.
  L'exécution de la présente ordonnance incombe au département.
- c. Abrogation du droit en vigueur
- d. La présente loi est sujette au référendum.

The creation of laws in a multilingual context also produces a special vocabulary in the legal and administrative language differing from that of the neighbouring countries. For this type of Swiss specialties, the term 'helvetism' has been coined both for French and German.[13] The following table shows a few examples:

13. For French helvetisms generally cf. Thibault and Knecht (1997), for German helvetisms cf. Meyer (1989).

Table 1. Common Swiss German-French helvetisms in legal language

German (Switzerland)	French (Switzerland)
Bund ('confederation')	confédération
Bundes- (z.B. Bundesgesetz, Bundeskanzlei) ('federal')	fédérale (p.e. loi fédérale, Chancellerie fédérale)
Nationalrat – Ständerat ('House of Representatives – Senate')	conseil national – conseil d'états
Kanton ('constituent state of the confederation')	canton (France: ,administrative district of a department')
(militärisches) Aufgebot ('command for militia solders to report for duty') (Germany: 'notice of an intended marriage'	convocation (France: general sense 'convocation, summoning')
Angebot (OR Art.232) ('offer in a bid')	mise (OR Art. 232) 2 Sont nulles les clauses qui obligeraient l'enchérisseur à maintenir sa mise au-delà des enchères; France: enchère
... ist gewährleistet (' ... is guaranteed')	.. est garantie
e.g. Art. 19 constitution: Der Anspruch auf ausreichenden und unentgeltlichen Grundschulunterricht ist gewährleistet.	art. 19 CF Le droit à un enseignement de base suffisant et gratuit est garanti.

Décharge erteilen (Germany: entlasten, Entlastung) ('release')	donner décharge (France: donner quitus)
Beitragsprimat Leistungsprimat	primauté des cotisations primauté des prestations
Schuldenbremse ('debt brake', a special quorum necessary for adoption of financial decrees above a certain limit)	frein à l'endettement
Ökologischer Leistungsnachweis (Art. 104 BV) ('proof of compliance with ecological requirements') Germany: CC = Cross Compliance	prestations écologiques
Invalidität	invalidité
bestimmen	déterminer

Helvetisms cover different areas, and often they are not very perspicuous. They imply for example only one special meaning of an expression known otherwise in the other countries. One part of this vocabulary concerns the particular political institutions of Switzerland. (In French these expressions are also called 'helvétismes statales'.) Expressions such as German *Bund* – French *fédération* and the corresponding derivations such as German *Bundes-* for compositions and the corresponding French adjective *fédérale* (*Bundesgesetz, Bundesrat, Bundesverwaltung – loi fédérale, conseil federal, administration fédérale* etc.) relate to the basic institutions defined by the Constitution, as *Kanton – canton, Nationalrat – conseil national, Ständerat – conseil d'états*. Although *Bund*, *Bundesrat* etc. are used in Germany and Austria for political institutions, too, these lexemes have different meanings in each country, depending on their political systems. The same is true for many other expressions.

German *Aufgebot* and French *convocation* are used in German and French more generally with various meanings. In Switzerland, both have a common special meaning in the context of the Swiss militia system, within which these terms specifically mean 'command for militia solders to report for duty'.

In many of these cases, exploring word history is an interesting task, especially with regard to the question which language has influenced the other, and how. An obvious case is the term *Kanton* as a designation for the constituent states of the Confederation, which is taken from the French *canton*. It has been introduced into Swiss political terminology in the course of the reorganization of the Swiss confederation by Napoleon in the beginning of the 19th century. In France, in the context of French centralism, this word has taken a different meaning as a designation for an administrative district in a department. With the foundation of the actual Confederation after the Sonderbundskrieg (1848), other new terms have been introduced into the political terminology, e.g. for the two chambers of the parliament *Nationalrat/Ständerat – conseil national/conseil* d'état. Whereas for the Nationalrat, a newly coined term with the same internationalism *national-* for both languages was chosen, the traditional expression for constituent states of the Confederation *Stand* was chosen for the representation of the cantons in German, nowadays an archaism that is only used in some fixed formulations. In French, the corresponding term is the more neutral expression *état*, which is, however, also the self-designation of some French speaking cantons in their constitutions and thus has some more specific connotations in this context. We may suspect the influence of loan translations in many of these helvetisms.

In the French version of Art. 231 of the obligation code, the expression *mise* is used as an expression for bid in an auction; the normal French expression would be mise aux enchères. It is assumed that this expression is taken from Swiss everyday language.

In the other direction, the German expression '... ist gewährleistet' '... is guaranteed' in several articles of the constitution is a translation of French '... est garanti', although not an impeccable one in that the French passive has been translated too literally:[14]

A peculiar mixing of a takeover (back and forth) is the use of French 'donner décharge' for French 'donner quitus' ('release') in the obligation code, which is coined following German 'Décharge erteilen'; but the German expression is a loan expression taken from French.

Of course, the cohabitation of French and German in the development of a specialised legal language continues in present times. Because of this,

14. In the German Grundgesetz, the corresponding expressions are "...wird gewährleistet", with a correct German passive construction, and "... sind unverletzlich" ('inviolable')

there probably is a number of new helvetisms being produced every year in the context of new laws, regulations in existing laws and new administrative procedures.

The creation of a common 'helvetic' specialised legal and administrative vocabulary is a continuous process. German influences French and vice versa. Swiss Standard German is more open to influences from French than e.g. the Standard German language in the German Federal Republic. We may assume that the specific Swiss expressions German *Beitragsprimat* und *Leistungsprimat* (primacy of contributions = defined contribution pension plan vs. primacy of payment obligation in the determination of a pension = defined benefit pension plan) in the Swiss terminology of employee pension plans have been coined following the French terminology *primauté des cotisations* and *primauté des prestations*. Other cases go in the opposite direction. *Schuldenbremse – frein à l'endettement* und *ökologischer Leistungsnachweis – prestations écologiques* (Art. 104 BV) have been introduced recently in the Constitution; in both cases the German expression probably came first.

In many cases the development of common French-German legal helvetisms takes place in rather hidden ways. Legal definitions give a special sense to many expressions that are used in everyday language as well, but in a more general sense. This semantic duality gives occasion to misunderstandings. One typical pair of terms that is prone to misconception is *Invalidität – invalidité*, others are *Unfall – accident* or *Hilflosigkeit – impotence* (also defined in the Law on the General Part of Social Security).

(13) Bundesgesetz über den Allgemeinen Teil des Sozialversicherungsrechts – Loi fédérale sur la partie générale du droit des assurances sociales (SR 830.1) *Art. 7* Abs. 1

German
[1] Invalidität ist die voraussichtlich bleibende oder längere Zeit dauernde ganze oder teilweise Erwerbsunfähigkeit.

French
[1] Est réputée invalidité l'incapacité de gain totale ou partielle qui est présumée permanente ou de longue durée.

Other expressions have gained their special meaning not by an explicit legal definition, but by constant use in legislation. The term 'bestimmen' in a formulation as the following has a very precise meaning: it implies that an authority has the competence to fix some items in an enumeration authoritatively, i.e. in an ordinance. The corresponding term 'déterminer' has the same value.

(14) Verordnung vom 7. Dezember 1998 über die Produktion und das Inverkehrbringen von pflanzlichem Vermehrungsmaterial – Ordonnance du 7 décembre 1998 sur la production et la mise en circulation du matériel végétal de multiplication (SR 916.151) Art. 9 al. 1

German
[1] Das Departement *bestimmt* die Arten, für die eine Sortenliste geführt wird, und legt Aufnahmebedingungen und Streichungsgründe fest.

French
[1] Le département *détermine* les espèces pour lesquelles une liste des variétés est établie; il fixe les conditions d'enregistrement et de retrait.

Similarly, in the Landwirtschaftsgesetz (Agriculture Act, SR 910.1) the expressions German 'fördern'/French 'encourager' systematically indicate all types of measures of support, including regulations , whereas German 'unterstützen'/French 'soutenir' denotes only financial subsidies.

7. Structural differences and problems of linguistic equivalence

Because of structural differences, it is sometimes difficult to achieve a satisfying degree of a linguistic equivalence on the level of expression. There are several aspects of this problem.

Occasionally, a good and simple formulation in one language cannot be chosen because there is no adequately corresponding formulation in the other language. E.g. the German term "Anordnung (einer Handlung durch eine Behörde)" as a nominalization of the verb *anordnen* 'to order' cannot be used in all contexts, because the corresponding French term *ordonnance* cannot be used as a nominalization of *ordonner* in the sense of *anordnen*, because it as another, specialized meaning: 'ordinance'. This is a consequence of the fact that differentiations of verbs and nouns by prefixes such as *an-* or *ver-* (*anordnen* – *verordnen*) cannot be replicated with French verbs.

In other cases, the fundamental principle of law drafting 'same meaning, same form' cannot be followed because of structural or lexical problems.

Often, one clear and unambiguous expression in one language cannot be consistently rendered by one single expression in the other language. In social security systems, the usual corresponding term for German 'Arbeitgeberbeiträge' (employer's contribution) in French is 'cotisation patronales'. But when an adjective is added, the parallelism cannot be kept. The transparent German construction 'freiwillige Arbeitgeberbeiträge' ('voluntary employer's contribution') has to be rendered as 'cotisations volontaires de l'employeur'. In other cases, a differentiation between two concepts in two expressions cannot be expressed in the other language and has to be represented in both cases by the same expression. The two German expressions 'Bedingungen' ('conditions') and 'Voraussetzungen' ('prerequisites') (in provisions regulating approvals) are rendered in French by the one word 'conditions'. This can cause difficulties when an author wants to differentiate between conditions and prerequisites.

On the other hand, the German term 'Ersatzabgabe' ('compensatory contribution/tax') is intransparent. It does not imply what duty shall be compensated by the contribution. In French, a difference is made between 'taxe de compensation' in the sense of 'tax to be paid in place of another contribution' and 'taxe d'exemption' in the sense of 'tax to be paid as a compensation for a duty one is exempt from'.

Generally, varying contexts can force different formulations in the particular languages for one and the same concept. German differs from French in being more flexible in word formation; this gives the possibility of creating complex words that can be used in very different grammatical contexts. In French, complex German word formations are usually rendered by grammatical constructions (e.g. complex noun phrases), whose usability depends much more on the particular grammatical context. The German expression 'Verursacher' (person, party responsible) has a several different counterparts in French. Depending on the context; a similar uniform expression is not possible in French:

(15) a. *Der Verursacher* trägt die Kosten der Sanierung
b. *Celui qui est à l'origine de l'assainissement* en assume les frais.

(16) a. Die Kosten von Maßnahmen, welche die Behörden ... treffen, werden dem *Verursacher* überbunden.
b. Les coûts resultant des measures prises par l'autorité ... sont à la charge de *celui qui a provoqué ces interventions*

(17) a. Kosten für Maßnahmen, welche infolge falscher oder fehlender Angaben anfallen, gehen zu Lasten der *Verursacher*.

b. Les frais lies aux measures s'imposant suite à des indications fausses ou incomplètes incombent à *l'auteur de ces indications.*

On the other hand, the French version is often more precise and explicit where the German version rather implicitly refers to a general principle of 'verursachen' ('cause' as a verb).

The same observation can be made with the German adjective 'beitragspflichtig' ('liable for a contribution'), which creates particular problems when it is negated as an attributive adjective in German:

(18) a. beitragspflichtig
b. tenu à contribution
tenu de payer des cotisations
tener de verser de cotisations
soumis à l'obligation de verse des cotisations

(19) a. Beiträge der Arbeitnehmer *nicht beitragspflichtiger Arbeitgeber*
b. cotisations des assures dont l'employeur n'est pas tenu de payer des cotisation

In the case of 'beitragspflichtig', it may be suspected that the diversity of the French wordings is partially the result of incoherence among the translators, and that more coherence would be possible. The incoherence is also due to the fact that there is no comparably simple expression in French as there is in German. If French had a similarly simple expression, such divergences would be less probable. But maintaining lexical consistency in legal terminology throughout the whole of the legislation is a difficult task even in one single language.

Another problem area is the equal treatment of men and women, where French is confronted with difficult grammatical problems. Fifteen years ago, the principle of equal grammatical treatment of genders was compulsorily introduced for the federal administration. All texts have to be formulated according to it, which implies that whenever physical persons are mentioned in a text it is not allowed to mention one particular gender only. This principle has not been fully implemented for French and Italian, however, because their structure makes it virtually impossible to find formulations that satisfy the principle and are still comprehensible and correct. This is mainly because of the obligatory agreement of adjectives with nouns and subjects in all positions (attributive and predicative), both in singular and in plural.[15]

Another type of difficulties for establishing equivalent wordings arises from different grammatical patterns for verbs or nouns among the languages involved. A verb may be used without a complement in one language, whereas in the other language an object must be added obligatorily for purely grammatical reasons, although such an addition may be redundant in the given context and mark an unnecessary precision:

(20) Bundesgesetz über die Landwirtschaft – Loi fédérale sur l'agriculture, (SR 910.1), *Art. 72*

German
Der Bund richtet als Entgelt für die gemeinwirtschaftlichen Leistungen Flächenbeiträge aus.

French
Afin de rétribuer les prestations fournies dans l'intérêt général, la Confédération verse *aux exploitants d'entreprises paysannes cultivant le sol* des contributions liées à la surface.

Of course, it is not only the French language that entails structural problems. The German sentence structure and especially the position of verbs and adjectives can cause structural difficulties for German where French offers simple forward or at least transparent sentence constructions. In French, attributive adjective groups, complements or adverbial groups are postponed to the verbal kernel of a sentence, whereas in German, in many cases, they are locked within the frame of the dominating structure (NP or VP). Frequently, such groups logically represent restrictive modifications of an assertion, which is one of the most frequent types of an elaboration of a provision. This often leads to clumsy and intransparent constructions in German, whereas in French the restrictions are systematically arranged at the end of a phrase and consequently are easily recognized.

(21) Verordnung der Eidgenössischen Kommunikationskommission betreffend das Fernmeldegesetz – Ordonnance de la Commission

15. E.g. one can find pairs such as "les retraités et les retraitées" ('retired persons' masc./fem.), which are not acceptable in official texts.

fédérale de la communication relative à la loi sur les télécommunications (784.101.112), *Art. 5*

German
Die Deckung *der* mit der Verbindungssteuerung zum Bestimmungsort der portierten Nummern verbundenen *Kosten wird* durch die Fernmeldedienstanbieterinnen in ihren Interkonnektionsverträgen *geregelt.*

French
La couverture *des coûts* liés à l'acheminement des communications à destination de numéros portés *est réglée* par les fournisseurs de services de télécommunication dans leurs accords d'interconnexion.

(22) Verordnung über die obligatorische Arbeitslosenversicherung und die Insolvenzentschädigung – Ordonnance sur l'assurance-chômage obligatoire et l'indemnité en cas d'insolvabilité (SR 837.02), *Art. 10b*

German
Die für die berufliche Vorsorge verwendeten *Beträge werden* von den zu berücksichtigenden freiwilligen Leistungen nach Art. 11a Abs. 2 AVIG bis höchstens zum Maximalbetrag des koordinierten Lohnes nach Artikel 8 Absatz 1 des Bundesgesetzes vom 25. Juni 19822 über die berufliche Alters-, Hinterlassenen- und Invalidenvorsorge *abgezogen.*

French
Les montants affectés à la prévoyance professionnelle *sont déduits* des prestations volontaires à prendre en compte selon l'art. 11a, al. 2, LACI jusqu'à concurrence du montant maximum du salaire coordonné fixé à l'art. 8, al. 1, de la loi fédérale du 25 juin 1982 sur la prévoyance professionnelle vieillesse, survivants et invalidité.

In the following case, the simple French preposition *selon* has to be rendered in German with a nominal group introducing an enumeration:

(23) Bundesgesetz vom 29. April 1998 über die Landwirtschaft – Loi fédérale du 29 avril 1998 sur l'agriculture, (SR 910.1), *Art. 22* Al. 2

German
[2] Die zuständige Behörde verteilt die Zollkontingente namentlich nach folgenden Verfahren und Kriterien:

a. durch Versteigerung;
b. nach Maßgabe der Inlandleistung;
c. aufgrund der beantragten Menge;
d. entsprechend der Reihenfolge des Einganges der Bewilligungsgesuche;
...

French
[2] L'autorité compétente répartit les contingents notamment selon:
a. la procédure de la mise aux enchères;
b. la prestation fournie en faveur de la production suisse;
c. la quantité demandée;
d. l'ordre d'arrivée des demandes d'autorisation;
...

Due to the specific verb position rules of German, enumerations tend to be formulated in ways that are grammatically inept. In contrast, French constructions correspond much better with the common grammatical rules:

(24) Verordnung vom 28. Mai 1997 über die Kontrolle des Handels mit Wein - Ordonnance du 28 mai 1997 sur le contrôle du commerce des vins (SR 916.146), Art. 2 al. 2

German
[3] Aus der Buchführung und den dazugehörigen Belegen müssen jederzeit ersichtlich sein:
a. die Ursprungs-, Herkunfts- und Sachbezeichnungen;
b. die Rebsorten und die Jahrgänge;
...

French
[3] La comptabilité et les pièces justificatives correspondantes doivent permettre de déterminer à tout moment:
a. les appellations d'origine, les provenances et les dénominations spécifiques;
b. les cépages et les millésimes;
...

(25) Verordnung vom 7. Dezember 1998 über die Produktion und das Inverkehrbringen von pflanzlichem Vermehrungsmaterial – Ordonnance du 7 décembre 1998 sur la production et la mise en circulation du matériel végétal de multiplication (SR 916.151) *Art. 11* al. 1

German
[1] Zur Anerkennung kann nur gelangen:
a. Prebasis-, Basis- und zertifiziertes Material;
b. Material einer Sorte, die in einem Sortenkatalog oder einer Sortenliste eingetragen ist, oder Material einer Kandidatensorte;
...

French
[1] Seul peut être certifié (s.l.):
a. le matériel de pré-base, le matériel de base et le matériel certifié;
b. le matériel d'une variété enregistrée dans un catalogue des variétés ou dans une liste des variétés ou le matériel d'une variété expérimentale;
...

Formulations in laws have to obey many restrictions. Often, there is no stylistically ideal solution due to terminological and formal constraints. In a multilingual context, these problems can be found in the corresponding languages in different ways and different areas. On the whole, the problems are distributed evenly, so that no language is affected by these difficulties more than the others.

Interpretation is not generally impaired by these problems, but they may reduce the terminological consistency of a version. They can also make it necessary to compare different formulations in different versions in order to establish a firm interpretation of one version. The efforts for finding equal solutions sometimes leads to formulations that are not optimal in view of one language only – but compromises are inevitable.

8. Conclusion

The aim of this contribution is not so much to develop a theory of multilingual law drafting, but rather to present some reflections on the daily work and practical problems of law drafting in a multilingual context. Text drafting always involves – or should do so – efforts to write a text that fulfils its purpose as well as possible and at the same time is as understandable as possible. Law drafting is in some respects particularly demanding, since laws have to be more precise and formally elaborated than other types of texts, which makes it even more difficult to achieve easy understanding.

Drafting multilingual laws adds another dimension to the requirements that have to be considered when elaborating on a good text. The multidimensionality of texts makes law drafting even more demanding in some ways. The challenges of this task can only be coped with by developing appropriate drafting methods and cooperative working methods, taking into account all versions of a text simultaneously.

If we consider the different versions of a text as equally authentic, this additional multidimensionality is not only a restriction. Rather, it can open more perspectives for detecting new possibilities of formulating a text. In the long run, as a result of a long tradition of multilingual text drafting, texts and languages do not remain isolated from each other. Instead, a network of parallel formulations, expressions and vocabulary and also drafting styles is developed that supports the parallel formulation of multilingual text versions. In this framework of multilinguality, the texts themselves become multilingal.

9. References

Albrecht, Urs. 2001. "Die mehrsprachige Redaktion in der Bundesverwaltung". *LeGes – Gesetzgebung & Evaluation* 12, H. 3, 99–114

Bertagnollo, Fabienne and Caroline Laurent. 2005. "Unkraut vergeht nicht: La corédaction dans l'administration fédérale suisse". *Jurilingistique: entre langues et droits – Jurilinguistics: Between Law and Language*, ed. by Jean-Claude Gémar and Nicholas Kasirer, Bruxelles: Bruylant. 119–126.

Born, Joachim and Wilfried Schütte. 1995. *Eurotexte. Textarbeit in einer Insitution der EG*. Tübingen: Narr.

Burr, Isolde. 2000. "Auslegung mehrsprachiger juristischer Texte: die Rolle des Italienischen in Urteilen des Schweizerischen Bundesgerichts". *Linguistica giuridica italiana e tedesca*, ed. by Daniela Veronesi, Padova: Unipress, 179–194

Caussignac, Gérard. 1995. "Corédaction, redaction parallèle et redaction bilingue des actes législatifs". *Français juridique et Science du Droit*, ed. by Gérard Snow and Jacques Vanderlinden, Bruxelles: Bruylan, 71ff..

Côté, Pierre-André. 2005. "La tension anter l'intelligibilité et l'uniformité dans l'interpretation des lois plurilingues". *Jurilingistique: entre langues et droits – Jurilinguistics: Between Law and Language*, ed. by Jean-Claude Gémar and Nicholas Kasirer, Bruxelles: Bruylant. 127–143.

Flückiger, Alexandre. 2005. "Le multilingualisme de l'Union Européenne: Un défi pour la qualité de la legislation." *Jurilingistique: entre langues et droits – Jurilinguistics: Between Law and Language*, ed. by Jean-Claude Gémar and Nicholas Kasirer, Bruxelles: Bruylant. 339–336.

Gallas, Tito. 2001. "La redaction legislative multilingue dan l'Union Européenne: bilan et perspective". *LeGes – Gesetzgebung & Evaluation* 12, H. 3, 115–129.

Gémar, Jean-Claude. 2001. "Le discours du législateur en situation multilingue: Traduire o corédiger?" *LeGes – Gesetzgebung & Evaluation* 12, H. 3, 13–32.

Guggeis, Manuela and Tito Gallas. "La traduction juridique dans l'experience des juriste-linguistes du conseil de l'Union Européenne". *Jurilingistique: entre langues et droits – Jurilinguistics: Between Law and Language*, ed. by Jean-Claude Gémar and Nicholas Kasirer, Bruxelles: Bruylant. 491–504.

Labelle, André. 2000. "La corédaction des lois fédérales au Canada". *La traduction juridique: Histoire, théorie(s) et pratique.* Genève/Berne: ETI-ASTTI, 269ff.

Lötscher, Andreas. 2000. "'Würde der Kreatur' – 'integrité des organismes vivants'. Sprachanalytische Beobachtungen zu Bedeutung und Auslegung zweier umstrittener Ausdrücke". *LeGes – Gesetzgebung & Evaluation* 11 H. 2, 137–155.

Meyer, Kurt. 1989. *Wie sagt man in der Schweiz? Wörterbuch der schweizerischen Besonderheiten.* Mannheim-Zürich et al.: Dudenverlag.

Oplatka-Steinlin, Helen. 1971. *Untersuchungen zur neuhochdeutschen Gesetzessprache : Befehlsintensität und Satzstruktur im Schweizerischen Zivilgesetzbuch und im Deutschen Bürgerlichen Gesetzbuch.* Zürich: Juris.

Prätorius, Ina and Peter Saladin. 1996. "Die Würde der Kreatur (Art. 24novies Abs. 3 BV)", *Schriftenreihe Umwelt Nr. 260: Recht / Organismen*, Buwal: Bern.

Šarcevic, Susan. 2005. "The quest for legislative bilingualism and multilingualism: Co-Drafting in Canada and Switzerland". *Jurilingistique: entre langues et droits – Jurilinguistics: Between Law and Language*, ed. by Jean-Claude Gémar and Nicholas Kasirer, Bruxelles: Bruylant. 276–292.

Schubarth, Martin. 2001. "Die Bedeutung der Mehrsprachigkeit für die höchstrichterliche Rechtsprechung", *LeGes – Gesetzgebung & Evaluation* 12, H. 3, 49–57.

Thibault, André and Pierre Knecht. 1997. *Dictionnaire Suisse Romand.* Carouge: Zoé.

A modular approach to legal drafting and translation

Jacqueline Visconti

1. Introduction*

A multilingual perspective on legal drafting and interpretation highlights new facets of the relationship between language and law. Since the Edinburgh European Council in 1992, the need for 'better' lawmaking – by clearer, simpler acts complying with principles of good legislative drafting – has been recognized at the highest political level. Both the Council and the Commission have taken steps to address the issue of the quality of the drafting of EU legislation (Declaration n. 39, Final Act, Amsterdam Treaty, 1997). As a result, the three institutions involved in the procedure for the adoption of Community acts, the European Parliament, the Council and the Commission, adopted common guidelines intended to improve the quality of drafting of Community legislation (Inter-institutional Agreement, December 1998). Yet the relationship between drafting and translating, between the ideal of simultaneous drafting of legislation in all official languages (art. 4, Language Charter, 1958) and the practice of translation, currently covering over 400 combinations for 23 official languages (cf. Gallas 2007: 30; Tosi and Visconti 2004: 152), raises a series of complex questions, which touch upon fundamental issues such as the need for transparency and accessibility in the interaction between European institutions and Member States citizens.

Many international research projects address the challenges set by such recent changes in the political shape of Europe.[1] Yet most literature dis-

---

* This paper discusses the results of two projects on legal language in a comparative perspective, funded respectively by the *European Commission* (University of Reading, 1995–97) and by the Italian *Ministero per l'Istruzione, l'Università e la Ricerca* (University of Genoa, 2003–2006). A preliminary version was presented at the International Conference on "*Approaching the Multilanguage Complexity of European Law: Methodologies in Comparison*" (Florence, IUE, 17 November 2006). Thanks to Isolde Burr, Angela Ferrari with her research group at the University of Basel and an anonymous referee for valuable feedback.

G. Grewendorf, M. Rathert (eds.): Formal Linguistics and Law, 401–426

cussing multilingualism and translation in the legal domain focuses on terminological issues. The problems at stake revolve around questions such as: is the translation of terms mirroring different legal conceptions legitimate? How is a term used in a EU context related to the corresponding terminology in a national context? Lawyers, in particular, comparatists, have been reflecting on the translation of terms such as trust, contract, property, etc. across legal systems (the obvious opposition concerning common vs. civil law) (e.g. Ioriatti Ferrari 2007; Jacomelli and Pozzo 2006; Sacco and Castellani 1999; Sacco 2002), problems with which translators working in a multilingual environments, such as the European institutions, are faced daily.[2]

Far from denying the importance of terminological issues, this paper widens the scope of the reflection to other linguistic structures of the legal text. The problematic character of legal translation is shown to concern not only concepts expressed by terms such as those indicated above – contract, property, etc., but also the semantic relationships expressed by connectives linking the propositions of a text. A fine-grained analysis of all linguistic levels of legal texts is argued to be a prerequisite for both translation and 'good' drafting practice in multilingual contexts. Such an analysis is best grounded in a modular approach, where lexical, morpho-syntactic and textual levels are seen as autonomous yet interacting modules. In the remainder of the paper, the textual dimension in its various facets (logical, argumentative, informational) will be shown to be of primary importance in shaping form and function of legal documents.

2. The textual dimension

Although essential, terminological reflection is not sufficient to achieve an accurate understanding of legal products. The textual dimension plays a fundamental role in such process. Adopted by a few individual studies on single languages (for instance Mortara Garavelli 2001; Sabatini 1990 for

1. Cf. e.g. the project *Uniform Terminology for European Contract Law* (http://normas.di.unito.it/syllabus and references herein to other research groups).

2. A recent initiative by the European Commission, the *Rete di Eccellenza dell'Italiano Istituzionale* (De Stefanis 2007), aims to building a bridge between the academic world and translators in the EU institutions: at a meeting organized by the Italian *Accademia della Crusca* (Florence, 5 July 2006), a team of lawyers and linguists was asked to suggest translations for terms such as *mobile worker, justiciability, class action, due diligence, grandfather clause, sunset clause...*

Italian; Heller 2003; Soffritti 1999 for German), a textual perspective ought to be made a systematic feature of any approach to legal interpretation and translation.[3] The relevant parameters in the organization of legal texts concern both the set of semantic and argumentative relationships that may be established between the propositions of a text (causal, conditional, etc.) (logico-argumentative level) (§ 2.1) and the information structure of the contents of the text (information structure level) (§ 2.2).[4] Although the interpretation of a text also relies on contextual, extra-linguistic, factors, in the following sections I shall be concerned with the linguistic inscription of textuality.

2.1 Connectives

Connectives have a crucial function in structuring the text.[5] In this section I shall look at conditional connectives, such as English *on condition that* or Italian *sempre che*. The account I propose shows the importance of widening the analysis beyond the terminological level, by looking at the interaction of lexical and structural factors in shaping the logico-argumentative skeleton of a text.

Conditionality plays a crucial role in legal language: a relationship between a conditioning fact and its legal consequence has been argued to be the underlying structure of all norms (Ross 1994: 125–132). Besides other means of expression, such as English *if* and its equivalents in other languages, or German *Verberst-Sätzen*,[6] a conditional relationship can be expressed by connectives such as English *provided (that)* or *as long as*, Italian *purché*, *a patto che*, French *pourvu que* or *à condition que*, German *falls* or *unter der Bedingung, dass*, as in examples (1) to (4):

---

3. The only other study, to my knowledge, highlighting the need for a "*vergleichende* [comparative] *Textlinguistik*" in the multilingual EU context is Burr (2006) (cf. Burr and Gallas 2004).
4. On layers of textual composition cf. *e.g.* Ferrari (2004: 19–25), who distinguishes between (i) logico-semantic, (ii) informational, (iii) topical and (iv) enonciative perspective. The *Topic-Comment* (*Theme-Rheme*) dimension – where *Topic* is defined, following Lambrecht (1994) in terms of *aboutness*, is a separate though related layer *vs* the information dimension that will be discussed in § 2.2.; the enonciative perspective has for obvious reasons little relevance in legal texts (cf. e.g. Cignetti 2005: § 5).
5. For a *compendium* cf. Pasch et al. (2003).
6. Cf. e.g. Heller (2003: 292–299).

(1) I will buy it, *provided/as long as* it is not too expensive.

(2) Lo compro, *purché/a patto che* non sia troppo caro.

(3) Je l'acheterai, *pourvu que/à condition que* ce/il ne soit pas trop cher.

(4) Ich werde es kaufen, *falls/unter der Bedingung, dass* es nicht zu teuer ist.

Such expressions, which, due to their structural complexity I have named "complex conditional connectives" (henceforth *ccc*s) (Visconti 2000a), introduce a more specific condition than *if*, thus not sharing the same contexts of use:

(5) If you're thirsty, there some juice in the fridge.

(6) **As long as* you're thirsty, there some juice in the fridge.

The semantic relationship conveyed by these connectives is moreover "richer". Compare, as an illustration, the following pair of examples:

(7) His party wanted to see a commitment to a reformed and modernised constitution. "*In so far as* there is a message for Labour, our message is: 'We are prepared to be clear about this. Are you?'" (Visconti 2000b: 44).

(8) His party wanted to see a commitment to a reformed and modernised constitution. "*If* there is a message for Labour, our message is: 'We are prepared to be clear about this. Are you?'".

In (8), with *if*, (the truth of) one proposition (q) is asserted to descend from (the truth of) the other (p); in (7), *in so far as* specifies the limits, the boundaries within which q is true, by inducing between the two propositions a relationship of proportional correlation, such that q descends from p 'to the extent that' p. The utterance assumes a tone of distance, of 'diplomacy', whereby the speaker transfers to the hearer the responsibility for deciding to what extent p is true: q is thus asserted only if and to the extent that p is accepted.

Not surprisingly do these connectives play an important role in legal language. Nevertheless, and although implementation of legislation in an international dimension crucially depends upon the equivalence of all versions, *ccc*s are not always rendered consistently. In the very *Treaty on*

European Union (Maastricht 1992), *in so far as* corresponds to (at least) four Italian connectives: *nella misura in cui* (10), *sempreché* (14), *in quanto* (18), *nei limiti in cui* (22); three French ones: *dans la mesure où* (11), (15), *pour autant que* (19), *dans les limites où* (23); one in German: *soweit* (12), (16), (20), (24):

Art. 86

(9) Any abuse by one or more undertakings of a dominant position within the common market or in a substantial part of it shall be prohibited as incompatible with the common market *in so far as* it may affect trade between Member States.

(10) È incompatibile con il mercato comune e vietato, *nella misura in cui* possa essere pregiudizievole al commercio tra Stati membri, lo sfruttamento abusivo da parte di una o più imprese di una posizione dominante sul mercato comune o su una parte sostanziale di questo.

(11) Est incompatible avec le marché commun et interdit, *dans la mesure où* le commerce entre États membres est susceptible d'en être affecté, le fait pour une ou plusieures entreprises d'exploiter de façon abusive une position dominante sur le marché commun ou dans une partie substantielle de celui-ci.

(12) Mit dem Gemeinsamen Markt unvereinbar und verboten ist die missbräuchliche Ausnutzung einer beherrschenden Stellung auf dem Gemeinsamen Markt oder auf einem wesentlichen Teil desselben durch ein oder mehrere Unternehmen, *soweit* dies dazu führen kann, den Handel zwischen Mitgliedstaaten zu beeinträchtigen.

Art. 73 H 3

(13) The progressive abolition of existing restrictions shall be effected in accordance with the provisions of Article 63 to 65, *in so far as* such abolition is not governed by the provisions contained in paragraphs 1 and 2.

(14) La graduale soppressione delle restrizioni esistenti si effettua conformemente alle disposizioni degli articoli 63 a 65 inclusi, *sempreché* non sia disciplinata dalle disposizioni dei paragrafi 1 e 2.

(15) La suppression progressive des restrictions existantes est effectuée conformément aux dispositions des articles 63 à 65 inclus, *dans la mesure où* elle n'est pas régie par le dispositions du présent chapitre.

(16) Die bestehenden Beschränkungen werden gemäß den Artikeln 63 bis 65 beseitigt, *soweit* hierfür nicht die Nummer 1 und 2 oder die sonstigen Bestimmungen dieses Kapitels maßgebend sind.

Art. 92. 3 C

(17) [...] However, the aids granted to shipbuildings as of 1 January 1957 shall, *in so far as* they serve only to compensate for the absence of customs protection, be progressively reduced under the same conditions as apply to the elimination of custom duties [...].

(18) [...] Tuttavia, gli aiuti alle costruzioni navali esistenti alla data del 1° gennaio 1957, *in quanto* determinati soltanto dall'assenza di una protezione doganale, sono progressivamente ridotti alle stesse condizioni che si applicano per l'abolizione dei dazi doganali [...].

(19) [...] Toutefois, les aides à la construction navale existant à la date du 1. 1. 1957, *pour autant qu'*elles ne correspondent qu'à l'absence d'une protection douanière, sont progressivement réduites dans les mêmes conditions que celles applicables à l'élimination des droits de douane [...].

(20) [...] Beihilfen für den Schiffbau, *soweit* sie am 1 Januar 1957 bestanden und lediglich einem fehlenden Zollschutz entsprechen, werden jedoch entsprechend den für die Abschaffung der Zölle geltenden Bestimmungen [...] schrittweise abgebaut.

Art. 90. 2

(21) Undertakings entrusted with the operation of services of general economic interest or having the character of a revenue-producing monopoly shall be subject to the rules contained in this Treaty [...], *in so far as* the application of such rules does not obstruct the performance, in law or in fact, of the particular tasks assigned to them.

(22) Le imprese incaricate della gestione di servizi d'interesse economico generale o aventi carattere di monopolio fiscale sono sottoposte alle norme del presente trattato [...], *nei limiti in cui* l'applicazione di tali norme non osti all'adempimento, in linea di diritto e di fatto, della specifica missione loro affidata.

(23) Les entreprises chargées de la gestion de services d'intérêt économique général ou présentant le caractère d'un monopole fiscal sont soumises aux règles du présent traité [...], *dans les limites où*

l'application de ces règles ne fait pas échec à l'accomplissement en droit ou en fait de la mission particulière qui leur a été impartie.

(24) Für Unternehmen, die mit Dienstleistungen von allgemeinem wirtschaftlichem Interesse betraut sind oder den Charakter eines Finanzmonopols haben, gelten die Vorschriften dieses Vertrages [...], *soweit* die Anwendung dieser Vorschriften nicht die Erfüllung der ihnen übertragenen besonderen Aufgabe rechtlich oder tatsächlich verhindert.

A systematic comparative analysis of such connectives confirms our initial concern (cf. Visconti 2000b). The analysis focuses on English, French, German, Italian, but it is conceived to be applied to other languages. In the following sections, I shall outline the main tenets of the account and draw on the insights it offers on both a theoretical and a methodological level.

An accurate monolingual analysis, *i.e.* the identification of the semantic properties of each connective in each language, is deemed to be a prerequisite for a sound comparative investigation. Such properties are identified on the basis of a *corpus* of authentic examples (not exclusively of legal language)[7].

The study is carried out in 4 steps:

(i) Monolingual examination, comprising: (a) classification of the *ccc*s; (b) semantic analysis of each connective; (c) 'formalization' of the results in a model lexical entry.

(ii) Cross-linguistic comparison on a system of scales elaborated on the basis of (i).

(iii) Verification of the correspondences obtained on comparable legal texts.

(iv) Organization of the results into a "glossary", where a system of cross-references between lexical entries and scales allows finding the most adequate translation.

In the following sections I shall provide an example of both the construction of a lexical entry (§ 2.1.1.) and the use of the glossary as an aid for translation (§ 2.1.2.).

---

7. The databases used are: *Italian Reference Corpus* [*IRC*] (Istituto di Linguistica Computazionale, Pisa); *British National Corpus* [*BNC*] (Oxford Computing Centre, Oxford); *Oxford English Dictionary Online* [*OED*]).

2.1.1 *A glossary of complex conditional connectives*

Visconti's (2000a: 81–86) classification of *cccs*, based on both a distributional and a functional criterion, distinguishes between "hypothetical":

> *{ammesso che, casomai, concesso che, dato che, in caso, nel caso che (in cui), nell'eventualità che, nell'ipotesi che, posto che, ove/dove/laddove, qualora, quando, supponendo che, supposto che}*
>
> *{assuming (that), given that, granted that, in case, in the event of (that), lest, supposing (that), when, where}*
>
> *{à supposer que, au (dans) (pour) (le) cas où (que), dans (pour) l'hypothèse où (que), dans la supposition que, en admettant que, en supposant que, posé que, quand, supposé que}*
>
> *{angenommen, dass; falls; (für den) in dem Fall(e), dass; zugegeben, dass}*

and "restrictive" *cccs*:

> *{a condizione che, a patto che, in quanto, nei limiti in cui, nella misura in cui, purché, sempre che*
> */sempreché}*
>
> *{as (so) long as, in as much that, in so far as, on condition that, provided (providing) that, to the extent that, with the proviso that, unless}*
>
> *{à (la) condition que, dans la mesure où, dans les limites où, pour autant que, pourvu que}*
>
> *{(in)sofern, (in)soweit, unter der Bedingung, dass; unter der Voraussetzung, dass; vorausgesetzt, dass}*

The former, typically preposed, introduce p as a 'framework' for q:

(25) *In the event that* the current Parliament was unable to select a new President, the task would fall to the new Parliament emerging from the April 8 general election ([*BNC*]).

The latter, typically postposed, introduce p as a limitation on the general validity of q:

(26) Ladies were allowed to attend College classes from 1884, *provided that* they were 'attended by some elder person' ([*OED*]).

As an example of punctual analysis, let us focus on the Italian restrictive connective *sempre che*. I shall try to isolate its properties in contrast to the other elements of the class: *purché, a patto che, a condizione che, in quanto, nei limiti in cui, nella misura in cui.*

Let us consider the connectives within the same context:

(27) Farò finta di niente, *a condizione che* l'incidente non si ripeta.

(28) Farò finta di niente, *a patto che* l'incidente non si ripeta.

(29) Farò finta di niente, *purché* l'incidente non si ripeta.

(30) Farò finta di niente, *sempre che* l'incidente non si ripeta.

(31) ??Farò finta di niente, *nella misura in cui* l'incidente non si ripeta.

(32) ??Farò finta di niente, *nei limiti in cui* l'incidente non si ripeta.

(33) * Farò finta di niente, *in quanto* l'incidente non si ripeta.
'I'll pretend nothing happened, *a condizione che/ a patto che/ purché...* the accident does not happen again.'

Notice, first of all, the unacceptability of example (33) and the marginality of (31) and (32). Whereas *a condizione che, a patto che, purché* and *sempre che* select the subjunctive mood and have a conditional value only, for *nella misura in cui, nei limiti in cui, in quanto* the conditional value arises out of the interaction of the semantics of the connective (*e.g.* causal, as *in quanto*) with the semantics of the Italian subjunctive mood, expressing the non factuality of p. Conditionality is thus 'derived', not an intrinsic feature for such connectives. *Nella misura in cui* also preferably selects the indicative mood and has a causal value, introducing moreover a proportional correlation between p and q (cf. *insofar as* in (7) above):

(34) Questa storia diviene d'altronde necessariamente una storia morale *nella misura in cui* le civiltà sono generalmente considerate dai teorici della decadenza come sistemi di costumi ([IRC]).

'History thus becomes necessarily a moral history nella misura in cui civilizations are generally considered by historians of decadence as being sets of customs'.

If we return to the 'purely' conditional *ccc*s, that is to examples (27) to (30), we notice how they evoke a condition which is not only sufficient but also necessary to the realization of q. Only if "the accident does not happen again" (or, at least, if the hearer commits her/himself to such a promise), will the speaker "pretend nothing happened". Otherwise, she/he will take the necessary steps. She/he is unlikely to add:

(35) ? Anzi, farò finta di niente in ogni caso.
'Actually, I'll pretend nothing happened anyway'.

I shall thus define more precisely 'restrictivity' as "the addition of a limitation to the general validity of a statement, via the expression of a condition that is not only sufficient but also necessary to its accomplishment".

However, such an addition is realized in different ways by the four connectives. What changes is the intensity of the 'imposition' of the restriction, which decreases from being peremptory for *a condizione che*, via the component of 'pact', 'agreement' in *a patto che*, to the minimality of the condition introduced by *purché* ('only that...'), to the value of 'afterthought' of *sempre che.* The latter differs moreover for the presence of an intonational break between the two clauses, the former being uttered with descending intonation.

Still attempting to isolate the properties of *sempre che*, we notice a feature opposing *a condizione che* and *a patto che vs purché* and *sempre che*: only *a condizione che* and *a patto che* are compatible with the focussing adverb *solo* ("only"):

(36) Farò finta di niente, solo *a condizione che* l'incidente non si ripeta.

(37) Farò finta di niente, solo *a patto che* l'incidente non si ripeta.

(38) ??Farò finta di niente, solo *purché* l'incidente non si ripeta.

(39) *Farò finta di niente, solo *sempre che* l'incidente non si ripeta.
'I'll pretend nothing happened, only *a condizione che/a patto che/purché...*the accident does not happen again.'

Such a compatibility indicates that *a condizione che* and *a patto che,* unlike *purché* or *sempreché*, can foreground the conditional relationship, a further argument in support of the hypothesis of a greater strength in the restriction they introduce.

What distinguishes *purché* from *sempreché*, which grammars and dictionaries of Italian present as semantically equivalent? Is it really only a difference in register (the latter being rarer and more formal)?

A first element has already been mentioned: unlike *purché*, which introduces a syntactically and intonationally integrated clause (cf. ex. 29), *sempre che* introduces an 'afterthought', provided of greater intonational and semantic independence (30). For this reason, example (40), for which the introduction – *après-coup* – of an afterthought is the most natural reading, is better than the corresponding one with *purché* (41):

(40) È arrivato alle otto, *sempre che* non abbia perso il treno.

(41) ? È arrivato alle otto, *purché* non abbia perso il treno.
'He arrived at eight, *sempre che/purché* he did not miss the train'

Secondly, *purché* has a volitional component, presenting the proposition introduced as the speaker's wish or request, as shown by examples (42) and (43):

(42) Faccia quel che vuole *purché* mi lasci in pace.
'He can do what he wants, *purchè* he leaves me in peace'

(43) *Purché* si penta gli perdono.
'*Purché* he regrets, I'll forgive him'

Such a component is absent in *sempre che*, as illustrates the oddness of the examples obtained by replacing *purché* with *sempre che*:

(44) ? Faccia quel che vuole *sempre che* mi lasci in pace.
'He can do what he wants, *sempre che* he leaves me in peace'

(45) ?? *Sempre che* si penta gli perdono.
'*Sempre che* he regrets, I'll forgive him'

Thirdly, *purché* but not *sempre che* confers an adversative component to the restriction introduced, as shown by the difference between (46) and (47):

(46) ? Verrò da te, *purché* tu sia d'accordo.

(47) Verrò da te, *sempre che* tu sia d'accordo.
'I'll come to see you, *purché/sempre che* you agree'.

(46) can be paraphrased by 'I'll come to see you, but you must agree', thus being inapt to the context of politeness due to the interaction between the volitional and the adversative element in *purché*, *vs* (47), in which *sempre che* introduces a polite reservation on the speaker's agreement.

Due to these features, which I summarize as: the association with an afterthought, not compatible with focalization (ex. 39) and bare of volitional components (exx. 44 and 45), the restriction introduced by *sempre che* has a lesser degree of imposition compared to the restriction introduced by *purché*.

To represent the semantic properties identified for *sempre che* I shall use the following model lexical entry (LE) (cf. Visconti 2000a: 220–226):

LE (sempre che):
(α) (a_1) logico-semantic level
<λR [ILL FUNCT ^{pot} (R (p, q)] (NEC & SUFF COND)>
(a_2) non logico-semantic level
(a_2') general features
[RESTR]
(a_2'') individual features
degree [0,2] of 'coercive strength' [*B]

The lexical entry above distinguishes between a more 'basic' level of meaning, named 'logico-semantic', and a less central component that lies outside the former.[8] The more 'basic' layer contains the logico-semantic relationship expressed by the connectives within the utterance and specifies the potential illocutionary function of the utterance itself. Such a lexical entry is grounded in a modular approach, where decoding and interpreting an utterance results from the interaction of different autonomous modules – (phonetic), morphosyntactic, semantic. The meaning of connectives is considered to be a function of both their structural manifestations and their lexical semantic features. Thus, in the case under examination, at the logico-semantic level (a_1) it is accounted for the fact that *sempre che*, like the other 'restrictive' *ccc*s, introduces between two propositions p and q a relationship (R) of 'necessary and sufficient condition' (NEC & SUFF COND). At the level of 'general features' (a_2'), where by 'general' it is meant 'shared by other *ccc*s', it is specified its inclusion into the category of 'restrictive' [RESTR], defined as above. The set of its distinctive features is summarized in (a_2'') as degree [0,2] of 'coercive strength' [*B], to

8. Cf. for discussion Visconti (2000a: Ch. 2) and references herein.

indicate, on a scale from 0 to 1, the (minimal) degree of imposition of the restriction. The asterisk in the lexical entry refers to scale B [*B], on which restrictive *ccc*s are ordered on the basis of the parameter of 'coercive strength':

SCALE B [degree of 'coercive strength']

0 1

--------• ----- •------------ •---------------• ------------------------• ---------------›

nella misura in cui *purché* *a patto che* *a condizione che*
nei limiti in cui
in quanto
sempre che
(sempreché)

Simultaneous consideration of the scales analogously elaborated for restrictive *ccc*s in English, French and German allows a general comparative outlook:

--------• ------------------- •---------------• ------------- •---------------• --------›

in so far as *as long as* *provided (that)* *on condition that*
to the extent that *providing (that)*
in as much as *with the proviso that*

--------• ----------------------------• -------------------------------• ---------------›

dans la mesure où *pourvu que* *à condition que*
dans les limites où
pour autant que

--------• ----------------------------------• --------------- •------------• -----------›

(in)soweit *vorausgesetzt, dass* *unter der Bedingung, dass*
(in)sofern *unter der Voraussetzung, dass*

If we reconsider the series of articles (9) to (24) above in the light of the analysis provided, we find that the correspondences found in the Treaty are confirmed, with one exception: *insofar as, nella misura in cui, in quanto, nei limiti in cui, dans la mesure ou, pour autant que, dans les limites ou* and *soweit* all share the same degree of 'coercive strength', whereas *sempreché*, having a slightly higher degree of imposition, introduces in the utterance a component not shared by the others.

2.1.2 Using the glossary

The glossary, divided into four monolingual sections, contains, for each connective, in each language:

I. A brief description of the *ccc*'s syntactic and semantic properties;
II. A lexical entry summarizing such properties;
III. Reference to a set of scales, ordered in comparative tables.

To illustrate the use of the dictionary as an aid for translation, let us consider the English connective *in the event that.* Suppose we are to translate into Italian the following example (Maastricht 1992):

Art. 100 C

(48) However, *in the event of* an emergency situation in a third country posing a threat of a sudden inflow of nationals from that country into the Community, the Council [...] may introduce, for a period not exceeding six months, a visa requirement for nationals from the country in question.

Following various bilingual dictionaries, which translate *in the event of (that)* by *nell'eventualità che*, we may be led to translate (48) as (49):

(49) Tuttavia, *nell'eventualità che* una situazione di emergenza insorta in un paese terzo minacci un improvviso afflusso nella Comunità di cittadini di detto paese, il Consiglio [...] può imporre, per un periodo non superiore a sei mesi, l'obbligo del visto per i cittadini provenienti dal paese in questione.

If we check the glossary, the lexical entry for *in the event of (that)* is:

LE (*in the event of/that*)
(α) (a_1) logico-semantic level
<λR [ILL FUNCT ^{pot} (R (p, q)] (SUFF COND)>
(a_2) non logico-semantic level
(a_2') general features
[HYP]
(a_2'') individual features
degree [0,5] of probability [*A]

The lexical entry, in the Italian section, for *nell'eventualità che* is:

LE (*nell'eventualità che*)
(α) (a_1) logico-semantic level
<λR [ILL FUNCT ^{pot} (R (p, q)] (SUFF COND)>
(a_2) non logico-semantic level
(a_2') general features
[HYP]
(a_2") individual features
degree [0,1] of probability [*A]

Such lexical entries result from punctual analyses analogous to the one outlined in the previous section. For instance, while *nell'eventualità che* presents p as 'unlikely', which explains the oddness of example (50):

(50) ? *Nell'eventualità che* Giampiero riesca ad affittare quella casa al mare – cosa che pare molto probabile – passeremo da lui una settimana in luglio (Mazzoleni 1991: 772).

'*Nell'eventualità che* Giampiero manages to rent that house by the sea – which he almost certainly will – we'll go and stay with him for a week in July'.

this is not the case for *in the event that*:

(51) *In the event that* Giampiero manages to rent that house by the sea – which he almost certainly will – we'll go and stay with him for a week in July.

The glossary thus suggests a possible equivalent, via a cross-referencing system of lexical entries and scales representing the *ccc*s' individual features. In this case, let us consider scale A, representing the degree of 'probability' of p expressed by the connectives:

SCALE A [degree of 'probability']

0 ------------------------------------•------•------------------------------------› 1

in case   *in the event of (that)*

--------•--------------------•------•------•--------------------------------------›

nell'eventualità che   *nel caso che (in cui)*

casomai   *nell'ipotesi che*

in caso

The scale suggests that, as far as this feature is concerned, *in the event of (that)* rather corresponds to *nel caso che (in cui)* than to *nell'eventualità che*. Both share the same degree of 'probability': [0,5], on a scale from 0 to 1, to indicate the neutrality of their modalization of p, *vs* degree [0,1] of *nell'eventualità che*, to indicate the modalization of p as unlikely. If we consult the Italian section of the glossary, the lexical entry of *in the event of (that)* corresponds to the one for *nel caso che (in cui)*:

LE (*nel caso che/in cui*)
(α) (a_1) logico-semantic level
<λR [ILL FUNCT ^{pot} (R (p, q)] (SUFF COND)>
(a_2) non logico-semantic level
(a_2') general features
[HYP]
(a_2'') individual features
degree [0,5] of probability [*A]

Moreover, by checking the French and German sections, we obtain as equivalents, respectively, *dans le cas où* and *falls*, or *im Falle, dass*:

LE (*dans le cas où*)
(α) (a_1) logico-semantic level
<λR [ILL FUNCT ^{pot} (R (p, q)] (SUFF COND)>
(a_2) non logico-semantic level
(a_2') general features
[HYP]
(a_2'') individual features
degree [0,5] of probability [*A]

LE (*falls*)

(α) (a_1) logico-semantic level

<λR [ILL FUNCT ^{pot} (R (p, q)] (SUFF COND)>

(a_2) non logico-semantic level

(a_2') general features

[HYP]

(a_2'') individual features

degree [0,5] of probability [*A]

Such is also the choice of equivalents in the four versions of the Treaty:

Art. 100 C

(52) However, *in the event of* an emergency situation in a third country posing a threat of a sudden inflow of nationals from that country into the Community, the Council [...] may introduce, for a period not exceeding six months, a visa requirement for nationals from the country in question.

(53) Tuttavia, *nel caso in cui* una situazione di emergenza insorta in un paese terzo minacci un improvviso afflusso nella Comunità di cittadini di detto paese, il Consiglio [...] può imporre, per un periodo non superiore a sei mesi, l'obbligo del visto per i cittadini provenienti dal paese in questione.

(54) Toutefois, *dans le cas où* survient dans un pays tiers une situation d'urgence confrontant la Communité à la menace d'un afflux soudain de ressortissants de ce pays, le Conseil peut, statuant à la majorité qualifiée sur recommandation de la Commission, rendre obligatoire, pour une période ne pouvant excéder six mois, l'obtention d'un visa par les ressortissants du pays en question.

(55) Bei einer Notlage in einem dritten Land, die zu einem plötzlichen Zustrom von Staatsangehörigen dieses Landes in die Gemeinschaft zu führen droht, kann der Rat jedoch auf Empfehlung der Kommission mit qualifizierter Mehrheit für einen Zeitraum von höchsten sechs Monaten den Visumzwang für Staatsangehörige des betreffenden Land einführen.[9]

9. The German version of the article uses the prepositional phrase (P[-DP]) 'bei einer Notlage'.

This example of comparative analysis, based on a careful investigation of the semantic properties of complex conditional connectives in each language, confirms our initial concern: the problematic nature of legal translation is not restricted to the concepts expressed by lexemes such as contract, property, etc., but crucially involves the logico-semantic relationships expressed by the linking elements among the propositions of a text.

The first step, if we want to extend the reflection beyond the terminological level, is the creation of a data base of similar lexical entries, built on monolingual analyses, for connectives expressing other semantic relationships, such as time, purpose, cause, etc. in all relevant languages.

2.2 Information structure

The second relevant level of analysis concerns the information structure of the text, *i.e.* the level pertaining to the foregrounding *vs* backgrounding of its content (cf. e.g. Lambrecht 1994). An adequate framework for our purposes is provided by Ferrari (2004, 2005), where word-order influences on information structure are incorporated in the very definition of information categories (cf. in particular, the notions of *Frame* and *Incipit* below). Tested so far on Italian only, such a model provides a fine-grained, innovative, approach, providing interesting results in a comparative perspective.

Following Ferrari (2005), an utterance can be subdivided into textual units organized according to a hierarchical-informational criterion, called Information Units ("Unità Informative"). The central unit is the Information Nucleus ("Nucleo Informativo"), which has the important function of defining the act of textual composition and the illocutionary act expressed by the utterance that contains it, as does the highlighted portion of text in (56):

(56) However, *in the event of* an emergency situation in a third country posing a threat of a sudden inflow of nationals from that country into the Community, /the Council [...] may introduce, for a period not exceeding six months, a visa requirement for nationals from the country in question/^{Nucleus}
(Maastricht Treaty, Art. 100 C).

Such a unit can (but need not) be joined by other, informationally subordinate, units, called *Frame* ("Quadro") and *Appendix* ("Appendice").[10]

The Frame is defined by a relationship of linear precedence to the Nucleus and introduces or reactivates the conceptual-semantic field in which the denotative, illocutionary and textual values of the nuclear information are interpreted. It is typically filled by an adverbial indication (temporal, spatial, causal, concessive, etc.) expressed by either a phrasal or a clausal structure, as in (57):

(57) However, /*in the event of* an emergency situation in a third country posing a threat of a sudden inflow of nationals from that country into the Community/^{Frame}, the Council [...] may introduce, for a period not exceeding six months, a visa requirement for nationals from the country in question
(Maastricht Treaty, Art. 100 C).

The Appendix, on the other hand, expresses information that the speaker decides to leave backgrounded and that specify and enrich the content of the information to which it is attached. As the Appendix can be attached recursively to both nuclear and subordinate information, it has an important function in creating different levels of information within the text. (58) provides an example of a nuclear Appendix:

(58) /Undertakings entrusted with the operation of services of general economic interest or having the character of a revenue-producing monopoly shall be subject to the rules contained in this Treaty,/^{Nucleus} /*in so far as* the application of such rules does not obstruct the performance, in law or in fact, of the particular tasks assigned to them/^{Appendix}
(Maastricht Treaty, Art. 90.2).

Nucleus, Frame and Appendix can be joined by "minor" information units, such as the *Incipit*, having as main functions to represent various aspects of the organization of the text (*dispositio*) and to convey the speaker's (epis-

10. Such a terminology (as well as my translation into English), is close to Mathesius ([1929] 1991) – *basis and nucleus*, – whose seminal work strongly influenced all subsequent reserch on information structure; it has the advantage of avoiding the confusion generated by terms such as *theme*, or *topic*, intended here, following Lambrecht (1994), in terms of *aboutness* (Ferrari 2005: 21) (cf. footnote 4).

temic, etc.) attitude towards the conveyed content. Such a unit is typically filled by functional linguistic categories, like adverbs or textual connectives:

(59) /However/ [Incipit], *in the event of* an emergency situation in a third country posing a threat of a sudden inflow of nationals from that country into the Community, the Council [...] may introduce, for a period not exceeding six months, a visa requirement for nationals from the country in question (Maastricht Treaty, Art. 100 C).

The organization of the information level of the text can be represented as follows (Ferrari 2005: 38 [my translation]):

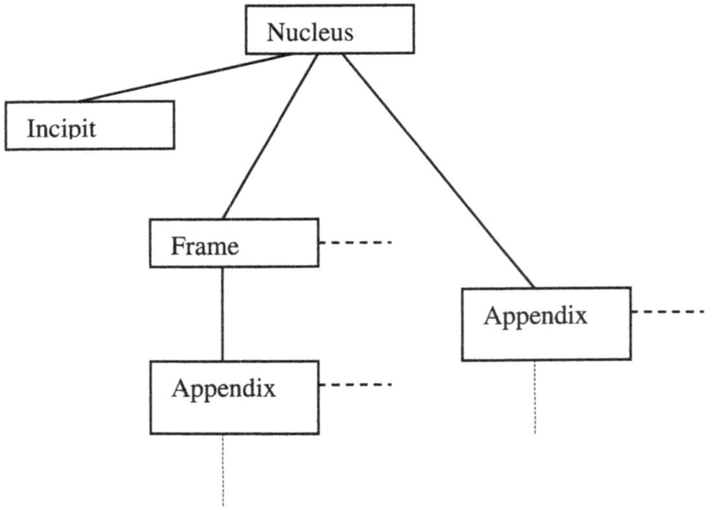

Figure 1. Utterance

A fine-grained analysis of the information structure of a text, I shall argue, is a prerequisite for its translation. Example (60) could only be rendered by an informationally isomorphic structure, such as (61):

(60) /Any abuse by one or more undertakings of a dominant position within the common market or in a substantial part of it shall be prohibited as incompatible with the common market/[Nucleus] *in so far as* it may affect trade between Member States/[Appendix].

(61) /Lo sfruttamento abusivo da parte di una o più imprese di una posizione dominante sul mercato comune o su una parte sostanziale di questo è incompatibile con il mercato comune e vietato,/[Nucleus] *nella misura in cui* possa essere pregiudizievole al commercio tra Stati membri./[Appendix]

A different information structure, such as the one imposed by the connective *solo se* 'only if', bearing focus on the conditional relationship and thus inducing one nuclear unit instead of a Nucleus-Appendix structure, changes both the logico-semantic and the illocutionary value of the text:

(62) /Lo sfruttamento abusivo da parte di una o più imprese di una posizione dominante sul mercato comune o su una parte sostanziale di questo è incompatibile con il mercato comune e vietato *solo se* possa essere pregiudizievole al commercio tra Stati membri./[Nucleus]
'Any abuse by one or more undertakings of a dominant position within the common market or in a substantial part of it shall be prohibited as incompatible with the common market *only if* it may affect trade between Member States./[Nucleus]

Information structure is also a fundamental parameter in the comparison of different versions of a legal document. Burr (2006: 193–194), for instance, remarks the 'apparent divergence' ("*Scheindivergenz*") of examples (63) and (64):

(63) Die Völker Europas sind entschlossen, auf der Grundlage gemeinsamer Werte eine friedliche Zukunft zu teilen, indem sie sich zu einer immer engeren Union verbinden
(*Europäische Grundrechtecharta, Präambel*).

(64) Les peuples de l'Europe, en établissant entre eux une union sans cesse plus étroite, ont décidé de partager un avenir pacifique fondé sur des valeurs communes.

Although a different foregrounding strategy could be perceived in the two examples – foregrounding of "*des valeurs communes*" in (64), of "*die immer enger werdende Union*" in (63), – such a difference, she argues, is only apparent and results from the constraints imposed by word-order and verbal constructions in the two languages. Our analysis of the examples provides a further explanatory level to her argument: despite the difference in linear order, the information structure of (63) and (64), represented below, is the same:

(63') //Die Völker Europas sind entschlossen, auf der Grundlage gemeinsamer Werte eine friedliche Zukunft zu teilen/[Nucleus], /indem sie sich zu einer immer engeren Union verbinden/ [Appendix] (*Europäische Grundrechtecharta, Präambel*).

(64') //Les peuples de l'Europe/, /en établissant entre eux une union sans cesse plus étroite, / [Appendix] ont décidé de partager un avenir pacifique fondé sur des valeurs communes.//[Nucleus]

The information structural dimension has, moreover, an important typological function. Cignetti (2005) shows how, within the same category of *normative* texts (Mortara Garavelli 2001: 26), *Italian Codici* differ from the *Italian Constitution* because of the different use of the Frame unit. A Frame is often found at the start of an article in the *Codici*, as in:

(65) /Se al momento della conclusione del contratto una parte dà all'altra, a titolo di caparra, una somma di danaro o una quantità di altre cose fungibili,/ [Frame] la caparra, in caso di adempimento, deve essere restituita o imputata alla prestazione dovuta (art. 1385 Codice Civile).

'If at the time of the conclusion of the contract one party trasfers to the other, as a deposit, a sum of money or other form of payment [...]'.

where it has often an important intertextual function, cross-referencing to other articles of the same document:

(66) /Nei casi previsti dagli articoli 361, 362, 363, 364, 365, 366, 369, 371 bis, 372, 373, 374 e 378,/[Frame] non è punibile chi ha commesso il fatto per esservi stato costretto dalla necessità di salvare se medesimo o un prossimo congiunto da un grave e inevitabile nocumento nella libertà e nell'onore.

/Nei casi previsti dagli articoli 371 bis, 372 e 373,/[Frame] la punibilità è esclusa se il fatto è commesso da chi per legge non avrebbe dovuto essere richiesto di fornire informazioni ai fini delle indagini o assunto come testimonio, perito, consulente tecnico o interprete ovvero avrebbe dovuto essere avvertito della facoltà di astenersi dal

rendere informazioni, testimonianza, perizia, consulenza o interpretazione
(C. Pen. Art. 384).

'In cases foreseen by articles 361, 362, 363, 364, 365, 366, 369, 371 bis, 372, 373, 374 e 378 [...]

In cases foreseen by 371 bis, 372 e 373 [...]'.

Such an information unit is never found at the beginning of an article in the Italian *Constitution*, which is always used to introduce a principle of general validity:

(67) /Il Presidente della Repubblica è eletto per sette anni./[Nucleus]
/Trenta giorni prima che scada il termine/ [Frame], il Presidente della Camera dei deputati convoca in seduta comune il Parlamento e i delegati regionali, per eleggere il nuovo Presidente della Repubblica (Art. 85, Costituzione).

'The President of the Republic is elected for seven years.
Thirty days before the expiration of the term, the president of the Chamber of Deputies shall summon a joint session of parliament and the regional delegates to elect the new president of the Republic.'

Based on general principles, such as the association of the nuclear information with an act of textual composition and an illocutionary act, the model presented has a comparative heuristic value. As illustrated by the examples in this section, seizing the underlying articulation of a text in the information units of Nucleus, Frame, Appendix, Incipit provides a sound, comparable, basis for both drafting and translation. Moreover, such an analysis would provide the ideal framework for investigating the role played by information structure in the specification of the illocutionary force of legal utterances. A recent study on spoken Italian (Tucci 2006) yields the findings that directives are only found in nuclear, never in subordinate information units. Comparing such findings with those obtained on a typology of legal texts would provide an interesting contribution to the question raised by the performative value pervasive of legal utterances and, in general, by the whole question of their illocutionary force (cf. Visconti in preparation). A fine-grained approach to all levels of the text highlights the way forward to improve our understanding of the structure and function of legal utterances, in both a monolingual and a comparative perspective.

3. Conclusion

The linguistic and legal challenges set by recent changes in the political shape of Europe, as the statement of the authenticity of the different linguistic versions of EU Treaties (art. 314, Amsterdam Treaty, 1997), require a level of granularity in the (micro-)analysis of legal documents such as the one proposed in this paper. Terminological reflection should be integrated in a modular framework, which considers the interaction of the lexicon and other linguistic structures in determining the meaning of legal utterances. Special attention should be paid to connectives, specifying the semantic relationships between the propositions of a text.

The ideas put forth in this paper form the core of a proposal for a large scale international project,[11] aiming to achieve, for each relevant EU language: (i) a database of connectives (§ 2.1); (ii) a database of legal documents labelled for both: (ii) information units); (iii) the illocutionary functions of the utterances composing them in relation to their information structure (§ 2.2). The attempt to 'formalize' the descriptions proposed, in the form of lexical entries or information units labels, make such proposal suitable to computational implementation.

4. References

Burr, Isolde. 2006. "Die Grundrechte-Charta: Ein europäischer Text". *Kölner Gemeinschaftskommentar zur europäische Grundrechte-Charta*, ed. by Peter Tettinger and Klaus Stern, München: C. H. Beck Verlag. 187–198.

Burr, Isolde, and Tito Gallas. 2004. "Zur Textproduktion im Gemeinschaftsrecht", *Rechtssprache Europas. Reflexion der Praxis von Sprache und Mehrsprachigkeit im supranationalen Recht*, ed. by Friedrich Müller and Isolde Burr, Berlin. Duncker and Humblot. 195–259.

Cignetti, Luca. 2005. "Sfondi e rilievi testuali nella Costituzione della Repubblica Italiana", *Rilievi. Le gerarchie semantico-pragmatiche di alcuni tipi di testo*, ed. by Angela Ferrari, Firenze: Cesati.

De Stefanis, Claudia. 2007. "REI: Rete di Eccellenza dell'italiano istituzionale", *La traduzione del diritto comunitario ed europeo: riflessioni metodologiche*, ed. by Elena Ioriatti Ferrari, Università degli Studi di Trento, Alcione, Trento. 9–15.

Ferrari, Angela. 2004. "La lingua nel testo, il testo nella lingua", *La lingua nel testo, il testo nella lingua*, ed. by Angela Ferrari, Supplemento al Bollettino dell'ALI n. 9, Turin: Istituto dell'Atlante Linguistico Italiano. 9–41.

11. Cf. Visconti (in preparation).

Ferrari, Angela. 2005. "Tipi di testo e tipi di gerarchie testuali, con particolare attenzione alla distinzione tra scritto e parlato", *Rilievi. Le gerarchie semantico-pragmatiche di alcuni tipi di testo*, ed. by Angela Ferrari, Florence: Cesati. 15–51.

Gallas, Tito. 2007. "Drafting multilingue: missione impossibile?" *La traduzione del diritto comunitario ed europeo: riflessioni metodologiche*, eb. By Elena Ioriatti Ferrari, Università degli Studi di Trento, Alcione, Trento. 27–40.

Heller, Dorothee. 2003. "Prinzipien der Textgestaltung und der Gebrauch von Konditionalsätzen im deutschen Schiedsverfahrenrecht", *Legal Discourse in Multilingual and Multicultural Contexts*, ed. by Vijay Bhatia, Christopher N. Candlin and Maurizio Gotti, Bern etc.: Peter Lang. 287–312.

Ioriatti Ferrari, Elena (ed.) 2007. *La traduzione del diritto comunitario ed europeo: riflessioni metodologiche*. Università degli Studi di Trento, Alcione, Trento.

Jacometti, Valentina and Barbara Pozzo (eds.) 2006. *Le politiche linguistiche delle istituzioni comunitarie dopo l'allargamento*. Milan: Giuffré.

Lambrecht, Knud. 1994. *Information Structure and Sentence Form: Topic, Focus, and the Mental Representation of Discourse Referents*. Cambridge: Cambridge University Press.

Mathesius, Vilem. 1991 [1929]. "La linguistica funzionale", *Il campo di tensione. La sintassi della Scuola di Praga*, ed. by Rosanna Sornicola and Ales Svoboda, Naples: Liguori. 97–112.

Mazzoleni, Marco. 1991. "Le frasi ipotetiche", *Grande grammatica italiana*, ed. by Lorenzo Renzi and Giampaolo Salvi, Bologna: Il Mulino. 751–784.

Mortara Garavelli, Bice. 2001. *Le parole e la giustizia. Divagazioni grammaticali e retoriche su testi giuridici italiani*. Turin: Einaudi.

Pasch, Renate, Ursula Brauße, Eva Breindl and Ulrich Hermann. 2003. *Handbuch der deutschen Konnektoren*. Berlin etc.: Walter de Gruyter.

Ross, Alf. 1994. "Tû-tû", *Il linguaggio del diritto*, ed. by Uberto Scarpelli and Paolo Di Lucia, Milan: LED. 119–134.

Sabatini, Francesco. 1990. "Analisi del linguaggio giuridico. Il testo normativo in una tipologia generale dei testi", *Corso di studi superiori legislativi (1988–89)*, ed. by M. D'Antonio, Padova: Cedam. 675–724.

Sacco, Rodolfo. 2002. *L'interprétation des textes juridiques rèdigés dans plus d'une langue*. Turin: L'Harmattan.

Sacco, Rodolfo and Luca Castellani. 1999. *Les multiples langues du droit européen uniforme*. Turin: L'Harmattan.

Soffritti, Marcello. 1999. "Textmerkmale deutscher und italienischer Gesetzebücher: Übersetzung und kontrastive Analyse", *Übersetzen von Rechtstexten: Fachkommunikation im Spannungsfeld zwischen Recthsordnung und Sprache*, ed. by Peter Sandrini, Tübingen: Gunter Narr. 119–135.

Tosi, Arturo and Jacqueline Visconti. 2004. "L''europeizzazione' della lingua italiana". *Lingua italiana contemporanea* I, 151–173.

Tucci, Ida. 2006. "Strategies of modalization in C-ORAL-ROM Italian", Paper read at the Third Workshop on Romance Corpus Linguistics (University of Freiburg, 12 September 2006).

Visconti, Jacqueline. 2000a. *I connettivi condizionali complessi in italiano e inglese. Uno studio contrastivo*. Alessandria: Edizioni dell'Orso.

Visconti, Jacqueline. 2000b. "La traduzione del testo giuridico. Problemi e prospettive di ricerca". *Terminology and Translation. A Journal of the Language Services of the European Institutions* 2, 38–66.

Visconti, Jacqueline (ed.). in preparation. "Speech acts in legal language". *Journal of Pragmatics*, Special Issue.

Index

A

B

C

D

E

F

G

H

I

J

K

M

N

O

P

U

V

W

X

Bei Fragen zur Produktsicherheit wenden Sie sich bitte an:
If you have any questions regarding product safety,
please contact:

Walter de Gruyter GmbH
Genthiner Straße 13
10785 Berlin
productsafety@degruyterbrill.com